Navigating the Sermon

Series II, Cycle A

Lectionary-based Commentaries

A Compilation of "Charting the Course" Columns from
Emphasis: A Preaching Journal for the Parish Pastor
a Component of **SermonSuite.com**

CSS Publishing Company, Inc.
Lima, Ohio

NAVIGATING THE SERMON, CYCLE A

FIRST EDITION
Copyright © 2022
by CSS Publishing Co., Inc.

Published by CSS Publishing Company, Inc., Lima, Ohio 45807. All rights reserved. No part of this publication may be reproduced in any manner whatsoever without the prior permission of the publisher, except in the case of brief quotations embodied in critical articles and reviews. Inquiries should be addressed to: CSS Publishing Company, Inc., Permissions Department, 5450 N. Dixie Highway, Lima, Ohio 45807.

Most scripture quotations are from the New Revised Standard Version (NRSV) of the Bible. Copyright 1989 by the Division of Christian Education of the National Council of the Churches of Christ in the USA. Used by permission.

Scripture quotations marked RSV are from the Revised Standard Version of the Bible, copyrighted 1946, 1952 ©, 1971, 1973, by the Division of Christian Education of the National Council of the Churches of Christ in the USA. Used by permission.

Scripture quotations marked TEV are from the Good News Bible, in Today's English Version. Copyright © American Bible Society 1966, 1971, 1976. Used by permission.

Scripture quotations marked NIV are taken from Holy Bible, New International Version, copyright © 1973, 1978, 1984 International Bible Society. Used by permission of Zondervan Bible Publishers. All rights reserved.

For more information about CSS Publishing Company resources, visit our website at www.csspub.com, email us at csr@csspub.com, or call (800) 241-4056.

e-book:
ISBN-13: 978-0-7880-2951-6
ISBN-10: 0-7880-2951-7

ISBN-13: 978-0-7880-2950-9
ISBN-10: 0-7880-2950-9

PRINTED IN USA

Introduction

Over fifty years ago, CSS Publishing Company was founded by two pastors and a Sunday school superintendent who had a vision to assist pastors "on the front lines" in their efforts to share the gospel of Jesus with people over the entire United States. The lectionary was taking hold over the country in an effort to bring a common message to people, no matter where they worshiped.

Over the years, CSS has published many different products. Of more that 1,700 publications that have been produced in the history of the company. *Emphasis: A Lectionary Preaching Journal* has been one of the most popular. In its history, thousands of pastors and their congregations have benefited from the commentaries and insights found within its pages.

Navigating The Sermon is a collection of commentaries from "Charting the Course," which is at the core of what **Emphasis** is about. For each Sunday in the Cycle A lectionary, the writers who contributed to these columns have provided thematic guidance drawing together the lessons for each Sunday in the church year. Not only have they provided one idea for each Sunday, but most days have multiple themes from which to choose.

We are excited to offer this new resource to the readers of **Emphasis,** both old and new, and pray that this book will be a blessing to you and an invaluable aid to your preaching ministry.

The editors of CSS Publishing Company

Contents

First Sunday of Advent	7
Second Sunday of Advent	10
Third Sunday of Advent	16
Fourth Sunday of Advent	19
The Nativity of Our Lord	25
First Sunday after Christmas Day	30
Second Sunday after Christmas	36
*The Baptism of our Lord	Epiphany 1	Ordinary Time 1*	40
*Epiphany 2	Ordinary Time 2*	45
*Epiphany 3	Ordinary Time 3*	51
*Epiphany 4	Ordinary Time 4*	56
*Epiphany 5	Ordinary Time 5*	58
*Epiphany 6	Ordinary Time 6*	64
Transfiguration Sunday	69
Ash Wednesday	75
First Sunday in Lent	78
Second Sunday in Lent	85
Third Sunday in Lent	90
Fourth Sunday in Lent	96
Fifth Sunday in Lent	100
Passion Sunday	102
Maundy Thursday	109
Good Friday	116
Resurrection of Our Lord (Easter Day)	121
Second Sunday of Easter	124
Third Sunday of Easter	128
Fourth Sunday of Easter	130
Fifth Sunday of Easter	136
Sixth Sunday of Easter	141
Seventh Sunday of Easter	144
Day of Pentecost	147
Trinity Sunday / 1st Sunday after Pentecost	152
*Proper 6	Ordinary Time 11*	157
*Proper 7	Ordinary Time 12*	162
*Proper 8	Ordinary Time 13*	165

Proper 9 | Ordinary Time 14 171

Proper 10 | Ordinary Time 15 173

Proper 11 | Ordinary Time 16 178

Proper 12 | Ordinary Time 17 184

Proper 13 | Ordinary Time 18 188

Proper 14 | Ordinary Time 19 190

Proper 15 | Ordinary Time 20 196

Proper 16 | Ordinary Time 21 201

Proper 17 | Ordinary Time 22 205

Proper 18 | Ordinary Time 23 209

Proper 19 | Ordinary Time 24 215

Proper 20 | Ordinary Time 25 221

Proper 21 | Ordinary Time 26 226

Proper 22 | Ordinary Time 27 232

Proper 23 | Ordinary Time 28 234

Proper 24 | Ordinary Time 29 239

Proper 25 | Ordinary Time 30 244

Reformation Sunday 250

All Saints Day 254

Proper 26 | Ordinary Time 31 257

Proper 27 | Ordinary Time 32 261

Proper 28 | Ordinary Time 33 267

Christ The King (Proper 29) 272

Thanksgiving Day 276

First Sunday of Advent

Isaiah 2:1-5

Romans 13:11-14

Matthew 24:36-44

by Herbert W. Chilstrom and James A. Nestingen

Crossing the bridge

If we had no church year calendar we would soon create one. Our sense of order demands it. Without it we would soon fall victim to a series of Sundays that would center on propaganda for causes rather than proclamation of the gospel. Even with our liturgical rhythm we feel that threat!

This First Sunday in Advent serves as a bridge from one year to the next. In the last Sundays of the previous year we reflected on eschatological sayings of Jesus and other biblical writers. Judgment day is coming.

All of today's lessons reflect that same accent. But those days cannot be separated from these days. The one who will come, has come.

That is why the Advent season stretches our preaching skills to the limit. We are not dealing with a single event, such as the exodus, the return from exile, the birth of Christ, the crucifixion, the resurrection, or the day of Pentecost. During Advent, we must combine several streams — the promise of our Lord's coming, Jesus' coming in his incarnation, his promise to come again in judgment, and how all of them touch this moment in the lives of those who hear us.

In the midst of the horrors of World War II, Helmut Thielicke watched his world disintegrate. Judgment fell on his native Germany, not only for the Nazis, but also for those, like Thielicke and Bonhoeffer, who resisted. But Thielicke discovered that even total chaos had its positive side. Mingled with his fear was an unexpected sense of hope.

Sometimes I gazed lovingly at the rows of books in my study and thought to myself, "I still have you. Perhaps you'll go up in flames tomorrow, but today is today." I experienced not the eschatological dissipation of the moment I had expected, but an enormous increase in the intensity of life. The "beautiful moment" acquired a heightened luminosity. The early Christians who were convinced of the imminent end of the world perhaps did not despise the world at all as much as I had thought. (Helmut Thielicke, *Notes From A Wayfarer*, Paragon Press, 1995, p. 162.)

Our task in Advent is to bring moments of "heightened luminosity" to a people facing judgment.

Grist For The Mill

Isaiah 2:1-5

Luther suggests that the root of all sin is unbelief, which results in turning away from God and toward self. The same is true for any corporate group, including a nation. That is what Isaiah saw happening in Israel. They had come to believe that they were so special that God cared only for them. Thus, when their fortunes turned sour they concluded that God had abandoned them.

The prophet's task is to call them back to the original Abrahamic vision — that they are blessed to be a blessing. The nations will stream to Jerusalem, not because Israel is superior to them, but that Israel "may teach us his ways and that we may walk in (the Lord's) paths" (2:3). **Through the chosen** people of God the nations will learn the way of peace and justice.

If the Christian church is the "new Israel," we who claim to be followers of Christ bear that same responsibility. We are to remind the world that all people live under judgment and grace. God calls all nations to accountability. "He shall judge between the nations" (2:4). From those who walk in the Lord's way will come insight on how to "beat their swords into plowshares, and their spears into pruning hooks" (2:4).

Across from the United Nations center in New York City one can find these words etched in stone. Does this mean that we pin our hopes on the work of the UN? Yes and no. Surely we must work for justice and peace now. The churches should be in the forefront of that endeavor.

But what about the "days to come" (2:2) of which Isaiah speaks? When will that day be here? Neither Isaiah nor we can know. It is like looking down a long road with trees on either side. They converge in the distance, but we cannot tell exactly where. We move ahead, doing the work of God for this time and trusting that God will have a final word.

Romans 13:11-14

Although God is not yet finished with Israel, Paul is convinced that the promise is now being fulfilled through the Gentiles. This should not cause pride. Whether Jew or Gentile, everything is by grace, says Paul. Because he believes the end is near, he urges the believers to get on vigorously with the work of the kingdom.

In order to make his point, Paul uses the technique of contrast: sleep/wake; night/day; darkness/light; honorable life/reveling, drunkenness, debauchery, licentiousness, quarreling, jealousy.

What about us? With so little sense of urgency about the coming of Christ, where is our motivation for sharing the Gospel and for living a Christ-centered life? The key is in Paul's understanding of the radical nature of life in Christ. In Romans 6:3-4 the contrast is between death and life. Those who are baptized into Christ go to the cross with him. They die. But they also come from the tomb. They live. Thus, whether Christ returns today or tomorrow or a thousand years from now is not the critical issue. Those who claim to be Christian are to live the new life each day. "The Christian," writes Reginald Fuller, "stands in the dark with his face lit by the coming dawn. He can therefore already cast off the works of darkness, and put on the armor of light. He can live 'as in the day,' although actually he is still in the night." (Reginald H. Fuller, Preaching the Lectionary: *The Word of God for the Church Today*, The Liturgical Press, 1974, p. 102.)

It was Romans 13:13-14 that led to the conversion of Augustine. Upon reading these words, he says, "I did not desire to read further, nor did I need to. Instantly ... a light of serenity flooded my heart and all the darkness of doubt vanished away." (Philip H. Pfatteicher, *Festivals and Commemorations*, Augsburg, 1980, p. 336.)

Matthew 24:36-44

As we near the third millennium we can expect prophecies that the year 2000 may mark the end of the world. The irony of it all is that Dionysius Exiguus, the sixth-century monk who created the B.C.-A.D. system of numbering, miscalculated the birth of Christ by several years, making it likely we may have passed the 2000th anniversary in 1994. This only underscores the point that for believers any year, any day, any moment is a time for the Lord's coming.

This makes the contrast between Matthew and Paul all the more striking. In Paul's letter to the Romans, it is those who practice all kinds of wickedness who will not be ready. Here in Matthew those not prepared are doing very ordinary things, as in the days of Noah: eating, drinking, marrying, working in the field, grinding at the mill. There is nothing inherently wicked about any of these activities. We do the same. We eat, drink, marry, bury, socialize, go to work, do the wash, mow the grass, vacuum the rugs .... But this is just the point Jesus wants to make: It is in the routine of our ordinary day that we are most likely to forget the urgency of being a Christian.

The letter to the Hebrews is thought to have been addressed to believers who were no longer living in the expectation of Christ's imminent return. They had fallen into an easy routine. They were content with spiritual "baby food" rather than a solid diet (Hebrews 5:12-14). Some were neglecting to worship on a regular basis (Hebrews 10:25). To them the author addresses the unsettling question: "How shall we escape if we neglect so great a salvation?" (Hebrews 2:3).

I have been a pastor for almost forty years. I can count on one hand the number of persons who have said to me, "Pastor, I once believed, but now I reject it all. I once testified that Christ was my Lord. Now I no longer believe in him." No, not many like that. But how many can I count who by simple neglect have drifted away from the church and from the faith?

Advent is a time to wake up!

FIRST LESSON FOCUS

By James A. Nestingen

Isaiah 2:1-5

In the wintry overcast of the Northern Plains, whites and grays meld, obscuring the horizon by obviating the break between sky and standing snows. Everything appears soft.

But there is a hard edge of violence hidden in the obscurity. Cold permeates, overtaking its victims without a sound. With a barely perceptible breeze, drifting snowflakes can quickly be whipped into a blinding blizzard of whites, stranding all movement.

There is another form of death that was hidden in the plains. When the cold war's fears justified them, cement pockets were installed along the Canadian border. Many of the installations were decoys, left empty. But enough were filled to turn sparsely populated states into the equivalent of world nuclear powers. They contained Minuteman missiles. It was never clear whether the name was given the people sending them, the weapons themselves or the intended targets. Neither was it ever sure which of these "silos," as they were called, were the more empty.

Antelope, like white-tailed deer, don't comprehend fences. To them, webbed wire, galvanized steel — human assertions of sovereignty — are minor nuisances in the run of open range.

So a herd grazed within a Minuteman compound, brown compactions of speed and grace dotting the snow, oblivious to anything but the possibility of frozen grasses. A doe stood with one leg on the cement lip of the missile tube, looked up and, content that her observers posed no threat, put her head down once more to continue her foraging.

The empty dreariness of every day accommodates us to continuing conflict. Their competing claims make it difficult to distinguish between peacemakers and peacebreakers. In the end, violence continues to cycle on itself, victims and victimizers rolling over one another in an unbreakable embrace.

Isaiah presents a vision of divine intervention. Having chosen them for the sake of the other peoples of the world, God has sent the children of Abraham and Sarah to carry this promise to the nations. Not all of the people saw what Isaiah did, peering through the obscurity. But as he looked over his people's shoulders, he saw God's future: a time when the cycle of violence will be broken, when all of the peoples of the world will follow Israel to Mount Zion, there to be taught by God. Though the form differs, Christians share this expectation: God will break through the strife, reforging weaponry to culture his creatures. Thus an antelope's nonchalance will be more than a glimpse of God's intention — the whole creation will abound in his peace.

Second Sunday of Advent

Isaiah 11:1-10

Romans 15:4-13

Matthew 3:1-12

by Wayne Brouwer

After the storm

What difference does my life make for others around me? What difference does anyone's life make? It's always a question related to parenting. Parents make choices which affect the manner in which their children form their identities. Harry Chapin put it well in his song "Cat's in the Cradle." When he was a young father he was too busy making a living to be bothered by his son. But when he was finally old enough to enjoy time with the family, his son had learned to be too busy for him!

Of course, the other side of the story is just as true. Maurice Boyd remembers one incident that sealed the impact of his father on his life forever. His father worked in a shipyard in Belfast, Northern Ireland. During the depression work dried up. Times were tough, and for three years his father was out of a job.

Then one of his old bosses at the shipyard approached him. The important man would find work for Mr. Boyd. He would guarantee it, no matter how much worse things got. All Mr. Boyd would have to do would be to buy a life insurance policy from the man. It would work to their mutual benefit: the boss's income would increase, and Mr. Boyd's work income would be guaranteed!

It was a great deal except for one thing: it was illegal. Maurice Boyd remembers his father sitting at the kitchen table with the whole family surrounding him. There at the table his father counted the cost. He reviewed their desperate financial situation. He ticked off the outstanding bills, and the money he ought to be making... could be making, if only he'd say yes to his boss.

His father wrote it all down on a sheet of paper: the gains and the losses; what he could make and what he could lose. Then he wrote down a category that Maurice Boyd will never forget: **integrity!** What did it matter if he gained the cash to pay the rent, but lost his ability to teach his children right from wrong? What did it matter if he gained the dignity of a job, but lost it each morning when he looked at himself in the mirror and knew that the only reason he could go off to work instead of someone else was because he cheated? Says Maurice Boyd: "He discovered that no one can make you feel inferior without your consent, and that one way you can keep your soul is by refusing to sell it. He realized that whatever else he lost, and God knows he lost enough, he didn't have to lose himself."

And when the one of integrity arrives, this world must change. This is why we celebrate Advent over and over, until the coming again of God's anointed one. When Bill Moyers interviewed Dr. Rachel Naomi Remen, she told him how it was for her. Dr. Remen has founded several institutes for the care of cancer patients. She said that sometimes she has a much greater sense of integrity within during those times when she isn't feeling all that well physically. Bill asked her what she meant by "integrity," and she replied "That I am what I am..." She said that even with her wounds and her weaknesses, "there's an essence and a uniqueness and a beauty" about her life that is whole and complete. Integrity. Pure in heart. The peaceable kingdom that we feel in part now, but long for following the storm of cleansing judgment still to come.

Second Sunday of Advent

Isaiah 11:1-10

A young girl was watching a parade with her parents when the Scottish bagpipe band came by. As her dad explained how the pipes worked, pointing to the bags under the arms of the players, the girl put her hands over her ears and shouted above the shrill sound: "Maybe if they stop squeezing, the bags will stop screaming!"

Sometimes we avoid the biblical prophets because all we hear is their piercing jeremiads. Yet if we take the time to meet them in their historical context, the prophets bring us back to divine messages we desperately need. There is an inherent consistency of message and focus among all of these diverse religious ruminations and rantings. First of all, the prophetic sermons are invariably rooted in the web of relationships created by the Sinai covenant. Israel belongs to Yahweh, and her lifestyle must be shaped by the stipulations of that suzerain-vassal treaty. Obedience to Yahweh triggers the blessings of the Sinai covenant, while disobedience is the first reason for Israel's experiences of its curses — drought, war, famine, enemy occupation, destruction of cities and fields, deportation, etc. For this reason, the prophetic writings are laced with moral diatribes that carry a strong emphasis on social ethics.

Second, the function and message of prophecy was very political. For Israel to come under the domination of other nations was always seen as a divine scourge resulting from the application of the covenant curses because of Israel's disobedience. How Israel handled its international relations showed plainly whether she trusted Yahweh, or had otherwise become enamored with power and politics rooted in lesser gods. Constantly the prophets asked whether Israel was Yahweh's witnessing people, or if she was merely another nation with no particular mission or divine purpose. Israel's self-understanding was thus always very religious, and at the same time very political.

Third, as the epochs of Israel's political fortunes unfolded, the message of the prophets became increasingly apocalyptic. There was a growing sense that because things had not gone the way they should have, producing heartfelt and ongoing national repentance and covenant restoration, Yahweh will have to intervene directly again, in a manner similar to that which happened during the time of Moses. When Yahweh interrupts human history the next time, however, along with judgments on the wickedness of the nations of the world, Israel will also fall heavily under divine punishment. But because Yahweh is on a mission to restore the fallen world, this next major divine intervention will be paired with a focus also on establishing a new world order, even as the old is falling away under the conflagration. In this coming messianic age, everything in both society and the natural realm will finally function in the manner the creator had intended in the beginning. Furthermore, because Yahweh is faithful to promises made, Israel will not be forgotten, and a remnant of God's servant nation will be at the center of all this renewal and restoration and great joy.

This increasingly forward-looking thrust of prophecy leads some to think of it as primarily foretelling, a kind of crystal-ball gaze into the future. In reality, however, the nature of prophecy in ancient Israel is more forth-telling, declaring again the meaning of the ancient Sinai covenant, explaining the mission of Yahweh as witness to the world, and describing the implications of the morality envisioned by the suzerain-vassal treaty stipulations.

By the time the seventh century BC rolled around, the prophets were rarely welcome in the royal palaces, even though all that was left of once proud and expansive Israel was the tiny mountainous territory of Judah. During the 600s, although Assyria kept threatening Jerusalem, it was increasingly occupied in defending itself against its rebellious eastern province of Babylon. During these years, while Jeremiah developed his gloomy diatribes in the heart of capital city, the messages of all the prophets had coalesced into an imminent intervention of Yahweh in the increasingly common term "The day of the Lord." Yet this global penetration of heaven's power would not be entirely destructive. As Isaiah often noted (including in today's reading), Yahweh's cleansing judgments are but the prelude to restoration and renewal, pointing to a future when the fortunes of Yahweh's people would be made full once again. Isaiah's words are the basis for all Advent celebrations: in a darkened world where the ways of God are no longer known, God will rescue the covenant community, restore their joys, and provide a light of grace that shines through them, beckoning the nations to enter the messianic celebration with them.

The true light, of course, would be Jesus, even though Zephaniah could not have apprehended at the time exactly how the divine message through him would be fulfilled. We, on the second Sunday of Advent, know exactly what God had in mind, and now wait in expectation for Jesus' culminating return to fully and perfectly realize the grandeur of the messianic kingdom. Someday the prophetic bagpipes will no longer be squeezed, and the music of the angels will shout the "Hallelujah" chorus.

Romans 15:4-13

Paul may well have had to wrestle his way through the problem of divine election (Romans 9-11) at least in part because of the mixed Jewish-Gentile makeup of the Roman congregation. This possible tension seems to reassert itself again in Paul's applications of Christian behavior in the chapters that follow. First, Paul urges a lifestyle of service rooted in sacrifice to Jesus (12:1-2), shaped by spiritual giftedness (12:3-8), and energized by love (12:9-21). Then Paul makes this servant behavior even more specific, by nodding to its public expressions (Romans 13): obey the government as a tool of God's care in the restraint of evil (13:1-6), and live as good neighbors who glow with the righteousness of God in some pretty dark neighborhoods (13:8-14). Finally, Paul revisits the issues surrounding the matter of the purchase and consumption of meat offered to idols (Romans 14:1--15:13), just has he had probed it in 1 Corinthians 8:1--11:1. Here, though, the overt tensions between legalistic and licentious extremes of Christian behavior seem less consuming than they did when Paul wrote to the Galatians and the Corinthians. Instead, his instructions flow more gently out of his social ethic of love and service.

Of course, all of this social ethic is based on just one thing for Paul: Jesus has come to change our darkness into light, our sadness into joy, and our selfishness into a grand paradise of caring good will. While the effects have only begun, during Advent we pray for the fullness of God's good pleasure to transform both ourselves and our society.

Matthew 3:1-12

Matthew's purpose for his gospel and the progression of his parallel lives — Israel and Jesus — is a clear script for the first seven chapters. Jesus relives the life of ancient Israel, but succeeds at what they were not able to do: bring fully the kingdom of heaven that will transform the earth.

It is in this intentional narrative that John the Baptist emerges as the consolidated voice of all of the Old Testament prophets. John the Baptist shouts his message to the crowds from Jerusalem who come to see his odd ministry at the Jordan River. The hardest thing to do in life is to maintain our integrity, he declares. Sin has entered the human soul precisely at this point. We are not, most of us, evil people. We're rather nice, aren't we? There's much that we do that's good and fine and noble and kind and wise, and no one can deny that.

But here's the problem: whatever else sin might do in our lives, it first and foremost perforates the lines of our hearts, and lets us tear off a piece here and a piece there, till we find ourselves segmented, fragmented, torn apart in separate snippets of self. It isn't that we become blackened by sin in large stroke. It isn't that we turn into some hideous monsters of greed and cruelty. It isn't that we dissolve the Dr. Jekylls of our personalities into dastardly Mr. Hydes. Instead, we keep most of our goodness intact, but we make small allowances in certain little areas. We cheat on our taxes a little, maybe... or we turn our eyes from the needs of someone we could help... or we compromise our communication till we speak from only our mouths instead of our souls.

The fragmentation of our lives makes us less than we should be, less than we could be. It makes us less than the people God made us to be. It is precisely because we and our world have lost our integrity that the great prophet of God must come and set things right.

There is a powerful scene in Robert Bolt's play *A Man for All Seasons*. The story is that of Sir Thomas More, loyal subject of the English crown. King Henry VIII wants to change things to suit his own devious plans, so he requires all his nobles to swear an oath of allegiance which violates the conscience of Sir Thomas More before his God. Since he will not swear the oath, More is put in jail. His daughter Margaret comes to visit him. "Meg," he calls her, with affection. She's his pride and joy, the one who thinks his thoughts after him.

Meg comes to plead with her father in prison. "Take the oath, Father!" she urges him. "Take it with your mouth, if you can't take it with your heart! Take it and return to us! You can't do us any good in here! And you can't be there for us if the king should execute you!"

She's right in so many ways! Yet her father answers her this way: "Meg, when a man swears an oath, he holds himself in his hands like water, and if he opens his fingers, how can he hope to find himself again?"

You know what he means, don't you? When our lives begin to fragment, it's like holding our lives like water in our hands, and then letting our fingers come apart, just a little bit. The water of our very selves dribbles away. We may look like the same people, but who we are inside has begun to change.

This is why John comes pointing the way to another kingdom. Here there will be no separation between the impulse of the heart, and the thought of the mind, and the word of the mouth, and the action of the hands. Somehow, everything about the coming kingdom is integrated. That's the meaning of the word "integrity," isn't it? Pure in heart!

Application

Jesus raises the banner of heaven's royal claims over both Gentile and Jewish territory, and thus is the source of political allegiances that supersede temporal boundaries. This is very good news during Advent, when the nations of the earth conspire against one another, and only the Christian church can effect a transnational celebration of the politics of grace: the peaceable kingdom.

Robert Coles is a child psychiatrist and professor at Harvard University who likes to try to figure out why we do the things we do. In his book *The Call of Service,* he wonders about people who try to make a difference in life; people who seek to reform themselves, even with the tenacity of sin that clings down deep; people who attempt to better society, in spite of the fact that it stubbornly refuses the challenge.

Why do they do it, Coles asks? The stories are all so different that it is hard to figure out a way to summarize them neatly in some framework. In fact, the people themselves often have a hard time defining what it is that makes them tick. One young teacher in an urban school gets challenged all the time. Street-smart students, weary of self-righteous "do-gooders," put the question to him: "What's in it for you?" they demand. And he really can't say.

But this he and all the rest of them can say: sometime earlier in their lives, each of them ran into a crisis situation, a situation that tested their identity and their willingness to do something about it; and in that crisis situation, each of them encountered someone who put his life on the line... someone who taught them the meaning of service... someone who gave of herself in a way that bucks the trend of selfishness and of self-preservation. And the influence of that someone else made it possible to be greater than each of them had previously considered. Enter the peaceable kingdom, where things change because we have brushed against the holiness of God, and Jesus becomes our Savior and mentor.

Years ago, when radio station WXYZ in Detroit was the big news in broadcasting, people spent hours each night listening to the latest episodes of "The Green Hornet" and S"ergeant Preston of the Yukon". Nearly every year the station brought out a new dramatic hero.

Station manager George Trendle often suggested the main ideas for these characters. In fact, he was the inspiration behind one of the most famous figures they ever created: the Lone Ranger. Trendle said this about the man he had in mind: "He's a sober-minded man with a righteous purpose. Make kids look up to him."

But that's easily lost on us. When Thomas Naylor was teaching business management at Duke University, he asked his students to draft a personal strategic plan. He reports that "with few exceptions, what they wanted fell into three categories: money, power, and things — very big things."

In fact, said Naylor, this was their request of the business faculty at Duke: "Teach me to be a moneymaking machine!" A moneymaking machine! A machine with no heart! That's the fragmentation of our lives taken to the extreme.

So here we are, in a sense, on the brink of another year, the liturgical year, the year of expectation of God's doing something good once again, the year of the coming of the kingdom announced by John. As they say, "Today is the first day of the rest of your life!" Let's imagine that there are 365 new days thrown back onto the credits side of the ledger. What do we do with them?

Alternative Application
Isaiah 11:1-10. Even though we like laughter and enjoy praise and celebration, especially at this time of year, it doesn't always come easily. One fellow tells of his work as a hospital volunteer. He couldn't believe the pain and suffering he saw there. Burn victims. Deformities. Terminal cancer. He watched the little ones cry. Some were so lonely: their parents couldn't take the trauma, so they never came to see their own children. How horrible!

He decided to get a clown's nose and a pair of oversized shoes. Then he painted his face and pulled on a wig. When he went to work dressed like that the next day, some of the children were scared, some were captivated, and some even showed hints of a smile for the first time in ages.

But others couldn't stop wailing. They were consumed by agony. What could he do for them? The next day the clown brought along some popcorn. When he came to the side of a crying child, he took a kernel of popcorn, placed it against the child's cheek, and soaked up the cascading tears with its fluff. Then he popped that kernel into his mouth and ate it.

It was a stroke of genius. The only time some of those children stopped crying was the moment they knew that somebody else cared enough to swallow their tears.

Advent brings us to a place like that. It takes us, at the end of our journey, to the "sanctuary" of God for a time of praise. "Sanctuary" is refuge, fortress, safe house, security, arms of love, a place where someone cares enough to swallow our tears and protect us from the worst that could harm us. This, certainly, is what the scenes of our Isaiah reading are all about.

Madeleine L'Engle paints a picture of such a sanctuary in one of her children's books. She tells of a young couple on a desert journey through wilderness in a rough caravan. They're on their way to Egypt. Someone is after them; someone wants to kill their little boy.

The journey is a rugged one. The desert is alive with ferocious beasts. All eyes cast about uneasily as darkness settles. There'll be little sleep in the camp tonight. They build a great fire to drive back the shadows and keep away the world that belongs to monsters with glowing eyes. Suddenly they start in terror; a great lion appears at the bonfire. The mother reaches for her child, desperately trying to draw him to safety.

But the child stands and laughs. He opens his arms wide to the lion. The lion lifts his front paws and hops around on his hind legs. He's dancing! And then, from the desert, come running several little mice and two donkeys and a snake and a couple of clumsy ostriches. Three great eagles swoop in from the purple skies. From the other side of the camp a unicorn emerges, and a pelican, and even two dragons.

They all bow before the child and then dance together round and round him. He stands at the center of their great circle, laughing in delight. It's a dance in the desert, as L'Engle calls it. In essence, it's the sum and substance of our worship here on earth, pilgrims passing through the wilderness of ghastly beasties and mournful hurts.

This is the second Sunday in Advent. Christmas seems close, but we are not there yet. We still spend time in the dark alongside those who wrestle with demons and shadows and beasties. But because of Advent confidence, we see the light and clap our hands in celebration of the child who comes to dance around our fires.

Third Sunday of Advent

Isaiah 35:1-10

James 5:7-10

Matthew 11:2-11

by Cathy Venkatesh

Easter in Advent

The third Sunday of Advent is traditionally one that emphasizes joy. Our readings invite us into the joy of new life with God *and* to examine our hearts to discover what may be keeping us from fully embracing that joy. Ultimately, in this season (as in all seasons) we are called to live into the hope of the resurrection.

Isaiah 35:1-10

Although today's oracle appears in the section scholars generally call First Isaiah (Chapters 1-39), its content suggests that it was originally part of Second Isaiah (Chapters 40-55), which dates to the 6th century BCE. In Second Isaiah, an unknown prophetic voice (only First Isaiah may be attributed to the prophet of that name) offers consolation to Israelites living in captivity in Babylon in light of their coming liberation under Cyrus of Persia. In today's reading, a vision of rejoicing exiles returning safely to Zion bears some similarities to the opening verses of Second Isaiah in chapter 40. A highway is made in a desert wilderness, and the wilderness is itself freed from the captivity of drought, just as the people are freed from the captivity of Babylon and the captivity of failing bodies. The commands "Strengthen the weak hands" and "Say to those of a fearful heart" may come from the heavenly council that appears in Isaiah 6 and again in Isaiah 40. The highway through the desert describes the land that separated Babylon and Judah, and is reminiscent of both the Exodus experience and the special roads Babylonians made for the festive processions of their own gods. The weak knees and fearful hearts must be strengthened for the joyous journey ahead. God's approach with vengeance and terrible recompense in verse four is good news to those who hear this oracle — God's vengeance will be against their oppressors, not them. Their ransom (verse ten) has been paid, and they will soon return home singing — possibly the songs of their homeland they were too grief-stricken to sing in captivity (Psalm 137)

James 5:7-10

This epistle — attributed to James, the brother of Jesus — echoes the wisdom writings of the Hebrew scriptures and holds a distinctive place in the New Testament canon. Though Martin Luther questioned its authority, most of the Christian church accepts the validity of its distinctive teaching. While Paul emphasized salvation by grace, not works, the writer of James was more concerned with the conduct of the faithful. What we do and how we live matters. Faith without works is dead (James 2:26). The writer may have been countering some of Paul's teachings, or misapplications of Paul's teaching, about grace. Both Paul and James are concerned about the conduct of the faithful, and neither of them advocate following Jewish law as necessary to salvation in Christ — a question that was alive for the early followers of Jesus. Instead, both Paul and James wish the followers of Christ to live justly and peaceably with one another, placing hearts and trust in God, not in the ways of the world.

Third Sunday of Advent

Today's passage comes from the final chapter of James, as the writer wraps up counsel and warnings and offers encouragement for continuing in the Christian life and community. In keeping with Advent expectation, the coming of the Lord is presumed to be near — the judge is at the door (James 5:9)! But the Judge has not yet stepped inside. In this waiting, in-between time, patience is an essential quality of faith in God and life with other believers. The author's mention of the suffering of the prophets hints that the community may be anticipating or experiencing persecution from without in addition to strife within. According to Josephus, James the brother to Jesus was put to death by the priestly authorities, probably around the year 62 (*Antiquities of the Jews* xx.9).

Matthew 11:2-11

I write this preceding our nation's presidential election — by the time these lessons roll around, I imagine our national mood will be different. Assuming a clear outcome, one month after the election we will be heading towards the holidays, biding our time between election and inauguration. But right now, anticipation keeps growing along with wonderings and whisperings, "Is he the one? Is she the one?" Anything one candidate says becomes immediate fodder for her or his opponent. It may be helpful to recall these anxious times as we explore today's reading

John is in prison, but he has a question: Is Jesus *the one*? The Messiah? The long hoped-for Savior? John's question may be direct, but Jesus' answer is not. It is too dangerous to answer directly in the political climate of Jesus' day. We know what happened to Jesus. To claim too early, too boldly that he is the Messiah would invite the wrath of the authorities and cut short his earthly ministry. Jesus is not ready to give the authorities who have imprisoned John words by which to imprison him too. He has more work to do. And so he answers with hints for those who know enough to hear them. John got his answer, and Jesus was able to continue his preaching and teaching. When Jesus tells John's disciples to report what they see, he is using words from Isaiah that we heard in today's reading, words that predict the coming liberation of the people by the Lord (Isaiah 35:5-6). Recall the preceding verse four, which states: "Say to those who are of a fearful heart, 'Be strong, do not fear! Here is your God.'" John and his disciples would have known that prophecy and the promise it made. "Yes," Jesus is telling them as he quotes the prophet.

Jesus then turns to address the crowd, and in a similar way hints at his messianic authority to those who know their scripture. From quoting Isaiah, he moves on to quote the prophet Malachi as he praises John the Baptist in Matthew 11:10 (see Malachi 3:1). In the final two verses of the Hebrew prophets, Malachi (4:5-6) promises the return of the prophet Elijah, and in Matthew 11:14 Jesus asserts of John, "he is Elijah who is to come." The description of John's rough clothes in the gospels is another allusion to Elijah (see Matthew 3:1 and 2 Kings 1:8), and the place where John was baptizing was a location associated with Elijah stories (*Harper Collins Study Bible*, p. 1671). If John is Elijah, it begs the question of who Jesus may be. If he is not Elijah, could Jesus be the Messiah? The way has been prepared. The judge is at the door.

Application

I went to seminary in California, and though I loved the seasons there, as someone who grew up in the northeastern U.S. I found them very strange. For me, Advent meant shortening gray days, bare branches on the trees, and hopes for snow at Christmas. In California we had some gray days during Advent as well, but that was because the rains had come. In December, when I was used to a dormant natural world, the landscape around me sprang to life. The dry golden hills turned bright green, and walks amidst the lush grasses after the rains had ceased revealed wildflowers blooming in profusion. Isaiah's vision of the parched desert springing to life rang true. The Currier & Ives images of traditional Christmas cards were replaced by desert blossoms.

Our readings today counsel patience, but they also counsel preparation to be able to fully embrace the joy that is to come. The exiles need to be strengthened for their joyful return to their homeland. Jesus, too, in his healing ministry is preparing the way for something new. Our Advent preparation for Jesus' coming means taking some inventory — what is parched in our individual and communal lives? Where are we weak and fearful? Blind or deaf, lame, leprous, or mute? We are invited into a season of joy, but our minds or bodies may not be ready to celebrate. With two weeks to go until Christmas Day, we still have time to take some inventory above and beyond any last-minute shopping lists.

In the Episcopal Church, this collect is appointed for the third Sunday of Advent: *Stir up your power, O Lord, and with great might come among us; and, because we are sorely hindered by our sins, let your bountiful grace and mercy speedily help and deliver us; through Jesus Christ our Lord, to whom, with you and the Holy Spirit, be honor and glory, now and forever. Amen.* In what ways do our sins, or wounds caused by the sins of others, hinder us from fully participating in God's kingdom? Now is the time to name them and to ask for God's healing, liberating aid. Each of us will have stories from our own lives and communities of healing and forgiveness, of putting down burdens of fear, shame, or long-held anger and grief, and discovering new nimbleness of spirit and heart. John the Baptist, with so many others of his time, was looking for a Messiah who would free his people from the oppression of Roman rule. Jesus was doing many remarkable things, but he didn't look and act quite like John expected or scripture foretold. "Are you the one?" he sent his disciples to ask Jesus. And Jesus' answer was yes, he is the liberator of God's people, but the liberation he brings is of a different, deeper sort than any political or military victory. Jesus has come to free people from the burden of sin and to heal those who are broken in body, heart, and spirit. There is much grim news in our world, but this news is not the reality of God among us. In Advent, as always, we are invited to listen to a different frequency than the world around us, one that leads us to dance and live in hope no matter our external circumstances.

While I commend the entire poem, the last stanza of *They Have Threatened Us with Resurrection* ("Nos han amenazado de Resurrección") by Julia Esquivel speaks deeply to this Christian hope:

To dream awake,
to keep watch asleep,
to live while dying,
and to know ourselves already
resurrected!

As we head towards the manger and Bethlehem, we also head towards Easter Day and the healing of the very worst that the world can do. Easter in Advent? As natural as the desert blooming after rain.

Fourth Sunday of Advent
Isaiah 7:10-16
Romans 1:1-7
Matthew 1:18-25
by Wayne Brouwer

Baby Changes Everything

As one congregation went through years of great growth and expansion, it became obvious that there could not be any more additions to its current facilities. A massive new capital campaign was launched, a ten-acre property was purchased, and architects began to design a new ministry center. Members of the church were involved at every step of the way, and many good ideas were incorporated into the layout and decorating schemes.

One Bible study group suggested that a scriptural text should be painted over the passages into each distinct ministry area of the new building. When the doors finally opened and members of the congregation wandered through the fresh facilities, many stopped to read and appreciate the dedicatory verses. Over the main entrance were the words "My house shall be a house of prayer for all nations" (Isaiah 56:7), and when people turned around to see the message that would face those who were leaving, they viewed Jesus' final command to his disciples: "Go and make disciples of all nations" (Matthew 28:19). Above the doors to the worship auditorium was the powerful phrase from the Psalmist: "Enter his gates with thanksgiving, and his courts with praise!" (Psalm 100:4). At the fellowship hall came the testimony "They broke bread and ate together with glad and sincere hearts" (Acts 2:46), and emblazoned over the doors into the educational wing was the reminder "The fear of the Lord is the beginning of wisdom" (Proverbs 1:7).

The general response to these Bible verses was very positive. But one of them raised more than a few eyebrows. At the reception desk of the infant nursery was posted "We shall not all sleep, but we shall be changed" (1 Corinthians 15:51)!

Those are fitting words for a room full of babies! But diapers are not the only things changed when the wee ones are around. Parents are changed. Houses are changed. Families are changed. Neighborhoods are changed. Society is changed.

Bret Harte described that whimsically well in his short story *The Luck of Roaring Camp*. In a California gold miners' camp, the local woman of ill-repute, Cherokee Sal, dies in childbirth. She never discloses who fathered the baby, so, with a guilty conscience, the entire dirty settlement owns him.

But the rough and reckless and raw existence of a mining camp is at odds with the helpless innocence of a newborn, now called Tommy Luck. First a bed needs to be made and clean sheets found. People have to take turns holding and feeding the baby, and even the noisy camp has to shut down during naptime. Within weeks, no visitor to Roaring Camp would recognize the place. A baby had changed everything.

Each of our lectionary passages for today is about a baby who changes everything. When the Assyrians threatened Ahaz' little kingdom of Judah, Yahweh promised deliverance through Isaiah, and sealed the deal with a birth announcement. Paul testifies to the Christian congregation in Rome that the coming of baby Jesus into our world has changed everything for him and for them. And when Matthew retells the story of Jesus' birth, he remembers how the event changed Joseph's life forever. This baby changes everything for everyone!

Isaiah 7:10-16

Who was Isaiah? His name meant "Salvation is of Yahweh," and this truly typified his words and prophecies. He was married (Isaiah 8:3) and had at least two children (Isaiah 7:3; 8:3), who were themselves illustrations of Isaiah's prophetic declarations. The commissioning scene of Isaiah 6, with its temple location, along with all of the liturgical language surrounding Isaiah's call, suggests that Isaiah might have been a priest, or at least a member of a Levite family. At the same time, his easy and constant access to successive kings (cf. Isaiah 7:3; 38:1; 39:1) might imply that he was an employee of the royal court, although his statement in 37:6 ("Say to your master...") could be interpreted as setting him outside of the political system, at least at some point. Nevertheless, with the narratives of chapters 36-39 incorporated directly into the book, Isaiah obviously was at minimum a court recorder or scribe or historian of some kind (see also 2 Chronicles 26:22). Most likely he was the chief historian in the royal house, and possibly even a member of the extended royal family. In his duties he appears to have functioned as the official scribe or court recorder. Using that platform as a pulpit, he expressed magnificently worded prophetic analyses and judgments about the religious and political actions of the kings.

Isaiah was overwhelmed by a divine commissioning (6) that took place in the temple during the year that King Uzziah died. He was guided by the theology of the Sinai covenant (2-5), which mandated that Israel was supposed to have a unique lifestyle among the nations, a set of behaviors that would serve as a missional call for others to join this holy community in a global return to the ways of their creator. He was confident that Yahweh could resolve all political problems (7-11), no matter how daunting they might seem. He believed Israel/Judah needed to repent (12), and recover their original identity and purpose as Yahweh's covenant partners and witnesses. He was certain that Yahweh was sovereign over all nations (13-35), even if Yahweh's primary focus was attached to Israel/Judah. He heard the heartbeat of divine love and compassion, wrestling for the soul and destiny of Israel/Judah as a loved companion and partner (36-41). He saw Yahweh transforming Israel's/Judah's identity and fortunes through a "suffering servant" leader (42-53). He envisioned a future age in which all the world and every society and even the universe itself would be restored to harmony with its creator and would resonate with magnificent glory (56-66).

Among the prophets of ancient Israel, Isaiah was truly a prince, and his writings shaped the language of theological reflection among his peers and on into the age of the New Testament church. And that is why so many snippets of Isaiah's ancient declarations continue to find their way into our modern Advent celebrations. Isaiah lived in a time of great crisis, when everyone was certain that the Assyrians were about to end all life as they knew it. The writing was on the wall. Very soon Judah's northern brother Israel would fall to that militaristic world power, and King Ahaz was dithering about like a plucked chicken with no place to hide.

It had been clear to Yahweh for some time that the kings of Israel following Solomon were not walking in the steps of great King David. In the north, beginning with Elijah and Elisha, God's leadership of the people had already shifted from the unfaithful kings to the stern prophets. In today's lectionary reading the same is taking place in the south. Ahaz, grandson of notorious King Ahab, is looking for a way to stem the inevitable flood of destruction, and by way of prophet Isaiah, Yahweh provides an out. Stay strong, stay free from allies, trust Yahweh, and deliverance will come.

With fake piety, Ahaz pretends not to want to bother God. But God wants to be bothered about things that truly matter. So God promises Ahaz a sign in spite of the kingly protests. A child will soon be born, said Isaiah, Yahweh's spokesperson. Within nine months, the threats from the north would dissipate, and Judah's salvation would be secured. The truth will be revealed: "Immanuel! God is with us!"

So it is that we who live in a world overshadowed by superpowers and super-viruses, terrorism and trauma, continue to wait on God's promises, and the coming of the divine deliverer. We still get scared in the dark. And we still hope for Immanuel.

Romans 1:1-7

Somewhere around late 53 AD, the social and economic impact of the Christian gospel began to be felt acutely in Ephesus (see Acts 19). Among the many cultural and civic resources of that city was its shrine to Artemis (known among the Romans as Diana). This temple was considered to be one of the seven wonders of the world. In fact, a great portion of the economy of Ephesus was derived from the cultic activities surrounding the temple, along with the religious tourist trade it brought to the city. As Christian adherents multiplied in Ephesus, and numbers of participants in the religious and social services related to the temple decreased, the local business world felt deeply challenged.

In response, "a silversmith named Demetrius" called together other craftsmen, and incited a public riot that brought the city to a standstill (Acts 19:23-41). Local government officials eventually diffused the situation, but Paul believed the time had come for him to move on. He traveled around the Aegean Sea, collecting the offerings that had been set aside in the churches for the large benevolence gift he was planning to bring to Jerusalem. Paul arrived in Corinth either late in 53 or early in 54 and stayed three months with his friend Gaius (Acts 19:1-3; Romans 16:23). When he found that another acquaintance (and a leader in the Christian congregation located in Cenchrea, one of Corinth's seaport suburbs) named Phoebe was making a trip to Rome (Romans 16:1), Paul quickly penned what has become the most orderly summary of early Christian theology.

Because Paul had not yet made a visit to Rome, this letter was less personal and more rationally organized than was often otherwise true. Paul intended this missive to be a working document; the congregation, already established in the capital city of the empire, would be able to read and discuss it together, in anticipation of Paul's arrival, which was planned for some months ahead (Romans 1:6-15). Paul summarized his working theme and emphasis up front: a new expression of the "righteousness of God" had been recently revealed, with great power, through the coming of Jesus Christ (Romans 1:17).

Jesus is Lord of all, Paul fairly shouts at the beginning, producing wonderful new life in all who are part of the church, both Jews who have long waited for their Messiah and also for Gentiles, newly incorporated into the family of faith. Probably because of the controversy revolving around Paul's sense of his mission to the Gentiles, a brief reminder comes that Jews and Gentiles are together on the same footing before God because of the powerful redemptive work of Jesus. As he begins to celebrate this amazing grace of God, Paul interrupts himself, reminding his readers of the specific calling he has received to know and communicate this divine revelation. Then Paul launches into an extended metaphor on what it means for the living Body of Christ (see Romans 12) to function in a dark world where, for too long, the righteousness of God (Romans 1:17) has been either hidden or ignored. Now that Jesus has arrived, grace and faith are expanding everywhere.

Matthew 1:18-25

When Matthew tells us of the manner in which Jesus came into this world, he declares, like Isaac, Samson, and Samuel, that this baby is a divinely sent deliverer. Each of these other great figures in Israel's history was miraculously born to mothers who were barren, and all of them provided new hope for their families and also the whole of the people of Yahweh. As with those earlier stories, here an angelic messenger explains the matter to one of the soon-to-be parents (Joseph), and provides a name for the child. "He will save his people," says the angel. Picking up on the word of Yahweh that came through Isaiah to ancient King Ahaz (Isaiah 7:11), Matthew informs us that history is repeating itself.

Each of these deliverers of God's people changed the course of history. Abram and Sarai were far too old to have a baby. They knew that themselves; it was the reason why Sarai sent her maid Hagar to have sexual intercourse with Abram and make a baby Sarai could claim for her own. Yet God managed the impossible, and Isaac was born to his ancient parents, causing them "laughter" (the meaning of Isaac's name) that they never had anticipated. Isaac's birth became the first step toward the amazing family growth story that was eventually Israel herself.

Samson came along, to otherwise barren parents, when the crisis of ungodliness and Philistine domination threatened the Israelites. Stronger than an ox, and more unruly than a cornered bear, Samson was nevertheless Yahweh's agent for Israelite deliverance. He tangled with the enemy and killed many of their soldiers. He shamed Philistine society and burned the fields. Samson was an embarrassment to his enemies, his own people, his family, his girlfriends, and himself, but he was also a divinely sent deliverer. And that became his ultimate claim to fame, particularly when he learned humility and renewed his connection with the God of his homeland.

Above all, it was Samuel who had God's ear. Born to a barren mother by a miraculous answer to prayer (1 Samuel 1), Samuel lived at a time when "the word of God was rare" (1 Samuel 3:1). This was a tragedy and great misfortune for a people who lived by the very word of the Lord. When God called out in the night, it was not the priest Eli who heard it, but little Samuel (1 Samuel 2). For decades he would become the hotline to heaven for the Israelites. And it was because God had the ear of Samuel that Samuel had the ear of God. When Samuel prayed, things changed. Samuel was the great deliverer of the Israelites.

So when Matthew explains the circumstances of Jesus' entrance into our world, he draws the connections carefully. A baby like this changes everything. He changes Joseph's life. He changes Mary's life. He changes life for the family and neighborhood. But most of all, he changes life for the whole of the people of God. "He will save his people from their sins." And the world has never been the same.

Application

Circumstances change. Happenings happen for a while, and then stop happening. We need to pin our goals and values on something deeper than shifting sands. That is precisely why the great change produced by Jesus is so earthshaking. This change links us to the great unchanging testimony of scripture, that God's love for us never changes, never dips, never flags, never fails. God's mercies are new every morning.

When we are in tune with the creator and the creation, temporary dissonance and discord are momentary ripples that soon will be smoothed into the larger patterns of life's fabric. Henry Francis Lyte was only 54, but several years of illness had kept him from functioning to full potential in his congregation in a small fishing village. His limitations seemed to have fostered problems in the church. At one time worship services were crowded, and over 800 children were taught by 70 teachers in the Sunday school program. At one time he knew the names of every boat in the harbor and every man who walked the docks. At one time his tireless care and enthusiasm drew even skeptics to Christ.

But now he was failing rapidly. His doctor told him to quit the ministry. His congregation was falling apart. And here he sat on a bluff above the sea, wondering what message to bring for his last Sunday evening sermon.

The points and outline wouldn't come. They were crowded out by the cares and troubles that surrounded him. But then a prayer began to form in his mind that softly caressed his vision back into focus. The prayer began to sing itself. And by the time his people gathered for worship, a new hymn called them into the presence of God.

Fourth Sunday of Advent

Henry Lyte died a few months later. But he died a blessed man. And people in churches around the world know that each time they open their hymnbooks to sing his prayer:

"Abide with Me!"
Abide with me! Fast falls the evening tide.
The darkness deepens; Lord, with me abide!
Change and decay in all around I see;
O Thou Who changest not, abide with me!
I need your presence every passing hour;
What but your grace can foil the tempter's power?
Who like yourself my guide and strength can be?
Through cloud and sunshine, O abide with me!

Not a bad testimony for us to make during Advent, when we know the changelessness of God's love toward us, the changes that happened to our world when the baby came, and the hope we have for faith's unchanging courage during these rapidly changing times.

An Alternative Application
Romans 1:1-7. There is a powerful scene in Robert Bolt's play *A Man for All Seasons*. The story is that of Sir Thomas More, loyal subject of the English crown. King Henry VIII wants to change things to suit his own devious plans, so he requires all his nobles to swear an oath of allegiance which violates the conscience of Sir Thomas More before his God. Since he will not swear the oath, More is put in jail. His daughter Margaret comes to visit him. "Meg," he calls her, with affection. She's his pride and joy, the one who thinks his thoughts after him.

Meg comes to plead with her father in prison. "Take the oath, Father!" she urges him. "Take it with your mouth, if you can't take it with your heart! Take it and return to us! You can't do us any good in here! And you can't be there for us if the king should execute you!"

She's right in so many ways! Yet her father answers her this way: "Meg, when a man swears an oath, he holds himself in his hands like water, and if he opens his fingers, how can he hope to find himself again?"

You know what he means, don't you? When our lives begin to fragment, it's like holding our lives like water in our hands, and then letting our fingers come apart just a little bit. The water of our very selves dribbles away. We may look like the same people, but who we are inside has begun to change.

This is why Paul comes pointing the way to another kingdom. Here there will be no separation between the impulse of the heart and the thought of the mind, and the word of the mouth and the action of the hands. Somehow, everything about the coming kingdom is integrated. That's the meaning of the words "righteousness" and "integrity," isn't it? Pure in heart!

When the one of righteousness and integrity arrives, this world must change. This is why we celebrate Advent over and over, until the coming again of God's anointed one. When Bill Moyers interviewed Dr. Rachel Naomi Remen, she told him how it was for her. Dr. Remen has founded several institutes for the care of cancer patients. She said that sometimes she has a much greater sense of integrity within during those times when she isn't feeling all that well physically. Bill asked her what she meant by "integrity," and she replied "that I am what I am..." She said that even with her wounds and her weaknesses "there's an essence and a uniqueness and a beauty" about her life that is whole and complete. Integrity. Pure in heart. The peaceable kingdom.

Jesus raises the banner of heaven's royal claims over both Gentile and Jewish territory, and thus is the source of political allegiances that supersede temporal boundaries. This is very good news during Advent, when the nations of the earth conspire against one another and only the Christian church can effect a trans-national celebration of the politics of grace. The peaceable kingdom.

The Nativity of Our Lord
Isaiah 9:2-7
Titus 2:11-14
Luke 2:1-14 (15-20)
by David Kalas

All that he is

The psalmist cries out "O, magnify the Lord with me" (Psalm 34:3), and we make take that as our invitation and our calling this holiday. The occasion and scriptures combine to give us that opportunity. They give us the chance to magnify the Lord.

When I was a boy, I misunderstood the phrase "magnify the Lord." It made no sense to me, for I thought that you can't make God bigger than he already is. And, of course, we can't. But what we can do with him is something akin to what we do with any magnifying glass: we can try to look at him more closely and to see him more clearly.

In that sense, of course, it is always the role of the preacher to be a magnifying glass for the congregation. And today's familiar passages are a great benefit to us in that work. Specifically, each passage enables us to look more closely at Jesus, and thus to see him more clearly.

Opponents notwithstanding, you and I still see a fair number of nativity scenes in stores, churches, front yards, and individual homes. They represent the Christmas event. But in those scenes, all we really see is that Jesus is a baby. And candidly, that may be all that so much of the culture around us knows about him this Christmas.

But Jesus is more than just a baby. He was then, which is why the angels, Herod, shepherds, and Magi all responded in the ways that they did. And he is certainly more than a baby now. So it is that Isaiah, Luke, and Paul cooperate with one another and with us today to help us proclaim all that he is!

Isaiah 9:2-7

Preaching is a privilege, to be sure. I'd be hard pressed to think of a greater one. Yet occasionally I wish that we worked in a different medium, for words — at least my words — seem inadequate for the task. And specifically just now I'm thinking of both music and painting.

The composer and the artist are able to do things, you see, that the preacher cannot. For when we speak, we are obliged to speak only one word, one phrase, one sentence at a time. To overlap words and phrases would become incoherent for our audiences. Yet the composer is able to arrange many notes together at a single moment in his piece. And the artist, meanwhile, is able to present an entire picture at once, with all of its colors and details there to be seen and discovered.

This familiar seasonal passage from Isaiah might be more effectively presented to our people in music or art than in words. Our challenge is to help our people see and hear simultaneously the truths that are contained here. They are gospel truths, and these few prophetic verses are packed full of them.

First, we note the familiar theme of light and darkness. From the first act of God at creation (Genesis 1:3) to the climactic descriptions of the new Jerusalem (Revelation 21:23-25), light and darkness are recurring themes in scripture. And we perceive that the issue is not merely the literal, physical state of light or dark. Rather, we recognize that those physical states become metaphors for deeper, spiritual conditions (e.g., Psalm 82:5; John 8:12). And that seems to be what is at stake here for the people referenced in Isaiah 9:2.

Second, we hear here the theme of rejoicing, which is surely a part of our association with this holiday. To capture the quality of that promised gladness, the prophet utilizes two contemporary images that would have had familiar and practical meaning for his audience: namely, harvesting crops and dividing spoils. Both connote abundance and success. Yet while we do not naturally associate Christmas with warfare, the prophet expands more on that imagery than on the harvest.

There is talk of oppressors, battles, warriors, and blood. This is not the stuff of secular Christmas songs — "White Christmas," "Winter Wonderland," or "Frosty the Snowman" — to be sure. Yet a thoughtful reading of our Christian corpus of Christmas music, on the other hand, reveals some very sober themes. Consider the imagery, for example, found in "O Come, O Come, Emmanuel," "Come, Thou Long-Expected Jesus," or "Joy to the World." Our hymnody recognizes that Christmas is no trite celebration. There are, indeed, issues of oppression, liberty, and victory involved.

Then we come to the most familiar — and probably most cherished — portion of the passage. George Frideric Handel has perhaps done more than any preacher to make famous Isaiah's language about the child that will be born and the names by which he will be called.

We will give more thought to these particulars below. For the present, though, it is sufficient for us to note simply the breadth of the promise. The child's impact seems to be both global and eternal; his roles run the gamut from exalted to intimate; and his attributes range from power to peace.

Words can't do justice, therefore, to all that is here. You and I would need the skill of a musician or painter to capture all at once all of the gospel truths contained in these few prophetic verses.

Titus 2:11-14

When we think of the Christmas story, we tend to think of its tangible elements — the ones that can be depicted in a crèche or nativity tableau. We think of angels and shepherds, wise men and gifts, stable and manger, parents and baby. Yet the apostle Paul offers a different take on the familiar scene. "The grace of God has appeared," he writes, "bringing salvation to all men."

Write that as the caption below the picture. When we see the cherished tableau or crèche, let this be our understanding of it. It is not merely that a baby has been born, but that the grace of God has appeared. It is not only that God sent his son, but that that baby has brought salvation for all.

As Paul expands on that salvation, he portrays a kind of reorientation of a human life. On the one side, there are the worldly desires and ungodliness. On the other side, there is sensible, righteous, and godly living. Likewise, at the end of the passage he juxtaposes "every lawless deed" and "good deeds." The salvation of God, you see, instructs us to turn from the one to the other.

The trick, of course, is found in the phrase "the present age." Paul understands that a global change awaits — a new age with a new way of living. In the meantime, however, the prevailing winds in this world blow mostly contrary to the ways of God. To deny the worldly desires and live righteously "in the present age," therefore, is a profound challenge. No fish has had to swim upstream against so strong a current as the man or woman of God seeking to live for him in a fallen world.

Finally, the apostle turns to a future prospect. Interestingly, he balances his earlier statement by utilizing the same word. The underlying Greek words, which we translate "appeared" and "appearing" are the source of our word Epiphany, and this epiphany evidently comes in two phases. The grace of God has already appeared; we still wait and hope, however, for the appearing of his glory.

Harry Emerson Fosdick's familiar hymn is not a Christmas carol, but it surely fits the spirit and themes of this passage. The salutation "God of grace and God of glory" captures the two-part nature of his appearing. "Grant us wisdom, grant us courage, for the living of these days,"1 meanwhile, speaks to our challenge of living between his first and his second comings.

The Nativity of Our Lord

Luke 2:1-14 (15-20)

It is Matthew, with his characteristic concern for the fulfillment of Old Testament prophecy, who reports the significance of Jesus' birth occurring in Bethlehem (Matthew 2:4-6). But it is Luke who tells us how it came to pass that a couple from Nazareth should have their baby in that prophesied town. The emperor in Rome had no idea how his decree was just a bumper in God's bank shot.

Interestingly, while Caesar Augustus was the big cheese in the world at the time, he places second in this narrative to a different king. And specifically, a king that had already been dead for a thousand years at that, for the truly dominant human monarch in this passage is David, who is mentioned three separate times in these fourteen verses. First, the narrator associates Bethlehem with David, and then Joseph with David. And later, the angel also makes the connection between Bethlehem and David.

The angelic reference is especially conspicuous. The shepherds, we assume, were located not far from Bethlehem. If you or I, therefore, had wanted to direct them to some site in Bethlehem, how would we have done it? Well, if I am just outside of town, I would simply say, "In town." And if I were a tad further removed, I would specify the town by name; I'd refer to it as Bethlehem. The angel, however, seems to go out of his way to introduce David into the news, eschewing the town's actual name and referring to it rather as "the city of David."

Even the audience for the angelic news tacitly recalls David. He, after all, is the most famous Bethlehem shepherd.

The prominence of David is no accident, of course, for by highlighting that particular man from history the story tells us a great deal about the baby in the present. And just as Jesus is implicitly tied to David here, the Palm Sunday crowds make the connection explicit, calling out "Hosanna to the Son of David" (Matthew 21:9). In human terms, Jesus is the son of Joseph, but Joseph is irrelevant to the crowds' expectations.

Not long after Palm Sunday, a conversation between Jesus and the Pharisees reveals what those specific expectations were. "What do you think of the Messiah?" Jesus asked them. "Whose son is he?" And without question or hesitation, the Pharisees responded, "The son of David" (Matthew 22:41). The prominence of David in the story of Jesus' birth, therefore, is a subtle witness to who Jesus is and what he will be.

Finally, the familiar scene in the field and night sky outside of Bethlehem paints a fascinating picture of reality. The human audience, we observe, was small, motley, and afraid. In the sky overhead, meanwhile, there was "a multitude of the heavenly host praising God." Perhaps that scene is not limited to Christmas night. Perhaps that is always the case. Perhaps the human audience for the good news of Jesus is always lagging behind the fabulous understanding and adoration of the heavenly host.

Application

The Isaiah and Luke passages go hand in hand: they both speak of a birth, and we see in retrospect that they speak of the same birth. The former declares "Unto us is born," and the latter proclaims "Unto you is born…" We observe, therefore, that it is a surprisingly personalized birth. In neither case is the audience the immediate family of the baby, you see, and yet still the birth is somehow "unto" them. This is the first layer of gospel to be revealed about all that Jesus is: namely, that he is personal; that he is "unto you."

Both the prophetic and angelic messengers tell about the birth of a child, and each one elaborates on the identity of that child. As we have noted above, both texts identify the child with David. The Luke passage makes its three different references to David, deliberately tying the baby's lineage and birthplace to that singularly important figure from Israel's history. Isaiah, meanwhile, anticipates that the child who is born will one day occupy "the throne of David and (rule) over his kingdom." And that is not expected to be the finite reign of an ordinary monarch, but "from then on and forevermore." This is a very special baby indeed.

Furthermore, Isaiah's prophecy offers a famous list of titles for this child: "Wonderful Counselor, Mighty God, Eternal Father, Prince of Peace." Within the ordinary context of human events it is an astounding prospect, you see. For it is no mere mortal that is being promised for David's throne and kingdom. Rather, in a remarkable turn, it is evidently God himself who will occupy David's throne and rule eternally over that kingdom.

As an aside, we may note that the natural tendency for a great many Christians is to keep God at a distance. And I don't necessarily mean, in this case, that we keep him at a distance personally, but rather that we keep him at a distance theologically. In our beliefs and doctrines, we associate him and his presence primarily with heaven. Yet from the God who comes walking in the Garden of Eden to the God who plans to occupy David's throne to the God who puts on flesh and is born in Bethlehem, we worship an astonishingly personal and present God. So while we tend to relegate him to heaven, the end-time declaration instead says this: "See, the home of God is among mortals. He will dwell with them; they will be his peoples, and God himself will be with them" (Revelation 21:3).

Meanwhile, the angel in Luke also weighs in on the identity of the baby. In addition to the Davidic references, the angel calls Jesus "Savior," "Christ," and "Lord." These three terms are so full of power and meaning that each deserves its own sermon. Perhaps one year I will preach a four-part Advent sermon series on what just what the angel says alone.

The news that "there has been born for you a Savior" speaks, first, of the human need for a Savior, as well as the truth that only God himself can be that savior (Isaiah 43:11). Also, it reminds us of the significance of Jesus' name (see Matthew 1:21), how he articulates his mission (Luke 19:10), and how the apostle Paul summarizes the reason for his coming (1 Timothy 1:15).

The title "Christ," of course, carries in Greek the same meaning as the Hebrew "Messiah." This baby is the long-awaited anointed one. He has been promised and foretold. For generations, the people had hung their hopes on the prospect of his coming. That single term, therefore, carries with it an accumulated meaning, enhanced and enriched by years of prophecies. And now the angel affirmed that the Christ, with all that means, was here.

Finally, the angel calls him "the Lord." This is likely to be an undervalued term in our vernacular, for it has almost no meaning apart from a religious context. In the world of the Bible, however, it was a word with real-world teeth. It connoted ownership, authority, and sovereignty. It was a human title with such potency that the people of God found it an apt title for him. And over the course of generations, it also became associated with the revered name of God. For the angel to call this baby "the Lord," therefore, was a statement of tremendous substance.

And so on this holiday, we may put the pieces together from the selected texts and preach the gospel. Indeed, more gospel than can be easily fit into a single message. For it is the profound good news of all that he is!

An Alternative Application

Luke 2:1-14 — "And the Government." The people of Jesus' day may have tended to over-politicize their understanding of the Messiah. Fixated on the political and military reality of the occupying Roman Empire, they expected God's promised one to function as a heroic military figure, a liberating revolutionary, and a strong monarch. And so they misunderstood and underestimated what the real work of Jesus would be.

Conversely, the people of our day by tend to under-politicize their understanding of Christ. That's not to say that Christians — or their preachers — necessarily ought to be more overtly or actively political. Rather, we need to rediscover the biblical truth that Jesus is Lord and that he will one day reign over all.

That political reality is plainly anticipated, of course, in the familiar language of Isaiah 9. David's throne is referenced, and an ever-growing kingdom is promised. No need to spiritualize the message, for its plain meaning is quite clear. Government is mentioned twice. And the expected child will be the centerpiece of that awaited government.

The Luke narrative, meanwhile, tells the story of that child's birth and openly identifies him as the Christ. But it is Luke's starting place for his story that adds a political hue to the picture. For I think we make a mistake if we dismiss the references to Caesar Augustus and Quirinius as mere narrative stage-setting. I believe there is a larger, theological component to the storyteller's choice.

The story begins with a sovereign's decree. What Caesar dictates sets people and events in motion. It has a seemingly global impact. Yet the decree from Caesar Augustus is juxtaposed in short order with a declaration from a different sovereign. The Lord God has a plan, and it is announced by no less than angel heralds. Moreover, the impact of the Lord's activity it is even more global than Caesar's sway, for it "shall be for all the people."

We may also detect a gently condescending tone in Luke's narrative. "This was the first census taken," he notes, "while Quirinius was governor of Syria." The human potentates and their actions are implicitly minimized. These rulers, after all, come and go. Their tenures have beginnings and ends. And their big-deal decrees can be condensed to enumeration.

In contrast, the activity of God that Luke reports is epochal. It is a once-in-history event, and it changes everything. And the important human rulers of their day are reduced to mere props — backdrop, scenery — in the story of Jesus' birth.

---

1. Harry E. Fosdick, *God of Grace and God of Glory*, United Methodist Hymnal, #577.

First Sunday after Christmas Day

Isaiah 63:7-9

Hebrews 2:10-18

Matthew 2:13-23

Psalm 148

by David Kalas and Schuyler Rhodes

Trapped in stained glass

I love stained glass. I grew up in churches that were very traditional, older structures, and stained-glass windows were essential parts of those sanctuaries. I have meditated on the messages contained in those windows through the years. And I have gained great insight, blessing, and inspiration from how stained-glass artists have depicted the events and characters of scripture.

For all of that, though, it may be important in our day to free Jesus from stained glass — at least in the minds of many people.

To an uninformed world outside — and to a sometimes minimally informed Sunday morning congregation inside — Jesus is seen as the exclusive property of religion. And mostly just one religion, at that. Just as the Bible became the privileged province of those educated few who could read Latin in medieval Europe, so Jesus has perhaps become the peculiar belonging of those who profess faith in him, with their mysterious liturgies, inscrutable traditions, and enigmatic doctrines.

Perhaps in the preaching, the teaching, and the emphases of the church through the generations, Jesus has taken a backseat to the two natural human preoccupations of religion: beliefs and behavior. One dogmatic group has insisted on right doctrine, while another, moralistic group has insisted on right living. And amid the kaleidoscope of peripherals, the world has not been able to see Jesus himself.

What an irony if the church has managed, inadvertently, to undo the incarnation. The Son of God put on flesh, but the church has put him in stained glass.

With the two New Testament lections we have for this week, we will have opportunity to put Jesus back where he belongs: as the flesh-and-blood center of God's good news for the world.

Isaiah 63:7-9

What things did you recount yesterday?

To recount is to recall in some detail. And we do a fair amount of recounting every day; some of which may be quite unhealthy.

If I am in an argument with someone, and the disagreement becomes personal, I might recount to him or her some unpleasant things. The times I have been right in the past, for example, or the times that he or she has been wrong. I might recount the other person's past failings, or I might recount their faults.

If I am in a complaining mood, I might recount to some poor victim in my proximity all of my aches and pains or all of my troubles or all of my worries. If I am in a bragging frame of mind, I might recount my accomplishments and achievements (or my children's). If I am feeling overwhelmed, I might lie in bed recounting all the things I have to do. If I am being prickly and critical, I might recount all that was wrong with that meal or that performance or that trip.

First Sunday after Christmas Day

On the happier and healthier side, I would do well to recount to my wife the things that I love about her, to recount to my children the many ways I am proud of them, to recount to my coworkers the things I appreciate about them, and so on.

The prophet Isaiah, meanwhile, takes the highest path of all: "I will recount the gracious deeds of the Lord, the praiseworthy acts of the Lord."

Surely we have seen clearly in other people — even if not always so clearly in ourselves — the effects of what a person chooses to dwell on. We have seen it in committee meetings, in marriage counseling, and in hospital calls. We have seen the positive examples, as well as the negative examples — and the cause-and-effect is clear.

Imagine, then, the effect on our faith, on our thanksgiving, on our hope, and on our overall outlook if we, each day, reviewed those two lists, and kept adding to them!

Next, the prophet makes an important theological point that should not be missed by our people. Pondering the deeds of the Lord, the prophet attributes them thus: "according to his mercy, according to the abundance of his love." That's an important truth, and it deserves elaboration.

Ask your congregation: "Why does the Lord do what he does?" A great many answers will likely spring to mind, including no doubt some cause-and-effect theology that includes our merit, our faith, our actions, our needs, and such. There is a place for those affirmations, of course, but those truths are not the whole truth.

The prophet says that the Lord does what he does "according to his mercy" and "the abundance of his love." In other words, he does what he does because he is what he is. That is tremendously good news for us.

Finally, it might be worth noting a few words and images that deserve to be recognized as part of the Old Testament lection. So many church folks operate with careless, broad-brush caricatures of the Old Testament and the New Testament. And, in so many hearts and minds, the Old Testament suffers by comparison. Yet, it was the Old Testament scriptures that Jesus explicated on the road to Emmaus, and that the apostles proclaimed throughout their preaching in the book of Acts. They found the good news there. And so we do well to observe here, in the midst of the Old Testament prophet, such lavish references to God's grace, his mercy, his steadfast love, and to the truth that he is a Savior who redeems his people.

Hebrews 2:10-18

In one of his most familiar songs from the 1960s, Ralph Carmichael noted some of the claims of Christ — seeing his handiwork in the stars, his majesty on the wind, the way he rules both land and sea — but then comes around to the practical question, "What is that to me?"

That question may serve as an approach to this week's epistle lection.

The writer of Hebrews has one great theme: Jesus Christ. These verses are just a small sample of the author's much longer and larger explication of the person and work of Christ.

In the midst of all of our sophisticated Christology and all of the doctrines that we affirm about Christ, the average man or woman in the pew — or on the street! — might rightly ask, "Yes, but what is that to me?"

And the writer of Hebrews has the answers.

First, this: Jesus identifies us as his brothers and sisters. In the midst of theological debates that can be absolutely deadening, this is a refreshingly personal word. Jesus is not trapped in stained glass. He does not sit far off, detached and unreachable. Instead, he regards us as part of the family. This image may be especially refreshing since it does not even include the authoritarian image of a parent, but the peer, shoulder-to-shoulder relationship of a sibling.

Second, just as we are reckoned as part of his family, he also became one of us, for "he himself likewise shared the same things" and he "had to become like his brothers and sisters in every respect." There is nothing quite so essential to a feeling of solidarity with another person as the certainty that they understand us. That is, they understand our situation, our experience, where we're coming from, and how we feel. The writer of Hebrews offers us that sense of solidarity between us and Jesus, for he became one of us.

Third, though he became like us, he was not immobilized by our limitations. Instead, "he is able to help those who are being tested." And, beyond that, he is able to "free those who all their lives were held in slavery by the fear of death," as well as to "make a sacrifice of atonement for the sins of the people." So he became like us in perhaps the same way that a lifeguard becomes like the person who is drowning: namely, they are both in and experiencing the same water. This lifeguard, however, is not overcome by the waters in which we are drowning; rather, he is able to come in and help us out.

Matthew 2:13-23

We have made the Christmas scene in Bethlehem a lovely and sentimental one. The little town is, in our mind's eye, peaceful and serene. The stable is quiet and quaint. The animals are gentle and attentive. The shepherds are reverent, the Magi majestic, and the whole scene is bathed in the light of a mysteriously bright star.

I expect our sentimentalizing of the scene is inaccurate to begin with. Even if it was so improbably tranquil, the whole lovely picture is shattered in an instant. The blessed couple with their newborn baby is suddenly on the lam — and the little town of Bethlehem becomes a bloodbath.

This whole episode with Herod's slaughter of the innocents seems like such an unwelcome and unnatural intrusion into the beauty of the Christmas story. But there it is, inextricably tied up with the beloved wise men, the plotline that leads to Egypt, and the familiar association of Jesus' boyhood with Nazareth. Yet, with lights still on most houses and trees still in most living rooms, who wants to have to preach such unpleasantness this Sunday morning?

At its core, the Christmas story is not at all about sentiment; it's about a Savior. Trouble and tragedy, therefore, are out of place in the story. We do, indeed, preach the gospel this Sunday. For the gospel is not, after all, good news introduced into a happy setting. It is, rather, light shining in the darkness; good news proclaimed in the midst of a bad world.

We might highlight the good news of this tragic passage in several ways.

First, there is the strong affirmation of God's providence and omniscience throughout all of human history. The recurring theme of fulfilled prophecies (three are explicitly cited in just these eleven verses) reminds us that nothing catches God by surprise. He is not bewildered by the headlines, and he is not thwarted by the machinations of human despots. His good will is achieved in spite of the malevolence and opposition of fallen humanity.

That, in turn, leads to the second piece of good news: God's ultimate victory. In Herod the Great, we see a potentate who is paranoid, shrewd, and cruel. On paper, the poor nobodies from Nazareth would seem to be no match for him. The juxtaposition of a helpless baby with Herod's sword-wielding legions suggests no contest at all. It is all injustice and oppression. Yet, still, God's will prevails. By the end of the episode, the antagonist is dead, and the chosen family is preserved.

There is also a layer of incarnational good news in this terrible story. The writer of Hebrews affirms that "we have one who in every respect has been tested as we are" (4:15), and this scene may be included under that umbrella. Jesus was not insulated from the dangers of this world. As the Son of God, he was not accorded some special lane on the highway, which permitted him to pass by the

First Sunday after Christmas Day

troubles that we experience. No, "he was despised and rejected by others; a man of suffering" (Isaiah 53:3). And that, we see on this Sunday after Christmas, is not an affirmation for Good Friday only. It was true for him from day one.

Application

A woman from my congregation came into my office not long ago to talk about her husband. She is a woman of sincere and profound personal faith, but her husband does not share that faith. He is not so much antagonistic as he is disinterested. She is in church every Sunday; he is in church when it's his turn to usher. She told me that he just doesn't like church. She told me that she is worried about his soul.

I did not dispute her concern or minimize it, but I did tell her that she didn't need to invest a lot of effort in trying to get her husband to like church. "I don't think he's wired up to like church," I said, "but I'm very sure he would like Jesus!"

The only Jesus this man has known, I'm afraid, is the stained-glass Jesus. The Jesus of institutional religion, of suits and ties, of hymns and organs. I don't disparage any of those things, for they have been vessels of God's grace in my own life. But I'm certain that this member's husband needs to meet and see Jesus outside of church. He needs to see that Jesus also leans on the lawn mower, wiping his brow; he puts his head under the hood to change the spark plugs; he laughs at jokes and tosses a ball.

The Jesus of the gospels is not made of stained glass; he's flesh and blood. Marvelously, perfectly flesh-and-blood. He had a mom, a dad, and a home. He had both friends and enemies. He got hungry, thirsty, and tired. He went to parties, he fished, and he told stories. And he became like us "in every respect" — struggling, suffering, and even dying.

The plight that we observed in our discussion of the gospel lection, as well as the whole theme and emphasis of the Hebrews passage, provide us with an opportunity this Sunday to tell our world what they need to hear and to show them what they need to see: Jesus Christ, the incarnate Son of God.

Alternative Applications

Isaiah 63:7-9; Hebrews 2:10-18. "Angels In And Out." Each of our three lections this week makes reference to angels. That's a rare coincidence. And while angels are meant to be instruments of God's work, not the center of our attention, the fact is that they do hold great interest among people today. Some skeptics want to deny their existence altogether, relegating them to the company of unicorns and mermaids. Others, meanwhile, are perhaps overly interested in angels and teach an angel paradigm that is way beyond what is plainly revealed in scripture. Perhaps the surprising theme of angels in our three selected passages offers us a chance to explore the topic a bit, and thus provide us with a unique angle for presenting the gospel.

The gospel lection offers us the picture of angels that we are most accustomed to seeing. In Matthew's post-Christmas story, an angel warns Joseph about Herod. Later, an angel alerts Joseph to the news of Herod's death. In both instances, the angel is instructing a human being in matters beyond that human being's natural knowledge, as well as giving direction ("Get up, take the child and his mother" is found in both v. 13 and v. 20). In short, therefore, the angels in the Matthew passage serve as instruments of God's work in human affairs. It is a utilitarian view of angels.

In the Old Testament passage, meanwhile, we encounter a passing reference to angels. In "recount(ing) the gracious deeds of the Lord," the prophet observes how God has — and how he has not — saved his people: "It was no messenger or angel but his presence that saved them." For all of the occasions in scripture when we see angels in the utilitarian role, the prophet makes a point of noting here that, ultimately, God's people are saved by God.

That is a very personal observation and affirmation. Such is the love and concern of almighty God for his people that, when it comes time to save them, he does not "staff it out." Gabriel is not God's errand boy, fetching, carrying, and delivering salvation for human beings. Michael is not dispatched. No, God does it himself. It is a marvelously personal picture.

Then, similarly, the writer of Hebrews also makes a personal point about God by his reference to angels. "For it is clear," he wrote, "that [Jesus] did not come to help angels, but the descendants of Abraham." Like the Old Testament prophet, the New Testament writer emphasizes the personal quality of God's saving act by demonstrating how angels are left out of the equation. Just as they are not the agents of salvation in Isaiah, neither are they the objects of salvation in Hebrews. God's saving work is not for their sake, but for ours.

People perhaps think more about angels at this time of the year than during any of the other eleven months. On this Sunday, we might turn our attention to the angels in these passages to see that — for as glorious and as instrumental as they are — their story only reveals still more God's tender love for us.

Isaiah 63:7-9. "The Gospel According To His Nature." In our discussion of the Isaiah passage above, we noted that the Lord does what he does because he is what he is. His marvelous acts are "according to his mercy" and "according to the abundance of his steadfast love." That is to say, his deeds are a function of his attributes.

That's a critical point for us, because it is central to the gospel message. We understand and preach, you see, that our salvation is a free gift of God's grace (Ephesians 2:8-9). That it is because God so loved the world that Christ came (John 3:16). And that the Son of Man came into the world to seek and to save the lost (Luke 19:10). In each of these basic affirmations, what the Lord does is a function of his attributes. Therefore, our relationship with him is a function of his attributes.

That should be liberating news to an age in which so much experience of human love is superficial and conditional. We have come to expect that another person's love for us depends quite heavily, if not entirely, upon our attributes. But not so with God. His love for us depends not on our attributes, but on his. Our relationship with him is lived out, not in the context of how good or lovable we are, but in the gracious context of how good and loving he is.

The sun is not warm and bright because I am tan. Rather, I am tan because the sun is warm and bright. And so it is with God and us.

Preaching the Psalm

by Schuyler Rhodes

Psalm 148. Into everyone's life comes a moment of complete abandonment of all the careful boundaries and filters we have put into place. For each person there is a moment of wild joy and unrestricted passion.

For us as a people of faith, these moments come as we abandon ourselves to unqualified praise of the almighty God. In some of our traditions, such abandonment causes discomfort. Passion is not easily controlled. But then, neither is the Holy Spirit.

It is this kind of wild praise that can be felt in this psalm. The call is clear and unambiguous. Praise the Lord! Everyone and everything is called upon to shout out the glory of the creating God! From sea monsters to the elements to topography and back again; all are called upon to enter into the dance of praise.

It is easy to imagine Saint Francis shouting out the words to this psalm as he danced through the forest and claimed a life of simple service and poverty. It is a little less easy to imagine one's pastor in such a paroxysm of praise. It is still harder to imagine oneself stomping and shouting out praises to God.

Yet, it is the call, not merely of this psalm, but of our faith.

God, after all, is God. The great "I AM" (Exodus 3:14). This is the creator God, the one who brings us redemption through (his Son) on this Christmas Day. This is the God who knows each person down to the number of hairs on the scalp. This is the God who loves each one of us just as we are.

If all this is true, which we claim today that it is, how can we do anything but jump and shout our praises? How can there be any other response than this? Let all creation issue forth a chorus of wonder and joy, a cacophony of celebration. How blessed and fortunate we are! For God has done great things for us and given us a Savior, born this day in Bethlehem. And his name is called Jesus.

What else can we do but sing our praises?

What other choice do we have but to set aside our puny agendas and complicated tasks and simply shout to the heavens, "PRAISE THE LORD!"

Second Sunday after Christmas

Jeremiah 31:7-14

Ephesians 1:3-14

John 1:(1-9) 10-18

by Cathy Venkatesh

Entering the mystery

It's a full ten days after Christmas; most of our world has moved on through New Year's celebrations and final cleaning up and putting away, but here we are in church, still keeping this Sunday as part of our Christmas observance. The *Godly Play* children's curriculum teaches that Christmas is so great a mystery that we need more than one day to fully enter into it — we need a full season to live into the deep mystery of Christ's coming. Today's readings invite us to enter the mystery.

Jeremiah 31:7-14

Jeremiah is known for his laments, and indeed in his life he had much to lament, personally and prophetically. Yet he could also be a prophet of hope, and it is in this mode that we meet him today. Today's reading comes from a collection of oracles in Jeremiah chapters 30-31 that scholars call the Book of Consolation. All of these oracles, today's included, speak of the future restoration of Israel and Judah after the exiles return from captivity in Babylon. In Jeremiah 31:7-9, the command to sing aloud opens a hymnic celebration of the exiles' gathering and return that carries echoes of Isaiah and Psalm 23. In Jeremiah 31:1, the Lord has proclaimed, "I will be the God of all the families of Israel, and they shall be my people." "Jacob" names the father of the twelve tribes of Israel, who is gladdened by the reunification of his family, and Ephraim signifies the northern kingdom, which had come under the control of the Assyrians before their ousting by the Babylonian empire. In Jeremiah 31:10-14, a second oracle addresses all the nations as far away as the coastlands, promising a renewed life together for all Israel that will culminate in songs of praise from Jerusalem and dances of joy replacing the sorrows of captivity.

Ephesians 1:3-14

Scholarly opinion is divided as to whether Paul himself wrote the letter we now call the letter to the Ephesians, or whether a disciple of Paul's wrote the letter pseudonymously sometime after Paul's death. Regardless of author, this letter likely was not limited to the church in Ephesus but circulated through a number of Christian communities. Here the writer celebrates the inclusion of Gentiles in God's plan of salvation through Christ, a plan that precedes even the foundation of the world (1:4). The Gentiles, adopted into God's family, share equally in God's inheritance as God's own people (1:11, 14). This passage contains several terms and phrases unique in the New Testament, such as naming Christ as the beloved (1:6) and the refrain "the praise of his glory" in verses 12 and 14, which reflects liturgical traditions. The seal of the promised Holy Spirit in verse 13 recalls the affirmation made at baptism in a number of Christian traditions as a cross is marked on the forehead of the newly baptized: "You are sealed by the Holy Spirit in baptism and marked as Christ's own forever."

Second Sunday after Christmas

John 1:(1-9)10-18

Christmas is the only time in the Revised Common Lectionary when we get to hear the poetry of John's prologue, and so I argue for a full, not abbreviated, reading of this remarkable piece of scripture that so many of our members know and love. Verse 1, "In the beginning," which can also be translated "before all time," echoes the first verse of Genesis, just as the imagery of light and dark echo God's work on the first day of creation. "The Word" is our inadequate English translation of the Greek *logos*, which in Greek philosophical thought had several connotations over the ages. The most pertinent to today's reading comes from the stoic school of philosophy, which saw *logos* as the "divine principle of reason that gives order to the universe and links the human mind to the mind of God" (*The Harper Collins Study Bible*, Revised and Updated [2006], p. 1816). Wikipedia offers the more succinct "the divine animating principle pervading the universe" as the stoic understanding of *Logos*. The Alexandrian Jewish philosopher Philo (c. 25 BCE-50 CE), who sought to reconcile Platonic and Jewish philosophies, further identified *logos* with divine wisdom in the Hebrew scriptures. The author of John's gospel takes a profound leap ahead of all these philosophies in naming Jesus as the earthly embodiment of this divine principle. Some preachers may wish to develop the themes of the scandal of the incarnation or the scandal of particularity — how radical a notion this is that the God of the entire universe came to inhabit the particular human body of Jesus. Developing this idea, one could also work with the final verse of the prologue, "And the word became flesh and lived among us" (John 1:14), which may also be translated "and made his dwelling among us," or even more vividly "pitched his tent among us." Thinking through the experience of pitching a tent, of living in one with the barest possible protection from the elements of wind and rain and snow, can invite listeners into a new perspective on the fragility and risk of God's choice to be born in human flesh.

Application

So often poetry gives voice to a level of truth that reasoned conversation can only attempt. Both John's prologue and the opening of the letter to the Ephesians seek to express experiences that are far beyond words: how in and through the life, death, and resurrection of a man named Jesus, the people who knew him, and those who knew those who knew him, and those who knew those who knew those who knew him caught a glimpse of the eternal God of all time and space. And the God that they glimpsed filled them with such deep assurance of their place in the universe that they were transformed. What had been beyond human comprehension somehow came within their grasp in knowing this man Jesus.

Christmas is about so much more than the shepherds and the angels, Mary and Joseph and the baby. In Christmas, the whole of Christ's life and being begin. In John, this beginning happens long before any historic birth; it happens before time itself is conceived. The baby who grew to be Jesus has been, is, and will be a part of God for all time and beyond all time. What a gift it is to have moved past (in the western church at least) all the busyness of Christmas decorations, gifts, and celebrations to come to these readings that point beyond the manger to the God of the cosmos, crying "glory" and "praise."

In her book *Teaching a Stone to Talk* (Harper & Row, 1982) Annie Dillard tells a remarkable Christmas story, "God in the Doorway," that evokes some of this sensibility and speaks to the awe that comes to anyone who genuinely encounters the Christmas story:

One cold Christmas Eve I was up unnaturally late because we had all gone out to dinner — my parents, my baby sister, and I. We had come home to a warm livingroom, and Christmas Eve. Our stockings drooped from the mantle; beside them, a special table bore a bottle of ginger ale and a plate of cookies....

There was a commotion at the front door; it opened, and cold winter blew around my dress.

Everyone was calling me. "Look who's here! Look who's here!" I looked. It was Santa Claus, whom I never-ever-wanted to meet. Santa Claus was looming in the doorway and looking around for me. My mother's voice was thrilled: "Look who's here!" I ran upstairs.

Like everyone in his right mind, I feared Santa Claus, thinking he was God. I was still thoughtless and brute, reactive. I knew right from wrong, but had barely tested the possibility of shaping my own behavior, and then only from fear, and not yet from love. Santa Claus was an old man whom you never saw, but who nevertheless saw you; he knew when you'd been bad or good. He knew when you'd been bad or good! And I had been bad.

My mother called and called, enthusiastic, pleading; I wouldn't come down. My father encouraged me; my sister howled. I wouldn't come down, but I could bend over the stairwell and see: Santa Claus stood in the doorway with night over his shoulder, letting in all the cold air of the sky; Santa Claus stood in the doorway monstrous and bright, powerless, ringing a loud bell and repeating Merry Christmas, Merry Christmas. I never came down. I don't know who ate the cookies.

For so many years now I have known that this Santa Claus was actually a rigged-up Miss White, who lived across the street, that I confuse the dramatis personae in my mind, making Santa Claus, God, and Miss White an awesome, vulnerable trinity. This is really a story about Miss White.

Miss White was old; she lived alone in the big house across the street. She liked having me around; she plied me with cookies, taught me things about the world, and tried to interest me in finger painting, in which she herself took great pleasure.... I liked her. She meant no harm on earth, and yet half a year after her failed visit as Santa Claus, I ran from her again.

That day, a day of the following summer, Miss White and I knelt in her yard while she showed me a magnifying glass. It was a large, strong hand lens. She lifted my hand and, holding it very still, focused a dab of sunshine on my palm. The glowing crescent wobbled, spread, and finally contracted to a point. It burned; I was burned; I ripped my hand away and ran home crying. Miss White called after me, sorry, explaining, but I didn't look back.

Even now I wonder: if I meet God, will he take and hold my bare hand in his, and focus his eye on my palm, and kindle that spot and let me burn?

But no. It is I who misunderstood everything and let everybody down. Miss White, God, I am sorry I ran from you. I am still running, running from that knowledge, that eye, that love from which there is no refuge, for you meant only love, and love, and I felt only fear and pain. So once in Israel love came to us incarnate, stood in the doorway between two worlds, and we were all afraid.

The even more amazing truth that the intimates and followers of Jesus found was that, in knowing him, they were not afraid. The closer they drew to him and he to them, the more fully they knew the love of God that he embodied. Some, encountering the deep mystery of Christmas, do feel afraid; but as a gathered community of Christians, we can support each other in drawing near to the mystery and encountering the love that gives life to all things. When our hearts turn from fear to praise and generous offering of our lives, we know that Christ is among us.

Second Sunday after Christmas

An Alternate Application

The theme of new creation is one that could be preached this Sunday, integrating the sense of a new start with the secular new year and the creation imagery in today's readings. Jeremiah is an especially powerful reading for those whose lives are broken in some way — it is the lame, the blind, those heavy with pregnancy or even struggling in labor who will create the new family of God in the restored Israel. God does not call the hearty and whole to rebuild, but the broken, who will find healing and nourishment, even dancing together. Ephesians and John celebrate the astonishing new creation that followers of Christ found and continue to find through him. Their very world and knowledge of their place in it are transformed by knowing Christ. Gentiles, once outside the fold, are adopted as God's own beloved children. The world itself is made whole.

The Baptism of our Lord | Epiphany 1 | Ordinary Time 1
Isaiah 42:1-9
Acts 10:34-43
Matthew 3:13-17
by Wayne Brouwer

From centripetal to centrifugal

In God's initial encounter with Abram, recorded in Genesis 12, it is clear that the relationship between God and Abram was missional in character. The Creator wished to "bless" all nations of the earth but would enact that blessing through Abram and his descendants. This became the source of Israel's unique identity: bound to Yahweh through the Sinai covenant and positioned on the great highway between the nations in the territory known as Canaan. For the mission to work, people would have to flow to and through this piece of property, and Israel would have to be the visible face of God and God's intentions.

But the world is expanding, and "Canaan" is no longer the center of civilizations. Also, the witness of Israel to the nations had become muted through historical circumstances and internal challenges. So the creator became a creature (John 1:1-14), taught and showed and expressed the divine mission, and then initiated the Christian church from among the people of Israel to become an international community of witness within every culture.

What began as a centripetal force, pulling all nations into Israel's witnessing orbit, was now flung out as a centrifugal spray, invading and influencing every territory on earth. This idea is central to each of today's lectionary passages. Through Isaiah, God takes and re-launches the redemptive mission of Israel in a very personal manner (the "suffering servant" personifying all of the divine being) to the nations of the earth. In the book of Acts, the "kingdom of God" as known to Israel now becomes globalized as Peter declares to Cornelius that Jesus alone is King of kings and Lord of lords. And even in the simple act of Jesus' baptism by John, the history of Israel as God's redemptive agent to the nations of the world is now filtered through the one who is baptized in the Jordan just where Israel was generations earlier on its road to fulfillment of the promises made to Abraham. God blesses Abraham. And through Abraham's descendants, all nations of the earth will be blessed.

Isaiah 42:1-9

Regardless of whether one person, or several from a community that was shaped by a larger-than-life teacher, wrote the various and combined oracles of Isaiah, the message is consistent throughout. Isaiah was overwhelmed by a divine commissioning (6) that took place in the temple during the year that King Uzziah died. He was guided by the theology of the Sinai covenant (2-5), which mandated that Israel was supposed to have a unique lifestyle among the nations, a set of behaviors that would serve as a missional call for others to join this holy community in a global return to the ways of their creator. He was confident that Yahweh could resolve all political problems (7-11), no matter how daunting they might seem. He believed Israel/Judah needed to repent (12), and recover their original identity and purpose as Yahweh's covenant partners and witnesses. He was certain that Yahweh was sovereign over all nations (13-35), even if Yahweh's primary focus was attached to Israel/Judah. He heard the heartbeat of divine love and compassion, wrestling for the soul and destiny of Israel/Judah as a loved companion and partner (36-41). He saw Yahweh transforming Israel's/Judah's identity and fortunes through a "suffering servant" leader (42-53). He envisioned a future age in which all the world and every society and even the universe itself would be restored to harmony with its creator and would resonate with magnificent glory (56-66).

The powerful "Servant Songs" in Isaiah 42-53 were first identified in a commentary on the prophecy by Bernhard Duhm in 1892. They personify both Israel and Yahweh in the tense drama unfolding among the nations of the ancient near east:

Isaiah 42:1-9 — Yahweh identifies and commissions his special envoy who will bring justice among the nations through quiet ministry to the marginalized and the disenfranchised. His work will be successful because the great creator has chosen this one to be the agent of divine renewal.

Isaiah 49:1-13 — The suffering servant testifies of his unique call and commissioning. His voice and message are then confirmed by successive oracles in which Yahweh speaks, announcing that his servant was ordained for this ministry from before his birth, and that kings and outcasts will experience divine favor through the work of this one. The outcome will be a restoration of joy to the entire world, which has too long suffered under the consequences of evil.

Isaiah 50:4-9 — Now the voice of the chosen one is heard even more clearly. The entire poem is in the first person, and is a reflection on both divine anointing for the tasks at hand and also the early backlash of those who do not want Yahweh to disturb their evil machinations. The confrontation thickens between good and evil, and the suffering servant stands at its vortex.

Isaiah 52:13--53:12 — The last and longest of the poems personifies the suffering servant most clearly. Here the focus is less on the grand justice that will result from his ministry and more on the agony that he will endure to accomplish his assigned task. What began as a shout of confidence and joy in the first song has now turned dark and almost defeatist here. Only the final lines of this song serve to remind us that Yahweh is still in control and that these things do matter for eternal purposes.

Jews believe that it is the people of God themselves who function in the role as the arbiter of God's justice among the nations, a task which ultimately crushes its vocalizer in the evil machines of human depravity. This is why the Jews remain the prophetic voice of God to the nations, and why they also mark their history with the awful pogroms and bloody reprisals that have been unleashed against them.

Christians, on the other hand, quickly found in these passages a kind of messianic blueprint describing the coming, anointing, teaching, ministry, suffering, and death of Jesus. There is no question but that the hints at divine initiative and personal character and contextual backlash all fit hand-in-glove with the events of Jesus' career.

Both interpretations are likely intertwined. Certainly the theme of today's combined lectionary readings brings the two strands together. If the God of creation and the God of redemption are fully met and expressed in Jesus, those who are saved by the messianic suffering servant and those who express the mission of the suffering servant are one and the same. "By his stripes we are healed" to become, ourselves, the wounded healer of others.

Acts 10:34-43

There is something wonderfully paradoxical about the Christian church. Its origin as a unique social phenomenon clearly dates from the Pentecost events described in Acts 2. Yet at the same time, Jesus' disciples, who were at the center of the church from its very beginning, would say that this "new" community of faith was simply part of a centuries-old, already-existing people of God, stretching back all the way to Abraham and his family. The connection between the old and the new is rooted in several theological axioms.

First, it is built upon the confession that there is a God who created this world and uniquely fashioned the human race with attributes that reflected its maker. Second, through human willfulness the world lost its pristine vitality and is now caught up in a civil war against its creator. Third, intruding directly into human affairs for the sake of reclaiming and restoring the world, the creator began a mission of redemption and renewal through the nation of Israel. Fourth, Israel's identity as a missional community was shaped by the Suzerain-Vassal covenant formed at Mount Sinai. Fifth, in order to be most effective in its witness to other nations, Israel was positioned at the crossroads of global societies and thus received, as its "promised land," the territory known as Canaan. Sixth, the effectiveness of this divine missional strategy through Israel was most evident in the eleventh century BC, during the reigns of David and Solomon, when the kingdom grew in size and influence among the peoples of the ancient near east and beyond. Seventh, this missional witness eroded away, almost to oblivion, through a combination of internal failures and external political threats, until most of the nation of Israel was wiped out by the Assyrians and only a remnant of the tribe of Judah (along with religious leaders from among the Levites, and a portion of the small tribe of Benjamin) retained its unique identity as the people of Yahweh. Eighth, because of the seeming inadequacy of this method of witness as the human race expanded rapidly, the creator revised the divine missional strategy and interrupted human history in a very visible manner again in the person of Jesus. Ninth, Jesus embodied the divine essence, taught the divine will, and went through death and resurrection to establish a new understanding of eschatological hope, which he passed along to his followers as the message to be communicated to the nations. Tenth, Jesus' teachings about this arriving messianic age were rooted in what the prophets of Israel called the "day of the lord," a time when divine judgment for sins would fall on all nations (including Israel), a remnant from Israel would be spared to become the restored seed community of a new global divine initiative, and the world would be transformed as God had intended for it to be so that people could again live out their intended purposes and destinies. Eleventh, instead of applying all aspects of this "day of the lord" in a single cataclysmic event, Jesus split it in two, bringing the beginnings of eternal blessings while withholding the full impact of divine judgment for a time. Twelfth, the Christian church is God's new agent for global missional recovery and restoration for the human race, superseding the territorially bound witness through Israel with a portable and expanding testimony influencing all nations and cultures. Thirteenth, since the "day of the lord" is begun but not finished, Jesus will return again to bring its culmination. Fourteenth, the church of Jesus exists in this time between Jesus' comings as the great divine missional witness.

Each of these themes is implied or explicit in the book of Acts and all are assumed in today's passage. God and sin and the divine mission are all part of the fabric of the narrative, while Israel's role in the divine mission, along with the changing strategies, is declared openly. Jesus is at the center of all these things, but the unique divine intrusion he brought into the human race is now being withdrawn as he ascends back to heaven. Now the church must become the ongoing embodiment of Jesus' life and teachings, so that it may live out the divine mission until the remainder of the "day of the lord" arrives when Jesus returns.

Peter's experiences with Cornelius in Acts 10-11 (or, perhaps even better, Cornelius' experiences with Jesus through Peter) are one of the most critical and world-changing events in human history. Peter was a good Jew. He was a pious believer in God. He was a leader among Jesus' disciples. But he remained convinced that God's work was primarily for and certainly always directed through the biological family of Abraham as channeled through Isaac and Jacob. Suddenly, however, first with the vision on the rooftop in Joppa, and then powerfully and personally through the Spirit-initiated connections with this Roman centurion, everything has changed. The God of Israel has become the God of humanity. The redemption of God's people has been transformed into the reconciliation of all nations. The salvation of Jews has broadened to encompass the renewal of all creation.

Matthew 3:13-17

Matthew opens his gospel with a quick-step through a variety of incidents in Jesus' early life, revealing a number of things about the essential character of this unique lad. Jesus, Matthew makes clear, is actually destined to replay or relive the life of Israel in a host of dimensions:

Jesus copies Israel's miraculous existence and purpose, born through divine intervention as savior of nations (1:18–25).

He is spared from the murderous intents of a scheming king (2:3-8) who goes on to slaughter the innocents (2:16-18), just as Moses was delivered in Exodus 2 while many Israelite boys were slaughtered.

Like the nation as a whole, Jesus is gathered out of Egypt (2:15).

From his earliest days, he is dedicated to a divine mission (so the play on the words "Nazirite" and "Nazarene" in 2:23).

His ministry is set in motion by passing through waters (3), right at the same spot where Israel crossed the Jordan River in order to begin its witness to the nations from the Promised Land.

Jesus also wanders in the wilderness for forty days (4:1-11) before he can fully assume his adult responsibilities, mirroring Israel's traumatic forty years described in the book of Numbers.

It is in this context that Matthew wants us to understand Jesus' baptism by John. There are certainly more layers of theology that can be read into these events, but we need, at minimum, to keep Matthew's primary focus in mind.

Application

The idea of "kingdom" implies citizenship, or at least allegiance to a governing authority. It possesses us. It is the kind of thing that J.R.R. Tolkien tried to picture in his powerful trilogy *The Lord of the Rings*. Writing in the recovery years after World War II, Tolkien imagined what powers there are in this world that can possess peoples and nations, for good or for ill. His tale of the struggles of Middle Earth allegorically reflected the biblical idea of kingdoms in conflict.

Our youngest daughter was born in Nigeria while I was teaching at the Reformed Theological College in Mkar. Because the Nigerian government does not automatically grant citizenship to all who are born on its soil, Kaitlyn was truly a person without a country in her earliest days. Until I could process her existence with the United States consulate in Kaduna she had no official identity, no traveling permissions, and no rights in society outside of our home. We took a picture of her at five days old, sleeping in my hands, and this became the photograph used on her passport for the first ten years of her life. The snapshot may have become outdated quickly as she grew through the stages of childhood, but the passport to which it was affixed declared that she belonged to the United States of America. She had rights. She had privileges. She had protection under the law. When the time came for us to leave Nigeria and travel through three continents to get back to North America, that little passport opened doors and prepared the way for her. She had never lived in the U.S., but the U.S. knew her by name and kept watch over her.

So it is and more with the kingdom of heaven, according to Jesus. It becomes the badge of identification for us, as well as the symbol of our protection and care. It is not enough to own a piece of fading substance; we need to be owned by something which transcends our time. We need God to lay hold on us.

This is why, in many of the earliest liturgical forms for baptism, those who were newly coming into the fellowship of believers were asked if they renounced the devil and all his works. Early on it was recognized that entering the kingdom of God was more than just adding another spiritual talisman to the mix of superstitious hex warders; it was a fundamental commitment of identity that could not be shared. No dual passports in this kingdom!

For God's "suffering servant," this complete allegiance was absolute. So, too, was Jesus' commitment through the act of baptism under John. And when Cornelius experienced God's grace through the preaching of Peter and the ministry of the Holy Spirit, the first response was for him to be baptized.

An Alternative Application

Acts 10:34-43. It is appropriately ironic that the first Gentile convert to Christianity was a Roman centurion. C.S. Lewis knew the battlefield connection underlying Christianity. He came about that insight in a very personal way. When he was nine years old his warm and loving mother contracted cancer. Within a very short time she was confined to bed, enduring harsh treatments, in terrible pain, and stinking because of the sores and horrible wasting of her body. At night she would cry out in anguish, and young Jack (as he was known) hid in terror under his covers. He had heard the minister say that God answers prayer, so he begged God for his mother's deliverance. But to no avail. She died gasping and screaming, and his belief in God went with her.

Years later, when as an Oxford professor he began to rationally think through the possibility of Christian belief, Lewis finally understood what was going on in his mother's painful illness. He came to see that this world is a battlefield between the kingdom of God and the powers of evil, and that Christianity was true precisely because it took this conflict seriously. The religion of the Bible was not a streamlined Santa Claus story of a jolly old grandfather figure who always brings gifts whether you are naughty or nice. Rather, it is an acknowledgement of the struggles present in this world and the necessary reality of God's intervention. Lewis' mother died not because God didn't grant a child's wish but because the evil one had twisted God's good world in such a way that even the very cells of her body no longer worked as they should. But though healing did not come in that instant of boyish spiritual lisping, the prayers did not go unheard, and his mother was not lost forever or forgotten.

Cornelius would share these marching orders in his new discovery of the kingdom of heaven. We are not saved so that we may politely pat ourselves on the back and smile at one another in the tiny corners we occupy. No, we are part of a movement that seeks and engages the nations of this world who might be campaigning for small victories to their own destruction.

Epiphany 2 | Ordinary Time 2

Isaiah 49:1-7

1 Corinthians 1:1-9

John 1:29-42

Psalm 40:1-11

by R. Craig Maccreary

Keeping up appearances

One of my favorite British situation comedies is *Keeping Up Appearances*. It chronicles the attempts of Hyacinth Bucket, pronounced "bouquet" on the show, to appear to have entered the British upper class by maintaining the manners and mores of that social set. The nearby presence of her sisters, Daisy and Rose, serve as a constant reminder that she has not gotten far from her origins in anything but the upper class.

At first I was quite put off by the show's title with an instant dislike for Hyacinth, and a fondness for Daisy, Onslow, and Rose who are what you see as vulnerable and with no capability of putting on airs. Certainly, Rose has a dream of finding perfect love and Daisy has a dream of making a passionate lover out of her oafish husband, Onslow. Yet, all of them clearly work within the confines of who they are. However, as my viewing of this show has gone along, I have grown more sympathetic to Hyacinth. Certainly, I have grown sympathetic to Hyacinth's husband, Richard, whose capacity to keep up the appearance of being the ever-ready dutiful husband maintains the only level of sanity in their relationship.

I have also grown more aware of how much of my life revolves around keeping up my own appearances. As pastor, it might be wise to keep up appearances that Saturday's death did not get to you as much as you are letting on at Sunday morning's baptism. Keeping up with the sense of humor of a six-year-old may require the stretching of appearances beyond reality. While I may want to be a non-anxious presence the appearance may come long before the reality is within my grasp. In the midst of crises, airline stewards and hospital emergency room personnel must put on the best face they can find in order to enable others to overcome their anxiety.

Keeping up appearances might not be an entirely bad thing after all. Certainly, at times it is the best that I can muster until something better can settle in. The measure of the trustworthiness of this is that Epiphany is the season of appearance. In Christian terms, keeping up appearances makes no sense and carries no worth unless it centers on the attempt to keep up with the appearance of the God who made the fullest appearance we know in the life of Jesus Christ.

The Hebrew text reveals the prophet as one who feels that there is a great distance between what God has called him to be and the way things are — "But I said, 'I have labored in vain, I have spent my strength for nothing and vanity; yet surely my cause is with the Lord, and my reward with my God.'" The Corinthian text "proclaims in every way you have been enriched in him, in speech and knowledge of every kind." As we join in the uncertainty of church life, does it feel that way? The John text reflects a refutation of the way things must have appeared to the many that followed John the Baptist, even thinking that he might be the Messiah. John says he is not the one. The future does not lie, contrary to all appearances, with repentance for sin but with the one who can take away the sin of the world. This is the one whose appearance we are called to keep up with even on those days when it is hard to keep up appearances.

Isaiah 49:1-7

Several recent national stories remind me of how hard it can be to keep up appearances in trying circumstances. A national story on the second anniversary of the Katrina hurricane reports how hard the trauma has been on clergy as they seek to care for their parishioners as well as themselves. The Episcopal diocese reports that every one of their clergy is in counseling. The bishop, the caretaker of those who take care, has been diagnosed with post-traumatic stress syndrome. The prophet says, "He made my mouth like a sharp sword, in the shadow of his hand he hid me; he made me a polished arrow, in his quiver he hid me away. And he said to me, 'You are my servant, Israel, in whom I will be glorified.' But I said, 'I have labored in vain, I have spent my strength for nothing and vanity.' " Hard to keep up appearances in the face of that until keeping up appearances can lead to the more genuine thing.

A story from the Associated Baptist Press reports that more and more seminary students are choosing to enter forms of ministry other than the traditional role of the pastorate. They have seen too much heartache, conflict, and wounded pastors to be attracted into parish ministry. They are attracted into chaplaincies, youth work, and the mission field. The trend is toward those fields where seminary graduates can experience being the sharp sword and polished arrow that one can feel like in ministries other than the parish.

All those who have not, at one time or the other, felt like they have labored in vain or spent their strength for nothing in the parish please raise your hand. There are going to be plenty of days when at best the parish will feel like it is about keeping up appearance in the face of vanity of all sorts, spending your strength in ways that leaves sleepless nights. A recent visit with interim clergy produced bobbing heads of approval when one said the chief difference between interim and settled ministry is the amount of sleep you get.

Keeping up appearances in such a context seems senselessly beyond the pale. Isaiah must have had similar feelings in the face of the challenges of rebuilding the nation following exile. Things certainly did not appear hopeful yet the patriarch Abraham is remembered as one: who "hoped against hope." He kept up with the appearance of a heavenly messenger and a vision that contrary to all, evident appearance would be fulfilled. The church is called to keep up with this appearance as it is fulfilled in the life and teaching of Jesus.

Some times this means investing in people who, contrary to all appearances, need to have people see more in them than they or others see in themselves. Keeping up with appearances means giving the appearance of a warm supporting environment even on days when you feel it is all vanity and all you can say is "yet surely my cause is with the Lord, and my reward with God." Keeping up with appearances of God in our lives comes when we recall how conflict can be used to create the kind of growth that brings people together at a deep level. The report on the clergy caught up in the aftermath of Katrina recounts that for those clergy who take care of themselves, there is the opportunity for more satisfying ministry than they have ever experienced before. Precisely because many clergy have been with people in a variety of contexts that the parish offers, they are better able to minister when crisis comes.

Certainly, there are many times, no doubt, when church feels like being in vain. We often long for congregations that can talk about the big issues and major concerns. Yet getting to the big talk is often contingent on engaging in the small talk that helps people feel they belong, are loved, and have worth. Such talk probably does as much to prepare people to faithfully face crisis as anything else we engage in.

Keeping up appearances has to do with keeping up with the one who has appeared among us, for surely our cause is with our Lord.

1 Corinthians 1:1-9

This doesn't appear exactly right. "For in every way you have been enriched in him, in speech and knowledge of every kind just as the testimony of Christ has been strengthened among you so that you are not lacking in any spiritual gift as you wait for the revealing of our Lord Jesus Christ." Does it feel like that among you or does it feel like that somewhere along the way the church has lost the gifts it once possessed? If anything it often seems that the church operates more out of a sense of depletion rather than abundance. This is further complicated because Paul is not merely describing the Corinthians but his words are meant to apply to the church wherever it is found, "To the church of God that is in Corinth, to those who are sanctified in Christ Jesus, called to be saints, together with all those who in every place call on the name of our Lord Jesus Christ, both their Lord and ours."

So the first letter to the Corinthians is a good case in point with lessons for the whole church. For a community that has been heavily, if not heavenly, endowed with gifts they do seem to find a way of getting into a lot of difficulties in Paul's eyes: Divisions and parties arise over worship, liturgical practices such as speaking in tongues, conflicts between haves and have-nots as to the timing of communion, the idealizing of individual leadership at the expense of the mission of the whole church, and a theological vigorousness that results in some extraordinary if not devious interpretations of scripture.

These gifted people seem to have run into some serious problems. What seems to have happened is that it is not the lack of gifts but the Corinthians use of the abundance of gifts that has gotten them into trouble. A rich past privileges a few; diversity creates barriers rather than bridges. Clear-eyed truth in one area blots out seeing the truth in others from another place. Charismatic leadership becomes a quick fix rather than the product of working at finding and celebrating the gifts of all.

To all appearances, an organization plagued by such problems would seem to have very little future ahead of it. Yet, keeping up with the one who has appeared among us has a way of running contrary to the way things may appear to be headed. Dietrich Bonhoeffer put it this way in *Life Together*: "What may appear weak and trifling to us may be great and glorious to God ... The more thankfully we daily receive what is given to us, the more surely and steadily will fellowship increase and grow from day to day as God pleases."

Over the years, I have had the opportunity to look over several church profiles as they went about the process of choosing a new pastor. My overall impression is that, for the most part, the impression that they wish to convey is not exactly what Dietrich Bonhoeffer had in mind as he described life in the church. I suspect that the average reader of this journal can name the number one phrase that most churches use to describe themselves: "We are a friendly church."

No one would want to be part of a church that was not friendly. However, the understanding of friendship that lays behind the phrase is that the church should keep up the appearance of being harmoniously conflict free. While the church can appear conflict free, much of the normal tensions that come along with being human beings go underground. I do not recall Paul ever writing that the churches should be friendlier. He is saying that we are equipped with every spiritual gift necessary to learn from differences, work through those wounds that come when we are a genuine community, and appreciate each other's truths.

A congregation that had that on its profile would capture my attention as it sought to give up keeping up with what appears the thing to say and chooses to follow the one whose appearance we celebrate in Epiphany.

John 1:29-42

Clearly scripture puts a lot of effort into interpreting the role of John the Baptist. He is rather hard to ignore. He makes quite an appearance — we are given detailed accounts of his dress, his mission, and his background. Scholars suggest that a certain rivalry arose between Jesus' and John's disciples. For a moment, let us make the case for John and explore just why scripture devotes so much premium space to John's story.

John comes with a cogent message and a clear plan. The crowds asked him, "What then should we do?" In reply, he said to them, "Whoever has two coats must share with anyone who has none; and whoever has food must do likewise." Even tax collectors came to be baptized, and they asked him, "Teacher, what should we do?" He said to them, "Collect no more than the amount prescribed for you." Soldiers also asked him, "And we, what should we do?" He said to them, "Do not extort money from anyone by threats or false accusation, and be satisfied with your wages." As the people were filled with expectation, and all were questioning in their hearts concerning John, whether he might be the Messiah, is it any wonder that some of John's hearers speculate as to whether John might be the Messiah? Not only does John have a clear brand as the one preaching a baptism of repentance but he also has a very clear detailed program. In Jungian terms, John has an appeal both to intuitive and sensate folks. Furthermore, his denunciation of the morality of those in high places shows his courage and willingness to apply his teaching to many levels. He had the knack of preaching a stern message that met with great success at least in terms of the numbers that went out to hear him. Clearly this is a voice that cannot be ignored.

One can imagine a church in search of a leader running across the profile of somebody like John the Baptist. Surely this must be the Messiah. High energy, able to attract a crowd, clear in his message, and willing to stand up to the powers that be: John has clearly got a future. Yet that is not the entire story. "This is he of whom I said, 'After me comes a man who ranks ahead of me because he was before me.' " John knows that he is not the Messiah, which is part of his message. Actually, such modesty makes John all the more attractive. I have known too many clergy and leaders that needed a reminder that they were not the Messiah.

The crucial thing to be noted here is that behind the modesty is the recognition that there is a significant difference between Jesus' and John's ministry. "I myself did not know him, but the one who sent me to baptize with water said to me, 'He on whom you see the Spirit descend and remain is the one who baptizes with theHoly Spirit.' " Jesus has the Spirit and can distribute it in a way that John cannot. Jesus has the Spirit that can take away the sin of the world, "Here is the Lamb of God who takes away the sin of the world! This is he of whom I said, 'After me comes a man who ranks ahead of me because he was before me.' "

It is one thing to lay out the sins of the world and denounce them. It is another to take away the sin. It is one thing to gather a crowd, another to take away its sins when people begin to jockey for position and place in the hierarchy. It is one thing to be able to denounce sin and it is quite another to have the spirit that, in taking time and taking care, can help to take away the sin. It is one thing to have a clear plan and it is another to have the spirit to deal with peoples' failures.

John recognizes that contrary to appearances he is not the Messiah but he can point to the one who is.

Application

The prophet Isaiah struggles with the gap between being made to be a sharp sword and a polished arrow yet meeting with a sense of laboring in vain having spent his strength for nothing and vanity. Given his feeling it is hard to imagine the mission of Israel to be as a light to the nations being fulfilled. We know the feeling.

The danger for the church is that we often try to fill this gap with our own resources. We fall prey to elevating leaders like John the Baptist because they can bring the crowds or they rescue us from any uncertainty by their definitive plans. Too often we take more pleasure in denouncing sin than in taking away the sin and the conditions that lead people to sin. We forget that, as Paul puts it, we are not lacking in any spiritual gift.

Yes, there will be times when we will feel the vanity of it all. There will be times when we cannot imagine the church as a vehicle of being a light to the nations. Certainly, there will be days when we go after the quick fix. However, contrary to appearances there will be enough spiritual gifts for, "From now on there is reserved for me the crown of righteousness, which the Lord, the righteous judge, will give me on that day, and not only to me but also to all who have longed for his appearing."

Alternative Application

John 1:29-42. What was it that moved Andrew and the other disciple to go beyond John's teaching and follow Jesus? The text indicates as much the conclusion they reached it was John's permission that helped them cross this threshold. "The next day John again was standing with two of his disciples, and as he watched Jesus walk by, he exclaimed, 'Look, here is the Lamb of God!' The two disciples heard him say this, and they followed Jesus."

John is remembered as somewhat stern and demanding as a preacher. On the one hand, the Christian scripture seems to find no inherent conflict between John's morality and the teaching and message of Jesus. One should not find in Jesus a reason to dismiss ethical and justice issues.

Secondly, while John is stern and steadfast, the story is moved along by John's willingness to grant permission for his disciples to follow Jesus in a new direction. This raises the question for me: Are there places where we need to grant permission to move in new directions in order to move the story along? Do we need to grant permission to ourselves to dwell with others of different faiths in order to see how God might have spoken to them? Who needs our permission to grow and change because we are holding them back? Do we need to grant permission to ourselves to rest and renew ourselves?

The scripture, above all, understands John the Baptist as one who did not make it hard for his disciples to follow Jesus — a standard worth emulating in our lives and churches.

Preaching the Psalm

by Schuyler Rhodes

Psalm 40:1-11. There is an unwritten law in lines at the local supermarket. The law states that if you change lines you will wait longer. No matter how carefully you check it out to see which line is shorter or how many things your neighbor has in their shopping cart, if you break ranks, if you step out of the line you're in and move to another line, it is decreed from somewhere that you will have a longer wait than if you had stayed in the line you first chose.

It's about patience — and it's no secret to anyone reading this that patience is in short supply in contemporary culture. Think about it. Wait just one second after the stoplight changes and someone behind you honks the horn. Walk down most any urban sidewalk and smell the rush and crush of getting wherever it is that has to be gotten in less time than is humanly reasonable. Hurry hurry, push push, and God help anyone who makes us wait. Patience is indeed in short supply in our daily lives.

And yet, patience is one of the magic elixirs that propels life forward with greater ease and joy. It is the patient person who usually succeeds with troublesome children. It is the patient person who wins the confidence of others who are caught up in the stress of the moment. It is the patient person who awaits the right opportunities for a host of things in this life. Whether it's the right job or the right relationship, patience is a universal assistant.

The benefits of patience are no less present in our fumbling attempts to reach for the holy. The spiritually impatient — a description which fits many — fire off a quick prayer and wonder why God hasn't answered. The too-often operative expectation is that God will morph God's self to meet our expectations. How does that old Janis Joplin song go? "Oh, Lord, won't you buy me a Mercedes Benz...." If the new car doesn't come, and quick, faith is shaken.

But "waiting patiently for the Lord" offers a thousand different benefits. Primary among them is that waiting usually requires quietude. We may not like it much, but there you are, waiting. And quietude makes it possible to hear things not usually audible in the daily rush of doing what we think is important.

What is it that patience brings? What comes when patience attends prayer? Perhaps it is patience that will provide; patience that will give space for God to "incline God's ear."

Epiphany 3 | Ordinary Time 3

Isaiah 9:1-4

1 Corinthians 1:10-18

Matthew 4:12-23

by David Coffin

Light enters into darkness

An older woman is home bound because of a bad hip. She sits in her rocking chair, gazing out the window at the various signs of life in her neighborhood. Parents and children are riding their bikes together. The neighbor is working on his garden. Another woman is climbing up a tree to fix a birdhouse. This older woman sits and ponders whether getting a hip replacement is worth the stress of facing surgery, therapy, medications, and visits to the doctor. She prays to God for guidance.

Finally, one day she sees another older woman whom she knows to have bad knees outdoors taking out the trash and playingwith her grandchildren. So this woman decides to take the risk and get the hip surgery. It was all of the things she thought it would be in terms of doctor and hospital visits as well as the surgery itself. But the physical therapist showed this woman body exercises and movements that she can practice so she too can resume a normal life. For once, this woman did not have to go back to her pain pills. If she keeps up on her therapy and maintains her daily routine, she now has the normal life of going shopping on the senior citizen bus. She now is part of the crowd who walks in the local shopping mall in the mornings. Somehow the wintry day of seeing another lady who had knee surgery playing with her grandchildren was the light that entered into her darkness. Here is an example of a person who was walking in the painful darkness who has seen a great light (Isaiah 9:1).

Isaiah 9:1-4

It is generally accepted that Isaiah was writing this to the northern kingdom of Israel in the years 734-732 BCE under the Assyrian ruler Tiglath-Pilesar III. Some recurring themes in all of the Isaiah works include that there will emerge a messianic king whose reign will be eternal. Also, his reign does not need violence to enforce the peace that he brings to all people. Such a people are made whole spiritually, physically, and economically as a community. Isaiah, like all of the prophets, speaks to a collective community, not necessarily to just individuals, though it remains accurate that individuals can find practical application from the prophet. Next, Isaiah believes that God works through a small group or remnant of believers. So if the major rank and file choose to assimilate, jump ship on the community, or seek other gods, the God of Abraham continues to work with the small remnant who is left. This should be a living word of encouragement to modern communities of faith who find their worship and Sunday school attendance numbers dwindling with time.

God is capable of reversals, especially the termination of hated political, military, and economic empires that use force and power to get their own way and remain the dominant influence of community and global concerns. Two metaphors are made here. First, the light enters into darkness. This hope can elicit an unrestrained rejoicing for those who yearn for the end of the yoke that is currently imposed on them. The older woman in the above illustration has the yoke that results in the physical limitations of a bad hip. Yet, this yoke could include some form of unemployment, underemployment, financial difficulty, or unresolved issues with various family members.

Isaiah believes that God can use a historical agent to reverse the current trends of discomfort, despair, and dread in any era. "Light" for Isaiah is linked to God's splendor, majesty, and sovereignty. It is disputed whether the new messianic king would be Hezekiah, possibly Josiah in a latter era, or Jesus as Messiah as the New Testament writers argued. The point is that God can deliver all people from the current darkness in which they presently reside. There is real reason for authentic hope, because Isaiah affirms a providential God whose ways remain mysterious but whose love is unconditional. This God keeps the promises made to the people of faith.

Second, the agricultural metaphor is used in verses 3-4. Today, the rough equivalent might be a metaphor for the source of economic income, security, and a future. This could apply to an industrial, academic, small business, agricultural, or any sort of community that has limited avenues to sustain its income base. This continues to make texts such as this a "living word" — regardless of the modern, even post-modern times we live in. God is capable of multiplying options for opportunity to grow and prosper as a community. The old yoke or constraints that might have made people feel "trapped" in a given work, family, school, or community situation can be broken. Today's oppressor can become tomorrow's bad dream that people wish to forget.

Regardless of any bad or dark situation Christians may find themselves in, God is fully capable of terminating it and ushering in a new era of peace and possibilities of growth. Such texts as this can be reheard with different ears to those in the period of Saint Matthew where Rome is the oppressor, just as easily as these words can be heard today or in any time or place where a military force, corporate entity, financial empire, or a bully boss on the job seems to dominate people's lives as well as blocking their peace and serenity. [Source: Walter Brueggemann, *Isaiah 1-39*(Westminster John Knox, 1998)]

1 Corinthians 1:10-18

Imagine a first-century version of a modern political pundit's talk show on one of the national news channels. This is essentially what Paul walked into in the urban city of Corinth. There might be people with strong Type-A, extrovert personalities, all trying to talk above the other people's voices saying, "I belong to Paul," or "I belong to Apollos," or "I belong to Cephas" or "I belong to Christ" (1:12). As with most of these aggressive debates, the people raise their voices and point their fingers at one another, as well as cut the other person off in mid-sentence. Everybody is staking a claim of legitimacy based on their own experience and ideas. So imagine the reaction if one were to talk about how God acts in the lives of humans with Paul's final verse of this text: "For the message about the cross is foolishness to those who are perishing, but to us who are being saved it is the power of God" (1:18).

This verse might be a helpful interpretative lens for this text as well as other readings in the Corinthian correspondence. It is also a reminder that Paul would probably not even be invited onto the program with all of the shouting pundits because he himself was perceived as being full of eloquent wisdom (1:17). He would not be "camera-friendly" for his day (unless he was on *COPS*).

Along with other cities of the times, Corinth craved wisdom and power. Some people thought they had found it by following one particularly charismatic or popular leader within the Christian movement. This resulted in division within the church, as well a poor witness to the community at large. Paul reminds the readers that God deliberately sets his saving activity against all of the perceived power brokers of the ages, that being wisdom and signs from heaven. God reveals God's presence in the form of a crucified Messiah, rather than the political king many zealots and others expected. This was a scandal (Greek word: *skandalon*). This means it was an offense to both Judeans and Gentiles. A crucified messiah was seen as an oxymoron (contradictory term) of that time. God takes human wisdom and power and turns it into folly, and shows strength in weakness. Paul will elaborate on this point later in 1 Corinthians 1:18-25. For the purposes of this week's lectionary text, there is to be no division of loyalties within the Christian church. It is all about Jesus Christ, his crucifixion, and the power of that crucifixion in how God meets us in our weakness, despair, sin, and difficulties in life. This is not the final word. There is new life (1 Corinthians 15).

Paul's objective in writing this text is stated in verse 10: "There be no divisions among you, but that you be united in the same mind and the same purpose." We as Christians might disagree over any number of doctrinal, worship practice, social, and moral issues. We might even have a strong passion about our views. Paul's encouragement is for Christians of all times not to take our eyes off the cross of Christ. This is the source of the power of the church. Paul does not want any Christian to forget that this whole Christian church movement began with a rejected, crucified messiah. This cross is where God chose to show God's power.

How are divisions overcome? How is community built? These are the two questions that Paul would want any congregational council or church mission outreach effort to engage in. For those in the world who walk in the darkness of various personal, financial, and family issues in their lives, the Christian church should shed light into the lives of such people with one common confession of being saved by the power of Christ on the cross. The cross remains a universal symbol of God's presence with those who are in the darkest of dark nights of their soul. Where is God? God is right next to them suffering with them, but pointing them to new light. This is the gospel of any Christian church, from the essential theology of Paul in 1 Corinthians 1. [Source: Ben Witherington III, *Conflict & Community in Corinth: A Socio-Rhetorical Commentary on 1 and 2 Corinthians*(Wm. B. Eerdmans, 1995)]

Matthew 4:12-23

A dark moment is announced with John the Baptist being arrested. His ministry is effectively over! "Jesus left Nazareth and made his home in Capernaum" (4:13). Matthew alone reports a hint that Jesus is cutting ties with his hometown and family. He does ministry in the lands of Zebulun and Naphtali, which were among the first to be conquered by the Assyrian ruler Tiglath-Pilesar III around 732 BCE (Isaiah 9:1-7). In Matthew, Jesus does have priorities for ministry. Just as the Jews receive the good news before the Gentiles, so also the lands (Zebulun and Naphtali) that were swallowed up (or suffer) first are also the first visited with the good news of this new messiah. For Matthew, Jesus' ministry fulfills God's purpose from the Hebrew Bible. Jesus is the light from Isaiah 9. Matthew believes his use of the prophet is an acceptable fit or complements Isaiah's prophecy. Matthew is not doing violence or taking such a text out of context, but simply suggesting that an interface with these two texts is compatible and makes sense to the readers at Matthew's time of writing this gospel. [Source: Robert Smith, *Augsburg Commentary on the New Testament: Matthew*(Augsburg Fortress, 1989)]

Jesus begins to preach repentance for the kingdom of heaven. Matthew is unique in labeling this reign of God as a "kingdom of heaven." It is disputed as to whether Matthew did not like using the specific names of "God" or "Lord" out of reverence, or if he was trying to find another name for "dominion or reign" that might have had political connotations at the time. This reign is different, as is its teacher.

Typical rabbis had students approach them to become followers or disciples. Jesus goes out and calls his own disciples. They may not have had the proper temple or religious preparation that a Jewish rabbi's student may have had. However, Jesus knew that his disciples would never "graduate," but that it would be a lifelong journey even beyond the grave. It is disputed as to whether the disciples left home for good, or if they were able to return home to attend to family business between missionary journeys. Most scholars opt for the latter option as more reasonable. There were visits to Peter's home (Matthew 8:14).

Jesus' kingdom of heaven is more than a passing on of information; requires a transformation of the heart. It is a lifestyle. It entails proclaiming the message elsewhere, even into unchartered lands of the Gentiles (Mathew 28:16-20). One practical observation for today is whether many people actually want to do the "missionary ministry." Has the consumer-driven society so conditioned people of many generations to simply show up and plug in to an already developed program or ministry, then move on with positive feelings until the next "experience or event"? Do people of faith really want to return to "missionary days" of setting up tables, chairs, coffee pots and donuts, then cleaning up afterward? Would a small worship service with a percussion instrument or a simple guitar be "good enough" in an age where people are connected with cyberspace 24/7? Any of these "call to be a missionary" texts raise this challenge in a western culture that prefers to watch past missionary pioneers rough it to blaze a new trail in a rustic frontier, while they themselves prefer to watch a movie of missionaries of the past.

Who is willing to go out into the darkness without much high-tech equipment? This might be one direction to go with this text. Also, which ministries are ending before our very eyes, and what glimmers of hopeful new light are we seeing? As many mainline churches struggle with budgets and worries about a lack of younger people to fill the Sunday school wings of the church, Matthew 4 suggests that Jesus still goes to those lands with people who sat in darkness (v. 16).

Application

It could be a dark, hidden secret in any family. Some family health careplans might try to create endless red tape of applications, approvals, and paperwork before covering it. Not many families, regardless of education or social status, are immune from this deeply hidden secret. That is mental illness and often addiction of many kinds intermixed into a family member's public behavior. Family matriarchs and patriarchs often have shame. Other family members are critical and judgmental. Mental illness and addiction can serve to darken career plans, sabotage family activities, and isolate those who are part of the "inner loop" of knowing what is really going on. Isaiah 9 reminds believers that God is capable of shining light into any darkness, if only the people own the reality of a fallen humanity. God can usher in a new era for such families.

God also suffers alongside all family members who experience mental illness and addictions. To worry about a loved one in such conditions feels like a cross on a body, as one feels the tense muscles from the shoulders out onto the hands, as well as leg muscles that are in constant tension from worrying about when the next emotional outburst or addiction rage will erupt. God is there alongside such family members to identity and comfort them. God also provides power in the refined faith and strength that is built up, as well as the authentic hope one finds in the resurrection. But it still hurts! This might be an application of the 1 Corinthians 1:10-18 text.

Matthew reminds faithful people of all times that God calls us not only to learn information about certain situations that bring darkness into the lives of families, but to work toward the transformation of such lives by pointing them and all people to the light that Jesus shines in the resurrection. Being called as a disciple can lead people into many types of valleys of darkness in terms of health, economic, family, or community hidden secrets.

An Alternative Application

Anybody can keep peace with the use of power and violence as an enforcement mechanism that is, to use weapons, money, rank, family name status, or manipulation to maintain an orderly community. True peace flows naturally, as light draws people out of darkness (Isaiah 9). A messiah who suffers alongside or works alongside those who are in the trenches earns more credibility than constantly pulling rank such as the Roman empire military might. Catching people through witnessing of what new life after death in the kingdom is, is to be preferred to any human-made traps or nets. Jesus' disciples did not have to spear or throw nets over people in darkness. They were drawn by the message of the Emmanuel who saves the people from their sins (Matthew 1:21).

Epiphany 4 | Ordinary Time 4
Micah 6:1-8
1 Corinthians 1:18-31
Matthew 5:1-12
by Ron Love

It's a dog's life

Pope Francis was selected as *Time* magazine's "Person of the Year." Regarding his selection, Nancy Gibbs, the magazine's managing editor, said, "He really stood out to us as someone who has changed the tone and the perception and the focus of one the world's largest institutions in an extraordinary way." All three lectionary readings speak of change. And it is a change that violates those seven deadly words of the church: "We've never done it that way before."

Pope Francis certainly is in violation of that established creed. He removed the fleet of Vatican luxury cars and replaced them with affordable midsize models. He has removed the title of monsignor from the hierarchy of the priesthood. He has selected cardinals from predominantely third-world countries. His vestments, though white, are plain and simple. The tailor-made red leather loafers that accentuated the status of the pope are an attire of the past, as simple black loafers will suffice. Then of course, he no longer resides in the Vatican palace but in the nearby guest hotel.

It is humility and self-effacing service that the three readings call us to. Micah wants us "to walk humbly with our God." Paul desires us to "consider our call" and "boast only of the Lord." Jesus instructs that "blessed are the meek... the merciful... the pure in heart... the peacemakers." These passages reflect a recurring message in the scriptures, personified when Hosea said, "For I desire steadfast love and not sacrifice, the knowledge of God rather than burnt offerings."

This is the liturgical season of Epiphany. The word *epiphany* means "manifestation" or "revelation." During the Sundays of Epiphany we acknowledge three aspects of Jesus' life and ministry. There is the visitation by the Magi, whose gifts not only declare the sovereignty of Jesus (gold), but also his humility (frankincense), and his sacrifice (myrrh). There is Jesus' baptism by John, where the symbolic dove of peace alights on his shoulder. There is Jesus' first miracle at the wedding feast, when legalistic practices are replaced by the new wine of grace.

The lectionary readings report a systematic message throughout the scriptures; that is, God desires humility and sacrificial service, not ornaments.

Micah 6:1-8

Micah offers a summons to the Israelites to recall and remember their Exodus experience. They are to understand that this was a pivotal point in their history when God reaffirmed the protection of the covenant and his unfailing love. The exodus did not create a liturgical creed, but more of a sacred story of deliverance. Now, when confronted by the Moabite King Balal, the Israelites are once again to find assurance in their sacred story of deliverance from the bondage of the Egyptians. When the Israelites found safety and security at the foot of Mount Sinai, there was no place for a golden calf, only commandments chiseled upon tablets of stone. Once again, with deliverance, God does not seek a burnt offering of rams and goats and sheep; God desires the offering of one's self, that is, "to do justice, and to love kindness, and to walk humbly with your God."

Epiphany 4 / Ordinary Time 4

1 Corinthians 1:18-31

Paul asks us to "consider our call" into ministry. In so doing we are not to think of ourselves as wise, such as the Greeks do, nor are we to look for signs as the Jews do. Instead, we are to view ourselves as foolish. This is not a call for self-deprecation but an acknowledgment of the superiority of God. It is the confession that all of our spiritual gifts come from God alone. This is why, unlike the haughtiness of the Roman priests and Jewish Pharisees, we humbly acknowledge "let the one who boasts, boast only in the Lord."

Matthew 5:1-12

The Beatitudes describe the eight blessings in the Sermon on the Mount. Each is a proverb-like proclamation. Each one of the Beatitudes consists of two phrases: the condition and the result. In almost every case the condition is from a familiar Old Testament context, but Jesus teaches a new interpretation. The Beatitudes present a new set of *Christian* ideals that focus on a spirit of love and humility. They echo the highest ideals of the teachings of Jesus on mercy, spirituality, and compassion. The Beatitudes acknowledge that the sacrifice Jesus seeks is not one of burnt offerings or pious displays, but is to be located in self-effacing humility of service. It is an attitude that emanates from the gratitude that we are a part of the sacred story of the exodus and crucifixion.

Application

To follow Jesus is to have an understanding of what we are called to do. First and foremost, it is to be aware of the needs of others.

Did you ever wonder why your dog is so attentive to your body language and voice modulations? It has recently been determined that a dog has the same recognition capacity as a one-year-old infant. As an infant follows a parent across the room with his eyes, so does a dog recognize the subtleties of body motion. As an infant recognizes the voice modulations of a parent, so does a dog recognize the voice commands of his devoted houseparent. Dogs are the only animals to have this ability that came from generations of domestication.

Dr. Adam Miklosi, a behavioral biologist who conducted a study on this, said, "Being in a human family gives a dog the ability to interact in a human way." When we decide to follow Jesus, let us be sensitive to the needs of those who are a part of our global human family.

Each of the three lectionary readings establishes the concept of a being a part of a human family. Each of the three readings helps define how we are to participate as members of that family. They each in part, or combined, can be summarized as having "the ability to interact in a human way."

An Alternative Application

To facilitate the process of education in the home and church, Martin Luther published two catechisms in 1529. Issuing the catechisms Luther implored: "I therefore beg of you for God's sake, my beloved brethren who are pastors and teachers, that you take the duties of your office seriously, that you have pity on the people who are entrusted to your care, and that you help me teach the catechism to the people, especially those who are young." This declaration authenticated Luther's didactic of individual freedom of thought in spiritual matters.

Both books focused on the same five premises: the Ten Commandments are a mirror of sin; the Apostles' Creed is a proclamation of forgiveness; the Lord's Prayer is an acceptance of mercy; the two sacraments of Baptism and the Lord's Supper are channels of grace.

Our three lectionary readings implore us to be mirrors of God by following his commandments accompanied with humility of service.

Epiphany 5 | Ordinary Time 5

Isaiah 58:1-9a (9b-12)

1 Corinthians 2:1-12 (13-16)

Matthew 5:13-20

by Wayne Brouwer

Fasting, faith, and focus

Bernarr Macfadden, who once had a wide following in North America, said that everybody should fast now and then, if only for the good health that it brings. Today's lectionary reading from Isaiah's prophecy might seem to concur.

We do not seem to know what true fasting is, however. Comedian Dick Gregory, for instance, used to stage hunger strikes in protest of the Vietnam War. The mayor of Cork, Ireland, died of a hunger strike against English rule in the 1920s, giving rise to much larger protests. History repeated itself in the 1980s, when Irish political prisoners in Maze Prison, near Belfast, carried on widely publicized hunger strikes. Several died in their protests against England.

Again, during the days of the Cold War when tension tightened in the old Soviet Union, some of the Jewish people who weren't able to get exit visas went on hunger strikes. The media turned on the spotlights, and the Soviet government was forced to comply.

While it is true that hunger strikes can be powerful tools for peaceful resistance in our societies, especially where they have "religious" motives, biblical fasting is actually something else.

Nor is fasting essentially a form of sacrificing for others. Some social justice organizations call for people to stop eating for a while, and then give the cost for your usual meals to hungry folk elsewhere. While the idea is noble, that is *not* what fasting is about. But our Old Testament reading today is a great opportunity to bring faith back into focus through fasting. The other readings provide great follow-through.

Isaiah 58:1-9a (9b-12)

In the world of Isaiah's day there were three specific reasons why people fasted. The first was repentance. You fasted because you sinned. You fasted because you did something wrong. You fasted to say to God: "I'm sorry! I'm really sorry!"

Great King David fasted after he did his thing with Bathsheba. He was up on his palace roof one summer's evening. The day had been hot, and he wanted to catch a breeze as the sun set. Then he saw her! Beautiful!

So he arranged to have an affair with her, and he cleared her military husband from the picture in a strategic move of battle. "Send Uriah in on a suicide mission!" he ordered Commander Joab. Next thing you know Bathsheba is living in his house, pregnant as the day is long. He's the king! He can get away with it! It all belongs to him anyway, right?

But kings can stumble and even great kings can sin greatly. When God checked in with David through Nathan the prophet, David collapsed in grief. "What have I done?" he wept. "How did I get myself into this? Where did I sell my soul to turn this corner?"

That's when David fasted. He fell on the floor of his room in prayer and repentance, and he would eat no food until God resolved the matter with him. He knew just how deep sin sinks into our lives and that without the struggles of pain in the body, there is sometimes no struggle of agony in the spirit.

The Bible tells us of other similar fasts. King Ahab fasted in repentance before God after he and Jezebel stole Naboth's reputation, life, and property. The people of Nineveh fasted in repentance to God after Jonah shouted his warning through the city streets. Fasting was even built into the regular rhythm of Israel's life as a nation. There was the annual Day of Atonement, when the whole nation fasted and prayed. They had a sense that it was possible to flit through life too carelessly, without taking stock of the grit of sin that sticks to the soles of our feet, as the writer of Hebrews described it, and the tether of evil that snags our hearts at inopportune moments.

The second reason people fasted in Bible times was to remember. When King Saul and Prince Jonathan died in battle with the Philistines, David, who took up the reins of power, called the nation of Israel to a day of fasting because something tragic had happened. When tragedy strikes only the careless and the cowardly and the callous are unmoved.

Daniel fasted when he remembered the destruction of Jerusalem and the loss of his people's homeland. And in Jesus' day there was an annual fast to remember the holocaust that nearly wiped out the Hebrew race when the hordes of Babylon swept down from the hills of Ephraim.

Fasting showed solidarity. Fasting declared shared involvement. Fasting said: "What happened was tragic, and I will not forget the pain of it!"

The third reason people fasted during the times of Isaiah was to rivet attention on God. This is the primary focus of today's passage.

When Queen Esther had to go to her husband, Persian King Xerxes, to plead for the life of her people, she asked her friends to fast with her. She couldn't do something like that without getting in tune with the spiritual dimensions of her soul.

In a similar incident, when Ezra was about to lead a contingent of Jews across the desert wastes to Jerusalem, they prepared well, gathering food for the journey, obtaining letters of legal documentation, and organizing the travel groups. But when they had finished their other preparations they fasted together for several days, riveting their attention on God, whose leading they hoped to follow.

Jesus fasted for forty days before he started his public ministry! Can you imagine that? The very son of God fasted in order to get in touch with his own father!

In Acts 13 we find Paul and Barnabas fasting and praying, and the whole congregation at Antioch with them, in order to find the future direction of the ministry God was calling them to. Fasting helps people get in touch with God.

1 Corinthians 2:1-12 (13-16)

During the time of the Reformation John Foxe of England was impressed by the testimony of the early Christians. He gleaned the pages of early historical writings, and wrote a book that has become a classic in the church: *Foxe's Book of Martyrs*.

One story he tells is about an early church leader named Lawrence. Lawrence acted as a pastor for a church community. He also collected the offerings for the poor each week.

A band of thieves found out that Lawrence received the offerings of the people from Sunday to Sunday, so one night as he was out taking a stroll they grabbed him and demanded the money. He told them that he didn't have it, because he had already given it all to the poor. They didn't believe him and told him they would give him a chance to find it. In three days they would come to his house and take from him the treasures of the church.

Three days later they did come. But Lawrence wasn't alone. The house was filled with the people of his congregation. When the thieves demanded the treasures of the church, Lawrence smiled. He opened wide his arms, and gestured to those who sat around him. "Here's the treasure of the church!" he said. "Here's the treasure of God that shines in the world!"

Lawrence was echoing Paul's testimony to the Corinthians.

Matthew 5:13-20

Think of the crowd to which Jesus was speaking. It wasn't a gathering of the United Nations. It wasn't a conference of the superpowers. It wasn't a sitting of Congress or Parliament, or even an assembly at City Hall. It was a crowd on a hillside in a tiny spot of land called Palestine. It was a group of common people with no high ambitions or positions. In fact, they were under occupation! They couldn't make their own laws! They couldn't plan their own futures! They couldn't determine their own destinies! Yet Jesus says to them: "*You* are the salt of the earth! *You* are the light of the world! *You* make a difference in this society!" It's an amazing assertion, isn't it?

Tony Campolo told about a friend of his who was walking through the midway at a county fair when he met a tiny girl. She was carrying a great big fluff of cotton candy on a stick, almost as large as herself! He said to her, "How can a little girl like you eat all that cotton candy?"

"Well," she said to him, "I'm really much bigger on the inside than I am on the outside!"

That's essentially what Jesus is saying here. "You are the salt of the earth! You are the light of the world!" Why? Because of your great power? Because of your positions in government? Because you are so smart or so strong or so gifted? "No!" Jesus would say. "It's because you belong to me!" On the outside you may seem to be nothing, but on the inside you're as big as the kingdom and the power and the glory of your God! You can make a difference!

"*You* are the salt of the earth! *You* are the light of the world!" You can make a difference in life! That's what Jesus says. But he adds a second thing to it. "If the salt loses its saltiness, how can it be made salty again?" asks Jesus. "It's good for nothing, and you throw it out into the streets."

Yet can salt lose its saltiness? Is it really possible for salt to become unsalty?

Not really. Any chemistry teacher will tell you that. Sodium chloride is one of the most stable compounds in the whole of the universe. It doesn't change. It doesn't lose its character.

Still, there is truth to what Jesus is saying. Much of the salt used in Palestine came from the area around the Dead Sea, which, at more than a mile-and-a-half *below* sea-level, is the lowest land area in the world. The waters of the Sea of Galilee flow into the Jordan River and run down there to the bottom of the earth. Once they get there, it's the end of the line. There's no place to go. The hot desert sun evaporates the water and leaves behind a chunky white powder made up of a combination of salts and minerals.

That powder contains enough salt to season meat or to add a little flavor to soup. For that reason the people of Palestine have always scooped it up to use in trade and in cooking. But the salt is mixed with minerals. It's not pure sodium chloride. Indeed, it is possible, under certain circumstances, with a little dampness in the air, for the salts to be dissolved first and leached away.

You may not notice it. What you have left looks the same, yet the taste is gone, and people throw it out. There may be a little salt left, but it isn't enough to make a difference; so the whole batch is chucked out into the street.

The comparison point Jesus makes, in essence, is that strength is found in community. A single grain of salt may make a slight difference, but it takes the concentration of a cluster of them to make a real impact. Similarly, one disciple with a sense of purpose may make a statement in the world, but it's the community of Christians that turns the world upside down.

It's hard sometimes to imagine just how important community is. We like to think of ourselves as independent and strong, full of personal vitality. Still, the first thing we hear from the lips of someone who is experiencing problems is often "Nobody cares! I'm all alone!"

The community is gone and with it went the power. The strength of their Christianity in testimony and witness has disappeared. When they talk about it they sound tired. They can't be salt anymore. They can't light up their world. They're alone and slowly dying, spiritually.

"You can make a difference!" says Jesus. "But you can do that best *together*, as a *community*, like the flicker of a thousand lights in the city on the hill or the powerful taste of a spoonful of salt in the potatoes. You can make a difference *together*!"

There's a third thing that Jesus tells us in these words. He tells us, "You can make a difference together *in the world*!"

Besides the power of flavor, there was an even greater strength of salt in the world of Jesus' day. Salt was used to confirm agreements, to seal treaties, and establish covenants. If you ate salt with someone, you became blood relatives. You had a stake in each other's lives. You were part of the same family.

King Abijah, in the Old Testament, reminds the people that they made a "treaty of salt" with David, and therefore they can't break it. The enemies of the Jews in the book of Ezra write a letter to King Artaxerxes of Persia, telling him that they will be his servants forever because they have eaten salt from his treasuries. They are his servants, confirmed by eating his salt.

In Arabic, the word for "salt" is the same word as the word for "treaty." Similarly, in Persian, the word for "traitor" means "someone who is faithless to salt." Not that many years ago this was all proved again in the modern state of Jordan. Informants for the king uncovered an assassination plot and discovered and reported to the king the name of the man who was supposed to kill him.

In response, the king devised an ingenious plan. Rather than sending his soldiers out to arrest the man, foiling the plot with guns and weapons, he invited the traitor to the royal palaces for a dinner! Since it is impossible to refuse a royal invitation, the man was obligated to enter the territory of his mark.

The king made certain that the meal was heavily salted. At that point things changed, because once they had eaten salt together there was a bond between them. The assassin became a brother, and he couldn't kill the king! They had eaten salt together!

Such a picture resonates with what Jesus gives us here. "You are the salt of the earth!" he says. You are the essence of God's relationship with the world around you. The church isn't just a little community off by itself somewhere. It is the confirmation that God still has an interest in our world!

The apostle Peter picks up that same theme (2 Peter 3). He says there is enough evil in society, enough wickedness in our world, for God to let loose the fires of his judgment. But he's not going to do that yet, says Peter, because he has people living throughout the whole world, and they make a difference. They confirm his relationship with his world. They are the salt of the earth!

And, of course, that brings us to the last thing that Jesus says to us here. "You can make a difference together in the world *for God*!"

It's not enough to be socially active, socially responsible, socially concerned. "Let your light shine before men," says Jesus here, "that they may see your good deeds and praise your Father in heaven!" Turn people's thoughts toward God, says Jesus. No mind is truly enlightened until it is flooded with the glory of heaven. No body is truly healed until it is touched by the power of the Creator. No person is truly set free until there is freedom of the Spirit of Christ.

William Carey was a pastor of a small congregation in Leicester, England. In 1792 he preached a powerful sermon called "Expect Great Things from God; Attempt Great Things for God!" People would remember it for years. His message not only moved hearts in his congregation, however; it also came home to challenge Pastor Carey's own soul. The next year he set sail for India and what he did in that country was simply astounding. He began a manufacturing plant to employ jobless workers. He translated the scriptures and set up shops to print them. He established schools for all ages helping people find a better place in society. He provided medical assistance for the diseased and the troubled and the ailing. He was nothing short of a miracle for the people of India.

Why did he do it? Because Jesus told him: "You are the salt of the earth! You are the light of the world!" And when he lay dying, these were his last words: "When I have gone, speak not of Carey but of Carey's Savior."

There was only one reason for it all: "... that they may see your good deeds, and glorify your Father in heaven!"

Application

There's a marvelous little story tucked away in the pages of Edward Gibbon's seven-volume work *The Decline and Fall of the Roman Empire*. It tells about a humble little monk named Telemachus living out in the farming regions of Asia.

Telemachus had no great ambitions in life. He loved his little garden and tilled it through the changing seasons. But one day in the year 391 he felt a sense of urgency, a call of God's direction in his life. Although he didn't know why, he felt that God wanted him to go to Rome, the heart and soul of the empire. In fact, the feelings of such a call frightened him, but he went anyway, praying along the way for God's direction.

When he finally got to the city it was in an uproar! The armies of Rome had just come home from the battlefield in victory, and the crowds were turning out for a great celebration. They flowed through the streets like a tidal wave, and Telemachus was caught in their frenzy and carried into the Colosseum.

He had never seen a gladiator contest before, but now his heart sickened. Down in the arena men hacked at each other with swords and clubs. The crowds roared at the sight of blood and urged their favorites on to the death.

Telemachus couldn't stand it. He knew it was wrong; this wasn't the way God wanted people to live or to die. So little Telemachus worked his way through the crowds to the wall down by the arena. "In the name of Christ, forbear!" he shouted.

Nobody heard him, so he crawled up onto the wall and shouted again: "In the name of Christ, forbear!" This time the few who heard him only laughed. But Telemachus was not to be ignored. He jumped into the arena and ran through the sands toward the gladiators. "In the name of Christ, forbear!"

The crowds laughed at the silly little man and threw stones at him. Telemachus, however, was on a mission. He threw himself between two gladiators to stop their fighting. "In the name of Christ, forbear!" he cried.

They hacked him apart! They cut his body from shoulder to stomach, and he fell onto the sand with the blood running out of his life.

The gladiators were stunned and stopped to watch him die. Then the crowds fell back in silence, and for a moment no one in the Colosseum moved. Telemachus' final words rang in their memories: "In the name of Christ, forbear!" At last they moved, slowly at first, but growing in numbers. The masses of Rome filed out of the Colosseum that day, and the historian Theodoret reports that *never again* was a gladiator contest held there! All because of the witness and the testimony of a single Christian!

An Alternative Application

Isaiah 58:1-9a (9b-12). Why should any of us fast? The word of the Lord through Isaiah suggests at least two reasons. The first is this: When I fast, I declare the religious truth that I am not merely a consumer. There's something more to me than just my appetites.

There's nothing wrong with wealth. But the danger of our society is to say that if you can afford something you like, you *deserve* to have it! You *need* to buy it!

Why are we "consumers"? Isn't it because the strength of our passions is so great? We desire, so we take! We want, and we have the wherewithal to make it happen, so we do! We're hungry, so we eat!

But fasting stops us. Fasting puts the brakes on. Fasting pulls us up short, because there is no greater craving of our souls than the hunger for food. Our days are organized around it: our coffee breaks, our lunch breaks, our supper hour, and our snacks. Our lives are organized around eating.

Only when we stop eating for a while do we make a religious statement. We say that there is more to us than just our appetites. There's something left of our wills. There's something bigger about our spirits.

Can you wear less than you can afford? Can you drive less than you have the means to buy? Can you develop a relationship with someone else without jumping into bed before marriage? Can you do it?

You won't know until you've tested your soul the way that fasting tests the hunger of your body. You and I are gripped with powerful diseases of the flesh beyond which we're often willing to admit, and the medicine of fasting is one way to check out just how deep the cancer cuts.

There's a second reason why we need to fast: We fast in order to find the contours of our personalities.

Who are you? Do you know? Yes, you are your ambitions. Yes, you are your abilities. Yes, you're even your relationships.

But you are also your *no!'s*. You and I are found, at least in part, in the *no!'s* of our lives. G.K. Chesterton put it this way: "Art and morality have this in common — they both know where to draw the lines!"

When you know where to draw the lines on the picture, it begins to have beauty and meaning. When you know where to draw the lines on a building, it begins to have definition and purpose. And when you know where to draw the line in your life, you begin to have character.

The person who will stop at nothing will say *yes!* to anything! The man who has no limits also has no identity of his own. He robs it from the victims of his cruelties! The woman who doesn't know how to say *no!* will never be able to say *yes!* to the things in life that matter most. And the child who isn't taught the boundaries of behavior grows up to be an adult without a conscience.

But lines are hard to draw, and character is difficult to fashion. Limits are tough to set, especially when society laughs at the pointlessness of it all.

Fasting is a spiritual discipline that takes us back to our roots and sets us down in the company of the great ones of the past teaching us the mastery of God over self and helps us find our way back home. Our identity is found, at least in great measure, exactly at the points in our lives where we will say no. The *yes!* of my life falls precisely within the limits of my *no!*, and fasting will test those limits for me.

Some years ago *People* magazine interviewed Dolly Parton. At one point the interviewer asked, "Where do you ever get such a strong character?"

Dolly said it came from her family and her Christian faith. "I quote the Bible real good!" she said.

What about psychiatry asked the interviewer? So many people find the need to get counseling, especially in the stresses of show business.

"No," replied Dolly, "I don't see a psychiatrist. I fast instead."

You what?

"I fast!"

Is that like a diet?

"No!" said Dolly. "I do it to get in touch with God! Sometimes I'll... fast 7, 14, or 21 days... I don't drink nothing but water and I don't ever say when I'm on a fast — scripture says you're not supposed to" (*People*, January 19, 1981).

Then she went on to say that she's never made a major decision without fasting and prayer. The interviewer was astounded, so much so that she made a point of it in the article.

But the truth of it remains: God expects us to fast, and when we do we find the contours of our souls. We find the definition of our characters. We find out who we really are.

Epiphany 6 | Ordinary Time 6

Deuteronomy 30:15-20

1 Corinthians 3:1-9

Matthew 5:21-37

by Cathy Venkatesh

Choosing to love

Here we are, the Sunday after the sentimentality and excesses of Valentine's Day. Some of us will arrive at church with fond memories of cards and chocolates, perhaps a special meal with a beloved partner or family. Others will arrive having done our best to ignore the holiday. And still others will arrive with renewed tenderness around loves lost to death or broken relationships or around months or years of living alone while longing for love. Children and teens may or may not have received valentines from cherished friends and secret crushes. In the face of popular culture in this season of romance, what does the church have to say about love?

I still remember the relief I felt at a Bible study in my early twenties when we looked at the command in Deuteronomy to love God and neighbor and discussed how this love is a choice we make rather than an emotion we feel. I knew how often I failed to feel love toward God and neighbor, and how guilty I felt about that failure, but here I was being told that no matter my feelings, I could choose to act in loving ways and that was what God was asking me to do. This was a revelation. Love was a choice I could make, something distinct from the tumult of my not always loving emotions.

Our lessons today speak to the power of choice in Christian life, to the power we have to choose love and life, both in our outward actions and inward dispositions. It can be the work of a lifetime to recognize and honor our emotions without being ruled by them. Throughout our lessons today, we hear invitations to mature, conscious, and godly love for self, others, and God.

Deuteronomy 30:15-20

Deuteronomy purports to be Moses' final address to the people of Israel as they prepare to enter the promised land. During their forty years in the wilderness, the generation born in slavery in Egypt has died and a new generation has been born into the covenant God has made with the people through Moses. In a covenant renewal ceremony for the entire gathered people, Moses reminds this new generation of their history, the law, and the promises God has made to them. In reality, Deuteronomy is a bit more complex in that it includes three distinct addresses of Moses to the people, each of which arise out of different historical periods. Our reading today is the culmination of Moses' third and final address (Deuteronomy 29:1--30:20), and it comes from exilic times (see Deuteronomy 30:1-10), when the people are longing to be restored to the promised land their ancestors once inhabited but they have now lost. It reminds the people that following God's laws and keeping the covenant are necessary to live peaceably in the land, and that the exile they now experience is the consequence of disobedience. As the prophets offered hope and comfort to those in exile, so too does this final address of Moses. Some preachers may wish to note the words of comfort that immediately precede today's passage: "Surely, this commandment that I am commanding you today [to obey God's law] is not too hard for you, nor is it too far away. 12 It is not in heaven, that you should say, 'Who will go up to heaven for us, and get it for us so that we may hear it and observe it?' 13 Neither is it beyond the sea, that you should say, 'Who will cross to the other side of the sea for us, and get it for us so that we may hear it and observe it?' 14 No, the word is very near to you; it is in your mouth and in your heart for you to observe" (Deuteronomy 30:11-14).

Today's passage provides an excellent opportunity to reflect on free will and the nature of God's law. Is God's law a threat — break a rule and be punished? Or is it a gift, offering an outline of how to live peaceably with self, neighbors, and the world? God does not mandate that we follow the law, but God does say that there will be negative consequences if we live apart from the law and positive consequences if we live under its guidance. And surely that is true. If we steal, murder, dishonor one another and God, we bring death into the world. If we choose to act according to God's law, we choose what gives life, stability, and hope to our own lives and the lives of the people around us. The people of Israel had been slaves in Egypt; before they were ready to enter the promised land, they had to be remade into free people who could establish just, peaceable lives as individuals and a society. The law that they received in the wilderness was a gift to guide them in living in this new land.

A modern corollary could be made in discussions of the slavery of addiction and the gift of the twelve steps for those who find new lives in sobriety. The twelve steps are not a threat but a gift, a lifeline thrown to those who are drowning and a constant means to find one's way back however many times one may falter or fall. God's law is the same. It is always there, offering a guide and a framework for our lives. When we go off-course, when our lives feel full of curses not blessings, it is worth returning to God's law and seeking to understand and remedy what went wrong — perhaps in our own lives, perhaps in the society in which we live. God lets us choose how to live, and God invites us to be conscious of the choices we make.

1 Corinthians 3:1-9

Paul writes to the church in Corinth to address several disputes and sources of strife. In this passage, we hear his concerns about divisions within the congregation over those who follow the teachings of one teacher or another (Apollos or Paul). According to the Acts of the Apostles (18:24--19:1), Apollos was a Jewish Christian from Alexandria, "an eloquent man, well-versed in the scriptures" who spoke with "burning enthusiasm" about Jesus in Ephesus and Corinth. No indication of any rivalry or theological dispute between Paul and Apollos appears in the scriptures, but clearly Apollos' charismatic presence earned him the allegiance of some in the Corinthian church, while others clung firmly to their prior, less eloquent teacher, Paul. (See 1 Corinthians 2:1-5 for Paul's depracating assessment of his own teaching, in implicit contrast to Apollos.) Sadly, this situation is familiar to many present-day churches and pastors, in which some congregation members favor one leader (past or present) over another and divisions ensue. Paul rightly points out that focus on the personality of the leader or teacher is misplaced. Our allegiance properly belongs only to God. And yet, in a religious tradition that so upholds the incarnation of God in human flesh, it is worth honoring the fact that many Christians find God's presence in and through the ministry of other human beings. It is natural to feel a special devotion to a person who has led us into a deeper experience of God, but the mature Christian recognizes that our ultimate allegiance is to God and God's community, not to any one leader. What an excellent text this one is for anyone engaged in interim ministry or other transitions of leadership in a parish setting!

Paul denounces the jealousy and quarreling in the Corinthian church while upholding his own ministry and that of Apollos and ultimately pointing the way to God. The Corinthians are acting like children, he says, fighting over inconsequential things and distracted from their true nature as children of God. Paul's letter is written to a church in a large, prosperous urban center with an ethnically, religiously, and culturally diverse population. Surely the Corinthian church reflected at least some of the diversity of the surrounding population, and this letter can be instructive to anyone seeking to minister in a diverse setting. As long as our focus is on one another, we will be divided. When we place our focus on God and God's work in Jesus, human divisions lessen and the unifying work of the Holy Spirit joins us in common purpose and understanding. As in Moses' address to the Israelites in Deuteronomy, the Corinthians (and often we) have choices to make in where we will direct our focus and energy: to what are often quite human and understandable disputes and tensions with each other, or to the loving God who made us.

Matthew 5:21-37

In today's gospel, we enter the third of four consecutive weeks of readings from Jesus' Sermon on the Mount. Note the parallel actions of Moses' ascent of the mountain to receive the law and Jesus' ascent of mountain to deliver new interpretations of the law. This and next week's readings contain six antitheses, each of which contrast "you have heard it said" (in the law of Moses) with Jesus' more radical teachings about anger, adultery, divorce, swearing oaths, retaliation, and love for enemies. For those who view the law as a threat — break it and be punished — Jesus ups the ante considerably in each teaching. But for those who view the law as a gift, Jesus' teachings offer new insights into peaceable life with self, others, and God. Here, as elsewhere in the Sermon on the Mount, Jesus is teaching beyond right outward actions, as delineated in the law of Moses. Jesus calls us toward holy inward orientations, which are the genuine foundation of a loving life with God, neighbor, and self.

In 5:21-26, Jesus says it is not sufficient simply not to commit murder; we must actively work toward forgiveness and reconciliation with those from whom we are estranged. If we come to worship with an angry heart, sorting out that anger and making peace take preeminence over staying in worship. If we said this each Sunday at the start of the worship service, and our parishioners truly listened, I wonder how many would be left in church by the end of the service! Let us not forget Jesus' propensity to overstatement as part of the Jewish rhetorical tradition. Sometimes we may need to come to God (and stay for the whole service) to gain strength and perspective to become peacemakers elsewhere in our lives. But none of us can argue that living with a heart full of anger is painful and difficult. Jesus seeks to relieve us of this burden that destroys our peace and quite often our health, relationships, and the people around us. We can choose to hold on to our anger, or we can choose to let it go. Examples from all times and places in Christian history abound, from St. Patrick, captured and enslaved in Ireland who returned to become its patron saint; from civil rights leaders and struggles in the United States, South Africa, and around the world; to Jesus himself on the cross: "Father forgive them, for they know not what they do."

Verses 27-30 concerning adultery again address inward dispositions over outward actions. Yes, committing adultery is wrong, but so too is contemplating it! What a challenge Jesus' message is to our sexualized media and culture that actively encourages lust as a means of selling products or providing entertainment. In approaching this topic, it may be useful to consider the power of prayer. If, as Christians, we believe that prayer, and especially praying for other people, is powerful and makes a difference in others' lives, then it follows that all our inward dispositions toward other people can make a difference. Perhaps they can be hard to name or detect, but if in our hearts we are treating other people as objects of our desire rather than unique children of God, there will be unhappy consequences for us and for them. Far better to throw out the television or the computer or whatever it is that leads us down this path than to live in a way that treats other people as objects. Martin Buber's *I and Thou* could provide further reflections on this theme.

Verses 31-32 may hit close to the heart for parishioners who are divorced, have marital troubles, or whose family members are divorced. It is worth considering this passage in conjunction with Matthew 19:1-9 in which Jesus makes similar statements about divorce in response to questioning by the Pharisees. In this case, Jesus explains why the Mosaic Law includes provisions for divorce: "It was because you were so hard-hearted that Moses allowed you to divorce your wives, but from the beginning [i.e., God's original creation in Eden], it was not so" (Matthew 19:8). With the Sermon on the Mount calling people to higher standards of interior life and love for God and neighbor (which would include one's spouse!), Jesus' condemnation of divorce is quite natural. Note that he is speaking only to husbands; women in his time presumably did not have the power to institute divorce themselves. Scholars believe that the provision for "except on the ground of unchastity" in Matthew 5:32 reflects the view of the gospel writer, not Jesus. In parallel comments in the earlier gospel of Mark (10:11), no such provision is made. Pastorally, it can be worth acknowledging that the Sermon on the Mount sets an ideal standard that none of us meets. The public nature of divorce is more readily seen than the inward disposition of our hearts, but for Jesus, all broken relationships are contrary to God's will and law. In the Eastern Orthodox tradition, the marriage ceremony for divorced spouses is penitential, compared with the joyful ceremony prescribed for first-time marriages and for those who have been widowed and are remarrying. Jesus condemns all failures to love and calls us to repent and return to love of God and neighbor and to know ourselves as beloved children of God. Those who know the pain of divorce may especially need the knowledge of God's love.

Verses 33-37 about making oaths may feel trite or obscure after dealing with such fraught subjects as anger, lust, adultery, and divorce. Yet there is a continuation of the theme raised in 5:28 of not making others objects of our own desires. Here, it is making use of God or God's name to reinforce the promises we make. Not only is it unnecessary, it is disrespectful and trivializes God. And to swear by one's own head (5:36) is for one, nonsensical, and for two, disrespectful of the God who made us and loves us so much that every hair on our heads is counted (Matthew 10:30). Let our yes be yes and our no be no. This may be easy for Jesus to say, but consider, even if we do not swear on God's name, how hard that can be for so many of us — we hedge, we qualify, we do not give clear or direct answers out of a desire to protect ourselves rather than genuine care for another person. Even in families and cultures in which oath-making is a rare event, this passage still provides plenty to consider when it comes to loving God and neighbor.

Any one of these teachings could inform an entire sermon, and this week we are given four! While particular congregational or pastoral circumstances may lead us to focus on a particular teaching, it is worth remembering Jesus' words in Matthew 5:17 that precede these teachings: "Do not think I have come to abolish the law or the prophets; I have come not to abolish but to fulfill." In these teachings, Jesus moves toward fulfilling the law, which he later summarizes for the Pharisees in Matthew 22:37-40: "You shall love the Lord your God with all your heart, and with all your soul, and with all your mind. This is the greatest and first commandment. And a second is like it: You shall love your neighbor as yourself. On these two commandments hang all the laws and the prophets." Jesus' teachings in the Sermon on the Mount are all elaborations on these two commandments, originally from Deuteronomy 6:5 and Leviticus 19:18. The Deuteronomic charge is a greater one than Jesus' simple words about loving God. In full, it reads: "You shall love the LORD your God with all your heart, and with all your soul, and with all your might. Keep these words that I am commanding you today in your heart. Recite them to your children and talk about them when you are at home and when you are away, when you lie down and when you rise. Bind them as a sign on your hand, fix them as an emblem on your forehead, and write them on the doorposts of your house and on your gates" (Deuteronomy 6:5-9). What sort of world would we live in if these laws were truly in our hearts?

Application

I am reminded of a story I heard some years ago. It is attributed to Native American origins, but I do not know its original source. In it, an old shaman lies dying. A student of the shaman enters and asks how the shaman is faring. He answers, "Oh my child, there is a terrible battle going on inside me. Inside me are a white wolf and a black wolf, and they are fighting to the death. The white wolf is all that is good and loving, brave and true. The black wolf is full of hatred and anger and seeks only to destroy. The battle is fierce and terrible." The student is horrified but eventually finds the courage to ask, "Which wolf is winning?" The old man answers, "The wolf that will win is the one that I feed."

Preachers who use this story may wish to make it more elaborate or change the racially charged black/white imagery, but there is great truth in the observation that all our hearts contain love and hatred, anger and forgiveness, greed and generosity... the list goes on. We may not be able to evict or eradicate our unloving and ungodly emotions, but we can choose which emotions we nurture and encourage to grow. We can choose to act in ways that nurture love, even if we are not actively feeling it. This takes attention and time and discipline and may work in a hundred different ways for different people. I know if I am hungry, I often get very short-tempered. I owe it to my family as well as myself to eat well so that we are not all penalized by my low blood sugar. I also know that things I read or watch or listen to affect me. Daily habits of TV watching or other media consumption that we may consider innocuous can shape us in ways we don't realize are happening. How often I've had to remind parishioners during times when it seems like one piece of bad news is reported after the other that all they are hearing is news because it is novel and not the normal course of events. Reporters don't get very far telling us how most days most people in the world love their children, go to work, care for their neighbors, and pray in their own traditions. The ordinary, good stuff of life doesn't make the news, so we need to look for that ourselves, and not let the media define our worldview. Here in Boston, nine months after the Marathon bombings, some people are reporting symptoms of post-traumatic stress from simply having watched the news and followed updates on social media intensively in the hours and days after the bombings. What we watch and how we choose to direct our attention have great power to affect our mental and spiritual well-being.

Disciplines of prayer, study of the Bible and other sacred readings, corporate worship, simplicity of life, tithing, and service are all gifts the Christian tradition offers to pull us out of our worst selves into the selves God would have us be. They all feed the good wolf. And as we grow in love and gratitude, we may come to love and honor even the least desirable parts of ourselves and what they have to teach us. In some longer versions of the story, even the black wolf is honored by the end for its gifts, while the loving, well-nourished white wolf guards and protects it. What aspects of your life do you feed? Where is God calling you to devote your time, your attention, your love, and your prayer?

Transfiguration Sunday
Exodus 24:12-18
2 Peter 1:16-21
Matthew 17:1-9
Psalm 2
by Wayne Brouwer and Schuyler Rhodes

A mountaintop experience

One of the cable networks has created a strange hit series. It began as *Ice Road Truckers*, monitoring the dangerous winter haulage north of Yellowknife on the frozen Canadian tundra. Then, after several years of gaining familiarity with the top tonnage truckers, the network displaced them to northern Alaska and introduced new challenges and new road masters. More recently, several of these rig lords and ladies have been transported to the Himalayan heights of upper India. Here the cameras have panned with toe-tingling shock and awe the dizzying cliffs and switchbacks that paint tiny trails against massive mountains. One wants to look up at splendor but becomes entranced by plummeting rocks and trucks bouncing toward certain annihilation.

But if one can reach the summit, all of heaven is at the doorstep. It certainly was that way for Moses and Peter, as they scaled the upper altitudes of earth's crust, beckoned by God into glory. Moses remained forever separated from the rest of humanity because of the experience, becoming the mediator of the Old Covenant. Peter was changed as well, but constantly nodded in the direction of the mediator of the New Covenant who brought him so close to grandeur. Jesus, of course, had already stepped through the gossamer tissue that veils eternity from time. And on this day we celebrate how he almost sneaked back but stayed on our side to make sure the door would never be closed to us.

Exodus 24:12-18

In clear and unambiguous testimony the Bible's own internal evidence is that the writing down of important ideas or history as a sourcebook of revelatory insight was begun when the Israelites encountered God in a unique way at Mount Sinai. It was there, according to the pages of Exodus, that God and Moses collaborated to create written documents which would travel with the community that became the nation of Israel.

So it is imperative to understand more clearly what was taking place at Mount Sinai. To do that, we need to know something of the broader history of the second millennium BC.

One of the dominant civilizations of the second millennium was the Hittite kingdom. Somewhat secluded in the mountainous plateaus of Anatolia (eastern Turkey today), the Hittites shaped a vast web of international relations, which at the height of their power in the fourteenth century BC, encompassed most of the ancient near east. While they were companions of other similar civilizations that shared commonalities of culture and conquests and cities, the Hittites linger in archaeological and historical studies for, among other things, their standardization of a written code used in the normalization of international relations. In order to establish appropriate structures that would spell out their on-going interactions with subjected peoples, a prescribed treaty form appears to have been widely used. The parameters of the typical Hittite Suzerain-Vassal Covenant included:

- A PREAMBLE declaring the identity and power of the ruler responsible for establishing this relationship.

- A HISTORICAL PROLOGUE outlining the events leading up to this relationship, so that it could be set into a particular context and shaped by a cultural or religious frame.
- STIPULATIONS specifying the responsibilities and actions associated with the relationship.
- CURSES AND BLESSINGS that evoked the negative and positive outcomes if this covenant were either breached or embraced by the parties.
- WITNESSES who were called to affirm the legitimacy of this covenant-making event, and who would then hold the parties accountable.
- DOCUMENT CLAUSE describing ratification ceremonies specified future public recitations of the treaty and noted the manner in which the copies of the covenant were to be kept.

What makes this bit of ancient historical trivia so intriguing for biblical scholars is the uncanny correspondence between the elements of this Hittite covenant code and the literature at the heart of Israel's encounter with God at Sinai. Note the following:

- When God is first heard to speak from the rumbling mountain, the words are essentially the PREAMBLE of a Suzerain-Vassal covenant: "I am the Lord your God" (Exodus 20:1).
- Immediately following is a brief HISTORICAL PROLOGUE reminding the people of the events that precipitated this encounter: "… who brought you out of the land of Egypt, out of the house of bondage" (Exodus 20:2).
- Then a recitation of STIPULATIONS that will shape the ethics, morality, and lifestyle of the community (Exodus 20:3--23:19).
- Following these are the CURSES AND BLESSINGS (Exodus 23:20-33) of a typical covenant document. What is unusual in this case is that the order is reversed so that the blessings precede the curses. This provides the same rigors of participatory onus, but gives it a freshness of grace and optimism that are often absent from the quick condemnation of the usual ordering.
- The WITNESSES are the Elders of the Israelite community (Exodus 24:1-2), bringing authentication of this process and these documents into the human realm, when it was often spiritualized in other covenants by listing local gods as moderators of these events.
- Finally there is the DOCUMENT CLAUSE (Exodus 24:3-18) that spells out the ratification ceremony. It will be followed by a further reflection on the repositories of the covenant document copies once the tabernacle has been built.
- The striking resonance between the usual form of the Hittite Suzerain-Vassal Covenant and the essential first speech of Yahweh to Israel at Mount Sinai makes it difficult not to assess the beginnings of conscious Israelite religion in terms other than that of a Suzerain (Yahweh) Vassal (Israel) covenant-making ceremony. Furthermore, this appears to elucidate the mode and function of the first biblical documents. They were not intended to be origins myths, ancestor hero stories, mere legal or ethical or civil codes, sermons, prophecies, or apocalyptic visions (though all of these would later accrete to the initial writings of the first community encounter with Yahweh); they were initially the written covenant documents formulating the relationship between a nation and the (divine) ruler who earned, in battle, the right to order her world. (For more on this see *Covenant Documents: Reading the Bible Again for the First Time*; Cognella, 2009.)

This is why the word "covenant" becomes an essential term for all the rest of the literature that will be garnered into the collection eventually known as the Bible. The Bible begins with a covenant-making ceremony that produces certain documents and then continues to grow as further explications of that covenant relationship are generated. One can read theology, ethics, politics, or history out of the Bible, but one cannot do so while ignoring the essential role of the Sinai Covenant between Yahweh and Israel. Even the idea of "kingdom," so prevalent and pervasive in the Bible, is predicated on the covenant, for it is by way of the covenant that Israel becomes the dominion of the great king. The kingdom of God is the context for all that is portrayed in the Bible, but the covenant is the administrative document through which the kingdom takes hold and adheres in the human societies that form the front ranks of Yahweh's citizenry.

This is strikingly important for explaining today's Old Testament passage. It is the culmination of the covenant-making ceremony, with Moses acting as mediator between the true king of Israel and the people themselves. In this role he anticipates the day, thirteen centuries later, when Jesus would function more fully in this manner, coming to us from the other side.

2 Peter 1:16-21

About the time that Paul was engaged in his final communications with Timothy and Titus, Peter made his own last swing through churches of northern and eastern Asia Minor. This was quite a trip for an older gentleman to take (exceeding the reach of all of Paul's journeys recorded in Acts) since Peter was based in Rome at the time. He calls it "Babylon" (1 Peter 5:13), but that was a code term already circulating throughout the Christian church, hinting at the persecutions looming from the ruler of the world in a way similar to the Babylonian pressures against Judah centuries before. It may well have been that Peter was invited to officiate at a number of large baptism ceremonies since the tone of his first letter is that of instruction for new members to the Christian community.

Peter reminds his readers that he was an eyewitness of Jesus' life and sufferings (1 Peter 5:1; see also 2:23 and today's lectionary reading) and directly echoes a number of Jesus' teachings in his words (compare 1 Peter 2:12 with Matthew 5:16; 1 Peter 2:21 with Matthew 10:38; 1 Peter 3:14 and 4:13-14 with Matthew 5:10-12). Some scholars believe this letter could not have been written by Peter since its use of the Greek language is too educated, too well crafted. But the double set of brothers from the fishing trade in Capernaum that Jesus called to follow him (Peter and Andrew, James and John), probably came from middle class families where education was important. Moreover, just as Paul had amanuenses writing out his letters, so in 1 Peter 5:12 the letter writing skills of Silvanus (a variant of Silas) are recognized.

Peter writes in powerful terms of the great salvation recently brought to humankind by Jesus. This new life is irreversibly guaranteed, by way of both Jesus' resurrection and ascension, for those who believe (1 Peter 1:3-12). Then follows an extended exhortation to holy living, because these believers in Jesus are God's special people (1 Peter 1:13--2:10), who follow in the footsteps of Jesus (1 Peter 2:11--3:12), and must face, with their master, the sufferings that will fall on all his disciples in these challenging times (1 Peter 3:12--4:19). Peter gives a special word of encouragement to the elders who lead the various congregations (1 Peter 5:1-4), and then expands these words of advice to the broader community (1 Peter 5:5-11) before closing with brief personal greetings (1 Peter 5:12-14).

The tone of Peter's letters is far darker than any of the writings of Paul. There is an ominous pall of suffering that clouds every perspective. Jesus suffered. You will suffer, if you are faithful. You must follow Jesus in and through suffering. New trials and greater suffering are coming. Whether by way of external hints or from the inner promptings of the Spirit, Peter seems to have been anticipating the sharp clout of Nero's official pogroms just ahead.

Yet through the murky shrieks and dark valleys, Peter never loses confidence in God's sovereignty or care. God is judge over evil, faithful creator, and the chief shepherd who will soon bring untarnishing crowns of glory for those who remain true.

This second letter attributed to Peter has been dogged by some controversy throughout the years. Its language and style seem different from 1 Peter, and it focuses on the second coming of Jesus (2

Peter 3) in a way that is not done anywhere else in the New Testament. Yet the majority of the church accepted it as Peter's letter from the very beginning. Once again, stylistic and vocabulary differences can be attributed to the secretarial assistance Peter used, and the particular false teaching that Peter wanted to address.

After all, the author identifies himself as Jesus' disciple Simon Peter (2 Peter 1:1), seems to be an old man looking back over a long career (2 Peter 1:12-15), speaks of being with Jesus during his earthy ministry (2 Peter 1:16-18), and uses these connections to confirm his teachings and authority (2 Peter 1:19-21). This does not prove the letter is from Peter, of course, but it has a ring of authenticity about it.

It seems that the letter was written because a number of pseudo-Christian teachers were compromising the core message of Jesus for their own personal gain (2 Peter 2). It is not clear whether they were seeking money for their teaching ministries, or if they just wanted fame and a high standing in their communities. In light of these developments, Peter presses the same apocalyptic ethic that Paul touted so often: Jesus is coming soon so be ready and live appropriately (1 Peter 3). What is particularly striking about Peter's version is that he clearly identifies the times in which he is living, coupled with the imminent return of Jesus, as the "day of the lord," which became the focus of Old Testament prophecy.

Peter anticipates his looming death (2 Peter 1:12-15), and certainly believes difficult times are ahead for all believers. For this reason he believes it is necessary to make one last reminder of his connection with Jesus and the validity of his ministry and message. In so doing, he remembers when he was first absolutely convinced of Jesus' divinity. It happened on the Mount of Transfiguration when all of heaven poured through his master, and Moses and Elijah confirmed the truth of what he and James and John were seeing. It is likely that Peter wrote this letter sometime in 64 AD, probably a year or so after his first letter and shortly before his arrest and crucifixion under Nero's persecution.

Matthew 17:1-9

When the gospels according to Mark and Matthew are placed side by side, it is very obvious that there is a strong literary dependence between them. Approximately 90% of the material in Mark's gospel shows up in Matthew's gospel. There are many good reasons to believe that Matthew used Mark's material in developing his own homiletic testimony about Jesus — editing a number of forms and expressions to make them come out more literarily polished, altering terms (like the "kingdom of God" to "kingdom of heaven") to fit a differentiated audience, adding teachings and incidents that expand upon Mark's rudimentary offerings, regrouping certain materials to collect them into more memorable theme sections, and providing additional personal details in the conclusion.

Following Mark's pattern, Matthew's large outline for unfolding the life and teachings of Jesus has three significant parts:

> *1-16 Jesus teaches the crowds about the kingdom*
> *— 17 Transitional Event–the Transfiguration*
> *17-20 Jesus teaches the disciples about discipleship*
> *— 21 Transitional Event–entry into Jerusalem*
> *21-28 Jesus moves through the Passion to his Coronation*

This shows the critical location of today's gospel reading. It forms the bridge between Jesus' public ministry declaring the significance of the kingdom of heaven and his more focused ministry with his disciples, helping them to understand their leadership role in it. On the mountain, Jesus' full divinity is revealed for his key lieutenants, confirmed by the endorsing appearance of the mediators of divine revelation in scripture as known in Jesus' day: Moses of the law and Elijah of the prophets. Moreover, the divine voice thunders heaven's unquestionable approval, striking overwhelming awe in the hearts of Peter, James, and John, just as the terrifying presence did for Israel at Sinai. Peter's desire to build "shelters" (Greek: *tabernacles*) confirms Matthew's penchant for parallels between the old and new expressions and events of the covenant.

While all of these details are interesting and interpretively helpful, at the center of all things remains Jesus. It is he upon whom we gaze, unable to tear away our eyes. He is the doorway between earth and heaven. He is the Lord of the covenant. He is the fulfillment of the law (Moses) and the prophets (Elijah). He is the one who commands his disciples to be about the business of the kingdom. And it is before him that we fall in worship with Peter, James, and John.

Application

British mountain-climber George Mallory tried a number of times to conquer the peak of Mount Everest. In fact, he lost his life in 1924 on those slopes and debate still rumbles in mountaineering circles about whether or not he reached the pinnacle before he died. He's the one who coined the phrase "because it is there" in response to the question of why anyone would want to climb a mountain.

"Because it is there" is a pretty fair psychological assessment of human interaction with high places. The ancients set their cities on hilltops to command the advantage in war. Rich folk have always wanted "a room with a view" and are able to buy the higher ground for their palatial homes. Historically "high places" were scenes of religious devotion, probably because of their isolation from the busyness of human society and their proximity to the heavens.

Even little children get in on the act. Who, in northern climates, at least, hasn't played "King of the Mountain" in a winter schoolyard, pushing all comers down icy slopes? And who among us doesn't relish "mountaintop experiences": times when we feel "elated" and "elevated" and "ecstatic," times when we are "flying high," "sitting on top of the world," and "on cloud nine" somewhere there in the heavenlies?

Religiously, it is a good thing for us to get back to the mountain. Moses is there, and Elijah, Peter, James, and John. Of course, the big attraction is Jesus. Have you seen him lately? Try the heights!

Alternative Application

Matthew 17:1-9. Mountains no longer carry with them the "religious" significance of earlier times. Now they are playgrounds for pleasure-seekers, tamed by skis and snowmobiles. Tunnels and superhighways ease travelers over the rugged places, and airplanes make them vanish altogether. The broad, the easy, the plain, and the simple beckon us. We do our climbing by way of elevators and escalators. Edward Kasner, renowned topologist at Columbia University for many years, knew more about mountains, on paper at least, than nearly anyone else in his day. He vacationed most often in Brussels, claiming that it was a convenient base from which to organize a mountain-climbing expedition to the highest point in Belgium. When people asked him how high that peak was, he replied, "Twelve feet above sea level." That was enough of a climb for him. And he has many compatriots in our age.

Yet those who travel again with Peter, James, and John to the heights with Jesus will never forget the experience. Some people can become so heavenly minded that they are no longer any earthly good. But seeing Jesus in all his glory as the crossover agent who brings heaven to earth can keep us focused here on the things that really matter. It certainly did for Peter.

Preaching the Psalm

by Schuyler Rhodes

Psalm 2. *Making God Laugh* by Schuyler Rhodes. There's an old saying that comes from some unknown quarter. It says, "If you want to make God laugh, make a plan." The implication here, of course, is that our plans may seem bold and even fail-proof, but at the end of the day things frequently go awry. Or, as this saying suggests, according to God's plan, not ours.

The second psalm takes this notion and goes in a somewhat different direction. Here, we are not talking about human plans but rather the conspiring of nations. The same principle, however, seems to apply. Whether corporate or individual, national or local, our human strivings mean little in the face of the Creator of the universe. It is not unlike the parents who sit back and shake their heads with wry smiles as pre-teens pronounce grand judgments about the world. "If only," the parents think to themselves, "If only they knew…."

Like these parents, God also sits back and laughs at our grandiose pronouncements and strategic plans. It's not our misguided planning, however, that triggers the derisive and holy laughter. It is, rather, our incessant attempts to be in charge. That's right. Human folly, indeed original sin itself, can be traced to this unabated drive that seems to be imbedded in our nature. The wreckage of human history is the tragically continuing story of the human struggle to control things. From dictators to popes to financiers and back again, we strain and wrestle for control. Whether it's a five-year-old on the play ground or a bishop jealous of his authority, we want to be in charge. We want to run things.

It's interesting to note that all of the world's great faith traditions recognize this human drive to control. It's for this reason that each of them has the concept of self-denial at their core. Islam, Buddhism, Hinduism, Judaism, and Christianity all call their adherents to deny the self and cleave to a more holy way. The words of Jesus echo this as he says, "Deny yourself, pick up your cross and follow me."

This psalm reminds us that, quite simply, it's God who's in charge. God, who created us and all that we see around us is the ruler and sovereign. At its root, this never-ending attempt to run things is, in God's eyes, idolatry.

One can't help but wonder how things would turn out in our world if human beings stepped back and surrendered the drive to be in charge and devoted themselves instead to service. Conjure up for a moment, a world filled with people dedicated, not to controlling, but to serving. Imagine how differently we would all behave if we surrendered our need to control.

Perhaps then God would stop laughing and lean forward in interest to see what we were doing.

Ash Wednesday
Joel 2:1-2, 12-17
2 Corinthians 5:20b--6:10
Matthew 6:1-6, 16-21
by Ron Love

Moksha

Evagrius Ponticus (also known as Evagrius the Solitary) was a Christian monk and ascetic who resided in a monastery in the Egyptian desert. Concerned with the temptations that besought people the most, in the year 375 he compiled a list of eight terrible thoughts, also referred to as the eight evil temptations. The eight patterns of evil thought he identified are gluttony, greed, sloth, sorrow, lust, anger, vainglory, and pride. The list was not to be one of condemnation; rather, it was to raise awareness about our most compelling temptations so that we would be self-disciplined enough to avert our attention from them. Almost two centuries later, in the year 590, Pope Gregory I (also known as Pope Gregory the Great) revisited the list and refined it to seven by combining two and adding two more of his own. Gregory's list is more commonly known as the Seven Deadly Sins, which are: pride, envy, anger, sloth, greed, gluttony, and lust.

Now some 1,400 years later, as we move into the 21st century, perhaps we ought to restore the list to eight — this time adding a temptation that had not appeared before but is appropriate for a technological society. The new temptation would be "fame." In a November 11, 2009 article in the *New York Times*, Alessandra Stanley wrote: "Fame has a spellbinding power in American society, the one thing that can trump wealth, talent, breeding, and even elected office. Reality shows and social websites like Facebook long ago knocked down barriers that kept ordinary people trapped in obscurity." For this reason, Stanley wrote, "...some people take huge risks for the freedom to be someone else — a celebrity." She lifted up as examples the Salahis (a couple who notoriously crashed a White House state dinner), the Heenes (who pretended their child was trapped in a runaway balloon), and the Gosselins (parents who showcased their eight children, all desiring to share the limelight of a reality television show).

May we pray that we are not led into the temptation of seeking celebrity status as our lasting "fame," the kingdom with which we choose to affiliate. Seeking notoriety as our dwelling place may highlight us in the tabloids of this day and even permanently record us on page B2 in the local newspaper. But wasn't this the kingdom Satan desired Jesus to preside over?

The recognition that Jesus sought was not to be found in the fleeting fame of celebrity stardom or in the limited tenure of public politics. Instead, Jesus desired to rule in the hearts of men and women through the ages, the authentic kingdom of God free of publicity but abounding in celestial recognition. If one should ever question his or her worth, ask by what standard it is being measured. Is being important authenticated by a marquee name or a name recorded in the Book of Life? Realizing this, Jesus easily discounted the unworthiness of Satan's offer to rule over earthly kingdoms. In so doing, Jesus directed our ambitions to focus on ministering to the lives of those with whom we are in contact on a daily basis. Indeed, this may be a small kingdom — but can there be any more important kingdom to which we can be assigned?

However you count them, be it six or seven or eight, sin is an act of disobedience to God. A sin is often measured as little or big, such as a "little white lie," which usually means a harmless lie; but is it possible for a sin to be harmless, measured on any scale? When we engage in the acts of pride, envy, anger, sloth, greed, gluttony, and lust, it demonstrates a disregard for God, a disdain for others, and even holding oneself in dis-esteem.

The religion of Hinduism understands the entrapment of living a self-centered life. Hinduism is the oldest established religion in the world and the third largest. At the end of the first century CE, the laws of Manu were established. These laws report the four basic goals that motivate humanity; thus they have also come to be called the "Four Ends of Human Life." A young man should transcend from a lower level to the next, until he discovers the true meaning of life.

The journey begins with *kama*, or pleasure. The aim is to discover purpose by gratifying the senses. At this stage *Kama-sutra* may be a familiar phrase to us, having become a part of the English lexicon. *Kama-sutra* is an often-quoted text for its picturesque descriptions of various positions for sexual intercourse. It is here, at *kama*, as a hedonist, that one begins the journey of life. Unfulfilled, the young man moves to *artha*, which means financial success or wealth. This is the first attempt to set some real goals, but it also reflects a misplaced ambition. He continues to sense an inner disquiet, because as well as being successful he equally desires to be respected. Therefore he strives for *dharma*, which is righteous living. As a viable contributor to the community he knows he is doing good for others; yet there still remains an emptiness. His goal now becomes *moksha*, which means liberation or spiritual freedom, and it is at this stage that the real purpose of life is realized. *Moksha* is attained by disidentification with the body and mind, which becomes the realization of our true identity.

Sin is not an abstract concept, as we all dwell behind the dark curtain of *kama*. Sin is not the evening news; it is what the front door of our dwelling conceals from friends and family. Sin is not absent from the temples of righteousness, as steeples cast a foreboding shadow upon the pretenders of virtue.

In the 1970s Karl Menninger wrote a book that was widely read, studied, and discussed. Menninger was a Harvard-educated psychiatrist who established the Menninger Sanitarium in 1925. As a psychiatrist he believed that mental heal this dependent upon physical, social, cultural, and moral (spiritual) health. A significant aspect of spiritual health is to be unencumbered by the ramifications of sin. Therefore his book, penned by a medical doctor, was titled *Whatever Became of Sin?* The following paragraph is the one that is most often quoted:

> *The very word "sin," which seems to have disappeared, was a proud word. It was once a strong word, an ominous and serious word. It described a central point in every civilized human being's life plan and lifestyle. But the word went away. It has almost disappeared — the word, along with the notion. Why? Doesn't anyone sin anymore? Doesn't anyone believe in sin?*

Has the word "sin" gone out of your vocabulary, or is it just reserved for the other person? Has sin gone out of your life, but lives abundant in your neighbors? Has sin avoided your church pew, but inhabit that which is behind, in front, and of course across the aisle? If sin is not to be found in your life, then where is it?

This is the significance of Ash Wednesday in our liturgical calendar. It is the understanding that we are sinners in need of repentance. As a sign of repentance we place ashes on our foreheads, to show that we have died to our sins and live for Christ. As the ashes are being placed upon us in the form of a cross, the celebrant will say: "Repent and believe in the gospel" (Mark 1:15).

Joel 2:1-2, 12-17

The trumpet is sounded as an alarm, warning the Israelites of God's impending judgment. No one can escape this judgment as all the people are to be gathered together, even the infants and the aged.

Ash Wednesday

Darkness and gloom cover the land because of the Israelites' disobedience. Judgment will come as the Assyrian army marches upon them and will devour them like a herd of locusts destroys a field of crops. Yet God "is gracious and merciful, slow to anger, and abounding in steadfast love, and relents from punishing." If the Israelites are truly repentant and re-establish their covenant with God, then the judgment of God shall pass over them.

2 Corinthians 5:20b--6:10

In our repentance we cannot receive the grace of Christ in vain, but we must be transformed by it. As Jesus was sinless, if we are to identify with him then we must strive to be sinless in our own lives. This means we are to persevere in the faith. This is what Paul tried to accomplish in his own life. Paul lists the ten weaknesses that he had to overcome to be pure and faithful to Christ (vv. 7-10).

Matthew 6:1-6, 16-21

We are cautioned by Jesus to guard against hypocrisy. The term "hypocrisy" comes from Greek theater, where an actor on stage pretends to be someone he is not. In all of his teachings, Jesus only judged hypocrites. He denounced sin, but did not judge the sinner. He only admonished the sinner to henceforth go and live a virtuous life. But hypocrites, like the Pharisees, he harshly judged.

Application

1. Discuss the meaning of sin, especially the meaning of hypocrisy.
2. Discuss repentance.
3. Discuss the liturgical significance of Ash Wednesday.

Alternate Applications

1. Discuss the judgment of God versus the grace of God.
2. Discuss how our sins can call forth the judgment of God. Discuss how we are less judged by God but must live by the consequences of our sinful behavior.
3. Discuss the liturgical significance of Ash Wednesday.

First Sunday in Lent
Genesis 2:15-17; 3:1-7
Romans 5:12-19
Matthew 4:1-11
by Wayne Brouwer

Tough beginnings

Ancient Israel's calendar of daily, weekly, monthly, and yearly markers was not so much a schedule of holidays that broke up the work seasons into manageable pieces. Rather it was the rhythm of married life with Yahweh. It was the way in which the covenant relationship was acknowledged daily and weekly, and then encouraged the deep permeation of the relationship as a kind of living testimony through the multiple anniversary remembrances throughout the year.

So it is with the liturgical year calendar of the Christian church. We mark the seasons not merely by way of the changing climatic conditions of snow and sun, seedtime and harvest, but rather by tracing the movement of God's redemptive activities in time:

- Advent — we wait expectantly through the dark night of earth's soul for the light of divine redemption.
- Epiphany — we celebrate the light of God's revelation among us in the glow of Jesus' presence.
- Lent — we stumble with Jesus under the weight of unresolved evil and judgment toward the "beautiful, scandalous night" of crucifixion, which will forever change human and cosmic destinies.
- Easter — we rise to new life with Jesus, aware that things can never be the same for those who are "born again."
- Pentecost — we are empowered by the Paraclete indwelling to live beyond mediocrity as daughters and sons of the great king, who share in the transformation of society as the kingdom of God presses against us with its hopes and dreams and expectations.

Each step in the journey is another opportunity to start over. We begin again on this Sunday during Lent to rethink our lives in the new ways of our Creator and redeemer. This is what comes out of the dark story of our first parents. This is the rebirth promised by Paul in his letter to the Roman church. This is the hope we share with Jesus as he spends time in the wilderness on the way to redemptive glory.

Genesis 2:15-17; 3:1-7

The "mythical" qualities of Genesis 1-11 ought not to be interpreted as synonymous with either "untrue" or "non-historical." Myths are stories that summarize worldviews in elided prose, giving snapshots of the value systems that drive a culture, or providing hooks on which to hang the unspoken but ubiquitous understanding of a social group's values and self-perception. This is why the stories told by way of myths may sometimes appear to be cartoon-like fairytales, or at other times a selection of emblematic events from the actual unfolding of a community's early history. In fact, many times they appear to be a combination of both. Myths by their very nature are not scientific descriptions or journalistic documentaries and should not be read in that manner. Myths serve instead to carry the fundamental values and worldview understandings of a culture in a manageable, memorable collection of tales.

It is in this way that Genesis functions as an extended historical prologue to the Sinai covenant. The stories of Genesis answer a number of important questions that arise simply because Israel has been shaken loose from 400 years of enslaved slumber and is now being reshaped as the marriage partner of God in a divine mission that has not yet been fully clarified. Genesis gives the context to the suzerain-vassal treaty formed in Exodus 20-24. It takes important moments from both Israel's distant and recent past and uses these as the shepherding banks by which to direct the flow of the people's river of identity into their new and uncertain future.

Because there is no authorial self-disclosure within the pages of Genesis, we are left to speculate about its specific origins. An interesting and important clue emerges from the text itself when the Hebrew nomenclature for God is analyzed. Most often, especially beginning with the stories of Abram in Genesis 12, "Yahweh" is used to name the divinity. According to the book of Exodus, this name emerged in Israel through the deity's self-disclosure to Moses in the encounter between them at Mount Horeb (Exodus 3). This would indicate that whoever wrote Genesis, and whenever the writing happened, this book was created no earlier than the lifetime of Moses and functions within the scope of the covenant-making events of Exodus. Thus, if one is to listen to the internal testimony of the literature of the Bible, Genesis must be understood to function as a companion volume to the covenant documents of Israel's national identity formation at Mount Sinai. Therefore Genesis must be read not as a volume preexisting in a disconnected primeval world, but rather as the interpretation of events leading up to the engagement of Yahweh and Israel at Sinai in the suzerain-vassal covenant established there. Genesis is the extended historical prologue of the Sinai covenant.

Viewed this way, the message of Genesis is readily accessible. To begin with, the cosmological origins myths of chapters 1-11 are apologetic devices that announce a very different worldview than that available among and within the cultures surrounding Israel. The two dominant cosmogonies in the ancient Near East were established by the civilizations of Mesopotamia (filtered largely through Babylonian recitations) and Egypt.

When placed alongside these other cosmogonic myths, the Genesis creation story is very spare and poetically balanced. In brief testimony it declares that God existed before the world that is apprehended by our senses was brought into being. It also asserts that creation happened by way of divine speech rather than through the sexual interaction of deities, or as the animation of guts and gore left over and emerging out of their conflicts. Moreover, creation was an intentional act that took place by way of orderly progression.

In the balanced rhythm of poetic prose, the Genesis creation story shows how divine planning and purpose brought the world into being specifically as a home for humanity. These creatures are not the byproduct of restless fighting among the gods. Nor are they a slave race produced in order to give the gods more leisure. In fact, according to the Genesis account human beings are the only creatures made in the image of God, thus sharing the best of divine qualities.

If, as the literature requires, the creation stories of Genesis 1-2 are part of a lengthy historical prologue to the meeting of Yahweh and Israel at Mount Sinai, these cosmogonic myths are not to be read as the end product of scientific or historical analysis. They are designed to place Israel in an entirely different worldview context than that which shaped their neighbors. Humanity's place in this natural realm is one of intimacy with God, rather than fear and slavery. The human race exists in harmony with nature, not as its bitter opponent or only a helpless minor element. Women and men together share creative responsibility with God over animals and plants.

Moreover, there is no hint of evil or sin in the creation stories themselves. In fact, the recurring refrain is that God saw the coming-into-being of each successive wave of creation and declared it to be good. There is no eternal dualism of opposing forces that in their conflict engendered the world as we know it. Nor is the creative energy of human life itself derived from inherent and co-equal powers of good and evil which, in their chasing of one another, produce the changes necessary to drive the system. Instead, evil appears only after a fully developed created realm is complete, and then enters as a usurping power that seeks to draw away the reflected creativity of the human race into alliance with forces denying the Creator's values and goals. Evil and sin are essentially linked to human perspectives that are in competition with the one declared true and genuine by the creation stories themselves.

In Genesis 3-11, following the devastating effects of evil that leach their way through the world, the Creator displays graciousness in delaying the sentence of death (2:17) upon them, and also by way of providing promises that this conflict need not end their existence. Instead the human creatures are driven out of the Garden of Eden, in what seems to be a divine desire to pull them to their senses through the restlessness of homelessness. They become exiles, and their descendants, in order to compensate, build cities as an apparent attempt to regain civility. All these efforts fail, however, and the cancer of disobedience explodes in acts of killing and violence.

Romans 5:12-19

Because Paul had not yet made a visit to Rome, this letter was less personal and more rationally organized than was often otherwise true. Paul intended this missive to be a working document; the congregation, already established in the capital city of the empire, would be able to read and discuss it together in anticipation of Paul's arrival, which was planned for some months ahead (Romans 1:6-15). Paul summarized his working theme and emphasis up front: a new expression of the "righteousness of God" had been recently revealed, with great power, through the coming of Jesus Christ (Romans 1:17).

Paul moves directly from his brief declaration about the righteousness of God into an extended discourse on the wrath of God as revealed against wickedness (Romans 1:18). Because of this, many have interpreted Paul's understanding of God's righteousness as an unattainable standard, against which the whole human race is measured and fails miserably. Only then, in the context of this desperate human situation, would the grand salvation of Christ be appreciated and enjoyed.

But more scholars believe that Paul's assertions about the righteousness of God actually have a positive and missional thrust. In their understanding of what Paul says, it is precisely because of the obvious corruption and sinfulness in our world, which are demeaning and destroying humanity, that God needed again, as God did through Israel, to assert the divine will. In so doing, the focus of God's righteousness is not to heap judgment upon humankind; instead God's brilliant display of grace and power in Jesus ought to draw people back to the creational goodness God had originally intended for them. In other words, the Creator has never changed purpose or plan. The divine mission through Israel was to display the righteousness of God so that all nations might return to the goodness of Yahweh. Again, in Jesus, the righteousness of God is revealed as a beacon of hope in a world ravaged by evil bullies. The power of God is our only sure bodyguard against the killing effects of sin and society and self.

This more positive perspective on the righteousness of God fits well with the flow of Paul's message. In chapters 1:18-3:20, Paul describes the crippling effect of sin. We are all alienated from God (1:18-25). But we are also alienated from each other (1:26-32), so that we begin to treat one another with contempt and painful arrogance, and destroy those around us in the malice that blinds us. We are even, says Paul, alienated from our own selves (2:1-11), not realizing how tarnished our sense and perspectives have become.

We make excuses about our condition (2:12-3:20), claiming that we are actually pretty good people (2:12-16), or accusing society and religion of raising moral standards to levels that are simply unrealistic (2:17-3:4), or even blaming God for all the nastiness around us and within us (3:5-20). Yet the result is merely self-deception and continued rottenness in a world that seems to have no outs.

Once the stage has been set for Paul's readers to realize again the pervasive grip of evil in this world, Paul marches Abraham out onto the stage as a model of divine religious reconstruction. God does not wish to be distant from the world, judgmental and vengeful. Rather, Jesus comes, the fullness of God's healing righteousness revealed.

The story of God's righteousness as grace and goodness begins with Abraham. God has always desired an ever-renewing relationship with the people of this world, creatures made in God's own image. Paul describes God's heart of love in 3:21-31, using illustrations from the courtroom (we are "justified" - 3:24), the marketplace (we receive "redemption" - 3:24), and the Temple ("a sacrifice of atonement" - 3:25). Moreover, while this ongoing expression of God's gracious goodness finds its initial point of contact through the Jews (Abraham and "the law" and Jesus), it is clearly intended for all of humankind (3:27-31).

This is nothing new, according to Paul. In fact, if we return to the story of Abraham, we find some very interesting notes that we may have glossed over. "Blessedness" was "credited" to Abraham before he had a chance to be "justified by works" (4:1-11). In other words, whenever the "righteousness of God" shows up, it is a good thing, a healing hope, an enriching experience that no one is able to buy or manipulate. God alone initiates a relationship of favor and grace with us (4:1-23). In fact, according to Paul, this purpose of God is no less spectacular than the divine quest to re-create the world, undoing the effects that the cancer of sin has blighted upon us (Romans 5). It feels like being reborn (5:1-11). It plays out like the world itself is being remade (5:12-21). This is the great righteousness of God at work!

Matthew 4:1-11

Matthew does a quick-step through a variety of incidents in Jesus' early life to reveal the essential character of this unique and specially born savior. Jesus, Matthew makes clear, is actually destined to replay or relive the life of Israel in a host of dimensions:

- Jesus copies Israel's miraculous existence and purpose, born through divine intervention as savior of nations (1:18-25).
- He is spared from the murderous intents of a scheming king (2:3-8) who goes on to slaughter the innocents (2:16-18), just as Moses was delivered in Exodus 2 while many Israelite boys were slaughtered.
- Like the nation as a whole, Jesus is gathered out of Egypt (2:15).
- From his earliest days, he is dedicated to a divine mission (so the play on the words "Nazirite" and "Nazarene" in 2:23).
- His ministry is set in motion by passing through waters (3), right at the same spot where Israel crossed the Jordan River in order to begin its witness to the nations from the Promised Land.
- Jesus also wanders in the wilderness for forty days (4:1-11) before he can fully assume his adult responsibilities, mirroring Israel's traumatic forty years described in the book of Numbers.

As we read this story of Jesus' temptations, we need to be guided by several interpretive principles that Matthew builds directly into his narrative flow. First, while Matthew never allows us to question whether these things actually happened, he also wants us to understand the symbolic significance of them. Jesus needed to be in the wilderness for forty days, just as Israel was. And what was the purpose of this time in wilderness? For Israel, it was a period of purification and preparation, when listening to the voice of God was paramount. Before the start of Jesus' own ministry to the nations of the world,

Jesus must be purified and prepared in the wilderness, just as Israel was, and live constantly by the divine word that sustains.

Second, the whole of reality is caught up in a spiritual conflict. The temptations of Jesus are not unique to him and never occur in the rest of time or society. Rather, the temptations of Jesus are the essence of reality. Notice that the key theme of the "Sermon on the Mount," which follows, is the conflict between the evil in ourselves and the kingdom of heaven. Jesus will put it succinctly: "Seek first the kingdom of heaven and its righteousness, and all these things will be added as well." Here Jesus is living out in his personal life the larger dimensions of reality that we too often ignore as superstitious or irrelevant.

Third, the temptations themselves are built into an increasing hierarchy of potency. First comes the call to survival: turn these stones into bread. After all, what good is a dead person in the work of the living God? Second comes the plea for faith's assurance: throw yourself off this pinnacle and either put yourself out of this existential misery or otherwise experience the miracle of faith you pretend to believe. Is faith relevant? Does God exist? Can religion be meaningful (see Psalm 73 for an extended meditation on this by Asaph)? Finally comes the meaning challenge: why not worship the god that pays the best dividends? From external survival to the assurances (or lack thereof) of faith to the questions of meaning itself, Jesus is taken on a ride. But each time he resists and relies not on his own insights but scripture itself. Each quote he offers is taken from Deuteronomy, the "gospel of Moses" as Samuel Schultz called it. Over against the challenge that we need to take care of our business, Jesus lives in the pious confidence that God makes our lives his business. Countering the existential leap of faith, Jesus has no time for the "god of the gaps," but sees all of life as religious devotion, even when there are no external signs. Responding to the religious choices of fidelity to the powers that appear most benevolent, Jesus lives out the testimony of Job and arms himself with Moses' fundamental call to prayer.

Fourth, note the brief conclusion at the end of this passage: "Then the devil left him, and angels came and attended him" (Matthew 4:11). Scripture has sustained Jesus' testimony. Confrontation has won Jesus the victory. And heaven is neither ignorant nor unmoved by these things.

Application

Chiam Potok's wonderful novel *In the Beginning* starts with these powerful words: "Beginnings are hard." Potok goes on to show how the start of a new life or a new venture, even when it is wrapped in excitement and promise, is often a very difficult transition.

Certainly the church's transition from Epiphany (or Ordinary Time) to Lent is difficult. We are snatched from a commonplace existence and thrust into a journey of pain that ends in death. While we know the other side of the story, the Easter celebration of resurrection and new life, the journey itself is difficult and takes us to places, with Jesus, where we don't really want to go.

Today in the congregational gathering are many who are living in the tough moments of the beginnings of difficult paths. The great comfort of Lent is that Jesus knows. Jesus walks with us so that we might walk with him into a better future. This is the gospel.

An Alternative Application

Matthew 4:1-11. The temptations of Jesus, while very different and certainly more intense than anything we usually face, are still a note of solidarity between himself and our journeys of faith and life and pain and challenge. These can be profitably explored at the start of the Lenten journey. Suffering is connected with pain, but pain can come in many varieties. Deepest, of course, is that of abandonment. It was abandonment, especially by God, that the devil used in his attempt to provoke Jesus' pain.

Pain is usually sharpest the instant it is inflicted. I can no longer call to mind the intensity of the pain I felt when I had a bicycle accident as a teenager. The Bible says that after a woman has given birth, she no longer remembers the excesses of her labor pains. It's the same with betrayal. The only way we can keep the pain alive is by replaying over and over in our minds the movement the agony was inflicted.

Every book by Jewish Nobel Peace Prize winner Elie Wiesel relives the horror of the Holocaust. Wiesel intends his writings to hurt, because he wants to keep the pain alive. He wants to remind people of the ungodly betrayal of Hitler, the unthinkable betrayal of the Nazis, and the incredible betrayal of German Christians. They turned their backs on their fellow human beings. They called on God to bless them and sent God's people to the gas chambers.

Although remembering our painful experiences can be constructive, it can also be destructive. Isn't life in the present challenging enough without dwelling on past hurts? Don't we already know in our hearts how great our agony is? Why cling to it and replay it without end?

Sometimes the healing of our hurts starts only when we find another song to sing. Take the story of Helen, for instance. She had her sights set on a law degree from Ohio Wesleyan College. But then the flu epidemic of 1918 hit, taking her father as a victim. Suddenly everything had changed. Helen couldn't go to college; she had to get a job to support her mother.

During the next ten years, Helen worked for an electrical utility company. Just when she thought she was destined to remain lonely and unmarried, young Franklin Rice stepped in. He was a dashing entrepreneur, an up-and-coming banker. When they married in 1928, Helen's future was bright with promise.

A year later the stock market crashed, and Franklin's financial world fell apart. He couldn't take the pressure, so he committed suicide.

Read the litany of Helen's life: a deceased father, a lost car, a vanished fortune, a dead husband, a lonely existence. Where is God when it hurts?

You may know Helen better than you realize. You see, she eventually took a job with the Gibson Greeting Card company. Helen Steiner Rice became a folk poet who spoke the language of thousands of Christians.

Some years ago Helen was asked which poem she thought was her best. She couldn't tell, she said, but she did know which one meant the most to her. It was this:

> *So together we stand at life's crossroads*
> *And view what we think is the end.*
> *But God has a much bigger vision*
> *And he tells us it's only a bend.*
> *For the road goes on and is smoother,*
> *And the pause in the song is a rest.*
> *And the part that's unsung and unfinished*
> *Is the sweetest and richest and best.*
> *So rest and relax and grow stronger.*
> *Let go and let God share your load.*
> *Your work is not finished or ended;*
> *You've just come to a bend in the road.*

Are you in pain today? Do you feel as if God has betrayed you? Then pause for a moment and ask yourself, "How long is my view?"

As Jesus reminds us, our souls need to know.

Second Sunday in Lent

Genesis 12:1-4a

Romans 4:1-5, 13-17

John 3:1-17

by David Kalas

Father of the faithful

When we meet him, his name is simply "Abram." In Hebrew, it means "exalted father." Along the way, though, God changes his name a bit. "Abraham" is the new appellation, and it means "father of a multitude."

Both names were filled with irony. For most of his life Abram was not a father at all, exalted or otherwise. By the time the Lord renamed him "father of a multitude," he was a rather old man with just one son.

One wonders how readily Abraham embraced his new name. Perhaps he wanted it to be more like a pet name — something that would be kept just between him and the Lord. Perhaps it was just about the time that he was finally not embarrassed by his given name that God gave him this new one, which could have been humiliating for him to call himself. Imagine having to jot that down on the self-adhesive nametags. "Hello, my name is Father of a Multitude," says the old guy with one kid.

Yet from the beginning of our record of their relationship, this was evidently God's will and plan for Abram all along. "I will make you a great nation," the Lord promised him in our Old Testament lection. In the episode later in his life that Paul recalls in our New Testament lection, the Lord tells Abraham that his number of descendants will rival the stars in the sky (Genesis 15:5). Father of a multitude, indeed!

We know the rest of the biological story, of course. By the time Abraham died he did have quite a number of children, although it would hardly qualify as a multitude. Yet his children and grandchildren did go on to become the ancestors of entire nations. To this day, millions upon millions of people proudly trace their lineage back to this once-childless old man.

When the apostle Paul considers Abraham's lineage, however, he sees something still more and much greater. For Paul, you see, the issue is not merely biology. Rather, the apostle sees a more profound heredity stemming from Abraham. For Paul, the real bloodline is a faith-line, and Abraham's real progeny are those who believe.

We see in the gospels that being children of Abraham was important to many of the Jews. Yet we hear both John the Baptist (Matthew 3:9) and Jesus (John 8:37-44) challenging the significance of that biological ancestry. Later then, Paul redefines what it means to be a descendant of Abraham.

Whatever our ethnicity, you and I may find ourselves on Abraham's family tree. With Paul's permission, we claim Abraham as our forefather. And this week's lections encourage us to ponder the chief hereditary feature: belief.

Genesis 12:1-4a

When we think of miracles in the Bible, we turn first to the spectacles. We think of the Red Sea parting, the fall of Jericho's walls, and the sun standing still. We recall Jesus walking on water, calming storms, feeding multitudes, and raising the dead. But miracles are not found only in the instantaneous spectacles.

I believe that some of the miraculous work of God goes undetected by us simply because it is unspectacular. It happens so gradually over so long a time that we don't see it. Does that make it less miraculous? Does that disqualify it from being the supernatural work of God? This week, we are invited to consider the long, slow miracle of God that is Abraham.

Most of the people who have lived and died on the earth never achieve the status of "important" beyond their own little circle. Perhaps they are important in their town, but most folks in the next town barely know who they are. If you travel another hundred miles from their home, you'd discover that they are altogether anonymous.

Then there is that small minority of people who manage to be important to a broader circle. In their time, they are known rather widely. Perhaps they might even qualify as famous. But we discover that most fame does not stand the test of time. The names of many folks who were important in our youth will garner only blank stares from our children and grandchildren.

That brings us to the next sphere of importance. There are in history those rare individuals whose importance is both broad and long. They are known all over and their names continue to reverberate through time. On the one hand, we could generate a very long list of those names. On the other hand, that long list must be recognized as a miniscule percentage of all the people who have lived and died on this earth.

If we made a list of the names of people whose importance is both broad and long, I believe that Abram — better known to us as Abraham — would appear on that list. His name is known around the world and has been for millennia. Yet I would argue that Abraham rises above almost all of his peers in that rather select group.

There is a kind of bell curve associated with most people's importance. Plato, Cleopatra, Shakespeare, Edison, and Gandhi were all individuals of tremendous significance and impact, but it would be hard to argue that their significance continues to grow. By contrast, consider the case of Abraham. Four thousand years after he lived and died, he is arguably more important today than ever.

When the Lord promised to make his name great, Abraham had no greater claim to fame than any of the other thousands of anonymous residents of Mesopotamia at that time. Yet that promise has been fulfilled beyond any human's wildest imagination. How could it be that a man who wrote no books, made no inventions, conquered no empires, led no movements, ruled no kingdoms, and owned virtually no land could emerge as one of the most important characters in the history of the world? It didn't happen suddenly but this is surely the miraculous work of God.

Romans 4:1-5, 13-17

Story always comes first. Not every passage of scripture is a story, of course, but even those that are not have a story behind them. Whether the passage is from a history book, a gospel, a section of law, a prophecy, or an epistle, the story always comes first.

Here we have a selection from Paul's epistle to the Romans. It reads as didactic material. It does not have plot, character, and dialogue — the elements that we associate with story. But it is part of a larger story and our people will need to know that story in order to hear this teaching preached.

The story has perhaps three parts. The first is related to the character we considered in our Old Testament lection: Abraham. His is the story to which Paul appeals in his teaching about salvation, faith, works, law, and grace. Our people will need to know the story of Abraham: both God's plans and promises for him and Abraham's faithful response.

The second part of the story is Paul's own biography. He tells the Philippians that he was a Pharisee, but that detail and its significance may be unknown to many of our people. His reputation is as persecutor and then evangelist, but most folks' association with Pharisees are from the negative light in which they appear in the gospels. But before his conversion, we must recognize that Paul was among that sect of Judaism most devoutly committed to the Old Testament law. And with regard to that law, Paul claimed that he was "blameless" (Philippians 3:6). Any reading we do of Paul's post-conversion teaching about the law, therefore, must be understood against the backdrop of his own story. He was not a person either dismissive of or unfamiliar with the Mosaic Law. He knew it, he believed in it, and he obeyed it.

Finally, the third part of the story belongs to Paul's audience. Each epistle, after all, is a snapshot from a relationship — in this case the relationship between Paul and the Christians in Rome — and a relationship suggests a story. In this case, we don't know a lot about the particulars of the relationship, though Paul's closing greetings do indicate a wealth of individual relationships (see Romans 16:1-15). What we do know a little more about, though, is the larger story that no doubt impacted the Christians in Rome. That larger story is the first-century church's struggle with the connection between Christian faith and Jewish law. The struggle was theological, though it was heavily influenced by cultures, traditions, and even individual personalities. What was the role of law in one's salvation? Does faith in Christ and his grace nullify the law?

Take those three stories, put them together, and then you have the context for this teaching from Paul. There was Abraham's example of faith, and God's reckoning to him as righteousness. There was Paul's own personal familiarity with and devotion to the law. There was the troubled context of Jewish and Gentile Christians trying to understand the relationship of that law to their salvation in Christ. In the midst of that larger context, Paul shares the gospel message. It begins with the gracious promise of God. Our opportunity is simply to believe his promises. And his continued grace is to justify us — reckon us righteous — on account of our faith in him.

John 3:1-17

I would rather preach a series of sermons on this episode from John than be forced to incorporate the entire passage into one Sunday, along with other lections, as well. If I were to preach it as a series, though, I would title it "Conversation in the Dark," and it would feature four sermons. Those certainly would not exhaust the passage, but I will share my vision with you, and you may make of it what you will.

The first sermon would be the "title track," if you will. It would be a sermon about Nicodemus and the symbolism involved with his coming to Jesus "by night" — a detail that John regards as significant enough to use it as Nicodemus' defining characteristic (John 19:39). Nicodemus is truly "in the dark," for he does not grasp what Jesus tells him. Jesus himself seems astonished by Nicodemus' spiritual obtuseness (John 3:10). This "teacher of Israel" does not compare favorably to the Samaritan woman of the next chapter. On the surface, she is much less qualified than Nicodemus to engage in a theological conversation with Jesus, but the end of her story is so much more fruitful than his. Nicodemus, it seems, starts and stays in the dark. But Jesus declares that whoever receives his words and follows him "will never walk in darkness but will have the light of life" (John 8:12).

"No Step Backward" would be my second title. Nicodemus' misunderstanding was that he thought he had to "enter a second time into his mother's womb and be born." His assumption, you see, was that he had to go back, when what God wants is for us to move forward. It is not a redoing of something old that he intends, but rather something new that needs to happen within us. He is the God who is doing a new thing (Isaiah 43:19) and who makes all things new (Revelation 21:15), including us (2 Corinthians 5:17).

"The Lesser Known Gospel" is the third sermon in the series I have in mind. A very high percentage of the folks in our pews will know John 3:16, but I wonder if any of them could recite or would recognize John 3:15. Did ever something so familiar live next door to something so unfamiliar? And yet it is Jesus' recalling of the episode of the serpent on the pole (Numbers 21:1-9) that gives rise to his magnificent statement in John 3:16. Because of that passage proximity, therefore, I take the obscure event from the wilderness to be an important element in our understanding of the gospel message. So I would preach a sermon about the cross in the wilderness: the story of the serpent on a pole.

Finally, my series from John 3 would conclude with "Divine Purpose." The gospel of John makes it explicit what God had in mind when he sent Christ into the world, and it is good news indeed. His purpose is not to judge the world. His purpose is that none should perish. His purpose, instead, is to save the world and to offer eternal life to "whoever believes." Why this undeserved magnanimity? It is because he loves the world so much. The purpose of God in sending his son is the gospel message we get to preach.

Application

Belief is the issue. It is what made Abraham righteous before God (Romans 4:3). It is what makes us Abraham's children (Romans 4:16-17). And it is what makes us God's children (John 1:12) and secures for us eternal life (John 3:16). Belief is the issue.

Unfortunately, belief has become a sloppy business in our day. We have come to equate belief with opinion. Witness the fact that so many poll questions include the word "believe."

Which candidate do you believe will be better for the economy? Which player do you believe the team should select with its first-round draft choice? What quality do you believe is most important in an employee? These are matters of opinion, you see. But is that what scripture has in mind when it talks about belief?

When we equate belief with opinion, that belief can become a pretty vague and detached thing. Such belief does not have to be central to my life, for hardly every opinion I hold impacts the kind of person that I am and the kind of life I live. I believe, for example, that football is a better sport than soccer. That's just my opinion, though, and it has no real significance in my life.

Furthermore, when we equate belief with opinion, we may make what we believe synonymous with what we support. I say, for example, that I believe in such-and-such a candidate or certain policy positions, and by that I mean that I agree with them or support them. It is tempting in our day to construe religious faith in this light, but I think it is a serious mistake. Such an understanding of belief, after all, tends to belittle the person or thing in which we believe. It may seem to be a compliment to a human candidate that I support him or her, but this attitude does not properly apply to God. He is neither a candidate nor a cause. God does not need my vote and his kingdom does not require my support.

Belief is the issue, yet we as preachers of the gospel must set belief free from its culturally discounted state. The writer of Hebrews says that "without faith it is impossible to please God" (Hebrews 11:6), yet James rightly warns us that inadequate faith cannot be truly pleasing to him either (James 2:17-19). Because of our impoverished versions of belief, it may be that much of our faith is inadequate. Will such a faith save you?

God made a promise to Abraham, and Abraham believed God. The promise was both exceedingly gracious and exceedingly improbable. But Abraham believed God. It was not a vague opinion that Abraham held or merely a cause that he supported. Rather, he hung his hopes, his identity, and his future on the promise of God.

The gospel invites us to believe. "Whoever believes," Jesus says. So let us help our people to understand what believing is, and then encourage them in the strong and fruitful choice of believing.

An Alternative Application

Genesis 12:1-4a. "And Lot Went With Him." The story in our Genesis passage is unmistakably the story of Abraham. He is the center of the narrative and his growing importance is anticipated by that narrative. Perhaps 2,000 years after he lived and died, he is still being cited by Paul as an exemplar of faith and obedience.

Yet Abraham is not the only character in this ever-so-brief scene. In the background, seeming to be little more than a prop on the stage, stands Lot. He has no lines and the narrative makes him hardly more than a tagalong. It is Abraham's story — and Lot went with him.

For as long as Lot went with Abraham, it seems, things went well for Lot. Inasmuch as Abraham stayed within God's will and plan, you see, he was someone you'd want to go with, someone you'd want to be near. Because he stayed in God's will, Abraham's location was always proximate to God's blessing, protection, and care.

Then came the juncture when Lot stopped going with Abraham. They parted company and made a decidedly un-Abraham-like choice. Lot made a selfish choice and unsurprisingly that selfishness landed Lot right in the midst of sin.

When Lot stopped going with Abraham, Lot settled in Sodom. Sodom along with neighboring Gomorrah were the twin cities of sin. Perhaps 4,000 years after the judgment of God wiped them off the face of the earth, their names are still known and still notorious.

While Lot was with Abraham, they enjoyed an overabundance of flocks and herds. After Lot stopped going with Abraham, however, we see no more evidence of Lot being wealthy. When Lot stopped going with Abraham, he had to be rescued — first by Abraham and later by angels. When Lot stopped going with Abraham, he is surrounded by troubles, he becomes a frightened fugitive, and his family turns into a disaster. While Abraham becomes the ancestor of Israel by a miracle, Lot becomes the ancestor of Moab and Ammon by ignominy and perversion.

The first narrative statement about Lot is an undistinguished one. Little did we know it would be his high water mark. He went with Abraham, but if only he had kept going.

Third Sunday in Lent

Exodus 17:1-7

Romans 5:1-11

John 4:5-42

Psalm 95

by R. Craig MacCreary

Turning things upside down

If you are like me, you come from an educational background that basically emphasized that the balanced life was a good life. This meant that my public school career included as much exposure to as many things as possible in its, including kindergarten, thirteen years. It is amazing the number of things that I know something about from music and art to physics. It is a credit to the teachers because much of this stuck in its own way. At 57, I was able to run six miles in under an hour. I favor Russian composers and have a mini- collection of Inuit art. There are Lauren Harris reproductions on my walls. I can reasonably follow the latest public television special on quantum physics. I read nonfiction as well as fiction. The YMCA slogan of body, mind, and spirit is emblazoned on my soul. How could it not be? We were being raised to be junior Leonardo da Vincis.

Let me say I feel richly blessed by the educational approach that was used on me as a child. As you might expect there is a down side, as well. There are times in life when the question is not how you will maintain your balance. Falling in love has nothing to do with maintaining your balance but the willingness to have your whole world turned upside down. Have a child and see what happens to the balance wheel of your life. Still, I like my life somewhat predictable and steady.

Then along comes these texts and they threaten to turn the basics upside down and tip the balance in unforeseeable directions. Certainly Jesus has that habit when he challenged people to leave the 99 and go after the one sheep. That does not look like good cost accounting to me. He had a habit of overturning things by switching the question from, "Who is my neighbor?" to asking, "Who proves to be a neighbor?" Turn the tables once too often and see what happens to your relationship to the powers that be. Jesus puzzled his listeners when he said that by going after the least, you got the most that life has to offer.

These texts also deconstruct our world and then reassemble it in a way that defies convention but promises more stability if we are willing to undergo the initial instability.

Water out of rocks seems like some sort of magic show to keep the masses coming. Anyone who has been to the Middle East for any length of time knows that we are dealing with serious business here. The great conflicts ahead will be over water not oil. It would be a godsend to have a staff like Moses had to turn things around.

Or does the balance need to be tipped in another direction for there to be the kind of lasting peace that all desire? What is God up to here? Has God given the Israelites an easy out or a reason never to look at their rock-strewn world ever again in the same way?

The balance of things for Paul has been upset in that God proves to have been active and engages the world through the very one whom he had despised. He does the seemingly despicable thing that "while we still were sinners Christ died for us." Not only has he become weak and vulnerable but he has died for sinners rather than as confirmation of the righteous. A world that tips the balance toward sinner is not the one that Paul was born into, raised up in, or trained for. It is one in which everything is stood on its head.

That Jesus had a conversation with the Samaritan woman is unbalancing enough but the whole conversation seems unsettling. Jesus concludes the section with "The reaper is already receiving wages and is gathering fruit for eternal life, so that sower and reaper may rejoice together. For here the saying holds true, 'One sows and another reaps.' I sent you to reap that for which you did not labor. Others have labored, and you have entered into their labor." Jesus tips the balance away from the self-made person toward reaping the harvest planted by others. Our beginning point is not with our own ambitions and dreams. This turns the world upside down for many.

The key question is, after reading and pondering these texts, whether your world is turned upside down but is now right side up or whether still right side up, you have things upside down.

Exodus 17:1-7

"He called the place Massah and Meribah, because the Israelites quarreled and tested the Lord, saying, 'Is the Lord among us or not?'" I don't know of a congregation that has not asked that question at one point in their life. Every congregation can recite what to them were the good old days. Pastors were loved, children were growing, and life was good. I cannot imagine a congregation that could write a history that would run something like this. We never had a pastor who cared for us or we cared for, children never darkened our door, the community despises us because we take up space and the denomination dislikes us because we have not paid apportionments for ten years. Such a pathetic history is not part of the journey.

Yet pastors and people know that, "Is the Lord among us or not?" is a question that is a part of the journey. Things are going well and the young charismatic pastor upon his resignation turns out not to have met the needs of everyone in the congregation. The pastor that did seem to have met the needs of everyone turns out to have engaged in inappropriate behavior. The neighborhood changes and churches do not. It does not take much for folks to have "Is the Lord among us or not?" on their lips.

Moses' response to the situation is to try asking God why these people are ready to stone him. The problem is not these people. The problem is that this kind of thing happens to all people.

The answer is, "Maybe not," if we resort to the kind of quick fixes and approaches that the Israelites use as they work their way through this time. There must be somebody to blame. The popular pastor must have resigned because of the ones who did not fall under his spell. There is always somebody trying to get attention by making such charges. We would still have the children if we had not abandoned the tried-and-true curriculum. Of course, when we are in the blame mode the answer is also simple: replace the pastor, go back to the old curriculum, hush up and dispose of charges of inappropriate behavior as quickly as possible.

God does not seem to delight in such answers. Moses does not get fired, the people do not get to go back to Egypt, but something does happen that moves the story along. Striking the rock and releasing the water creates a whole new dynamic for the Israelites to live with. Never again can they look at the surrounding territory in the same fashion. Surely they will have to acquire a taste for manna and for the water that comes from cracking open rocks, but the Lord is very definitely still among them. As much as God parted the waters that the Israelites might walk in freedom God is still among them.

Yes there were the good old days, but that rock needs to be cracked open a bit. The Lord was among us in those days but how is the Lord among us now?

Most congregations view an interim time as something to get through as quickly as possible and get back to normal. The work of the Alban Institute and others reveal that it is important to crack that rock open. Interim times can be times of inspection, growth, and some painful reflection; so that some unhelpful patterns are broken. This turns things upside down from the usual way of looking at things. Heretofore, most religious intuitions believed that it was best to keep the reality of pastoral abuse hidden. The Lord is still among us even when the rock is broken open to reveal some painful things. In recent years, the church has found itself facing questions about war, human sexuality, and justice. The Lord is still among us even though we find ourselves facing challenging issues. There is the opportunity to pray, to learn from each other, and to learn about ourselves and where we are really coming from. The Lord is still among us. It may involve getting used to a different diet and acquiring a taste for something new to quench our thirst.

It does seem to be an upside-down world that finds itself imbibing from rocks, or is it upside down that it might become right side up?

Romans 5:1-11

Paul, when he was Saul, experienced Christianity as a crazy religion that was deeply unbalanced. He came to see its claims to be part of his tradition as downright blasphemous and dangerous, warranting persecution. Paul makes plain in verses 6-8 his core objection. "For while we were still weak, at the right time Christ died for the ungodly. Indeed, rarely will anyone die for a righteous person — though perhaps for a good person someone might actually dare to die. But God proves his love for us in that while we still were sinners Christ died for us." Many of us might find some resonance in Paul's objection. God is less about affirming the righteous than being invested in sinners to the point that Christ dies for them.

If you had a track record like Paul, having kept to the law and out "Phariseed" everyone in sight you can understand Paul's consternation. Many who believe that they have led reasonable, respectful, and decent lives, find their world turned upside down; they are put off to find that the balance is tipped in the favor of sinners. It comes as even more destabilizing to many of us, to be reminded that we are all sinners. Paul discovered that even in his keeping of the law he was sinner.

If there was anything that was ever counterintuitive this must surely be it. Is there a power that is only available to those who are willing to have their world turned upside down by this notion?

Surely there is a certain power that is available to those who maintain their advantage in life, who demonstrate their imperviousness to being touched by their own pain or the pain of others. No doubt we envy those who can keep going in life no matter what the opposition.

However, there is a power that only comes to those men who entered a program to help them understand what their wives were going through during pregnancy. The program included the men strapping on extra weight and trying to maneuver through the day.

These men switched from a day in which they exercised power in several instances to put people into place into evening in which they engaged in putting themselves in the place of another. Literally, these men in the space of a few hours had their world turned upside down. Or was it right side up?

Some have learned about working with the physically challenged by having their whole world challenged, being forced to wear glasses that distort the world or use straps that restrict bodily movement.

This is not a panacea. There are no panaceas in this life. It must surely be a sign that when one's life is turned upside down that you should ask what God may be up to in the moment. It took a special revelation and three years in the desert according to Paul's own account to get to that point.

Yet, it does seem that lives turned upside down often seem to be lives that are on their way to coming right side up: Gandhi was literally tossed upside down onto a train platform; Franklin Roosevelt's world was turned upside down by polio; Eleanor Roosevelt's life was turned upside down by betrayal. Often these lives are better able to enter into the experience of others because of their own moment with having their world turned upside down.

Paul was better able to enter into the experience of others because he experienced having his world turned upside down on the road to Damascus. No longer could he divide the world into righteous and unrighteous. While he was yet a sinner God had acted not to put him in his place but to put God's self in the place of one who in his self-righteousness needed to be forgiven in order that he might forgive.

John 4:5-42

"Come and see a man who told me everything I have ever done! He cannot be the Messiah, can he? They left the city and were on their way to him." As one reads John's gospel it behooves the reader to remember the context in which the question of the meaning of Jesus is asked. I find that most of the congregations contain a spectrum of belief that ranges from the soundly orthodox to what some might consider outrageously radical. Most of us find this not only tolerable but useful. It certainly can make for interesting Bible discussion. Some might be less than enthusiastic about this situation but few are deeply threatened by it.

This was not so for John's church at a time when Jesus' followers and the synagogue were reaching their point of separation. It was one thing to believe that Jesus was informative, interesting, and worth studying. It was another to come to the conclusion that he was the Messiah. The latter meant ejection from family, friends, and much that connected you to the surrounding world. Make the profession and you have crossed much more than an intellectual line with consequences barely discernable in our world.

"Could he be the Messiah?" is no idle rhetorical question. As a matter of fact, the construction suggests the expectation of a negative answer. Perhaps one should give due consideration to the negative response before a positive one literally turns your whole world upside down. Consider the negative in our day. How can Jesus be the Messiah when he is hopelessly wrapped up in this first-century agrarian world? How can he be the Messiah if the church to which he entrusted his teaching and spirit is such a mess and is so divided? How can he be the Messiah if his followers can't name five stories he told? How can he be the Messiah with all the Jewish-Christian baggage he brings into a highly religiously pluralistic world? How can this male figure understand the experience of women? As it turns out the Samaritan woman has raised a question of importance well beyond the first-century Jewish community.

However, stand on end these objections and they may become reasons to name Jesus as the Messiah. No human being grows to maturity without the evidence of where and when they were raised becoming evident. If God has entered our world in human fashion, then it is a reminder that we need to recognize all the advantages and limitations of where we and others began our journey. Jesus' experience invited us to take a look at our own experience. This seems to be saving work. Is the church always impoverished by its differences or is it enriched by the fact that Jesus' life has given rise to so many responses? I can't remember five things my junior high football coach said to me but I do know that the spirit of the man is a saving presence in my life. Jesus came as a Jew, which reminds me that if there is to be salvation in our world it will come from hearing each other without erasing our own understanding. While Jesus was male, he seems to have integrated feminine and masculine in ways that was redemptive. Can any more be expected of us?

As I stand these objections on their head there is reason to begin to turn my life upside down in order that I might get it right side up. The question, "Can Jesus be the Messiah?" generally does not get much play in our time. However, it gets the whole city running out to see Jesus. The woman expects a negative answer after all that has happened to her. After all that has happened, how can he not be the Messiah?

Application

We expect Lent to be a time of confession and spiritual change, but by and large we do not expect any changes that do occur to go too far or change too much. We would be rather astounded if most people jumped out of the fairly familiar grooves of their lives. Perhaps we expect too little.

First, if people's lives are already upside down with the blood rushing to their heads then we do them no favor if we make no effort to give them an opportunity to right themselves. Secondly, the scriptures speak of a spirituality that clearly involved people's lives and thinking taking a 180-degree turn from what it had been. We, by and large, do not expect much more than a 45-degree turn. Perhaps as a pastor preparing for Lent, one should consider just how many degrees of turn one is expecting to take place. How many degrees can one live with before one can't handle the heat? Is there an upper limit on one's capacity to invite and challenge people to turn their lives upside down in order that they might get them right side up?

Alternative Application

Romans 5:1-11. Being a cancer patient, I often find myself tripping over Paul's word about knowing that suffering produces endurance, and endurance produces character, and character produces hope. I know where he is coming from, yet I know it is not that easy. Every industrial process produces by-products. Suffering does produce endurance, yes, but it also produces tears, screaming, incoherence, anger, and long silent periods of staring out the window. I think that working with those who are suffering is not about helping them to endure so much as handling the by-products of the process.

Yes, endurance produces character but there are an awful lot of by-products along the way that need to be dealt with. I suspect that what those who are suffering expect and long for are those who handle the by-products: who accept the long silent periods, who let the tears do their work, those who don't insist on coherence just because the coherent person is the one they knew how to love, who can capitalize on coherent moments when they are there, and who understand that the nastiness comes because this is a nasty business.

All of this makes it a lot easier to swallow Paul's words.

Preaching the Psalm

by Schuyler Rhodes

Psalm 95. In democratic culture, individualism reigns supreme. Each man and woman is trumpeted as master of his or her destiny, and is free to pursue happiness as they deem fit. It is this kind of cultural assumption that lies behind the question that gets asked of every six-year-old, "What do you want to be when you grow up?" The answers that come are delightful, of course. Beaming parents field answers like, ballerina, firefighter, police officer, and a hundred other options. But the operative assumption in this ritual is that each of these six-year-old children has a better than even chance of becoming anything they desire.

Before the fall of the Soviet Union and the demise of its client states, a group of children in an elementary school in Dresden, Germany, were asked the same question, "What do you want to be when you grow up?" Instead of a response, there was a stony, mystified silence in the room. "What do I want to be? What's that got to do with anything?" As it turned out, such a question focusing on the fulfillment of individual desires or wants was so alien that it never even occurred to these children.

The question these children were asked was not what they *wanted*, but instead what did their nation need? To devote one's life energy to pursuing a personal goal was thought in this culture to be selfish, even destructive.

These two poles of individual and communal orientation lead directly to the reading of this wonderful psalm. Here is a full-blown explosion of praise to the creator God! All stops are pulled out in favor of a glorious, passionate expression of praise. It doesn't even matter if the choir is on key. Just make a joyful noise! Give glory and honor to God! Enter God's presence with thanksgiving!

In short, the psalm is a powerful utterance that speaks the location of allegiance. Here there are no individual desires staked out with prayer requests. Neither are there calls to communal commitment, wondering what the collective needs most. No, instead the writer simply lays out an ultimate commitment to God.

So it is that a person of faith, whether growing up in middle-class USA or the worker's paradise of the German Democratic Republic would not be concerned with either individual or collective needs. Instead, the person of faith who shouts out God's praise and dances with a passion for the Lord asks quite another question altogether. Indeed it is formed more like a prayer than a question.

It's not what I want, God, nor is it what the state expects. But in all things, Lord, let me be led by you. Amen.

Fourth Sunday in Lent

1 Samuel 16:1-13

Ephesians 5:8-14

John 9:1-41

by David Coffin

New light in darkness

A group of younger workers are seated next to one another at a workplace where they have to deal with the public both person-to-person and over the telephone. They are having difficulty dealing with clients and customers who are older than they are in terms of communication skills, etiquette, and basic manners. These workers console one another once the older clients leave the office by criticizing the older people and trying to avoid them the next time. In the next office sits an older worker who is of the generation these younger workers are trying to avoid. If they were to simply talk to their elder colleague, they could get good tips on communication and etiquette skills. But these younger people only communicate to others in their spare time on social media and hand held computer devices. The older worker is willing to assist in order to make the workplace more user-friendly to the public. She can provide new light to assist her younger colleagues on relating to older people and the public in general.

This same older person has to stop at the public library to get some information about personal and family health issues. She finds out that the younger librarian escorts her to a computer monitor and chair in the library. The friendly librarian gives this person her own password code and plastic library card. This older person now has to see new light in the world of computer information.

In that same community, some boarded-up storefront buildings are now in repair and are being painted, restored, and a new business is going up. The business owners appear to be from an Asian country. They do not speak English very well. But they too are attempting to bring new light into the community in revitalizing the boarded-up buildings. All three texts suggest that new light might come from different sources than expected by the people of faith.

1 Samuel 16:1-13

This text begins the "rise of David." One would not envy the task of Samuel the prophet this week. He has to anoint a new king of Israel while the old office is still not vacant. Also, the old king likes his job and plans on giving it to his son Jonathon. What Samuel is attempting in this lesson could be construed as treacherous in the eyes of King Saul, the current monarch. However, God is doing a different act to bring new light to Israel in the anointing of David, the shepherd boy and musician. Other brothers such as Eliab might have been more obvious candidates for king, but Samuel awaits all of the sons of Jesse to make an appearance, even making the rest of the family wait until the obscure shepherd boy named David arrives.

David was the youngest of his brothers and did not have the physique of a typical soldier or warrior of the time. He lacks credentials as warriors and leaders go, is without social standing, and unseasoned as a veteran of Israel's political machinery. However, just as God did a new action with Samuel's mother Hannah in giving birth to a man of God not of the current priest Eli's lineage, God is leaving the tribe of Benjamin and going on to the tribe of Judah for a new king.

Some recurring theological themes in this text as they relate to the Hebrew Bible (Old Testament) include that God is sovereign and does have control over the affairs of the community of faith. God's prophets such as Samuel serve as both king makers and king-breakers. The anointing of any office in the Hebrew Bible has a sacramental, binding nature to it. David is anointed with oil (v. 13). The text says, "[T]he spirit of the LORD came mightily upon David from that day forward." Nobody, not even a military monarch, can stop a spirit or wind from God the Creator.

This new king would have a "right heart." He would have his share of conflicts and would commit awful sins as well as celebrate great victories. David was part of God's divine intention for the nation. Neither King Saul nor his cruel tactics of retribution against David would stop God's will. This is an opportunity to preach about God's ultimate will prevailing in the lives of believers and communities of faith. However, in this season of Lent God can and may use new sources of light that are unfamiliar to many people, such as cyberspace, immigrants settling in the community, and people of other generations as illustrated above. [Source: Walter Brueggemann, *Interpretation, A Bible Commentary for Teaching and Preaching: First and Second Samuel*(John Knox Press, 1990)]

Ephesians 5:8-14

Authorship questions related to authentic or latter Pauline writers or the apostle himself remain contested and present among many scholars. This does not change the content or themes of this text. "Paul" will be used as the writer in this work. The text is an exhortation to live as children of light. The triad of such a lifestyle is in Ephesians 5:9: "all that is good and right and true." The challenge this text addresses is daily Christian behavior in any society where a Christian's moral guidelines are always under fire, be it in a work, living, community, education, or family situation. The metaphor used is seen in copies of the Dead Sea Scrolls as they contrast "children of light" and "children of darkness." Another illustration might be the book of Daniel, where people of faith are constantly being challenged to uphold their faithfulness in their God against a culture whose behavioral norms are radically different than that of people of faith.

Christians are to do what they know to be pleasing to God. They are to expose unfruitful works of darkness. They are to keep in mind that whenever somebody does anything they think will be under the cover of darkness or secrecy, it will eventually be exposed. Modern political scandals prove this often in the era when any cell phone can become an instant recording device. Verse 14 says, "Sleeper, awake! Rise from the dead, and Christ will shine on you." This is often viewed as a baptismal formula for Christians to keep alert in daily Christian living. A persistent, active faith is one core theme of Paul's theology in all of the epistles.

A helpful tool one can use to preach any of these Ephesians texts is to move forward to Ephesians 6:10-20, or the "whole armor of God" text and apply it to any situation of temptation, darkness, or awkward circumstances that happen to be occurring at a given time. For example, a company develops a policy and secretly tries to implement it while nobody is looking. This sort of text could be a basis to ask the question of "What happens if this policy becomes public?" Another example is when an organization chooses not to renew the contracts of some of its workers but does not make mention of it in any public arena. The workers who are released could use Paul's Ephesians light and darkness metaphor in order to expose such a decision and to make sure those in power are still held accountable. [Source: Ralph Martin, *Interpretation, A Bible Commentary for Teaching and Preaching: Ephesians, Colossians and Philemon*(John Knox Press, 1991)]

John 9:1-41

This lengthy pericope has a two-leveled scholarly analysis to it. First, there is the level of the events themselves (around 30-33 CE), where a blind man is healed by the spittle of Jesus (a Greco-Roman practice), then the Jewish council leaders interrogate both the healed man and his parents. Fear of being ejected from the synagogue is at stake if one confesses Jesus as the one from God who performed such a miracle. The second level, which most commentators attribute to the classic work of J. Louis Martyn, identifies the actual events of the Johannine community who wrote this gospel (around 90 CE). The Jewish temple had issued an edict that Christians were heretics (among other groups), so these John 9:1-41 verses are also addressing the hurt feelings of those Christians now ejected out of the Jewish temple. One has to be careful as to how the Jewish council leaders are identified. A more common practice these days is to call them "Judeans," rather than mistake them for the local worshipers at the Jewish synagogue in any given modern community. This is an attempt to minimize anti-Semitic attitudes as a result of this text.

One interpretative lens for this and other Johannine texts is John 1:1: "In the beginning was the word, and the word was with God, and the word was God." In this lesson and throughout John, it is all about "Who is Jesus?" If Jesus is God revealed to humanity, then John believes we have it right. If one rejects Jesus as God's revelation to the cosmos, then they are living in darkness and have chosen to remain in sin. In this story the man, who did not solicit Jesus' healing, does gain his sight. His parents are interrogated by the Judean leadership, but back off for fear of being sent out of the temple (vv. 20-23). The healed man holds his ground to acknowledge the healing from Jesus. So insults are hurled at him (v. 28). There are three interrogation scenes in this text. This text also follows a pattern of a situation of need and the miracle and attestation of the miracle. It is all about Jesus, despite any other questions that are brought to the table.

In this text, the basic theodicy question of the cause of the man's blindness is shifted in conversation by asking: "Where God is acting now?" John's answer is that God is working through Jesus. Also, God's work is through belief in Jesus. So John's response to "why is a person blinded, suffering, and so forth?" is that God is at work through Jesus. Regardless of one's beliefs on whether they inherit the sins of their ancestors, John wants readers to know that God is working now in Jesus! Light and darkness are concepts embedded in the characters of this text. The healed man sees more and more light as the Judean leaders plunge deeper into darkness. Good and evil are defined in John's gospel according to one's response to Jesus.

Other major theological themes this text in John raises include salvation is less about expiation or sacrifice on the cross and more about one's right relationship to Jesus as God's revealed "word" (1:1). Many have viewed the man's healing as supporting a baptismal motif of the water and new life. However, some commentators of a non-sacramental tradition may differ. Salvation is in Jesus alone for John. His life is as much (or more) a part of the salvation formula as his death on the cross. However, Jesus' life brings new life to those who follow him (John 10:10 is a good cross-reference here).

If one views "meaninglessness" and "despair" as common enemies of humans during this season of Lent, John's gospel is full of good news. Jesus is God's revelation who provided anybody in a vulnerable situation a source of new life, such as the blind man in John 9. The text invites Christians to discover how Jesus brings new light and life to the communities we live in right now. New light from Jesus was challenged in John 9 by the Judeans because they did not identify it with the tradition of Moses. God is capable of bringing new sources of light bring new life into any time of rejection, crisis, or loss. This text is a challenge to stand one's ground, to defend what they have experienced and believe to be true about the source of their light and life. In this case, it is how one responds to Jesus. [Sources: Leander Keck, editor, *The New Interpreter's Bible, Volume IX: Luke John* (Abingdon Press, 1995); J. Louis Martyn, *History and Theology of the Fourth Gospel* (Abingdon Press, 1979)]

Application

So who is Jesus today? For some other religions and personal spiritualities, Jesus is a great teacher whose examples and words would make anybody's life better. Jesus' model of ethics could improve any community's quality of life. This is not a wrong idea. Christians have confessed that Jesus is God in the flesh (John 1:14). To see Jesus is to see God (incarnate). In Lent, John 9 would challenge a reductionist view that might say "Jesus died on the cross for my sins and rose from the grave three days later so I and others can have eternal life when we die." This is not "wrong" *per se*. But John 9 wants readers to realize that Jesus' life brings each person new life now in the dark, dreary days of Lenten wintry months or wherever one is living in the months before spring season. One day another power outage occurs. The local media remind folks to have plenty of flashlights and batteries on hand. But for some who lead very hectic, busy lives, they may have to rely on a simple candle for light. This too allows people to see in the darkness.

One never knows when new people might come into our lives that we barely know or are unfamiliar to us. Is God using such people to point us to new light? A family who tends be to "migrant" in their living habits enters into a community for a season of work while the job lasts. They volunteer to work on the church grounds. On one hand, they will probably not be on the church property committee for any length of time. On the other hand, the church leaders should be grateful that God is showing kindness and a new surge of energy to clean the church through this migrant family for however long they are in the community.

An Alternative Application

A new person has just been hired mid-year into a company. The new employee is not like the person he or she has replaced. The former worker was able to lift heavy boxes, help unload trucks, and drive to do errands. This new worker is short and skinny. The new person has a good spirit but is not the multi-purpose worker of their predecessor. This scenario could be any person who arrives at a job or volunteer situation in the middle of the year, after the rest of the crowd "got used to the person who just left the organization." This is the world of David in the book of 1 Samuel.

In another organization down the street, an office worker is trying to orient into their new job. On Friday night, he or she is invited to go out for drinks at a local tavern. They know they have a family at home who is waiting for dinner, so they excuse themselves "for this week." However, should this person be pressured into making the Friday tavern night part of their weekly routine in order to be in good standing with the peer group at the new job? This is an application of the Ephesians 5 text.

Fifth Sunday in Lent
Ezekiel 37:1-14
Romans 8:6-11
John 11:1-45
by Ron Love

787

J. Philip Wogaman, a professor of ethics and the former dean of Wesley Theological Seminary in Washington DC, began the first day of my class with this question: "What is the central theme of the Bible?" He heard from the students the expected responses of love, forgiveness, and salvation. I am sure you could name the continuing list of replies. The one answer he did not receive was the word "hope." The professor then lectured that hope is the central message of the scriptures. Hope is the message of the resurrection. It is the message that there is always a new day in the morning. It is the message that no matter how tragic life may be there is the possibility for a new beginning. This does not lessen the sorrow or suffering of the befallen tragedy. It does not discount the severity of the present agony. What it does mean is that in the midst of these horrible circumstances there is the possibility for a new beginning.

Hope is the central message of our three lectionary readings today. Each reading relates to us the possibility of a new life lived in Christ if we only allow for the indwelling of the Holy Spirit; if we only allow the breath of God to renew us; if we only allow the promises of God to prevail amidst our despair.

You could not see it in the sky, but if you were an air traffic controller it was very visible on their radar screen. It was the outline of the number 787 and the logo for Boeing stretching from Washington state to Iowa. Boeing decided to place this design in the sky to commemorate the recently launched 787 *Dreamliner*. The jet required an 18-hour extended operations flight in order to be certified. So as long as the plane was going to be in the air, the Boeing executives decided to advertise their new aircraft and company at the same time. The design took nineteen hours to create and covered over 9,000 nautical miles.

In times of despair and disillusionment it may seem as if God is a distant God, even an absent God, but like that unseen 787 stretching across our continent, God is always very much present.

Lent is a journey of suffering. It is a journey to the cross where we recall the passion of Christ and the many sorrows and indignities he had to suffer. Yet we know at the end of the journey there is the resurrection. There is new life. This is our hope. This is our 787.

Ezekiel 37:1-14

Ezekiel looked upon the dried-up bones of the defeated soldiers of Israel, slaughtered by the Chaldeans. As he wandered through the valley he wondered and worried if the nation of Israel could ever again be restored. He contemplated if there would ever again be a renewal for a fallen and disobedient people. He questioned if he was looking upon the final act of justice by God; the final statement of God for a wayward people. Were the chosen people finally and indefinitely cast aside?

Then Ezekiel heard a voice. It was the voice of God. It came as a question, but it was really more of a statement: "Can these bones live?" They can live. They once again can be restored if they hear the prophetic word of the Lord. So Ezekiel spoke in God's name, and the bones came together. Then with

Fifth Sunday in Lent

the breath of the prophetic word, just like the moment of creation, the bones came alive.

But let us remember the bones came alive and Israel was restored only because Ezekiel acted as an intermediary on God's behalf.

Romans 8:6-11

If we are to live, we are to live for the Lord. If we set our minds on the flesh we shall die, not physically, but spiritually. Our lives, though seemingly playful and joyful as we indulge in the inequities of decadent behavior, will be lifeless.

It is only when we set forth to live in the Spirit of God that we have true joy as we are focused on the true meaning of creation, which is to love God and live in harmony with others.

We will be able to get off of the merry-go-round of life, escaping the anxiety of trying to grab the brass ring of wanting more. Instead, we will be able to take a ride on the pony, fenced in, having a handler, moving at a slow and steady gentle pace.

John 11:1-45

Lazarus was Jesus' best friend. So it is little wonder that Jesus wept upon learning of Lazarus' death. Sorrow, heartbreak, and tribulation did not even escape our Lord. Jesus traveled the same path through life as you and I do. It was a life of both ecstasy and sadness.

Yet at the gravesite, with the rolling away of the stone and with the call for Lazarus to come out, Jesus gave us the promise of new life. It was the promise of resurrection. It was the declaration of a life restored. So even though Jesus wept, he still lived in the promise of a new creation.

Application

The natural calamities of life, unpreventable disasters, and illness can all place us in the valley of despair, as spoken to by Ezekiel. Our own illicit behavior can cause us unforeseen problems, as presented by Paul. Sadness may follow us like a dark shadow, as seen when Jesus wept for his friend.

But as each lectionary reading demonstrates there can be and will be new life, if we can keep our focus upon the promises of God.

An Alternative Application

Amidst the sufferings and uncertainties of life, you and I are an intricate ingredient in the ministry of God. It was only when Ezekiel spoke that the bones came alive. It was only when Paul taught that the people received a message of a new life. It was only when Martha came to Jesus that Lazarus was able to come forth from his grave. We are an indispensable part of the ministry of our Lord.

Passion Sunday

Isaiah 50:4-9a

Philippians 2:5-11

Matthew 26:14-27:66

Psalm 31:9-16

by Arthur Kolsti

The road to redemption

Last summer my family and I moved from the East Coast to the Midwest. Our only previous travel to our new home was by airplane, but this time we were driving two cars. In preparation for our journey and because we wanted to visit some friends along the way, I arranged to secure maps and driving directions from the AAA. Now normally I would have mapped our journey myself (or more likely just headed out in the general direction of our destination and allowed my instincts to get us there), but my wife insisted that we get professional help (travel help, that is).

All went well the first day. We arrived at our friend's home with no trouble and without needing to stop and call for assistance. The next day's trip was another matter. For starters it was raining — not just a light drizzle, but a blowing, blinding rain that lasted all day long. When we crossed the state line into Kentucky, I began consulting the map for our cut-off that would carry us to Indiana. On the map the cut-off was listed as a U.S. Highway, which I remembered being just one step down from an interstate. When I found the road we wanted, it turned out to be not at all what I expected.

For one thing the road was a two-lane road, not a four-lane. For another it was a mountain road full of hills and curves. Not only was it a two-lane mountain road, it was a rural two-lane mountain road which meant two things — one, there wasn't much civilization around and two, what civilization was around was driving a combine tractor 10 miles per hour in front of us. It was raining. The driving was painfully, exasperatingly slow. We did not know where we were or how long it was going to take us to get where we were going. All I had was the AAA map and the names of occasional villages to help assure me I was going in the right direction.

We eventually arrived at our new home, safe and not too much worn for the wear, but the journey was a true test of patience and faith. The road to redemption is like that. Sometimes all we have is a destination and occasional directional markers — the success of the journey is a matter of faith.

Isaiah 50:4-9a

Call it a "guy thing," but there comes a time in every boy's life when he gets "The Lecture" from his dad. The lecture is almost always precipitated by a crisis and the crisis has to do with the moment when power and vulnerability collide. Or to put it more commonly, the moment when the local bully decides that you are going to be his next trophy. The lecture can take many forms using a wide range of vocabulary and emotions, but every lecture always boils down to this — "Son, don't let anyone ever push you around. Stand up. Fight back. It's better to go down fighting than to run away from a confrontation."

This aggression by the perpetrator and the counter-aggression by the intended victim permeate much of life as we experience it. Whether in sports, politics or business, the mentality that motivates so much of interpersonal interaction is one that says we either beat or get beaten; we either retaliate in kind or risk being humiliated in our cowardice. We dare not show weakness. We dare not show vulnerability. We dare not walk away from a fight.

I do not wish to minimize the appropriateness of self-defense, but neither do I wish to so broaden the definition of self-defense that it becomes a license for any aggressive act we believe to be in our self-interest. What I do want to do — no, what I believe this text is asking us to do, is to move beyond the self-defeating cycle of meeting violence with violence and to entrust ourselves to the vindicating love of God.

This is certainly the path chosen by the servant who was able to meet the strength of violence with the greater strength of non-retaliation. The servant was able to do this because (1) he was willing to give the voice of God priority in his hearing; (2) his listening to God was a daily habit, not an occasional exercise; (3) he affirmed by teaching that which he heard from God, and what he taught, he lived; and (4) he knew that all persons were answerable to God for their actions — not just the beard-pulling, foul-mouthed, expectorating adversary, but even the servant himself.

Lest we think that all of this has nothing to do with us, let us remember that this model of a servant is lifted from this text and re-incarnated in the example of Jesus Christ and through him is made applicable to us.

Life lived according to this servant model is not what we were taught by our fathers, but it is what we are taught by our Father.

Philippians 2:5-11

There is probably no passage in Philippians more quoted or used as the basis for more sermons than today's epistle lesson. That familiarity can be either a blessing or a curse. We will strive for the former.

At various moments in penning his thoughts to one congregation or another, Paul becomes so wrapped up in what he is trying to say that he breaks out in songs of praise to God. Our text is one of those moments. In the midst of a call for unity among the faithful at Philippi, the words of an early Christian hymn grab hold of Paul and will not let him go. He can hardly concentrate for thinking about this song, so he decides to make the song a part of his correspondence.

There are several ways this hymn-text can be approached and a few of them are addressed in the Alternative Applications section below. However, the approach I invite you to consider focuses on verse 5, "Let the same mind be in you that was in Christ Jesus." Often when we read this text we move immediately to examine the character traits exemplified by Jesus and to admonish and encourage one another toward emulating those traits. However, as each of us knows, it is far easier to occasionally act with selflessness, humility and obedience than it is to exhibit these traits consistently. The reason for this is found in verse 5.

Paul invites his readers to ground their actions not in a desire to do good, or even in a command to do so, but to ground one's actions in a different way of thinking. Behavior can be tied to any number of stimuli — guilt, fear, duty, peer-pressure, the desire to be better than others — but the energy and motivation required to follow Christ's example is simply not sustainable based on these or similar stimuli. That is why Paul said to let Christ's mind be in you. He understood that the place to begin was with how one viewed the world, how one thought about life, how one mentally processed and assessed society's power arrangements. We cannot follow Christ's example if we are worried about place and prestige or about rights and rewards. We cannot follow Christ's example if we are keeping one eye on our neighbor's progress and the other eye on our neighbor's possessions. We cannot follow Christ's example if we elevate the status of the slave to that of a servant or elevate cruciform death to momentary inconvenience. We can only follow Christ's example if first we are willing to change our mind about what is important and adopt the worldview of Jesus.

The road to redemption is not successfully navigated without the transformation that comes by the renewing of our minds (Romans 12:2).

Matthew 26:14—27:66

The Sunday preceding Easter is celebrated as Palm Sunday in some faith traditions and as Passion Sunday in others. The gospel lesson for today honors the Passion Sunday tradition. The difficulty facing the interpreter is the length of today's passage and the richness of the material covered by it. It is hard to imagine how one might do justice to this text in one sermonic endeavor. One could certainly understand if the preacher simply chose to read with dramatic intonation the entire passage without comment and allow the passage to speak for itself. But since this is a preaching journal and since you rightly expect more rather than less from us, perhaps some helpful comments are in order after all.

Whatever portion of this text one chooses to build a sermon upon, there are certain characteristics of the book as a whole relevant to its proclamation. One characteristic is Matthew's use of supportive references to the Hebrew scriptures. The nature of Matthew's community and the purpose of his gospel have been discussed in previous installments and need not be repeated here. Suffice it to say, however, that Matthew's use of the Hebrew scriptures is not primarily an effort to validate those scriptures through Jesus, but to validate Jesus through the scriptures. In other words, it is not the scriptures' relevancy that needs to be proven, but Jesus'. In this passage there are no fewer than six direct references to the Hebrew scriptures, usually accompanied by some version of "in order to fulfill what was written." Additionally, there are several indirect allusions to the scriptures, usually as a part of a speech sequence. As the interpreter deals with today's text it is important to keep in context Matthew's use of the Hebrew scriptures and not to treat these scriptures as little more than a Christological ouija board.

Another characteristic of Matthew's gospel is its anti-Judaic references. Once again context is important. Matthew was written at a time of intense rivalry among the various Jewish sects (of which the Jesus movement was one) over which group best represented post-temple Judaism. In the effort to make a case for the Jesus movement, the gospel writer draws the opposition (Pharisaic and Sadduciac Judaism) in unflattering caricatures.

Additionally, at the time of writing this gospel, the Jesus movement was attempting to gain legitimacy in the eyes of the Roman occupiers of Judea and Galilee. The combination of this anti-Judaism and philo-Romanism led the Gospel writer to polemicize the events surrounding the death of Jesus. For example, those who operate in the shadows are the chief priest (26:14), Judas in collusion with the temple hierarchy, the scribes and the elders (26:57f) and, amazingly, the Jewish people themselves (27:25) in a phrase that would be used against the Jews for centuries to come. The ones who come off looking like heroes in this account are Pilate, Pilate's wife and a centurion (27:54). To employ an overused phrase, "What's wrong with this picture?"

One can understand and even appreciate Matthew's context and purpose without falling victim to them. To use the text today in such a way that vilifies the Jews and exonerates the Romans is not only ahistorical, but also perpetuates stereotypes that have no place in the gospel truth. Remember, the central event in this text is the self-giving love of Jesus Christ through which we experience the forgiveness of sins and a renewed relationship with God.

Today's gospel lesson could be used to flesh-out the theme of road to redemption by considering the manner in which Christ met the various challenges during that long night. A question to frame this consideration might be: What are the essentials for a journey down the road to redemption? The following suggestions attempt to touch down at several of the key events covered by our text.

The first essential is community (26:17-30). Redemption is not possible without a community of caring fellow travelers whose support and encouragement not only make it possible for us to begin the journey, but who sustain us on our way.

A second essential is commitment (26:36-46). The journey will not always be easy and sometimes what we are called upon to do seems beyond our ability to carry through. Nevertheless, constant and faithful commitment toward the goal will keep us moving forward.

A third essential is compassion (26:47-54), not only toward those who befriend us, but to those who would be our enemies as well.

A fourth essential for the journey down the road to redemption is the courage of one's convictions (26:57-68; 27:11-26). When the forces that would undo us bring against us all the power at their disposal, it takes extraordinary courage not to cave in under the pressure. Yet, if we are to negotiate successfully the road to redemption we must be courageously true to those convictions that form our core beliefs.

A fifth and final essential is cruciform love (27:32-50) — a willingness to give even one's own life on behalf of others as an expression of one's love for humankind and obedience to God.

May Christ's passion be our passion as we journey along the road to redemption.

Application

Today begins Holy Week — the final journey on the Lenten road to Easter. For most congregations there will be several services to mark the significance of this season. Some congregations will hold a Good Friday service in which the liturgy will be built around the seven last words of Jesus. Others will conduct a service in which the Stations of the Cross will be featured. And still other congregations will hold services that will mark the conclusion of their focus on Lent. What all of these services have in common is the theme of moving toward a destination.

As persons of faith, we, too, are moving toward a destination. For us the destination is redemption, but we are not there yet. We are still on the journey. What we are sometimes slow to understand is that the journey itself is just as important as the destination. What we make of the journey, how we conduct ourselves on the journey and the attitude that guides us on the journey are all vitally important.

We can take our cues for successful journeying from the example of Jesus as he faced his final hours before the crucifixion. We do not know how much Jesus knew in advance about those hours leading to Golgatha, but we can be fairly certain that he knew the brief road ahead of him was going to be difficult. He knew that, as much as his disciples cared for him, in the final analysis they would likely be locked in a paralyzing confusion. He knew of the brutality associated with the Roman soldiers, especially directed at those who were a threat to the peace of Rome. He knew from his previous encounters with the various Jewish sects, that if they had the chance, they would make life difficult for him, just as they made life difficult for each other. He knew that if he asked, God would likely spare him from the coming ordeal, but he also knew that he would not ask. And he knew that everything, literally everything, depended on how he responded in his hour of crisis.

So his response was to gather his friends for a final meal even though they might soon fail him. His response was not to meet aggression with aggression, threats with curses, or insults with retaliation. His response was to stand firm in the integrity of his being when confronted by his accusers and even when the accusations were a collection of half-truths and non-truths. His response was to pray for strength to drink deeply from the bitter cup and to do so willingly. His response was to take upon himself the burden of humanity and to do so in a way that others might be led to be of the same mind.

In our journey down the road to redemption, Jesus, in both his life and death, is our guide. We cannot expect clear skies and four-lane highways every mile of our journey. There will be times when our hour of testing hits us squarely in the eyes, and at that moment, we will need to decide whether to drink deeply from the bitter cup and follow the example of Jesus or pass the cup off to another and detour from the road to redemption. When that time arrives may the same mind be in us that was in Christ Jesus.

Alternative Applications

1) Isaiah: It is interesting to note that the purposes of God's grace gifts to the servant are not at all what one might expect. In verse 4 the servant is given the tongue of a teacher, but not that the servant might impart wisdom or knowledge. Rather, the servant has the tongue of a teacher in order to sustain the weary. In verse 5 the servant is given an ear to hear, but not that the servant might possess more facts. Rather the servant has an ear to hear in order to withstand oppression. In verse 7 the servant is helped by God, but not that the servant might have an unencumbered life. Rather the servant is helped in order that injustice can be confronted.

God grants grace gifts to each one of us, but we should not assume to know automatically the purpose of those gifts. Rather we are to allow God to teach us, to speak to us and to help us that we might know how to be faithful servants.

2) Philippians: In addition to the approach taken in the application section above, this text could be used to celebrate the Incarnation. The focus here would be on Jesus — his self-emptying (kenosis), humility, obedience and exaltation. This focus has the advantage of not only being appropriate to the text, but appropriate as a theme for Passion Sunday as well. One might argue that the only way to exaltation (for Jesus and us) is by means of self-emptying, obedience and humility.

3) Matthew: The possibilities offered by this lengthy passage are endless. One could examine the motivations that prompted the followers of Jesus to abandon him. For Judas either greed or political necessity was a motivator. For Peter it was the fear factor. For others the motivation may well have been self-interest. However, for all of them, personal expediency of one form or another was more important than faithfulness to Christ. The issues prompting our disobedience today are not much different.

4) Matthew: What do you make of Jesus' cry from the cross in 27:46? Was Jesus abandoned by God? If so, how does that fact square with Paul's insistence that God was in Christ reconciling the world to himself? Is this question really about abandonment or is it about hope? If the quotation from an opening stanza of a psalm is meant to call to mind the entire psalm and not just the passage quoted, how does that affect how we understand Jesus' cry?

FIRST LESSON FOCUS

By James A. Nestingen

Isaiah 50:4-9a

This text presents a challenge to the preacher because it is the stated Old Testament text for Passion Sunday in all three cycles of the three-year Revised Common Lectionary. Thus, year by year, the preacher is confronted with how to deal with it. The preacher does have the option, of course, of basing the sermon on the epistle or gospel lesson instead. But this is too important a text to be ignored for too long.

As has long been noted, this is one of the four "servant songs" to be found in the preaching of second Isaiah (Isaiah 40-55), although the lectionary reading unfortunately has omitted the second half of verse 9. The lectionary committee seems very squeamish about including anything judgmental from the scriptures, ignoring the fact that God does indeed bring his judgment upon his enemies and, sometime, upon the enemies of his chosen people. The song was spoken by the prophet sometime between 550 and 538 B.C. in Babylonian exile.

What we have in this song is a description of suffering for the sake of the Word of God. Very likely the servant is being subjected to a legal trial (v. 8), but verse 6 describes the abuse that the servant suffers before being hauled into court. He is flogged, and he is scorned, his tormentors brazenly standing in his face, to yank on his beard and to spit on him. The servant, however, has not flinched or cowered as he has undergone such suffering. Instead he has silently and bravely endured it all. Why? Because he thinks it is the will of God that he do so.

Such abuse may very well have been what second Isaiah himself suffered as he delivered the Word of God to his people. Certainly it is a role to which the prophet is calling his people, because the servant in second Isaiah is very likely to be identified with an idealized Israel — with Israel as God wants him to be and as God will make him to be (cf. Isaiah 41:9; 44:1-2; 44:21; 45:4; 49:3, all texts in which Israel is named the servant). But of course we cannot read this text without almost automatically applying it to the passion of our Lord Jesus Christ. In the days before his crucifixion, our Lord suffers such abuse at the hands of his accusers, and he does so willingly. He is not "rebellious," but in faithfulness to his God, gives his back to the smiters and his face to those who scorn and spit on him. He utters not a word, but is like a lamb that before its shearers is dumb. And he does not cower before the abuse that is heaped upon him. Why? Because it is the will of the Lord that he suffer so.

God asks of his servants that they willingly undergo suffering for the sake of the gospel. To our society, which seems to believe that persons' religion should make them happy, prosperous and well-liked, that is a strange and odious thought. Who wants to follow a faith that brings with it suffering and scorn? "What's in it for me?" would be the question of many. But at the heart of the Christian faith and, indeed, in the Bible as a whole, the necessity of suffering for the will of God is prominent. After all, the central symbol of the Christian faith is a cross. And the command of our Lord is to take up our cross and follow him — to die to ourselves as he died. When we hear that, our response is often, "Well, just a minute. I'll bring around the station wagon, and we can put the cross in the back."

But no. The servants of God are to be, as 2 Timothy also says, willing to take their share of suffering for the sake of the gospel (2 Timothy 1:8).

The reason for that is clear. Our society and our world do not welcome the gospel. If our Lord lived today, most people would still want to crucify him. For he turns all of our accustomed ways upside down, doesn't he? He tells us to love our enemies, of all people, to forgive 70 times seven, to love one another as he has loved us. He announces that the meek will inherit the earth, and whoever heard of that in our world? It's the fellow who knows how to promote himself who will climb the ladder of success, isn't it? Jesus tells us not to pile up treasures for ourselves on earth, but we all know that the bigger the portfolio, the better. He tells us that we can't do one thing to work our way into eternal life, and that everything depends on the grace of the Father. But doesn't God value the good persons we try to be? Doesn't he approve of all of the things we have done for the church? And won't that be rewarded in heaven? Let's face it. The gospel of Jesus Christ, like his passion and cross, are scandalous in our world. And yet, we are called to give our lives for the sake of testifying to it.

In short, God calls his servants to lives out-of-joint with the rest of society, because God wants to save his world. He wants to forgive the transgressions of humankind. He wants to deliver everyone from death. He wants to pour out his love on every soul whom he has created on the face of this planet. And God can do that only if his servants are willing to suffer, as his prophet suffered, and as his son finally suffered for us all. Only by a cross, that nailed all of this world's evil to its wood, did God manifest his amazing love that was willing to die for you and me. And only as his servants are equally willing is the message of that incredible love spread throughout creation.

How is it possible for us to be such willing and loving servants of our Lord? Our text tells us the answer. Second Isaiah recounts to us that "morning by morning" God "wakens" his ear (v. 4). Indeed, when he is weary, he listens — listens to the Lord — and is sustained. And there we have the foundation of the Christian servant-life. In a daily communion with his God, in constant listening to the Lord's word, now preserved for us in the scriptures, in prayer and meditation, there are given to us unworthy servants of our God the strength, the sustenance, the guidance, the courage to do the will of our Lord. By constant fellowship with our God, we Christians are enabled to face any scornful challenge that the world may throw up to us, to undergo any suffering that may come our way, and to cheerfully know that no matter what the situation may be, the Lord is our help and our stay. Servants like that never know defeat, good Christians, because God is never defeated. And servants like that never wonder what their purpose is in life, because God's purpose is their guide and goal — God's purpose of love.

Preaching the Psalm

by Stan Purdum

Psalm 31:9-16. On this day when preachers have to decide whether to pursue the psalms or the Passion, it should be noted that Psalm 31:9-16 is part of the Liturgy of Passion, not the Liturgy of the Palms, and it occupies that place for all three years of the Revised Common Lectionary. But even if one did not know that, the tone of these verses would surely push one away from any triumphalism. These words are the cry of a person in agony.

A couple of preaching possibilities:

1) Verse 9 and especially verse 10 can be taken literally, as references to serious illness. Many sufferers have found courage and hope in viewing the voluntary suffering of Jesus. One pastor mentioned visiting a Christian woman who was in the end stages of cancer, and was in terrible pain. Yet she said to the pastor, "If Jesus suffered for me, I can suffer for him." To himself, the pastor thought the woman's comment simplistic. How could her suffering, caused not by sin but by rogue cells, be doing anything for God? But the fact was, that understanding was helping the woman handle her ordeal. Wisely, the pastor did nothing to challenge her view. But maybe the woman was right anyway. Here's a place to talk about redemptive suffering.

2) Verse 12, "I have passed out of mind like one who is dead," could easily be the lament of a person "downsized" out of a job and unable to find new employment. Those who have been there testify that it really does feel like being forgotten by one's former workmates, employers and even the crowd that one ran with while employed. What will it take to get the person in such straits to trust that "my times are in your hands" (v. 15)?

Maundy Thursday
Exodus 12:1-4 (5-10) 11-14
1 Corinthians 11:23-26
John 13:1-17, 31b-35
by *Wayne Brouwer*

A world turned upside down

In 17th-century England, under the leadership of Oliver Cromwell and his righteous Puritanism, Parliament passed laws ensuring that Christmas would be observed as a solemn occasion. Not all in the country agreed, particularly since Christmas had been one of the great festivals of social silliness where class distinctions were put aside for a few hours. Responding to the uptight rigor of governmentally imposed holiday restrictions, a new protest song swept through neighborhoods and quickly became the song of the day. It was called "World Turned Upside Down," and included these lyrics:

Listen to me and you shall hear, news hath not been this thousand year:
Since Herod, Caesar, and many more, you never heard the like before.
Holy-dayes are despis'd, new fashions are devis'd.
Old Christmas is kicked out of Town
Yet let's be content, and the times lament, you see the world turn'd upside down.

The song took on new significance a century later, when the American colonies rebelled. After the battle of Yorktown in 1781, ending the Revolutionary War, the British military band is reported to have played this song, signaling the strangeness of mighty England's ungainly defeat. The world, it seemed, had indeed turned upside down.

So too in today's lectionary readings. Yahweh battles Pharaoh in the ten plagues showdown, leading to the death of Egypt's firstborn, and the Passover celebration starting a new world order. Paul reminds the new Christians of Corinth that social orders come undone in the world turned upside down by the gospel of Christ. And Jesus himself models for his disciples what love means when the mighty serve and the humble are honored. Perhaps this is not a world turned upside down, but an upside-down world finally turned right side up!

Exodus 12:1-4 (5-10) 11-14

Exodus 1-19 forms an extended "historical prologue" to the Sinai covenant by declaring Israel's precarious situation in Egypt (ch. 1), the birth and training of the leader who would become Yahweh's agent for recovering Yahweh's enslaved people (ch. 2), the calling of this deliverer (chs. 3-4), and the battle of the superpowers (the Pharaoh and Yahweh) who each lay claim to suzerain status over this vassal nation (chs. 5-19). Exodus 25-40 focuses on the creation of a suitable residence for Israel's suzerain. Thus the whole of Exodus may be quickly outlined as struggles (1-19), stipulations (20-24), and symbols (25-40) surrounding the Sinai covenant-making event.

The struggles of chapters 1-19 involve a number of things. At the start there is the nasty relationship that has developed between the Pharaoh of Egypt and the Israelites. An editorial note declares that "Joseph" has been forgotten, and this small reference forms the bridge that later draws Genesis into an even more broadly extended historical prologue to the Sinai covenant. We will find out, by reading backward, that Joseph was the critical link between the Egyptians and this other ethnic community living within its borders. When the good that Joseph did for both races was forgotten, the dominant Egyptian culture attempted to dehumanize and then destroy these Israelite aliens.

The deadly solution proposed by the Pharaoh in dealing with the rising population of his slave community may sound harsh, but it was likely a very modest and welcomed political maneuver among his primary subjects. Because there is virtually no rain in Egypt, with most of its territory lying in or on the edge of the great Saharan desert, the Nile is and was the critical source of water that sustained life throughout the region. The Nile "miraculously" ebbed and flowed annually, responding to the rains of central Africa thousands of miles away. Far removed from Egypt's farmlands and cities, this process was attributed to the gods that nurtured Egyptian civilization. Thus it was fitting for the people to pay homage to these gods, especially by giving appropriate sacrifices to the power of the Nile. In that manner, having the boy babies of the Hebrews tossed into the Nile's currents would not have been considered genocide, but instead it would be deemed a suitable civic and cultural responsibility. Such a practice provided the Nile god with fittingly dear tribute and at the same time allowed the bulk of the Egyptian population to save its own babies by substituting those of this surrogate vassal people living within their borders.

Moses' own name ties him to the royal family of Egypt and its influence (note the frequent occurrence of the letters MSS in the names of Pharaohs of the 18th through 20th dynasties — Thutmoses, Ramses, and so on), and his training in the palace schools would provide him with skills that set him apart from the rest of the Israelites in preparation for his unique leadership responsibilities. Moses' time in the wilderness, on the other hand, made him familiar with Bedouin life and similarly fortified his ability to stand at the head of a wandering community once Israel was released from slavery.

In Moses' unique encounter with God at Mount Horeb (chs. 3-4), he experienced the power of the forgotten deity of Israel and learned a name by which this divinity would soon become known again to the people. "Yahweh" is a variation on the Hebrew verb of existence, and that is why translators bring it into English with terms like "I am" or "I will be." Furthermore, through the voice from the burning bush, this God immediately connected the current events with a specific past through a historical recitation that would later be explicated at length in the extended Genesis historical prologue to the Sinai covenant: Yahweh is the God of Abraham, Isaac, and Jacob. Because of the promises made to that family, Moses is now to become the agent through whom the Israelites will be returned to the land promised to their ancestors. Of course, this is what triggered the battle for control of the nation and eventually set the stage for Yahweh to claim suzerainty over Israel at Mount Sinai.

The conflict intensifies in Exodus 5:1-6:12 when Moses makes his first dramatic appearance back in Egypt. The Pharaoh's initial reaction is disdain; why should he listen to the apocalyptic ravings of a wilderness wild man, even if he seems unusually aware of Egyptian language and protocol?

At this point the famous plagues enter the story. While these miracles of divine judgment make for great Hollywood screenplay, the reason for this extended weird display of divine power is not always apparent to those of us who live in very different cultural contexts, especially when it is interspersed with notes that Pharaoh's heart was hardened, sometimes, in fact, seemingly as an act of Yahweh. Could not Yahweh have provided a less destructive and deadly exit strategy for Israel?

The plagues begin to make sense when they are viewed in reference to Egypt's climate and culture. After the initial sparring between Moses and the pharaoh's sorcerers (Exodus 7:10-13) with snakes to show magical skills, the stakes are raised far beyond human ability merely to manipulate the natural order. First the waters are turned to blood; then the marshes send out a massive, unwelcome pilgrimage of frogs; next the dust is beat into gnats, soon to be followed by even peskier flies; subsequently the livestock gets sick from the dust, and this illness then spreads to human life in the form of boils and open sores; penultimately the heavens send down mortar shells of hail, transport in a foreign army of locusts, and then withhold the light of the sun; finally, in an awful culmination, the firstborn humans and animals across Egypt die suddenly.

This is strange but not quite so when seen in three successive groupings. Among the many deities worshiped in ancient Egypt, none superseded a triumvirate composed by the Nile, the good earth, and the heavens that were the home of the sun. So it was that the initial plagues of bloody water and frogs both turned the Nile against the Egyptians and showed the dominance of Yahweh over this critical source of national life.

The ante was then upped when Yahweh took on the farmland of Egypt, one of the great bread baskets of the world. Instead of producing crops, Moses showed, by way of plagues three through six, how Yahweh could cause these fertile alluvial plains to generate all manner of irritating and deadly pestilence, making it an enemy instead of a friend. Finally, in the third stage of plagues, the heavens themselves became menacing. Rather than providing the sheltering confidence of benign sameness, one day the heavens attacked with the hailstone mortar fire of an unseen enemy. Next these same heavens served as the highway of an invading army of locusts. Then old friend *Ra*(the sun), the crowning deity of Egyptian religion, simply vanished for three days. The gloom that terrified the Egyptians was no mere fear of darkness but rather the ominous trepidation that their primary deity had been bested by the God of the Israelites.

All of this culminated in the final foray of this cosmic battle, when the link of life between generations and human connectedness with ultimate reality was severed through the killing of Egypt's firstborn. The Egyptians believed that the firstborn carried the cultural significance of each family and species, so in a sudden and dramatic moment the very chain of life was destroyed. Furthermore, since the pharaohs themselves were presumed to be deity incarnate, descending directly from the sun by way of firstborn inheritance, cutting this link eviscerated the life-potency of the Egyptian civilization not only for the present but also for the future. It was a true cultural, religious, political, and social knockout punch.

This explains why the plagues originally served not as gory illustration material for modern Sunday school papers, but rather as the divine initiatives in an escalating battle between Yahweh and the Pharaoh of Egypt over claims on the people of Israel. The plagues were a necessary prologue to the Sinai covenant because they displayed and substantiated the sovereignty of Yahweh as suzerain not only over Israel but also over other contenders. Israel belongs to Yahweh both because of historic promises made to Abraham, and also by way of chivalrous combat in which Yahweh won back the prize of lover and human companion from the usurper who had stolen her away from the divine heart. Furthermore, Yahweh accomplished this act *without* the help of Israel's own resources (no armies, no resistance movements, no terrorist tactics, no great escape plans), and in a decisive manner that announced the limitations of the Egyptian religious and cultural resources.

This is why the final plague is paired with the institution of the Passover festival (Exodus 12). The annual festival would become an ongoing reminder that Israel was bought back by way of a blood-price redemption, and that the nation owed its very existence to the love and fighting jealousy of its divine champion. In one momentous confrontation, Egypt lost its firstborn and its cultural heritage, while Israel became Yahweh's firstborn and rightful inheritance.

1 Corinthians 11:23-26

Probably sometime in late 51 AD or early 52 AD Paul sent a letter of strongly worded reproof to the Corinthian congregation. No copies have survived, but from what Paul himself says about this communication in 1 Corinthians 5:9 it is easy to see why some might take exception to it. Indeed, it appears that a number of people in the congregation began to disown Paul's authority after reading that letter, and then began to instigate factionalism in the community. Cliques grew based upon personal preferences about which leaders were better preachers, and who had a right to claim greater sway among them (see 1 Corinthians 2-4). Meanwhile, a delegation of three men (Stephanus, Fortunatus, and Achaicus), all highly respectful of Paul's apostolic authority, traveled from Corinth to Ephesus, bringing to Paul an oral report about the difficulties going on in the church. They also carried a written list of questions that members of the congregation were raising.

Paul quickly wrote a letter of response. Although it was actually his second letter to the Corinthian congregation, because the earlier communication has been lost, this one survives as 1 Corinthians in our New Testaments. Immediately in the opening passages, Paul addresses the difficulties some have at his continued influence in the congregation. He chastises the members for dividing up into parties where each waves a banner acclaiming the worthiness of a different leader. These groupings were sinful and disruptive, according to Paul, for they denied the honor that ought to be given only to the true head of the church, Jesus Christ. Such schisms also played favorites among human leaders, setting them over against each other, rather than recognizing their complementary gifts for helping the church as a whole to grow. By chapter 4, Paul was ready to give a declaration for his own apostolic authority, pleading with the Corinthians to receive his teachings as God's own initiatives toward them.

In chapters 5 and 6, Paul painfully rehearsed some of the examples of immorality within the congregation that must have been the focus of his earlier letter. Several social sins, including blatantly inappropriate sexual relations and lawsuits between Christians, are marched out onto the platform in descriptions that must have left little doubt as to who Paul was talking about. The reflections about sexual behavior may have reminded Paul of the queries on the list brought by Stephanus, Fortunatus, and Achaicus. To these he turns next.

Paul's response to questions about worship practices (11:2-33) contains a reflection on two social value systems. First, with regard to differing roles for women and men in society, Paul wants to ensure that the genders are not blurred. There is a creational distinction between females and males, according to Paul, and this must not be erased, even by the freedoms found in Christ. At the same time, this gender distinction ought not to undermine the broad equality by which the gifts of the Spirit are distributed. Both women and men can and should prophesy. Spiritual leadership in the church is not limited by gender.

Second, in a review of the church's celebration of "the Lord's Supper," as it was becoming known, another facet of social interaction was addressed. The "differences" within the congregation were not only of the kind where parties became loyal to different leaders (1 Corinthians 1-3), but also the manifestation of divergent socio-economic groupings present in Corinthian society. The reason why some who attended these Lord's Supper gatherings "go ahead without waiting for anybody else" and others "remain hungry," was due to the divergent lifestyle practices of the rich and the poor among them. Wealthy people were able to come and go as they pleased, including showing up to worship services, potluck dinners, and Lord's Supper celebrations right at the start. The poor and the slaves, however (some likely coming from the same households), were often late to arrive because they had to fulfill their domestic work obligations first. Paul declared that "recognizing the body of the Lord" was necessary if the Lord's Supper was to be celebrated properly. This did not mean having the capacity to understand an appropriate theological theory of the atonement or some other such cognitive ability. Instead, it amounted to remembering that all who belong to Jesus are welcome at his table, and none have more rights than others. If this socially and economically diverse group of society was indeed the body of Christ, each must live and act accordingly, making room at the table for all.

Maundy Thursday

John 13:1-17, 31b-35

Once the transition takes place in John's gospel from the "Book of Signs" to the "Book of Glory," only two major events happen. First, Jesus meets for an extended meal and conversation with his disciples (chs. 13-17). This lengthy monologue seems somewhat meandering and repetitive until it is viewed through the Hebrew communication lens of chiasm. Then the "Farewell Discourse," as it is known, takes on new depth as it weaves back and forth and climaxes in the middle. This parting exhortation becomes an obviously deeply moving instruction to Jesus' followers to remain connected to him by way of the powerful "Paraclete" (a Greek term meaning "counselor" or "advocate"), in the face of the troubling that will come upon them because of his imminent physical departure, and the rising persecutions targeted toward them by the world that remains in darkness. In chiastic summary, the Farewell Discourse can be portrayed in this manner:

Gathering experience of unity —*13:1-35*
Prediction of disciple's denial —*13:36-38*
Jesus' departure tempered by Father's power —*14:1-14*
Promise of the "Paraclete" —*14:15-24*
Troubling encounter with the world —*14:25-31*
"Abide in Me!" teaching —*15:1-17*
Troubling encounter with the world —*15:18--16:4a*
Promise of the "Paraclete" —*16:4b-15*
Jesus' departure tempered by Father's power —*16:16-28*
Prediction of disciple's denial —*16:29-33*
Departing experience of unity —*17:1-26*

Every element of this "Farewell Discourse" is doubled with a parallel passage except for Jesus' central teaching that his disciples should "abide in me."

Furthermore, these parallel passages are arranged in reverse order in the second half to their initial expression in the first half. At the heart of it all comes the unparalleled vine and branches teaching, which functions as the chiastic center and ultimate focus of the discourse as a whole. In effect, John shows us how the transforming power of Jesus as the light of the world is to take effect. Jesus comes into this darkened world as a brilliant ray of re-creative light and life. But if he goes about his business all by himself the light will have limited penetrating value, over against the expansive and pervasive darkness that has consumed this world. So a multiplication and amplification has to happen. Jesus himself spoke about this at the end of the "Book of Signs." He said: "The hour has come for the Son of Man to be glorified. I tell you the truth, unless a kernel of wheat falls to the ground and dies, it remains only a single seed. But if it dies, it produces many seeds. The man who loves his life will lose it, while the man who hates his life in this world will keep it for eternal life. Whoever serves me must follow me..." (12:26).

In this chiastic "Farewell Discourse," Jesus makes clear the meaning of everything. His disciples have been transformed from darkness to light (and thus from death to life) through Jesus' incorporation of them into fellowship with himself and the Father (chs. 13, 17). This does not free them immediately from struggles, as seen in Judas' betrayal and the coming denial of them all. But the connection between the Father and the disciples is secure, because it is initiated by the Father, and will last even when Jesus disappears from them very shortly, because the powerful "Paraclete" will arrive to dispense Jesus' ongoing presence with them all, wherever they go, and in whatever circumstances they find themselves. Of course, that will only trigger further conflicts and confrontations with "the world." So (and here's the central element of the discourse), "abide in me!" Either you are with the darkness or you are with the light. Either you are dead because of the power of the world, or you are alive in me. And, of course, if you "abide in me," you will glow with my light and the multiplication of the seed sown will take place. Eventually through you, the light that comes into the world through Jesus will bring light to everyone. It is a picture of the mission of God, promised to Abraham, enacted geographically through Israel, but now become a global movement through Jesus' disciples who "abide" in him through the power of the "Paraclete."

In today's gospel passage, it all begins when Jesus' disciples are served by their master and washed into holy union with him and his mission. The world we thought we knew has been turned upside down.

Application

Donna Hoffman, a young mother who battled cancer for a number of years, wrote this little poem in her journal. She was in the hospital at the time. The cancer seemed so strong, and tomorrow seemed like an uncertain dream or a tragic nightmare. She called her poem *Journey*:

> *My soul runs arms outstretched*
> *down the corridor to you.*
> *Ah, my feet may stumble*
> *but how my heart can stride!*

Only God's grace can sustain us in a world turned upside down, even when our feet stumble and when the journey seems too long, too troublesome. "My soul runs. How my heart can stride!"

Years ago, young William Borden testified of the same. He was the wealthy son of a powerful family who graduated with top honors from Yale University. He could do anything in life that he chose. Many were surprised that he chose to become a missionary of the gospel of Jesus Christ.

His friends thought he was crazy. "Why throw your life away like that?" they said. "You've got so much to live for here."

But Borden knew who held his tomorrows. He made his choices, and God gave him the inner strength to live his convictions.

He set out on a long journey to China. It took months in those days, and by the time he got to Egypt, some disease managed to make him sick. He was placed in a hospital and soon it became obvious that he wouldn't recover. William Borden would die a foreigner in Egypt. He never reached his goal. He never went back home.

He could have been troubled by the tragedy of it all. But his last conscious act was to write a little note. Seven words — seven words that were spoken at his funeral. Seven words that summarized his life, his identity: "No reserve, no retreat, and no regrets!"

An Alternative Application

John 13:1-17, 31b-35. On this Maundy Thursday, the gospel passage stands at the center of our attention. We are served by Jesus and receive his new command (so "Maundy"): "Love one another as I have loved you." This is not something to be exegeted but to be enacted.

Walter Wangerin Jr. powerfully summarized the meaning of Jesus as Messiah in his allegory of the Ragman. Wangerin pictures himself in a city on a Friday morning. A handsome young man comes to town, dragging behind him a cart made of wood. The cart is piled high with new, clean clothes, bright and shiny and freshly pressed.

Wandering through the streets the trader marches, crying out his strange deal: "Rags! New rags for old! Give me your old rags, your tired rags, your torn and soiled rags!"

He sees a woman on the back porch of a house. She is old and tired and weary of living. She has a dirty handkerchief pressed to her nose, and she is crying a thousand tears, sobbing over the pains of her life.

The Ragman takes a clean linen handkerchief from his wagon and brings it to the woman. He lays it across her arm. She blinks at him, wondering what he is up to. Gently the young man opens her fingers and releases the old, dirty, soaking handkerchief from her knotted fist.

Then comes the wonder. The Ragman touches the old rag to his own eyes and begins to weep her tears. Meanwhile, behind him on her porch stands the old woman, tears gone, eyes full of peace.

It happens again. "New rags for old!" he cries, and he comes to a young girl wearing a bloody bandage on her head. He takes the caked and soiled wrap away and gives her a new bonnet from his cart. Then he wraps the old rags around his head. As he does this, the girl's cuts disappear and her skin turns rosy. She dances away with laughter and returns to her friends to play. But the Ragman begins to moan and from her rags on his head the blood spills down.

He next meets a man. "Do you have a job?" the Ragman asks. With a sneer the man replies, "Are you kidding?" and holds up his shirtsleeve. There is no arm in it. He cannot work. He is disabled.

But the Ragman says, "Give me your shirt. I'll give you mine."

The man's shirt hangs limp as he takes it off, but the Ragman's shirt hangs firm and full because one of the Ragman's arms is still in the sleeve. It goes with the shirt. When the man puts it on, he has a new arm. But the Ragman walks away with one sleeve dangling.

It happens over and over again. The Ragman takes the clothes from the tired, the hurting, the lost, and the lonely. He gathers them to his own body and takes the pains into his own heart. Then he gives new clothes to new lives with new purpose and new joy.

Finally, around midday the Ragman finds himself at the center of the city, where nothing remains but a stinking garbage heap. It is the accumulated refuse of a society lost to anxiety and torture. On Friday afternoon the Ragman climbs the hill, stumbling as he drags his cart behind him. He is tired and sore and pained and bleeding. He falls on the wooden beams of the cart, alone and dying from the disease and disaster he has garnered from others.

Wangerin wonders at the sight. In exhaustion and uncertainty he falls asleep. He lies dreaming nightmares through all of Saturday until he is shaken from his fitful slumbers early on Sunday morning. The ground quakes and Wangerin looks up. In surprise he sees the Ragman stand up. He is alive! The sores are gone, though the scars remain. But the Ragman's clothes are new and clean. Death has been swallowed up and transformed by life!

Still worn and troubled in his spirit, Wangerin cries up to the Ragman, "Dress me, Ragman! Give me your clothes to wear! Make me new!"

We know the picture. It is Jesus coming into our world to share our sufferings and to bear our shame and guilt. Jesus stands in our place, dying our death so that we might gain a new and renewing relationship with God.

Sure, it is hard to explain. But it is also something, according to the Bible, that we cannot live without.

Good Friday

Isaiah 52:13--53:12

Hebrews 10:16-25

John 18:1--19:42

Psalm 22

by G. David Yeager and Schuyler Rhodes

What's so good about Good Friday?

One of my favorite movies of all time is the 1956 classic titled *Twelve Angry Men* featuring an all-star cast including Henry Fonda, E.G. Marshall, and Lee J. Cobb. The entire movie takes place in a jury room where the twelve jurors try to arrive at a verdict in a murder case (hence the title of the movie).

When the first ballot is taken, the vote is 11 to 1 to convict. The lone holdout (Henry Fonda) refuses to accept the prosecutor's case at face value because of inconsistencies he detected in the prosecution's case. As he discusses his concerns other jurors become less sure of the accused's guilt. Complicating the dynamics between those certain of the accused's guilt and those less certain is the stifling summertime heat in the non-air-conditioned jury room.

In the deliberations the anger becomes intense, tempers flare, and short fuses become quick triggers. All of the anger, threats, and intimidations are directed primarily to the one juror who would not go along with the majority over, what is for most, an inconsequential matter. Slowly, the motivations of those favoring a guilty verdict come to the surface, suggesting that the search for truth begins with a search of the self. Fonda stands by his convictions and one by one the jurors are forced to face their own prejudices and inner conflicts until at last the vote is unanimous — 12-0 to acquit.

There are many interesting (and I think important) layers to this movie, but certainly among the most interesting is the Fonda character's unwillingness to let the opinions of others or even his own unpopularity dissuade him from doing what he thought was right. And that's what's good about this movie — in the midst of confusion and doubt and fear and uncertainty it offers the hope that one person, standing by what they believe to be right, can make a difference.

Isaiah 52:13--53:12

The first lesson text reminds us that the servant passage of today's lesson had a life before its use in helping to define the person and work of Jesus.

The gospel writers are called upon in this and other passages within the Hebrew scriptures to describe the meaning of the cross event. In spite of Jesus' attempts to prepare his followers for what would happen, the idea of a crucified Messiah was totally beyond their frame of reference. When the crucifixion did occur, the disciples were left to make sense of what had happened and one source to which they naturally turned was their scriptures. If, as they believed, Jesus were the Messiah of God then surely the scriptures, which were given by God, would provide a clue to understanding this unexpected turn of events. As the early disciples looked more carefully at their sacred text, they began to see references that matched their experiences of Jesus. They used these references in their teaching and proclamation to assist others in understanding the life and ministry of Jesus.

Good Friday

Hebrews 10:16-25

The letter to the Hebrews could probably more accurately be described as the sermon to the Hebrews, since as many commentators have noted, it has fewer characteristics of written correspondence and more characteristics of an oration. The letter/sermon was written to Jewish believers in Jesus at a time when to be a follower of Jesus was dangerous business. Persecutions and harassment seemed to be the order of the day for those who were followers of the way. Consequently, some converts, old and new, were downplaying their belief in Jesus, while others were abandoning the faith altogether and returning to Judaism. This sermon/letter was delivered in an attempt to encourage the persecuted believers to remain faithful to Christ and to the confession of faith they had embraced. The form this encouragement took was to pile example upon example to demonstrate the superior nature of Christ.

In today's lesson the author is laying a foundation upon which he wants to construct his argument. That foundation is the once and for all forgiveness of sins offered through Jesus Christ. The Jewish Christians were familiar with the sacrificial ritual in the temple where every day as part of the daily liturgy the priestly representative would offer a sacrifice for the sins of the people. The preacher will argue that this repeated act is ineffective as atonement for sin because of its repeatable nature. Something that has to be done every day, so the argument goes, cannot be nearly as effective as something that by its very nature does not need to be repeated. In contrast to the daily, repeated sin sacrifices offered by the priests, Jesus has offered himself as a once and for all sin sacrifice the results of which are a full and complete forgiveness.

With the reality and permanence of that forgiveness as a foundation, the author moves on to the "So what?" question. Therefore, because one is forgiven, there need be no hesitancy in approaching the presence of God. There is no "Off Limits" section in Christ's sanctuary. There is no longer a curtain separating the seeker of God from God's holy presence. The one with true intentions of the heart and with deeply felt needs can confidently approach the presence of God because of the priestly function of cleansing performed within the individual by Christ.

Because one is forgiven one should lay hold of one's confession of faith with an unrelenting tenacity. There will no doubt be many situations to arise that will severely test one's faith, but the believer's faithfulness should be as unwavering as the one in whom the believer's hope resides.

Because one is forgiven one should take advantage of the opportunity to turn attention away from oneself and toward that brother or sister in the faith whose steadfastness is also undergoing a challenge. Rather than stoking one another's fears, each should provoke the other toward a confident love. Rather than the paralysis brought on by anxiety, one should encourage the other to acts of goodness. Rather than shunning the gathered community of Christ so as to preserve one's deniability, one should welcome the opportunity to worship with and encourage one another.

Because one is forgiven, one can face whatever life throws at him/her because one knows that no matter what forces of darkness rule the moment, God rules tomorrow. The day of the Lord is approaching when forgiveness will be complete, when hope will be fulfilled and when the enemies of Christ will be made a footstool for his feet (10:13).

John 18:1--19:42

In the last third of the first century, the gospel writers put pen to parchment in order to preserve a record of the life, ministry, death, and resurrection of Jesus. We should not be surprised that one remembered different facts than the others or that they remembered the same fact differently — that's the nature of memory and perspective. Nor should we hasten to make one version out of four. Each of the gospel writers used the facts that were available to them, added to the facts their own recollections and produced an account that primarily served the purposes and needs of their particular audience. I believe, therefore, that we are better served by allowing each of the gospel writers their own voice, rather than trying to synthesize their voices and memories into a seamless whole.

The purpose, then, of what follows is to help us understand the cross event from John's perspective. To do that I will attempt to point out John's unique contributions to the Jesus story. One of the first things to notice is that for John, Jesus is in control throughout the ordeal. Jesus is depicted controlling the conversation and the events surrounding the arrest (18:1-11); engaged in an in-your-face dialogue with Annas (18:19-23); turning Pilate's questions back on Pilate (18:33-38); carrying his own cross all the way to the place of execution (19:17); giving instructions for the care of his mother even as he is hanging on the cross (19:26-27); and finally relinquishing his spirit himself (19:30). All of this accords well with John's focus elsewhere (10:18) that no one takes Jesus' life from him, rather Jesus lays down his life of his own will. Therefore, there is no question but that John understands the cross event as a completely self-giving act on the part of Jesus.

Another thing to notice is the detail John provides to significant events. If indeed he is the unnamed disciple throughout this gospel, then not only did he have a front row seat to many of the events (notice the use of "another disciple" and "the disciple whom he loved"), but he had political connections as well (18:15) that gave him entrance not available to other disciples. The specifics added to the story of Peter's denial (18:15-27), of the indecisiveness of Pilate (18:28--19:16), and of the rationale for the actions taken after Jesus' death (19:31-42), add a background to the tapestry not found in the other gospel accounts. This does not mean that John's account is more reliable — after all John seems to use facts in a random order to suit his gospel purpose — but it does personalize the story in a way that is not done elsewhere.

Perhaps the most important thing to notice about John's version of the cross event is the timing of the crucifixion. The synoptic gospel writers clearly identify the Last Supper as a Passover meal. John places the meal before Passover and for a very important reason — he wants to present the crucifixion of Jesus as taking place during the same time period in which the Passover animal would have been sacrificed. What this does for John is to unambiguously identify Jesus as a Passover sacrifice. Note that Pilate offers to release a Jewish prisoner in honor of Passover (18:39), presumably before the festival begins. Pilate brings Jesus out for one last attempt at releasing him and John provides us with a time reference, about noon on the day of preparation for Passover (19:14). The significance of this reference would seem to be that the ensuing events occurred between noon on Passover eve and the beginning of Passover (19:31, 42), or as the Passover animals were being prepared for the evening celebration. This theological arrangement is, again, very much in keeping with John's style throughout his gospel.

As a final matter, it is interesting to note that Joseph of Arimathea and Nicodemus use a garden tomb near the execution site more out of expediency than plan. Passover was quickly approaching and they needed a temporary place to secure the body — they just didn't know how temporary.

Application

What makes Good Friday good? This was the question posed by one of my children several years ago as they watched me struggling to put together an Easter Sunday sermon. It was one of those out-of-the-mouth-of-babes moments. What does make Good Friday good? For that matter what makes anything good? Is something good simply because of its personal benefits or is there a deeper, more objective quality to goodness? What makes Good Friday good?

The most reflexive answer to that question is that Good Friday is good because of the eternal and universal consequences of Jesus' sacrifice. That is a true answer and an important answer, but it is also an answer we can give without much thought or reflection. It is, in a sense, the easy answer. If we thought about the question for more than half a second, might there be additional answers we could offer?

I would like to make a contribution to the answer pool and it is this: Good Friday is good because it gives us reason to hope that the world can be different. Hope will continue to flicker as long as there are persons among us like the servant of Isaiah 52-53. In a world that celebrates the ideal, the beautiful, the near perfect, the servant offers hope that the rest of us — the mere mortals, the uncomely, the flawed — are not overlooked or abandoned by God. In a world that lives by the sword and that is quick to retaliate against suspected offenders, the servant offers hope that by choosing a different path, a path of suffering reconciliation, the righteousness of God might be revealed. In a world in which each person seeks one's own self-interest to the neglect and oppression of the other, the servant offers hope that through selflessness and concern for the other the righteousness of one will lead to the righteousness of many.

Hope will continue to flicker as long as there are persons among us like the preacher of Hebrews. Each of us experience moments when life seems to overwhelm us, when faith no longer makes sense, when we cannot muster the energy it takes to continue on, when the forces set in opposition to us flex their muscle and our 98-pound frame quivers in their shadow. At such times we need the hope provided by one like the preacher to the Hebrews. A hope that reminds us that through forgiveness we are welcomed into the very presence of God. A hope that keeps before us our confession of faith. A hope that is fed and nourished by a community for whom we truly matter. When life hands us lemons, we need one like the preacher to teach us how to make lemonade.

Hope will continue to flicker as long as the presence of Jesus resides among us. In Jesus we find one who controls events and is not controlled by them. In Jesus we find one who, in spite of our denials and faithlessness, continues to count us among his own. In Jesus we find one who is willing to lay down his life for us so that those enemies of mortality, sin and death, might not hold sway over us.

Good Friday is good because hope still lives. Hope lives in the one willing to be a servant and in the one who calls us to faithfulness. But more than these, hope lives in the presence of Christ within us. And that is what makes Good Friday good.

Alternative Applications

Isaiah 52:13--53:12. The prophet reminds us of a truth that the apostle Paul will echo in his letter to the Corinthian Christians, namely that God doesn't go to *GQ* or *Cosmopolitan* for his models of faithfulness. God does not limit his pool of useful servants to the beautiful people. What that tells us is if we want to see God at work in our world, we might pay closer attention to the despised and rejected, to the ordinary folks and to the no-accounts, to those bruised by life and to those crushed by oppression.

Additionally, the preacher cannot walk away from this text without giving much reflective thought to verses 4-6. Whether or not these verses are used for a sermonic offering, preachers would do well to sit before this text as they prepare to lead their congregations through a Good Friday service in preparation for Resurrection Sunday.

Hebrews 10:16-25. The author of Hebrews attempts to build a case for faithfulness upon the foundation of forgiveness. On this Good Friday, when minds are focused on the forgiveness offered by God through Christ, the preacher might consider with the congregation the implications of forgiveness in contemporary society. Has forgiveness gone out of style? What does forgiveness look like these days? Why should we bother with forgiveness in the first place? If one does decide to forgive, what's in it for the forgiver? Is that even an appropriate calculation? For the preacher of Hebrews, forgiveness of sins was the linchpin for the work of Jesus. What does forgiveness mean to us?

John 18:1--19:42. John's account of Peter's denial is one that we can identify with all too well. Peter's failure is also our failure. The only difference is that his failure is recorded for all the ages to see and we can quietly walk away from ours. At its core Peter's denial of Christ was a capitulation to peer pressure. In the presence of Jesus, Peter was bold. In the community of the disciples, Peter was a rock. Left on his own among an unsympathetic audience, Peter's courage melted away. Isn't that the way it is with us as well? At the office, in the market, at school, or chatting with a neighbor when we are asked about our faith, isn't our first reaction to try and change the conversation, to deny in some way that faith is much of an issue with us? A sermon exploring our propensity to deny an intimate connection with Christ might help our hearers to see themselves in that courtyard standing around the charcoal fire.

Preaching the Psalm

by Schuyler Rhodes

Psalm 22. A God who does not answer... by Schuyler Rhodes How hard it is to have faith! To actually set down the reservations and the doubt and release the need for control and to simply trust. This is no mean feat. Trusting God is difficult in any season. However, when enemies attack and adversaries let loose, this trust is harder than usual. And when the cry goes up to God for help and it goes unanswered, then it seems that trust must be broken. In this Psalm it is not so.

Out of utter agony the question comes. "Why are you so far from helping me?" "I cry by day, but you do not answer, and by night, but find no rest...." For most people, the lack of response in a time of terror would cut the cord. The monologue goes something like this. "You want me to trust in you, God? To have faith? Well, then try being trustworthy!" As it turns out, though, the psalmist does not lose trust so easily.

Even as dark forces surround, the whispered utterance comes. "Yet you are holy."

Abandoned, alone, suffering terribly and still faith survives. It begs the question of how long we would hold out in the same situation. Battered, bruised, and beaten with our prayers for aid continually unanswered, how long would it take for us to fold?

The eager and the misty-eyed will quickly step up and swear that they will never lose faith. "No matter what, Lord, I will never lose my faith in you!" The truth, though, is that it takes stern stuff to hang in with this God. It takes courage that we never thought we had and persistence that we never tried to exercise.

Maybe it's for this reason that we practice the discipline of God's presence. Perhaps this is why we enter always into prayer and meditation and seek the company of those who will strive with us to strengthen and live out this faith.

Indeed, faith is difficult. It takes courage and strength; boldness and patience. Yet through it all, this God is worthy. Through it all, our faith is never misplaced. Through all this God remains the God of hope, the God of salvation.

Resurrection of Our Lord (Easter Day)

Acts 10:34-43

Colossians 3:1-4

John 20:1-18

by Arthur Kolsti and James A. Nestingen

Promise and fulfillment

Some years ago someone asked me whether I believed that the resurrected Jesus was the Jesus whose corpuscles and muscles and cells and lungs had died and then were miraculously reinflated, reinvested with life, retriggered, and the like. Being a Bible-believer, I said no, because the Bible makes a point of the different character of the Jesus who makes appearances after death. Paul and the gospel writers struggle to find new language to match a new reality, and cannot find it. But they do not want to see the risen Jesus as the same old thing. Ever since, I've read in some of the right-wing press that I disbelieved the resurrection.

There is another way to fall off faith's tightwire: to say that the resurrection was "nothing but ..." a psychological transformation in the disciples. When you hear the word "nothing but" connected with faith, run for the door. The scriptures keep coming forth with narratives, proclamations, and twists that suggest a new kind of reality is present in the resurrection.

Just as important as the newness is the motif that connects the resurrection with the baptized, the believers. We shall see how in the Colossians text the resurrection is not something simply awaited by believers. In some senses it has already occurred. If so, Paul will be telling them, this ought to show. They ought to live different kinds of lives than before.

The Easter cycle that follows rings changes on that notion of new kinds of creation, new kinds of life. I am not sure that the reconstitution of the same old, arthritic, cremated body-in-ashes will do more for hope and love and faith than would resurrection as an idea in the mind of God and of humans. No, correct that: I am sure it would not. All this is new.

Grist For The Mill

Acts 10:34-43

The Hebrew Scriptures, our Old Testament, have few references to resurrection or life to come. Sheol offers little life and no hope. A passage in Isaiah, another in Ezekiel, a miracle resuscitation story or two, a hymnlet in Job — these have to suffice. In the intertestamental period there are witnesses to resurrection within Judaism. But the celebration of a new creation, a resurrection that represents more and other, not less and same, awaits the activity of God in Christ. So for the Easter cycle the first reading comes not from the Old Testament but from preaching in the Book of Acts, much of it referring to roots in the Hebrew Scriptures.

Acts 10 tells the story of "the awakening of Peter," which ought to be as familiar as the Acts narrative of "the conversion of Paul." Both of them are stories about acceptance of vocations. Peter's is an opening to a God who "shows no partiality," but who works among Jews, Gentiles, and Romans like Cornelius. Cornelius, yes, a non-Jew who "feared God," was "well-spoken by the Jewish nation," and more. But he was an unfinished product, so Peter is glimpsed and overheard condensing the gospel, as Luke-Acts digested it.

There is a climax: "They put [Jesus] to death by hanging him on a tree; but God raised him on the third day and allowed him to appear ... to us ... who ate and drank with him after he rose from the dead." The New Testament can be read as a library occasioned by what was referred to in those two lines. Many events in the gospel antecede the death and resurrection, but most would not have been recorded or preserved apart from the hanging and raising. With good reason we pay attention to the readings that follow.

Colossians 3:1-4

People who grow up with New Testament preaching tend to have learned how to live with a jumbling of tenses. Past, future, present, future, past: they tumble together and seem to fall randomly. The preacher has to take some pains helping newcomers sort out or old-timers think through these juxtapositions. Commentaries are full of word combinations like "having and not having," "now and not-yet," "having and hoping," and the like.

Once the resurrection of Christ occurs, the deliberate, sometimes casual, sometimes formal mixing of tense usages increases. In the present case, people alive at Colossae are being told that they "have died," mine, as they say. Their lives are hidden with Christ in God. But they will be revealed with Christ in glory when he is revealed.

What sense does that make? Very much, as soon as one gets clear the understanding of Paul that faith in Christ, baptism in Christ, and identification with Christ mean that in real senses death is already behind. God looks at one in this identification with Christ. The Colossians are supposed to, too.

Scholars call sections like this "paranesis." This pattern of moral injunction, advice on how to be and to be good, can turn quite boring in the modern pulpit. Now, in the last three minutes, all the predictable and forgettable things get said. Not so in the letter to the Colossians.

Paul interrupts quiet talk about how to live with a shattering, dazzling vision of the future because the reader or hearer has died. Comedian Woody Allen once said he did not mind death so much; he just didn't want to be around when it happened. The Colossians had been around when it happened, and now their lives were "hid with Christ in God." So it goes, still.

John 20:1-18

A strange phrase colors the Johannine Easter story, a story enlivened by the poignant scene between Mary Magdalene, who mistakes Jesus for the gardener, and Jesus, risen, not a gardener. That phrase says that "as yet they [Peter and the Beloved Disciple] did not understand the scripture, that he must rise from the dead."

We who read scriptures written decades after the event, documents that come to our attention centuries after the event, cannot think our way back into the world of the disciples, as described in the gospels. Certainly, in the evangelists' telling, Jesus threw out enough clues what the scriptures had written about — scriptures has to mean our Old Testament — was to be fulfilled in his rising. Still, we have found few anticipations of resurrections in the Old Testament and very few that could connect with Jesus. (For clues, look in Acts 2:4-28, next Sunday, or Luke 24, two Sundays from now).

Now, Mary has come to the tomb, and had seen it open; she has run to have her vision of things confirmed. The beloved disciple, favored in this gospel, won the race to the tomb but was deferential and let Peter look in. The "other disciple" believed; Peter did not, being among those who did not yet understand the scriptures.

Finding an empty tomb by itself was not the great event. Finding the tomb empty as a confirmation of scriptural promise made all the difference. Not that someone rose from the dead mattered. Who it was, and why it was, that the one who "must rise from the dead" had risen from the dead was the point from which proclamation began, and faith grew. Promise and fulfillment, scriptural anticipation and event: these connected for the first believers.

FIRST LESSON FOCUS

By James A. Nestingen

Acts 10:34-43

Being forgiven is a little bit like falling in love — it is only after the fact that a person realizes, with joy, how it exceeds all sense of expectation.

The ecumenical and liturgical theologians responsible for the lectionary apparently declared that such expectation, and anything else that might be found in the Old Testament, is out of place in the Easter season. So they have set it aside in favor of texts from the Book of Acts. Eschatology generally doesn't have much place when ecclesiology takes over.

But the Apostle Peter, even in the more idealized portrait presented in Acts, isn't going to be bound by these or any other restraints. He is alive with the hope of the resurrection to the point where it is spilling over the edges of his sermon, particularly as he speaks of the gift of Good Friday and Easter, "that everyone who believes in him receives forgiveness of sins through his name" (v. 43).

It could be argued that there would have been good reason for Peter's appetite for forgiveness. The gospels single him out in the accounts of passion week, devoting particular attention to his behavior through the tribulations that beset Jesus. So we hear him swearing loyalty and then snoring in the Garden of Gethsemane, see him pulling a sword on an unprepared soldier and then later betraying his Lord before a young woman tending a fire. Peter the Rock became Peter the Shale before it was over.

Forgiveness would be about his only protection. He knew what he needed and so do we, at times.

But this is where the gestalt, need-fulfillment, problem-solution structure of common assumption breaks down. No doubt forgiveness does have a way of fulfilling a need. But lovers know what those sunk deep in the forgiveness of sin also discover:

> *that there is more to the relationship than the fulfillment of personal need, a remarkably shallow way to talk of something — better, somebody — so rich.*

Forgiveness is a matter of clearing a disturbed past, but the clearance is for the sake of the future, particularly for the sake of living in the constancy of an undisturbed love of the one responsible for the relationship itself. It is a gift worth dying for, dying and rising, in fact, so that our crucified and risen Lord appears to us in his Easter enthronement as Lord of all. He now holds both past and future in his hands, restoring one, bestowing the other on the basis of his sheer, abounding grace.

Second Sunday of Easter
Acts 2:14a; 22-32
1 Peter 1:3-9
John 20:19-31
by David Coffin

Pound of flesh demanded

It is the time of year for the last push of demands before the summer season beckons upon the horizon. The children's school system is squeezing in as many meetings as possible for parents. Teachers are trying to push assignment and test dates before the even warmer days arrive in May and June. Many church organizations have their denominational gathering about this time of year. They have business they hope to have wrapped up so staff and volunteers can take the summer off out of the area or on mission trips.

Some people are still paying off their credit cards from the holidays. Other families are experiencing a sudden surge of bill collectors, advertisers, and volunteer organizations requiring their time, money, or commitments. This is the time of year that many groups demand a major pound of flesh in whatever form that takes. Easter Sunday was last week. Now what? Not many people get days off from work or school aside from "Good Friday." It is as if the daily grind and rat race resumes the Monday morning after Easter eggs, new clothing, and for some the biannual trip to "church" (until Christmas). The "constant" in this universe liturgically is the remembered "Doubting Thomas" text in John 20:19-31. However, these texts address those people and families who are living in the reality when a pound of flesh is demanded from their daily lives and personal resources.

Acts 2:14a; 22-32

It is the same thing, different day at any given workplace, school, and family or community environment. So what has actually changed if it is "Easter" or the season of a "new life"? As a matter of fact, the Messiah who rode into Jerusalem about a week ago has been arrested and executed. There was no "Arab Spring" of a change in political powers as occurred in the Middle East some time ago. Peter, the disciple who denied Jesus three times, has a newfound courage and preaches to the Judeans in Acts 2:14. The Roman empire who exacts heavy taxes and burdens upon people, or a "pound of flesh," has indeed been defeated. How does one declare Easter to the average peasant, ship's galley slave like in the movie *Ben Hur*, or household who still has to work much of the day for food?

The good news is that Jesus' dead body was never found by the Roman officials. The body remains gone! Peter and 120 people had witnessed the risen Jesus and his Ascension (Acts 1:15), which would be a credible measurement if any Roman tax census takers had happened to be there that day. So chalk one up for the people of the new Lord Jesus, and minus one for the lord of the Roman empire. Add to this that it was God's plan all along, according to Peter.

For David says concerning him, "I saw the Lord always before me, for he is at my right hand so that I will not be shaken" (Acts 2:25; taken from Psalm 110:1). Also "foreseeing this, David spoke of the resurrection of the Messiah, saying, 'He was not abandoned to Hades, nor did his flesh experience corruption,' " applied as being a fulfillment of Psalm 16:10. David also has a prophetic role (as well as monarch and priestly offices) in the eyes of the people of faith (vv. 25, 30). The God of the Hebrew

Bible (Old Testament) is not asleep on the job. In this Easter season, this God is active right now in the resurrection of Jesus as the Christ who has defeated sin, death, and that which represents death to anybody of any time era. This might include the loss of a job, family, house, value of higher education (with loans still due!), as well as health concerns. To a world that still exacts a pound of flesh from hard-working, sincere, faithful people, Jesus or God's Messiah has beat the system at the grave. This Jesus is raised up (v. 32).

God was at work through this Jesus of Nazareth (v. 22) and remains at work through him. God had planned this since the earlier Hebrew Bible times and is now carrying out these plans. Whoever has a faith in this God also shares this God's new life after every death. No longer does one have to worry if their faith in Jesus will disappoint them before or at the grave. A "spiritual community" that supersedes any institutional structures has risen that practices unconditional love and new life after every death. While the lords of this world demand another pound of flesh for whatever returns they may or may not deliver, this Lord of Easter provides new life.

This text is also a support for the creedal phrase of "he descended into hell (or the dead)." Scholars still contest if this is a strong enough text to support such a creedal claim, but it is a viable interpretation for many scholars of the church. There was also a popular belief that souls went to the land of the dead (Sheol) for a short period; then to their eternal destiny. Luke believes that period must have been short because Jesus told the repentant thief "Today you will be with me in paradise" (Luke 23:43). This Jesus is Messiah because his body was not decomposed like that of the deceased King David of Israel.

Though the Easter candy, eggs, and dinner have been mostly digested by the family and guests, the body of Jesus is still gone. More than 120 people who saw the risen Jesus are sticking to their story. The very energy-sucking group who are demanding a pound of flesh on this spring day might well be gone when autumn or winter arrives this same year. But Christians still have new life. This is the good news of Easter. [Sources: Ernst Haenchen, *The Acts of the Apostles: A Commentary*(Westminster Press, 1971); Paul Tillich, *Systematic Theology, Volume 3*(University of Chicago Press, 1963)]

1 Peter 1:3-9

So, how does one keep rejoicing while they are still enduring hard times, trials, and threats upon their lives, income, or way of living in the foreseeable future? It is still Easter, the season of new life. The communities of 1 Peter's epistle were exiles in dispersion (1 Peter 1:1-2). Authorship for the epistle is contested between the apostle himself and a pseudonymous writer of a following generation. One moderating position might be that Silvanus, one of the early Christian followers of that time, had written these words on Peter's behalf (Kelly, pp. 32-33). This question does not minimize the content of the text.

The threefold results of being baptized into the household of faith include: 1) A living hope made possible through Jesus being raised from the grave, 2) an inheritance in heaven that cannot be destroyed, and 3) salvation that is being revealed through the risen Christ. God is guarding the Christians through his power in the new age, but this does not insulate Christians from being tested and suffering.

First Peter's response to the basic "theodicy" question of righteous suffering by believers is that such trials serve to purify people in the genuineness of their faith. The metaphor of refining gold through the fiery tests is used to show how faith in Jesus Christ is refined in a similar manner. So if a person is going through many trials in any given community, 1 Peter's response would it that this refines one's faith and shows the genuineness of what they actually believe. Such faith is even more pure than gold. This should be reason for rejoicing.

Salvation of the soul occurs now; this is another reason for rejoicing in times of trial. While there is a future sense of this glory and honor when Jesus Christ is revealed (v. 7), there is reason to be confident that this Christ and the eternal inheritance will not let Christians down. Some authors believe that this is a catechism formula from an unknown source, which both Paul and Peter have drawn. Also verse 8's reference to "although you have not seen him, you love him; and even though you do not see him now" might suggest that this text is written to a later generation of Christians. This is not a necessary conclusion, but it is a viable option that could suggest that the readers are of a later generation who continue to experience local and possibly governmental suffering.

For people who feel as if others are always trying to take "a pound of flesh" by demanding more time, money, commitments, and other resources, 1 Peter says this is another way of testing the genuine nature of one's faith. Therefore they should rejoice that their sufferings point to an inheritance that is kept for them. This might be one response to the theodicy question of "righteous people suffering." Any church, community group, or people who seem to always encounter one set of problems after another may be comforted that such experiences are ways to refine their faith in the crucified and risen Jesus Christ. Hence, though it is Easter season, the shadow of the cross remains present in the form of continual times of testing and suffering. This is the basic response of 1 Peter to the any would-be "Job" situations in our midst. [Source: J.N.D. Kelly, *Thornapple Commentaries: A Commentary on the Epistles of Peter and Jude*(Baker Book House, 1969)]

John 20:19-31

One of the "constants" in the lectionary universe remains the "Doubting Thomas" text on the Sunday after Easter. The text has at least three basic themes to it, so if desired one is not forced to dwell on the Thomas theme. The text opens with the disciples being locked behind closed doors in the evening for fear of the "Jews" (or I prefer the trend to call them the "Judeans"). Then Jesus appears in their presence to wish them "peace." In any time of stress, worry, or fear for one's well-being, the message of "peace" from a risen God in the flesh (1:1-14) is welcome. This theme recurs in verses 21 and 26. This is an opportunity to preach about God's wholesome peace that makes one complete and fills their inner emptiness or "estrangement" from realizing their place in the cosmos as well as with humankind. John 10:10 declares that Jesus comes to provide abundant life both in quantity and quality. This is one train of good news in this text. There are still other strands one may pursue.

John's "Pentecost" is here, where Jesus breathes the Holy Spirit into the disciples (v. 22). This is immediately followed by the church's call to forgive or retain the sins of people. One of the implications of this command is the question of which sins were around in the New Testament times and which ones had not even occurred to the writers. Are congregations facing issues that are not so black-and-white and do require some reflection, discernment, and rethinking of what is considered "sinful" and what is not "sinful"? Another way to split hairs here is to suggest that all of humanity is fallen; which areas of this fallen nature are subject to forgiveness (with repentance)? Since the age of the enlightenment, science, and so on, how does the church discern what Martin Luther called its "Office of the Keys"? Examples of such areas might include: marriage and divorce, sexuality issues, economic realities that lead to bankruptcy, genetic concerns for repopulation of the planet, and "what if" there is life on other planets in the universe. The Holy Spirit of Jesus the Christ will not leave us "orphaned or parentless" (14:18). In fact, this Holy Spirit continues to remind and teach the community of faith Jesus' ways (14:25-26). It can also be seen as the beginning of a "mission" for the church from John's perspective. Depending on how theologically savvy people wish to be on this Sunday, there is still another theme.

When he finally realizes who Jesus is, Thomas answered him, "My Lord and my God!" (v. 28). Coupled with such texts as John 1:14, there is a solid case for both the Holy Trinity, as well as the deity of Christ — in forms of a high Christology (i.e.: Jesus is God for John). Verse 31 states that the purpose of this writing is "so that you may come to believe that Jesus is the Messiah, the Son of God, and that through believing you may have life in his name." The Messiah is being defined in John as God in the flesh that brings peace or completion to those whose lives lack meaning. This Messiah dwells with humans in a Holy Spirit. And this Messiah is none other than God in the flesh. This strand of thought could elicit a sermon on "who exactly is this Jesus for us today?" Do people really want a "God" that fulfills John's vision for a deity or is there is a stronger temptation to sidestep the Johannine writings and simply create one's own personal deity in life?

The detail of Thomas, the twin, is unique in the gospels. Many articles have been written to suggest that his "doubt" is actually the other side of "deeper faith" once he realizes who Jesus really is as God in the flesh. This text also famously reminds Christians of succeeding generations that even though they have not seen Jesus in the flesh personally, "Blessed are those who have not seen and yet have come to believe" (v. 29). Apocryphal works suggest that Thomas was the patron saint in the nation of India and was skinned alive for his confession in Jesus as the Christ. This might put the "Doubting Thomas" label to rest permanently if preached in a passionate manner. This text also invites people of faith to seek out and become friends with doubters of any notion of faith, religion, or a deity on the job, at school, in the community, or with one's relatives at a social gathering. [Source: George R. Beasley-Murray, *World Biblical Commentary: John*(Word Books, 1987)]

Application

For people who are living under some form of stress or worry, all three texts commend themselves as "good news" for the weary, even though the calendar says it is still the Easter season. Acts 2 reminds us that the same God of King David whom the prophet Samuel anointed (1 Samuel 16) remains active and provides new life to those whose lives are tangled up in balls of endless demands and worries that mercilessly exact a pound of flesh from their sore bodies. First Peter 1 is a reminder to those who have asked to "grow spiritually" that this is accomplished through trials and sufferings. John 20 assures believers of all times that the Holy Spirit continues to breathe in new life every day, as God continues to want all people to have peace and fulfillment through the risen Jesus.

An Alternative Application

Acts 2 asks the question if God can do a new thing that is not from Moses. How is newness defined today? Do people simply want the past revisited, or are they prepared for a truly new reality? In the Roman empire of 1 Peter's epistles it was a "winner takes all" economy where Rome was the enforcer and beneficiary of the lands conquered. Suppose true blessing was found in suffering? Are Christians prepared for the possibility of seeing their church basements without children, bills overdue, inability to pay a pastor, and then eventual closing of their building as God blessing them through trials and sufferings? While John's gospel ends on a positive account, the latter Johannine epistles paint a picture of more problems. Yet the Holy Spirit is available to remind and teach the church about new life every day of the year!

Third Sunday of Easter

Acts 2:14a, 36-41

1 Peter 1:17-23

Luke 24:13-35

by Ron Love

A time to reflect

Jimmy Carter, in his memoir *An Hour Before Daylight*, recounted the number of tramps that frequented their home in depression-era Georgia. He admired his mother who never turned one away, always providing food and water for the unexpected guests. Equally admirable, in the eyes of the future president, was that most of these men were polite, honest, and educated, sincerely on a quest to find gainful employment. Confused by the unusual number of visitors she received, Mrs. Lillian Carter inquired with the matron of the neighboring farm as to the number who frequented her residence. "None," replied the neighbor.

The next time a vagrant visited, Carter's mother asked why they came to her home and not others along the dirt road. The gentleman replied that they placed a symbol on the mail posts of households that would not mistreat them. After his visit mother and son went to the post and discovered some unobtrusive scratches, and "Mama told us not to change them." The Carter household would always be one of hospitality.

Hospitality, friendliness, and the fellowship of the flock have always been associated with sheep. Perhaps this is one of the reasons they are an endeared animal at a child's petting zoo. The lamb has always been a symbol of innocence, meekness, lowliness, kindness, and gentleness of life that would never cause hurt to another. It is these distinguished attributes of a lamb that readily avail themselves to symbolically representing Christians. In Christian writings the symbol of a lamb has been weaved into the life of Jesus. The word "lamb" has in it all the mercy, purity, and innocence which belonged to the life of Jesus of Nazareth.

This calling should not escape us as followers of the lamb. On the doorposts before our hearts there must be inscribed the symbol that friends and strangers alike are welcomed, that none will be turned away. Humbly, we extend ourselves in service administering to the most basic needs, be they physical or spiritual. Companionship becomes our byword.

The three lectionary readings this Sunday all speak to the same message — we are forgiven. The blood of the lamb is upon our doorposts, the blood of the lamb is heard in our sermons, the blood of the lamb is found on our communion table. It is the blood of redemption, forgiveness, and new life. It is present, but we must first be able to see it, we next must be able to comprehend it, and lastly we must be willing to accept it. At that moment — at the moment of acceptance — we realize and actualize our redemption.

Acts 2:14a, 36-41

Jesus has been crucified, resurrected, and finally ascended to heaven. Peter is left as the keeper of the keys — the *de facto* leader of the church. The story of Jesus could have ended at this point, but Peter was convinced and overcome with the in dwelling of the Holy Spirit to allow this not to be the last chapter. With the departure of Judas and the selection of Matthias, the church moved forward into the world. Though Peter directs his sermon to the Jews, it is really a global message that Jesus is the

Messiah. Though Peter is strong in speech he is not antagonistic, for those who heard him were "cut to the heart" and became believers. They became believers only when they accepted the invitation to "repent and be baptized."

1 Peter 1:17-23

Peter writes that the final assurance for the forgiveness of our sins has come upon us. We no longer hold to the legalism of Judaism but accept for ourselves the free gift of salvation that comes through the death and resurrection of Jesus. The blood of the lamb no longer needs to be smeared on our doorposts but now is on our hearts. From the beginning of creation we had waited for this moment, this place in time, for our final redemption. Through the rituals of Judaism we have been preparing for this moment, and now it has come upon us. We now have in Jesus the perfect lamb, the perfect sacrifice without blemish, for the forgiveness of our sins. What is required of us is "obedience to the truth."

Luke 24:13-35

It was three weeks after the ascension and people were still dismayed, in disbelief, and questioning. Could Jesus possibly be the chosen messiah for the people of Israel? Two men, accompanied by a third, a stranger, were on a seven-mile walk to the village Emmaus. It was a long walk at a leisurely pace, which allowed for much discussion. It seems that day the conversation consuming them was the same that was being discussed throughout Jerusalem — was Jesus the Messiah or should we look for another? It was only when they took the time to pause at the table, to seriously look at the guest among them, and to break bread with him that they came to understand. Their realization did not come from a dialogue or a theological discourse, but rather when they paused and entered into a meaningful fellowship.

Application

Why Jesus had to be crucified is often asked and debated. The discussion can now end, for John provides the answer: As the priests were making sin offerings in the temple square, God was making the conclusive sin offering on the cross. As blood was shed to avenge the Angel of Death of the firstborn, blood was now shed for the ultimate deliverance of all God's children. Jesus was being executed at exactly the same time as the Passover lambs were being slaughtered in the temple. The priests who haughtily enforced the death of the Lamb of God recessed to the temple to commence the legalistic sacrifice of the paschal lambs. Beyond question, the symbolism is that Jesus is God's Passover Lamb, sacrificed for the deliverance of God's people. Jesus is the culmination of the sacrificial system, never to be repeated, only to be remembered and revered. This is why Peter could confess that we were ransomed from our sins as the new revelation. It was for this reason that Peter could preach to the Jews and the entire world community to repent and be baptized. It is the reason why two men recognized the stranger among them. It is the same timeless message that we are to share this day.

An Alternative Application

Though Jesus did come as our Savior and his sacrificial death did redeem us from our sins, there is still a personal responsibility associated with the event. We must listen to the sermon and repent and be baptized. We must be obedient to the new truth and be born anew. We must be willing to walk, listen, pause, and believe. The gift of salvation is before us. We must be willing to accept it.

Fourth Sunday of Easter
Acts 2:42-47
1 Peter 2:19-25
John 10:1-10
by Wayne Brouwer

Easter living

"A grave is a sobering thing," said Wordsworth. We try to mark each with snippets of meaning that will defuse the scandalous superficiality of life that Emily bemoaned in Thornton Wilder's *Our Town*. "If I was so quickly done for," asks the wee voice etched on a child's grave memorial, "what on earth was I begun for?"

Ancient Romans tossed away the scandal of our brief and meaningless lives. When archaeologists first sifted through grave yards of the early centuries of the great empire, they were caught up short by a plethora of burial plot stones inscribed with the same seven letters: **N F F N S N C**. These certainly spelled no known Latinword, and other connections escaped would-be interpreters. Until, that is, they uncovered older quadrants of cemeteries where many grave markers carried seven-word inscriptions beginning with these otherwise meaningless letters: *Non Fui. Fui. Non Sum. Non Curo.* Suddenly the intent was clear. So many Romans had found this phrase as the best representation of life and death that even poor people with small stones could abbreviate it down to just seven letters and all would understand: "I was not. I was. I am not. I don't care."

Tragic. Cynical. Hopeless.

I have officiated at hundreds of funerals over the past 35 years and never met a family that would have dared place that testimony over the grave of a loved one. We cry. We weep. We wail. One young man even jumped on top of the casket as it was being lowered into the cold earth, pounding in horrible grief on the unforgiving final home of his brother's body.

Even when death is "good," and an elderly grandmother slips willingly from time into eternity, tears of loss trace our cheeks. We were born to live, not to die.

This is the theme of each of our lectionary texts today, on this fourth Sunday of Easter. "Life" emanates and oozes from the new community of Jesus' followers in Pentecostal Jerusalem. Even when life gets tough with suffering, Peter reminds us to live in the footsteps of the resurrected Jesus', who promises more and a better life to come. And Jesus himself calls on us to shift our focus from the wary wolves and even bad shepherd death by hearing his voice and following him into pastures of life.

Acts 2:42-47

There is something wonderfully paradoxical about the Christian church. Its origin as a unique social phenomenon clearly dates from the Pentecost events described in Acts 2. Yet at the same time, Jesus› disciples, who were at the center of the church from its very beginning, would say that this "new" community of faith was simply part of a centuries-old, already-existing people of God, stretching back all the way to Abraham and his family. The connection between the old and the new is rooted in several theological axioms.

First, it is built upon the confession that there is a God who created this world and uniquely fashioned the human race with attributes that reflected its maker. Second, through human willfulness the world lost its pristine evitality and is now caught up in a civil war against its Creator. Third, intruding directly into human affairs for the sake of reclaiming and restoring the world, the Creator began a mission of redemption and renewal through the nation of Israel. Fourth, Israel's identity as a missional community was shaped by the suzerain-vassal covenant formed at Mount Sinai. Fifth, in order to be most effective in its witness to other nations, Israel was positioned at the crossroads of global societies, and thus received as its "promised land" the territory known as Canaan. Sixth, the effectiveness of this divine missional strategy through Israel was most evident in the tenth century BC, during the reigns of David and Solomon, when the kingdom grew in size and influence among the peoples of the ancient near east and beyond. Seventh, this missional witness eroded away, almost to oblivion, through a combination of internal failures and external political threats until most of the nation of Israel was wiped out by the Assyrians, and only a remnant of the tribe of Judah (along with religious leaders from among the Levites, and a portion of the small tribe of Benjamin) retained its unique identity as the people of Yahweh. Eighth, because of the seeming inadequacy of this method of witness as the human race expanded rapidly, the Creator revised the divine missional strategy and interrupted human history in a visible manner again in the person of Jesus. Ninth, Jesus embodied the divine essence, taught the divine will, and went through death and resurrection to establish a new understanding of eschatological hope, which he passed along to his followers as the message to be communicated to the nations. Tenth, Jesus' teachings about this arriving messianic age were rooted in what the prophets of Israel called the "Day of the Lord," a time when divine judgment for sins would fall on all nations (including Israel), a remnant from Israel would be spared to become the restored seed community of a new global divine initiative, and the world would be transformed as God had intended for it to be so that people could again live out their intended purposes and destinies. Eleventh, instead of applying all aspects of this "Day of the Lord" in a single cataclysmic event, Jesus split it in two, bringing the beginnings of eternal blessings while withholding the full impact of divine judgment for a time. Twelfth, the Christian church is God's new agent for global missional recovery and restoration for the human race, superseding the territorially bound witness through Israel with a portable and expanding testimony influencing all nations and cultures. Thirteenth, since the "Day of the Lord" is begun but not finished, Jesus will return again to bring its culmination. Fourteenth, the church of Jesus exists in this time between Jesus' comings as the great divine missional witness.

Each of these themes is implied or explicit in the first two chapters of the book of the Acts of the Apostles. God and sin and the divine mission are all part of the fabric of the narrative, while Israel's role in the divine mission, along with the changing strategies, is declared openly. Jesus is at the center of all these things, but the unique divine intrusion he brought into the human race is now being withdrawn as he ascends back to heaven. Now the church must become the ongoing embodiment of Jesus' life and teachings, so that it may live out the divine mission until the remainder of the "Day of the Lord" arrives when Jesus returns. This is the picture in the lectionary reading for today.

1 Peter 2:19-25

About the time that Paul was engaged in his final communications with Timothy and Titus, Peter made his own last swing through churches of northern and eastern Asia Minor. This was quite a trip for an older man to take(exceeding the reach of all of Paul's journeys recorded in Acts), since Peter was based in Rome at the time. He calls Rome "Babylon' (1 Peter 5:13), a code term already circulating throughout the Christian church, hinting at the persecutions looming from the ruling center of the world in a way similar to the Babylonian pressures mounted against Judah centuries before. It may well have been that Peter was invited to officiate at a number of large baptism ceremonies in the congregations to which these letters are written, since Peter's tone is that of instruction for new believers, and baptism is a central concern (1 Peter 3:13-22).

Peter reminds his readers that he was an eyewitness of Jesus' life and sufferings (1 Peter 5:1; see also v. 23) and directly echoes a number of Jesus' teachings in his words (compare 1 Peter 2:12 with Matthew 5:16; 1 Peter 2:21 with Matthew 10:38; 1 Peter 3:14 and 4:13-14 with Matthew 5:10-12). Some scholars believe this letter could not have been written by Peter since its use of the Greek language is too educated, too well crafted. But the double pairs of brothers from the fishing trade in Capernaum that Jesus called to follow him (Peter and Andrew, James and John) probably came from middle-class families where education was important. Moreover, just as Paul had Amanuenses writing out his letters, so in 1 Peter 5:12 the letter-writing skills of Silvanus (a variant of Silas) are recognized. Peter may well have been accomplished in his use of the Greek language, and certainly Peter's letter-writing scribe was.

Peter writes in powerful terms of the great salvation recently brought to humankind by Jesus. This new life is irreversibly guaranteed by way of both Jesus' resurrection and ascension for those who believe (1 Peter 1:3-12). Peter next provides an extended exhortation to holy living, because these believers in Jesus are God's special people (1 Peter 1:13-2:10), who follow in the footsteps of Jesus (1 Peter 2:11-3:12) and must face, with their master, the sufferings that will fall on all his disciples in challenging times (1 Peter 3:12-4:19). Peter gives a special word of encouragement to the elders who lead the various congregations (1 Peter 5:1-4), and then expands these same ideas for the broader community (1 Peter 5:5-11) before closing with brief personal greetings (1 Peter 5:12-14).

The tone of Peter's letter is far darker than any of the writings of Paul. There is an ominous pall of suffering that clouds every perspective. Jesus suffered. You will suffer, if you are faithful. You must follow Jesus in and through suffering. New trials and greater suffering are coming. Whether by way of external hints or from the inner promptings of the Spirit, Peter seems to have been anticipating the sharp clout of Nero's official pogroms just ahead.

Yet through the murky shrieks and sinister valleys, Peter never loses confidence in God's sovereignty or care. God is judge over evil, the ever-faithful Creator, and the chief shepherd who will soon bring untarnished crowns of glory for those who remain true.

John 10:1-10

Archaeologists of ancient Roman artifacts were surprised by some of the memorials found next to the burial niches in the catacombs where Christians laid their dead. There were inscribed verses of scripture, to be sure, but also symbols and pictures. The one, however, that most mystified showed the upper body of a man holding a harp. It seemed to represent Jesus, but standard mythological representations usually tied this one to Orpheus.

Orpheus was the darling of Greek love and music and tragedy. Orpheus was the master musician of his time and well could have had 39 out of the top 40 tunes on the charts at once. When Orpheus sang, the birds swooped in just to flit on his lilting melodies. When Orpheus sang, the clouds rolled back from the skies and the sun shone more brightly and the beasts crept out of the shadows to dance their fancy footwork. When Orpheus came to town, people floated out of homes and shops to jig in the streets and fall in love.

Of course, when Orpheus himself fell in love, passion intensified. It was Eurydice who caught his eye and heart, and before long they were fawning and fainting after one another. When Orpheus and Eurydice wed, the world shimmered with significance, and couples everywhere twitterpated.

But a week later all meaning was lost. While Eurydice romped with her friends through a field, a snake slithered through the grass and struck her heel. Almost instantly Eurydice was gone, robbed of her nascent marriage and life itself.

Deep in grief, the song died in Orpheus' heart. Now he only moaned and groaned, and the world hung heavy with pain. Willows drooped their branches in empathy, and the wild beasts slunk back into the shadows. Dark clouds covered the sun's smile and birds roosted, unable to take flight in the oppressive air.

Orpheus moped and wallowed. Consolation fled. Lament took the orchestra's podium.

Reaching for nerves that rejected grief's cancerous alloy, Orpheus set out on a mission to the undiscovered country. He found the door to the underworld and slid down, down, down, down, down, down into the kingdom of death. Confronting elusive Hades, Orpheus demanded back the woman he had loved too shortly. Hades, of course, would have none of it. His contracts were lethally binding.

So Orpheus did what only he could do. He sang a love song. Strumming his harp, Orpheus put his heart to music in a way that sent shivers through the shifting shades and shadows. As his voice reverberated against the wailing walls, one ghost began to thicken and color. A few more stanzas of amore and Eurydice stood solid before him once again. They kissed and hugged and held hands all the way to earth's surface, gripped by smiles of incredulous ardor.

The legend of Orpheus grew over time so that even the most skeptical linked his name to true love. But why would early Christians reconfigure Jesus in the guise of Orpheus? How could they profane the sacred so scandalously?

Obviously they did not believe in Orpheus. They were martyrs of Christ and traded all trite tales of the marketplace to buy the pearl of great price. But some metaphors command instant understanding, and when these groaning souls recalled the words and deeds of Jesus, it was precisely in the cemetery that conflating Orpheus and Christ made perfect sense.

Christians remembered the day when Jesus traveled to Bethany to mourn his friend Lazarus' death. Jesus should have been there earlier to heal Lazarus of his illness and stay death's untimely call, and everybody knew it. Lazarus' sister Martha came blazing out of the town when she heard that Jesus was approaching. She had sent word of Lazarus' illness to Jesus while there was still time for the great one to make a difference, like he did with so many others throughout Palestine. But Jesus had dithered and dallied, and now Martha was angry.

"If you had been here my brother wouldn't have had to die!" she shouted at Jesus. He knew she was right and did not try to defend himself. In great grief they lumbered slowly to the family home. Professional wailers at the door assaulted their ears, accusing Jesus with fiery eyes. Stooping to enter, Jesus found the other sibling, Mary, covered with torn rags and ashes. "If you had been here my brother wouldn't have had to die!" she simpered, cutting Jesus deeper than her sister's diatribe.

Jesus cared without self-defense and brought his entourage out to the cemetery. Only a week before he had inspired the Galilee crowds with his delightful homily about shepherds, getting knowing nods about the nasty hirelings who lead sheep astray and bring them into the fold of death, the baddest shepherd of all. Leaning on the best of Israelite heritage, Jesus mounted the shoulders of shepherd boy/King David and reclaimed the dignity of the office Ezekiel celebrated in chapter 34 of his prophecy. Jesus said his sheep knew his voice and would follow him anywhere. He also mentioned, cryptically, that he had other sheep — not of the flock in front of him — and that he had to go and call them.

The disciples must have thought about these things as they now stood with Jesus in the local cemetery. He challenged the keepers of the place, demanding that they roll back the stone covering the carved cavern where Lazarus' body had been laid, allowing the maggots to do their work. The cemetery tenders shook their heads. "You don't want to do that," they replied. "He stinks!"

But Jesus repeated his request with demanding authority and the workers shrugged. When the grave yawned, it burped death's stench. Only Jesus did not cringe and retreat. Standing resolutely in the land of the living, he cried out with the voice of the Good Shepherd to his friend now taken captive in death's dark fold: "Lazarus!" And down, down, down, down, down, down, down in the depths of the netherworld, owned by that baddest of the bad shepherds, death itself, Lazarus heard his master's voice and came through the dark window of the grave to stand once again in the sun next to his shepherd.

This is why the Christians in Rome conflated the myth of Orpheus with the reality of Jesus. They did not trust in human legends. But they did hang their hopes on the one who said to Martha and Mary "I am the resurrection and the life!" and then proved it that day in Bethany. In fact, the Roman Christians knew that Jesus had confirmed all of this a short while after the incidents of John 10-11 when he himself went down, down, down, down, down, down, down into the depth of death and came up again on Easter morning as the Lord of life.

Now, as wives bade farewell to husbands who had been torn apart by the beasts in the Coliseum, as children wrapped the bodies of parents in burial clothes, as friends mourned the deaths of their kindred spirits, the great metaphor of Jesus as the true Orpheus told the most magnificent promise of all. For even in these dark days of deathly haunts, followers of Jesus knew that one time soon the good and great shepherd would shout the names of their loved ones down to Hades itself, and even though captured in shepherd death's lockdown fold, their family and friends would hear their master's voice, and they would rise to life and follow him into the eternal kingdom.

We all try to evade and fool death, stymying him with tummy tucks and fleeing him through our exercise routines and vitamins. But come death shall with fateful inclusiveness, whispering our names at night or noon, and against our wheedling and pleading will march us into his awful gloom. Then the hope of our faith will endure its final test. For if the gospel is true, our good and great and chief shepherd will not forget us but will march down, down, down, down, down, down, down to Sheol and sing us his song of love. We, who know the voice of our master, with rise into the dawn of eternity and follow the one who calls us by name.

Application

Leslie Weatherhead once called Christianity "the religion of the dawn." He pointed to the first dawning of light at creation as the irreversible testimony of God to this world. "It is a religion of unquenchable faith and hope and patience; unquenchable because it believes that the permanent thing is light and the passable thing is darkness; that however long the night, whether it be in world affairs or the poignant private world of the human heart, the night will pass." He pointed to the astounding power of Easter dawn. "After the great darkness, this amazing dawn! Within seven weeks they — the hunted, frightened fugitives — had become flaming missionaries and willing martyrs ready to lay down their lives rather than deny the truth of his risen glory and his transforming power... From the East the dawn-light spread across the skies of the world. The religion of the dawn!"

On this fourth Sunday of Easter, in the light of that great resurrection event, we glow in the prophetic grace of our Lord, who said of us: "You are the light of the world!"

An Alternative Application

John 10:1-10. Some years ago, the pastor of a Presbyterian congregation in Mendota, Illinois, decided that the church's nativity scene needed a little repair work. The shepherd figures held staffs made of electrical conduit, bent and rebent and kinked over the years.

"Let's get real ones," he thought. But no farm supply store had such a thing. Intrigued, the pastor asked around until he gained the name of a man who not only owned a large herd of sheep, but was also an expert on their care.

"Where can I get a genuine shepherd's staff?" he asked.

"Nowhere," came the reply. "You have to remember that here in the west, sheep are *driven* by dogs. It's only in the east that they are *led* by a shepherd."

Ours often seems to be a driven society. The ideals of the French Revolution have permeated our culture: Life! Liberty! Land! We North Americans have turned the last into a steady pleasure trip by translating it this way: the pursuit of happiness. All too often we're scrambling after more and better and bigger thrills.

One picture from the French Revolution, with its mob mania, perhaps best typifies the whole enterprise of western life. A wild-eyed man comes charging up to a citizen pausing on a Paris street corner.

"Where's the crowd?" he cries. "Tell me, quick! Which way have they gone? I must follow them. I'm their leader."

Driven by madness! Driven by the dogs! The dogs of desire, the dogs of fame and fortune, the dogs of war... It's a dog-eat-dog world.

Maybe it's time to return to the east. Not the east of mysticism and transcendental meditation, helpful as they might be, but rather the one who grew up in the east, the one called "the good shepherd" (John 10:1-18), "the great shepherd" (Hebrews 13:20-21), and "the chief shepherd" (1 Peter 5:4). Maybe it's time to stop being driven and be led again in the simplicity of devotion.

Fifth Sunday of Easter
Acts 7:55-60
1 Peter 2:2-10
John 14:1-14
by David Kalas

Not only the builders

Take a survey of your congregation. Ask your folks to list their favorite Bible verses. It would be interesting, for starters, to see what percentage comes from the Old Testament. My guess is that the Old Testament would not be represented proportionately — that is to say, though the Old Testament comprises about two thirds of the Bible, I doubt that it would account for two thirds of our people's favorite verses.

Meanwhile, of the folks who did choose a verse from the Old Testament, I wonder if any would cite Psalm 118:22. Probably not. And yet that seemingly obscure verse from the book of Psalms is arguably one of the favorite verses of the writers of the New Testament.

Five different times Psalm 118:22 appears in the New Testament. Matthew, Mark, and Luke all include the episode from Jesus' ministry when he cited that verse at the conclusion of the parable of the tenants. Peter challenges the members of the council with that provocative verse in Acts 4. And he celebrates the truth of it later in our epistle lection.

The verse considers a certain stone. Though there is no extended metaphor, the guiding image is of a building project. We can imagine the scene, therefore, as the eligible materials are gathered and piled at the work site. Certain men, presumably expert in their craft, are in charge of the whole enterprise. They are the builders, and they evaluate each quarried stone to see whether it is suitable for the project.

All of that would have been standard operating procedure, of course. Under ordinary circumstances we would not presume any crookedness or malevolence on the part of such builders. They would simply try to make the best choices for the project at hand. And, in the course of their work, the psalmist sees one particular stone that those builders rejected.

But then comes the surprising turn of events. "The stone that the builders rejected," the psalmist reports, "has become the chief cornerstone" (Psalm 118:22). It is an improbable ascension from the scrap heap to the spot of greatest prominence, from being left out of the building to occupying the place of greatest significance in that building. What prompted such an unlikely reversal? "This is the Lord's doing; it is marvelous in our eyes" (v. 23).

It is hard to imagine just what the psalmist had in mind when he penned those words a thousand or so years before the time of Christ. But Jesus declared the fulfillment of the psalmist's prophetic words, and Peter reiterated the truth. And now, this week, we may lead our people in considering that stone and the risk of rejecting it.

Acts 7:55-60

Our passage begins with two characteristic Luke-isms. First, he describes Stephen as "being full of the Holy Spirit." Then he reports that Stephen "gazed intently into heaven."

As we read the gospel of Luke and its companion volume, Acts, we recognize how prominent the Holy Spirit is in Luke's narratives. Specifically, that there is no higher recommendation Luke can give a person than to say he or she is filled with the Spirit. Five times in his two books Luke refers to people as "full of the Holy Spirit" and nine times as "filled with the Holy Spirit."

Meanwhile, the Greek word *atenizo* appears just fourteen times in the New Testament, and twelve of those times it is used by the narrator Luke. He uses it here to characterize Stephen's gaze into heaven, and it suggests no ordinary looking. There are simpler, more common words to describe someone looking or seeing. But Luke chooses this term that suggests a special kind of intensity.

What Stephen sees is astonishing — perhaps even unprecedented. Several English translations eschew the prepositions "to" and "toward" for the more provocative "into." Stephen "gazed intently into heaven." This is not merely looking upward, you see. Stephen is enjoying a peek into another realm.

Reginald Heber famously sang, "Holy, holy, holy! Though the darkness hide thee; though the eye of sinful man thy glory may not see..." ("Holy, Holy, Holy"). That human limitation did not apply to Stephen, however. While by every ordinary measure Stephen was in an unfavorable spot, from where he stood he saw the glory of God. We'll consider that paradox in more detail below.

Meanwhile, what Stephen saw — and shared — only exacerbated the anger of the crowd around him. It is hard to have a higher Christology than to assert that Jesus is at the right hand of God. But such an affirmation about Jesus was the last thing this zealous mob wanted to hear. So, in a scene that would seem laughably juvenile if not for its consequences, "they covered their ears, and with a loud shout all rushed together against him."

Then began the stoning. Stephen is known as the first Christian martyr, and this episode recalls the event. At the human level, of course, it is unsettlingly violent and gory. At the same time, however, we see in the midst of it the beauty of faithfulness, boldness, peace, and love.

Luke is generally regarded as the best storyteller of the four gospel writers, and he shows his flair here too. In the midst of a scene that is dominated by the face of Stephen and a faceless mob, Luke momentarily directs our attention to one other individual. "And the witnesses laid their coats," Luke reports, "at the feet of a young man named Saul." That young man is almost incidental to this episode, and yet this episode evidently was not incidental to that young man. Later, Luke will report that "Saul was ravaging the church" (Acts 8:3) and "breathing threats and murder against the disciples of the Lord" (9:1). So it is that the skillful storyteller introduces us to a face in the crowd that seems unimportant in chapter 7, but who becomes inestimably important in most of the chapters that follow.

Finally, James Montgomery, in his profound hymn meditating on the passion and resurrection of Christ, invites us to "learn of Jesus how to die" ("Go To Dark Gethsemane"). We don't have any textual or circumstantial evidence to suggest that Stephen was a witness to Christ's death, and yet this martyr certainly seemed to learn how to die from his Lord. Acts reports two final words from Stephen as he was being stoned to death and they echo two of Jesus' seven last words (see Luke 23:34, 46). If it is right for the followers of Christ to resemble him in how they live, then it should also be expected that they will resemble him in how they die. Stephen did.

1 Peter 2:2-10

Most children and some adults are known to prefer books with pictures. Our selected text from 1 Peter should have that sort of appeal for us and our congregations. For while Peter's epistle was not illustrated, so far as we know, his language is picturesque. Indeed, it might be most effective to study this passage by thinking of ourselves flipping through a picture book.

On the first page, we see a picture of a baby. It connotes innocence and dependence. In its purity, the baby's needs and wants are both identical and few. And prominent among those needs is milk. Peter says that we should be "like newborn babes," with a wholesome appetite for the spiritual milk that is God's word.

Peter quickly turns the page to a new, second picture. This one is a picture of a stone, and the reference to it being "rejected by men" quickly identifies it as the stone of Psalm 118. That stone is not cast aside for long, though, for it was "chosen and precious in God's sight."

The third picture is built quickly upon the second. Now Peter's audience themselves are brought into the picture, as they are encouraged to be "like living stones." The God who chose the aforementioned rejected stone has a larger building project in mind — "a spiritual house" — and we may be included in it.

We find ourselves flipping the pages quickly as yet another picture is introduced suddenly: "a holy priesthood, to offer spiritual sacrifices." It is for Peter a natural extension of the "spiritual house" theme, for the principle is the same. Our opportunity and calling is to become holy and live in the service of God.

Next, Peter returns to the image of the stone and this time he develops it further. He quotes three Old Testament passages about stones (Isaiah 28:16; Psalm 118:22; Isaiah 8:14) to illustrate two principles. First, there is a stone ordained by God and significant in his plan. Second, how a person responds to that stone makes all the difference. Notably, the stone is "precious" to the believer, just as it was "precious in God's sight" earlier.

This matter of how a person responds to this particular stone is central to our theme this week. Jesus is presented by Peter as a kind of watershed. Those who believe and those who do not believe fall on opposite sides of this stone. So it has always been (see John 1:11-12), and so it will always be until the day comes when every knee shall bow and every tongue confess that Jesus is Lord (Philippians 2:10-11).

The author-illustrator next revisits images of a holy people and a priesthood dedicated in service to God. Yet in the very next moment, there is a recognition that Peter's audience did not begin with such a status. Rather, they were in darkness, but it is by God's gracious call that they have become what they are. Finally, that principle of a people whose status has been changed by God is illustrated by an allusion to Hosea (1:9-10).

This final point is good news indeed. It reminds us that the two groups — those who believe and those who do not; those who accept the "stone" and those who reject him — are not innate and they are not permanent. No one really begins on the right side. But by God's grace, we are called and we are changed.

John 14:1-14

In the course of just a few verses, we find some of the most comforting, most challenging, most encouraging, and most troubling words of Jesus. Here is one person's favorite verse juxtaposed with another's least favorite. And it may be that both people will be in my pews and yours this Sunday.

Our gospel lection comes from John's account of the Last Supper. John's account, we observe, dwarfs what we find in Matthew, Mark, and Luke. Each of them devotes less than a single chapter to this Holy Week episode, while five of John's 21 chapters are given to that single event.

As Jesus speaks to his disciples on this momentous occasion, he is fully aware of what lies ahead. They, in spite of being forewarned in several times and ways, seem completely surprised by what follows. But because Jesus knows, he addresses them out of that knowledge, offering them hope, perspective, and reassurance.

Interestingly, Jesus' chief concern does not seem to be the suffering that awaits him but rather the loss that awaits his followers. He is aware that he is leaving them and so these chapters are filled with promises about the comfort, power, blessings, and fruitfulness that are ahead for them. And he promises them that he will return.

The cherished words of comfort, so often affirmed during funeral and memorial services, reveal both Jesus' going away and his return. The lovely promises are that he leaves to prepare a place for us, he will come back for us, and we will be with him forever. The passage is so familiar; yet its beauty remains inexpressible, full of love, hope, comfort, and heaven.

For as widely embraced as the first three verses of John 14 are, the next three are not so universally welcome. Jesus makes unique claims about himself that some hearers will find offensive. In some instances, any unique claims would be rejected as too sectarian. In other instances, the concern is for those implicitly left out by Christ's claim.

The juxtaposition of these two passages may reveal the consumerist approach that contemporary American Christians take to scripture. We treat the word of God like a buffet, gladly picking what we like and unapologetically passing on what we do not like. Sometimes folks like to disguise or excuse their pick-and-choose methodology by playing Old Testament against New Testament or Paul against Jesus. But here we have two statements from the same person in the same passage; by what intellectually honest hermeneutic may we highlight the one and scratch out the other?

In truth, of course, Jesus' claims and his promises are natural and inseparable companions. There is always a vital relationship between the content of a promise and the identity of the person who makes it. For the value of any promise, after all, is predicated on the ability of its maker to fulfill it. I could promise my daughter that there will be perfect weather for her wedding day, but such a promise is nearly worthless since I have no ability to determine the weather. On the other hand, if I promise to pay for the expenses of that wedding, the promise has some credibility and value.

As part of our larger conversation this week, we are invited to consider the stone that is Christ. It is, at once, rejected by the builders, a stone of offense, yet uniquely chosen by God. That entire spectrum should be kept in mind when we read and preach these distinctive claims of Christ.

Application

In Psalms, the stone is unidentified. In the New Testament, however, it is plainly proclaimed. Jesus is that stone. We are given two salient facts about him: He was rejected by "the builders," but he was the Lord's ordained choice for the most important component in his project.

When both Jesus and Peter cited that verse from Psalm, they were making a provocative point. Their words condemned the leaders in Jerusalem at that time, for they were understood to be the "builders" who had missed God's plan and purpose. The problem was even more sinister than that: Those leaders had actively opposed the one who was central to the plan and purpose of God.

It is important to understand any biblical text in its original context, of course. But in some cases, it is tempting to leave the text in its original context, lest it become equally provocative for us. Yet Peter's extended discourse on this "stone" forces us to extend the application beyond those Jewish leaders who conspired to have Jesus arrested and killed. Peter challenges us to consider the application to ourselves and to our day.

The psalmist, we recall, said that the stone was rejected by "the builders." In his epistle, however, Peter says that the stone was "rejected by men." And that is where the rubber meets the road for us. Jesus continues to be widely rejected — by the culture at large and by individuals within it. As in the days of Stephen, they still angrily cover their ears to the proclamation of his name and his truth. Yet he also continues to be the one specially chosen and used by God.

As preachers of the gospel, then, we must not fail to understand what is at stake here. We mustn't let the prevailing winds of the culture around us put us on the wrong side of this watershed stone. Rather, we are unsurprised that he continues to be "a stone of stumbling and a rock of offense," and we remain "bold to confess thy glorious name before a world of foes" ("Jesus! The Name High Over All").

An Alternative Application

Acts 7:55-60. "Patron Saint of Paradox." There came a moment in the evolution of the early church in Jerusalem when the apostles needed to delegate some responsibilities. It was the sort of clarification and definition of roles that every organization requires from time to time. For the sake of efficiency, we need to be clear about who is supposed to do what. The apostles determined that someone else needed to be waiting tables in order that they might devote themselves to the preaching of the word (see Acts 6:1-6). Interestingly, though, it was one of those who were appointed to be table waiters that ended up having the longest sermon recorded in the book of Acts.

His name was Stephen, and almost as soon as Luke reports that the twelve would devote themselves to prayer and the ministry of the word, the story follows Stephen the waiter. He performs miracles, his wisdom is irresistible, and his effectiveness is so intolerable that he becomes the first Christian martyr.

It strikes me as a very lovely paradox that one appointed to wait tables becomes one of the most notable preachers in Acts. Likewise, that one whose assigned role seems so innocuous should become an insufferable force among the enemies of Christ. And 2,000 years later, Stephen's name and reputation exceed all but the most famous of those twelve apostles.

The paradoxes continue into our brief excerpt from Acts. As we noted above, Stephen "gazed into heaven and saw the glory of God and Jesus standing at the right hand of God." While his opponents would have expected him to see anger and danger, he saw heaven. While they were trying to show him their displeasure, he saw God's glory. And while they were treating him with violence and murder, he prayed for their forgiveness. He is a paradox in the midst of his foes.

The truth, of course, is not actually that these paradoxes belong to Stephen. They belong to God. He, after all, is the one who turned the rejected stone into the most important one of all. Stephen's life and experience bear witness to the divine providence that gives rise to such lovely paradoxes.

Sixth Sunday of Easter
Acts 17:22-31
1 Peter 3:13-22
John 14:15-21
by Cathy Venkatesh

Lives transformed

What if the resurrection happened and no one told anyone about it? There wouldn't be a church; no one would know Jesus ever existed; the world would be an entirely different place. I've heard it said that the church is always just one generation away from extinction. Often this is said out of fear that this generation will be the last, but when I hear this, I marvel at how Christianity has passed from one generation to the next for two millennia. Today, and throughout the Easter season, we have the opportunity to celebrate the first bearers of the good news of Jesus' resurrection, and we have the opportunity to celebrate how the gospel transforms human lives and societies in every generation from the first apostles to our own.

Acts 17:22-31

Paul, that avid persecutor of the followers of Jesus, has been converted and is well into his ministry by the time we meet him in today's reading. He has been ridiculed, driven out of town after town, beaten, stoned and left for dead, and imprisoned, yet he persists in every town he visits in going to the synagogue to tell the Jews about Jesus. With assistance from believers, Paul has escaped to Athens from Beroea (a city in Macedonia close to Thessalonica) after the Jews from Thessalonica where he had preached before followed him and incited the crowds in Bereoa against him. Separated from his traveling companions Silas and Timothy, Paul waits for them to join him in Athens. While he bides his time, he looks around Athens and talks about Jesus to anyone who will listen, both in the synagogue and in the marketplace. He debates with Epicurean and Stoic philosophers who are confused by his message. "So they took him and brought him to the Areopagus and asked him 'May we know what this new teaching is that you are presenting? It sounds rather strange to us, so we would like to know what it means'" (Acts 17:20). The Areopagus is a rocky hill northwest of the Acropolis that historically served as a meeting place for councils and courts. It is unclear whether the reference in Acts is to the geographic place or to a council that Paul addressed, though we are told in Acts 17:34 that one of Paul's converts was Dionysius, a judge of the Areopagus.

Acts 17:21 tells us, "Now all the Athenians and the foreigners living there would spend their time in nothing but telling or hearing something new," a description of Athenian culture found in other ancient sources, so we can assume that Paul drew a crowd with his novel teaching. His address at the Areopagus is the only major speech in Acts to a Gentile audience, and thus omits references to the Hebrew scriptures and history typically found in other speeches. Indeed, Jesus is not even mentioned until the end of his speech and then only obliquely, as "a man" (Acts 17:31). Instead, Paul meets the Athenians on their own ground, praising their religiosity, noting especially an altar "to an unknown god" and quoting their own poets (Acts 17:28) as he builds his argument in a manner in keeping with the philosophical debates and eloquent Greek of the Athenians. His philosophically-inclined audience would have agreed with his proclamations that God does not live in shrines made by human hands and that God, the Creator of heaven and earth, has no need for sacrifices (Acts 17:24-25). It is only at the very end of his speech that Paul diverges from the common ground he shares with his audience to issue a call to repentance founded on the resurrection of Jesus (17:30-31).

1 Peter 3:13-22

First Peter, which we have been reading through the Easter season, is a circular letter addressed to "the exiles of the dispersion in Pontus, Galatia, Cappadocia, Asia, and Bithynia" (1 Peter 1:1), five provinces that made up most of Asia Minor (now modern-day Turkey). Likely written by a follower of Peter rather than the apostle himself, it still serves as a reminder of the stature of Peter in the early church. The churches addressed were mainly Gentile in origin, and the letter concerns itself with helping these new Christians live into their conversions in the face of social pressure against them. Christians are to model their lives on Christ himself, accepting suffering as Christ did, living humbly and acting in love. While exhortations in chapters 2 and 3 for slaves to accept the authority of their masters and wives to accept the authority of their husbands may raise modern hackles, the author of 1 Peter was concerned with helping Christians continue to live in a hierarchical society that they were already challenging by the fact of their religious beliefs and practices. Today's passage exhorts Christians to do good and be above reproach so that whoever may try to malign them will be seen to have no cause. This moves into a discussion of Christ's saving action, even of those evildoers who were destroyed by the flood in Noah's day. The flood, which wiped out all that was evil from the face of the earth, prefigures baptism, which is another, personal assurance of the power of Christ to save the believer.

John 14:15-21

Last week and this, we read most of John 14, part of Jesus' counsel and comfort offered to his disciples after he washes their feet at the Last Supper. He is preparing them for his death and assuring them that his death will not be the end of their relationship. John uses distinctive terms for the Holy Spirit, who the Father will send to accompany the disciples: Advocate (also translated Paraclete, Comforter, Counselor, Helper) and Spirit of Truth. Jesus exhorts the disciples to keep his commandments after his death, and the command Jesus has given the disciples to observe is deceptively simple: Love one another (John 13:34, repeated in John 15:12). Today's passage prepares us for the coming days of Ascension and Pentecost, when Jesus' post-resurrection departure and the coming of the Holy Spirit empower the disciples to live in the love Jesus showed them.

Application

For the disciples, Easter Day was not a day of trumpets, lilies, and joyful celebration, but a day of wondering and confusion, fear, grief, and doubts. From Easter Day through the Day of Ascension, observed on Thursday this week and recounted in our readings next Sunday, we see a gradual dawning of hope and understanding among the disciples that Jesus was not dead, but alive in a new way. Then, on Pentecost, the coming of the Holy Spirit completed the transformation of the disciples into apostles... from those who followed Jesus to those who were sent out by Christ into the world in his name, filled with his resurrection power.

Today we encounter words attributed to both Peter and Paul, and it is worth remembering their stories: How Paul was transformed from chief persecutor of Jesus' followers to chief missionary and evangelist; how Peter who denied Jesus three times before Jesus' death was charged three times by the post-resurrection Jesus to care for his flock (John 21:15-19; we read this passage only on Easter 3 in Year C). The bumbling, slow-to-understand, sometimes cowardly disciples we meet in the gospels become in Acts the courageous, assured apostles who preach and heal in Jesus' name, enduring persecution and even death with joy. Their lives were transformed, just as lives have been transformed by Jesus and Jesus' followers in every generation since. We all know stories of people who lived in the power of the Holy Spirit and passed it on to the next generation; we may even know or live with some of them in our homes, churches, and neighborhoods. Today can be a day to name and honor them and the work God does through them.

Today can also be a day to consider how we may "always be ready to make your defense to anyone who demands from you an accounting of the hope that is in you; yet do it with gentleness and reverence" (1 Peter 3:15-16). Paul's speech before the Areogapus provides a model for talking about our faith with non-believers when we are invited to do so. Paul does not harangue and challenge, but begins by naming what is admirable and godly among the Athenians, honoring the human longing for the divine that he sees in their midst. He recognizes what is unnamed and seeks to give it a name as a means of inviting the Athenians into communion with Christ. In his epistle, Peter urges gentleness and right living as the model for Christian life: actions speak louder than words, or as some claim Saint Francis said, "Preach the gospel at all times. When necessary, use words."

While we can use our readings today to celebrate the amazing transformations that happen through life with Christ, we can also acknowledge the varying realities among the people in the pews. Coming to full knowledge of the love, power, and resurrection of Christ may be the stunning work of a moment, as it was for Paul, but it may be the incomplete work of a lifetime for others. Recognizing that Easter is a season in which the disciples grappled with all kinds of misgivings, fears, and doubts before they came to their own deep knowledge of resurrection may be something even the most faithful church members need to hear.

This Sunday before the Ascension is also, of course, Memorial Day, which will be observed variously in different congregations. While the message of Christ is peace, faithful Christians have fought in good conscience and died in war after war. Like Jesus, their sacrifice was of life itself and prayers for the fallen and their families as well as for a world in which war will cease can guide this day. An alternate extra-scriptural theme some may wish to observe is that of the Rogation Days, traditionally observed on the days leading up to Ascension Day. These were marked in the Catholic and English churches by processions and prayers for the crops, the success or failure of which would determine the health and even survival of the community through the year to come.

Seventh Sunday of Easter
Acts 1:6-14
1 Peter 4:12-14; 5:6-11
John 17:1-11
by Ron Love

The lion roars

Encratis lived in Portugal, but her father had given her in marriage to a nobleman in Roussillon, France. Wanting to preserve her virginity for the honor of God, she fled from her father's home to avoid the arranged marriage. She privately went to Saragossa, Spain. In Saragossa she encountered the Diocletian Persecution of 304, conducted by Dacian. Because of the cruelties of the barbarians, she personally reproached Dacian for his actions against Christians. Because of her outspokenness and confrontation, Dacian had Encratis tortured in the most inhumane way possible: her sides were torn with iron hooks; one of her breasts was cut off exposing her inner chest to be viewed; and her liver was then pulled out through her upper chest cavity. In this condition she was sent back to prison, still alive, where she died of her wounds.

When we think of persecution, we often put it into the shape of stories like Encratis from the early church. But the persecution endured by the church of the first four centuries is not absent from many churches scattered around the globe today. In April 2014, in Somalia, a group of armed men burst into a home in Mogadishu and murdered "Sufia." They dragged her outside, shooting at neighbors who tried to rescue her. After killing the young woman, the men fled. The victim was given the name "Sufia" out of fear that her attackers will return to kill her family.

Somalia has suffered from civil war for more than two decades. Ninety-nine percent of the population is Sunni Muslim, and Christians are targeted by all of the Muslim factions fighting for control. The most dangerous of these groups is the militant Islamist group known as al-Shabab, which controls much of southern and central Somalia. Al-Shabab, which means "The Youth" in Arabic, has sworn to rid Somalia of all Christians and impose its strict interpretation of Shariah law. All Christians are viewed as apostates by the Muslim majority. Every church building in the country was destroyed during the civil war, so believers meet for fellowship in small home groups. When Christians are discovered by al-Shabab, they are sometimes beheaded on the spot, as occurred with a seventeen-year-old boy in 2011 in Mogadishu.

The story coming out of Somalia is repeated in North Korea, China, Rwanda, India, Pakistan, and Egypt to name only a few where devastation and destruction, killing and maiming are daily occurrences inflicted upon Christians.

There are several themes coexisting on Ascension Sunday that we celebrate this day. Luke, who is the author of Acts, instructs us that with Jesus' departure we are to be his witnesses to his life and teaching, guided by the Holy Spirit. John instructs us that in doing so we shall be persecuted; but, in our persecution we will be giving glory to God. Peter informs us since all congregations compose the body of Christ, the persecution of one church is the persecution of all congregations. The death of "Sufia" is our death as well.

Though we live in the sanctuary of the United States, we should not feel so content and at ease. If we are adamant in our witness for the Lord and promotion of social justice, our persecution may not come in the form and machetes and bullets, but it will certainly come in the form of being jeered and ostracized.

Seventh Sunday of Easter

Acts 1:6-14

Our reading from Acts outlines for us our spiritual journey. Two themes are apparent in Peter's account. The first is that the disciples stayed together. The second is that the disciples prayed together. We know they stayed together for they went as a group to a place that was familiar to them and where they were reminded of their relationship with Jesus — the upper room. It was in this place of refuge they found solace with one another. It was in this room where they shared what has become known as the Last Supper that they prayed together. It was in this solidarity that the era of the church began.

The disciples embarking as the body of Christ, or as we understand it the church, is symbolized by the presence of Mary, the mother of Jesus. As Mary was present at the birth of the Messiah, she was now present at the birth of the church.

The journey that the disciples undertake will not be aimless. The disciples received the indwelling of the Holy Spirit, which next Sunday, Pentecost Sunday, will come upon the multitudes. The Holy Spirit will be the presence of Christ within all believers, empowering and directing, instructing and enlightening.

Verse 8 is often referred to as the apostolic charge: "And you will be my witnesses in Jerusalem, in all Judea and Samaria, and to the ends of the earth." Having witnessed Jesus' ascension into the cloud of heaven, having received the Holy Spirit, having the assurance of the cohesiveness found in the upper room, and having Mary as a reminder that they are the body of Christ in the world today, they do take the message of the resurrection "to the ends of the earth."

1 Peter 4:12-14; 5:6-11

Our reading from 1 Peter outlines for us our journey into persecution. "As Christ suffered so shall we" suffer is the message that is presented by Peter. Although Jesus was accepted by many, he was also despised by many. We read of the multitudes that followed him and worshiped him. We only read of a few names of individuals who actually opposed him and two groups in general: the Pharisees and Sadducees. Unrecorded, but we know to be present, are the Roman citizens dwelling in Palestine who had a disdain for Jesus. Then there were the Roman soldiers who joked among themselves that if they ever encountered this Jesus, they would adorn this fabricated king in a purple robe and a crown of thorns. Then there were the Jews in general who thought of Jesus as some sort of sooth sayer. In this milieu of hatred and resentment Jesus walked. The disciples, as his ambassadors following the ascension, walked on this same ground.

The devil, Satan, is compared to a roaring lion ready to devour its prey. Lions hunt in a pack, single out one animal from the herd, and then pronounce its death. This is why the disciples must stay alert. This is why as the body of Christ the disciples were connected to all congregations in Jerusalem, Judea, and Samaria. The cohesiveness of the upper room spreads beyond the doors of the room, beyond the city limits, and across borders.

The severity of the persecution that will confront the disciples is described by Peter as the need for them to endure "the fiery ordeal." These words should be taken at their full meaning that only hardship and headache will be encountered as the gospel message is taken to the ends of the earth.

Peter calls his fellow believers to "resist Satan, and be steadfast in your faith." These are easy words to speak; almost impossible words to live by as the lion roars.

John 17:1-11

Our reading from John outlines for us a journey in discipleship. Jesus tells them that the same intimacy and interdependence that he had with his heavenly Father the disciples will now have with Jesus through the power of the Holy Spirit. The call to discipleship has now begun for Jesus declares that the same words that God gave to him he has given to his disciples. It is those words that the disciples are to take to the ends of the earth. The ministry of the disciples is displayed in unity when Jesus said: "So that they may be one, as we are one."

Application

Persecution is a theme that is present in all three readings. Discuss how the church has been persecuted through the centuries and continues to be persecuted this day in many foreign lands. Then emphasize that we, who are living in the serenity of the United States, should be experiencing some persecution, some discomfort for our beliefs, as we witness to others the gospel message and promote social justice. Discuss how the disciples were able to endure through fellowship and prayer and how we need to institute those same principles in our own congregations.

An Alternative Application

Sharing the gospel message with others is present in all three readings. We must be willing to tell others about Jesus and invite them into the fellowship of the church. Realizing the message is to go to the ends of the earth, we need to explore ways to evangelize the entire community in which our church resides. Within the church we need meaningful worship, an educational program, prayer groups, small groups, and as many ways as possible to provide spiritual nurturing. It is through these spiritual disciplines that we will be receptive to the indwelling of the Holy Spirit, providing the strength and guidance we will need for our mission.

Day of Pentecost
Acts 2:1-21
1 Corinthians 12:3b-13
John 20:19-23
by Wayne Brouwer

Harvest time

An ancient Jewish legend declares, "Pentecost is the day on which Torah was given." One wonders whether James might have had that in mind as he penned these words. According to the Jewish teaching it was on the day that eventually became the feast of Pentecost that God gave birth to the Hebrew nation by speaking the divine covenant to them at Mount Sinai.

As the book of Acts makes clear, Pentecost was the day on which the New Testament church was given birth. Just as God spoke through Moses to bring the nation of Israel into being at Mount Sinai, so God spoke through Peter to create the first elements of the new faith community.

It was symbolically powerful for these events to take place on Pentecost. In its first use "Pentecost" was essentially a nickname or label. The feast of Passover was one of the most significant holidays in the Jewish community since it recalled the manner in which God miraculously brought the nation out of Egypt. Seven Sabbaths and a day later ($7 \times 7 + 1 = 50$) the people celebrated this next major religious event as harvest season began in Palestine. Since it occurred fifty days after the Passover, people started referring to it as the "Feast after Fifty" or Pentecost.

Yet the real significance of the event was more clearly understood through its original name — Feast of Firstfruits. Regulations for the celebration required all Israelites to assemble at the temple in Jerusalem bringing with them the first sheaf of grain from their fields. As the time of harvest approached across the land, even before the regular reaping started, a single bundle of grain was cut on each farm and toted off to the temple.

There it was "waved" before the Lord as an offering (Leviticus 23:11) along with two loaves of bread that were baked from the newly-harvested grain (Leviticus 23:17). Furthermore, to broaden the impact of the event, two male lambs were also brought from the first castings of each flock (Leviticus 23:12).

As these gifts were presented to God in the temple courts, all of the men danced around the altar that carried the smoke of the gifts toward heaven. The crowds of women, children, and elderly men too old to jump around wildly formed a large circle around these revelers and sang Psalms 113-118. According to historical reports the celebration was often wild and uninhibited.

We might ask what the purpose was behind these religious revelries. The instructions of Moses declared that the feast was a theological testimony. The nation was making a confession that no general harvesting for profit would begin until God had laid claim to the "firstfruits" of the fields and the flocks. By devoting the first of the new produce to God, the people were acknowledging that everything came from God and belonged to God. Whatever benefit they might receive from the harvest that year was a direct result of God's care and providential intervention.

With that background the significance of Pentecost as the birthday of the Christian church takes on new meaning. A new era of God's kingdom began that day, as God claimed the firstfruits of a worldwide faith harvest. The mission of the church began only after God had first miraculously owned the original converts from each nation represented in Jerusalem that day.

At the dawn of creation God sowed a world of hope and possibility. Evil storms and tragic seasons may have slowed the harvest of greatness on planet Earth. But if anyone wants to know what the true and best harvest will look like, he should check out the church.

That may seem funny to us. We would have a hard time seeing the church as a picture of God's profit margins. Yet for God the church is the firstfruits of the great harvest.

Maybe that's why we ought to take ourselves less seriously and more seriously at the same time in the church. Less seriously because there is an awful lot of humor in what God is doing. More seriously because God's humor is the first smile of love that the rest of creation around us needs desperately to see.

Acts 2:1-21

The momentum of the stories told in the book of Acts is derived from a single critical incident that took place in Jerusalem during the Jewish religious festival known as Pentecost. Jesus' instruction for his disciples to stay in Jerusalem and wait for a special gift (Acts 1:4) must have seemed vague at the time, but the arrival of the explosive power of the Holy Spirit during the Pentecost feast made sense. This celebration was both a harvest festival and a time for recalling the gift of the original covenant documents to Moses at Mount Sinai. These two themes intersected marvelously with what was taking place. First, there was the dawning of a new age of revelation and divine mission, paralleling the first covenant declaration in the book of Exodus. Second, during the Pentecost harvest festival, the first sheaves of grain were presented at the temple, anticipating that God would then bring in the full harvest. This expression of faith served as a clear analogy to the greater missional harvest of the church, which was begun through a miraculous "firstfruits" in Jerusalem that day.

Peter capitalized on these themes when he preached a sermon explaining Joel's prophecy of the "Day of the Lord." Peter tied together God's extensive mission, the history of Israel, the coming of Jesus, and the splitting of the day of the Lord so that the blessings of the messianic age could begin before the final divine judgment fell. The pattern for entering the new community of faith was clearly outlined: repent and be baptized. The former indicated a transforming presence of the Holy Spirit in individual hearts, while the latter became the initiation rite by which the ranks of this missional society were identified (replacing the badge of circumcision in its unique application to the nation of Israel — see Colossians 2:11-12).

Although not explicitly stated, there seems to be a conscious undoing of the troubles that started at Babel through the miracle of multiple-language communications at Pentecost. In Genesis 11, the human race was becoming unified against its Creator, and the divine solution to dissipate this rebellion was to multiply the languages spoken, forcing the community to become segmented into competing groups. At Pentecost this action was reversed and the many people who communicated in their diverse local languages suddenly all heard the same message of grace at once and were knit together into a new common humanity of the church. Babel was undone by Pentecost.

What had been a centripetal energizing motion during the first phase of God's recovery mission on planet Earth (that is, drawing all nations toward a re-engagement with their Creator through the strategically placed people of Israel) was now shifted into a centrifugal motion of divine sending out these blessings of testimony to the world in ever-widening circles of witness. The Christian church, born as a Jewish messianic sect, became a global religion.

1 Corinthians 12:3b-13

Probably sometime in late 51 AD or early 52 AD, from his new mission in Ephesus, Paul sent a letter of strongly worded reproof to the Corinthian congregation. No copies have survived but from what Paul himself says about this communication in 1 Corinthians 5:9, it is easy to see why some might take exception to it. Indeed it appears that a number of people in the congregation began to disown Paul's authority after reading that letter, and then began to instigate factionalism in the community. Cliques grew, based upon personal preferences about which leaders were better preachers, and who had a right to claim greater sway among them (see 1 Corinthians 2-4). Meanwhile, a delegation of three men (Stephanus, Fortunatus, and Achaicus), all highly respectful of Paul's apostolic authority, traveled from Corinth to Ephesus bringing to Paul an oral report about the difficulties going on in the church. They also carried a written list of questions that members of the congregation were raising.

Paul quickly wrote a letter of response. Although it was actually his second letter to the Corinthian congregation, because the earlier communication has been lost, this one survives as 1 Corinthians in our New Testaments. Immediately in the opening passages, Paul addresses the difficulties some have at his continued influence in the congregation. He chastises the members for dividing up into parties where each waves a banner acclaiming the worthiness of a different leader. These groupings were sinful and disruptive, according to Paul, for they denied the honor that ought to be given only to the true head of the church, Jesus Christ. Such schisms also played favorites among human leaders, setting them over against each other, rather than recognizing their complementary gifts for helping the church as a whole to grow.

In a review of the church's celebration of "the Lord's Supper," as it was becoming known, another facet of social interaction was addressed. The "differences" within the congregation were not only of the kind where parties became loyal to different leaders (1 Corinthians 1-3), but also the manifestation of divergent socioeconomic groupings present in Corinthian society. The reason why some who attended these Lord's Supper gatherings "go ahead without waiting for anybody else" and others "remain hungry," was due to the divergent lifestyle practices of the rich and the poor among them. Wealthy people were able to come and go as they pleased, including showing up to worship services, potluck dinners, and Lord's Supper celebrations right at the start. The poor and the slaves, however (some likely coming from the same households), were often late to arrive because they had to fulfill their domestic work obligations first. Paul declared that "recognizing the body of the Lord" was necessary if the Lord's Supper was to be celebrated properly. This did not mean having the capacity to understand an appropriate theological theory of the atonement or some other such cognitive ability. Instead, it amounted to remembering that all who belong to Jesus are welcome at his table, and none have more rights than others. If this socially and economically diverse group of society was indeed the body of Christ, each must live and act accordingly, making room at the table for all.

This reflection on the expression of the body of Christ at the communion meal may have significantly shaped Paul's next reflections. When answering the Corinthians' question about spiritual gifts (1 Corinthians 12–14), Paul further develops the body of Christ metaphor, making it the core analogy by which both the identification and expression of unique gifts was to happen. At the center of this discussion, Paul pens one of the most beautiful hymns about love ever recorded (1 Corinthians 13). Although it is often lifted from its context to become a wedding text, this passage is actually the glue that holds together all of Paul's testimony concerning spiritual gifts. Only when these are used out of love and expressed through love is the true community of faith is formed and nurtured.

John 20:19-23

When describing the events of resurrection morning, John gives us some wonderful analogies to see its meaning on several levels. For one thing, when Mary looks into the empty tomb (John 20:10-12), the scene as John describes it immediately calls to mind the Ark of the Covenant that symbolized Yahweh's presence in the tabernacle and later the temple. While the other gospel writers tell of angels being present, John views them through Mary Magdalene's eyes and sees two such creatures in exactly the same position as the cherubim that stood guard over the Mercy Seat throne. This time, however, the divine presence was missing, indicating the dawning of a new age in which the Creator's power and presence would not be confined to or limited by a particular geographic location. The second strategy in the divine mission had come, and the gospel was now to be preached to the whole world through Jesus' disciples.

When Mary Magdalene weeps because she misses her "Lord" (which is the Greek version of "Yahweh"), a man appears on her periphery, and she assumes that he is "the gardener." Of course, Mary's perception is incorrect, because the man is actually Jesus. But is she really wrong? John never says that she was mistaken; only that Mary Magdalene had assumed he was the gardener. In fact, John appears to want his readers to get the subtle message that Jesus is indeed the gardener. After all, at the beginning of time, the Creator placed Adam and Even in a garden and came to walk and talk with them (Genesis 2). Now, in the re-creation of all things, it is quite appropriate for new life to begin anew in a garden where the great gardener is again meandering and sharing intimacy with those who are favored friends. John confirms this symbolic intent when he tells about Jesus speaking Mary's name. Just as Adam and Eve, along with all the animals and all elements of creation, came into being when they were named in the first beginning, so now Mary is restored to life in a new way as her identity is regenerated when Jesus speaks her name. Jesus, however, cannot be held in this garden (John 20:17) as partner in only one local friendship, for the process of re-creating all things is only just beginning, and he must leave to finish the task. Only when he goes, as he said in the "Farewell Discourse," will he be able to multiply his presence through the gift of the *paraclete*.

This coming of the *paraclete* is enacted next, when Jesus meets with the rest of his disciples later that day. John tells us that he "breathed on them" (v. 21), imparting to them the divine Spirit, and sending them out as his ambassadors, exactly in the manner of which he prayed in chapter 17. Is this, as some have suggested, John's different version of Pentecost (Acts 2)? No, it is a final expression of the re-creation process. Just as Adam only came alive to his life and livelihood at the beginning of time when God breathed into him the divine breath (Genesis 2), so now this tiny gathering of the new humanity cannot function until they are divinely enthused in a similar, very literal manner. The Creator who breathed the breath of life into Adam in the first creation now breathes the same breath of life into his disciples in this re-creation. The dead of the world are coming back to life!

Application

Pentecost reminds us that no mind is truly enlightened until it is flooded with the glory of heaven. No body is truly healed until it is touched by the power of the Creator. No person is truly set free until there is freedom of the Spirit of Christ.

William Carey was a pastor of a small congregation in Leiceter, England. In 1792, he preached a powerful sermon called "Expect Great Things from God; Attempt Great Things for God!" People would remember it for years. His message not only moved hearts in his congregation; however, it also came home to challenge Pastor Carey's own soul. The next year he set sail for India, and what he did in that country was simply astounding. He began a manufacturing plant to employ jobless workers. He translated the scriptures and set up shops to print them. He established schools for all ages, helping people find a better place in society. He provided medical assistance for the diseased and the troubled and the ailing. He was nothing short of a miracle for the people of India.

Why did he do it? Because he was transformed by the pentecostal spirit of Jesus. And when he lay dying, these were his last words: "When I have gone, speak not of Carey but of Carey's Savior."

Day of Pentecost

During the time of the Reformation, John Foxe of England was impressed by the testimony of the early Christians. He gleaned the pages of early historical writings, and wrote a book that has become a classic in the church: *Foxe's Book of Martyrs*.

One story he tells is about an early church leader named Lawrence. Lawrence acted as a pastor for a church community. He also collected the offerings for the poor each week.

A band of thieves found out that Lawrence received the offerings of the people from Sunday to Sunday, so one night, as he was out taking a stroll, they grabbed him and demanded the money. He told them that he didn't have it, because he had already given it all to the poor. They didn't believe him and told him they would give him a chance to find it. In three days they would come to his house and take from him the treasures of the church.

Three days later they did come. But Lawrence wasn't alone. The house was filled with the people of his congregation. When the thieves demanded the treasures of the church, Lawrence smiled. He opened wide his arms and gestured to those who sat around him. "Here's the treasure of the church!" he said. "Here's the treasure of God that shines in the world!"

An Alternative Application

Acts 2:1-21. The symbols that appeared with the great Pentecost empowerment are very creative. They provide visible representations of the divine activity:

Sound of wind: a single word, both in the Hebrew (*ruach*) and Greek (*pneuma*) languages, serves to designate "wind," "breath," and "spirit." Thus the sound of a rushing wind captured the attention of all who were about to breathe in the Spirit of God. In a real sense, this is the second creation (or recreation) of humankind. At the beginning of time, it was the breath of God invading Adam's newly-formed earthen body that transformed him into a true divine-image-bearing life.

Single blaze of fire becoming multiple flames above heads: Jesus' cousin John had said that he baptized with water, but that Jesus would baptize with the Holy Spirit and with fire (Luke 1:16). This vision represented the single divine Spirit baptizing all at the same time.

In a grand "Show & Tell," the new age of God's mission was announced with great power!

Trinity Sunday / 1st Sunday after Pentecost

Genesis 1:1--2:4a

2 Corinthians 13:11-13

Matthew 28:16-20

by David Kalas

Changing the conversation

You probably have, as I do, certain email applications that allow you to view your emails as "conversations" or "threads." For example, the emails that my staff and I have exchanged on a certain subject are all grouped together in my inbox, even if they are separated by months in terms of when they were written. And if I happen to write a reply to any one of the emails other than the very latest in a given thread, my email application will tell me that I am not responding to the most recent part of the conversation.

This Sunday, you and I are presented with the creation story in Genesis. As we are, we may naturally think in terms of the larger thread of our cultural conversation about creation. And we may feel an implicit pressure to respond to the latest part of the conversation.

But perhaps we should change the conversation instead.

You and I, along with our people, live in the midst of a long-standing and deeply-entrenched debate on the subject of creation. I am not going to end that debate by what I say from the pulpit this Sunday, and so I do not want to weaken my pulpit by becoming just one more predictable voice in that debate. Let me resist being among those who use the pulpit to condemn science for being anti-faith, or who condemn faith for being anti-science. I suspect that that entire dichotomy is rooted in a misunderstanding to begin with. So rather than feeling the need to respond to the latest email in this long conversation, I would prefer to change the conversation for my people.

The apostle Paul said to Timothy, "The goal of our instruction is love from a pure heart and a good conscience and a sincere faith. For some men, straying from these things, have turned aside to fruitless discussion" (1Timothy1:5-6NASB). Only the enemy is pleased and served when I let my pulpit become an instrument of fruitless discussion. So I will endeavor to change the conversation for my people this week — setting them and God's word free from controversy and debate — by preaching the gospel that is found in the story of creation.

Genesis 1:1--2:4a

The book of Genesis presents two accounts of creation. Scholars have offered a variety of insights into the reason behind the two accounts, and I'm sure that only a small minority of the people in our pews care about those theories and debates. For myself, I don't think in terms of two accounts so much as two perspectives.

Sports fans are familiar with the significance of different camera angles. When watching a sporting event on television, we routinely see the same play from several different angles because every play is recorded by several different cameras. Then we discover that those different cameras offer different perspectives on the same play.

So it is in Genesis. The material that comes after our assigned passage offers a close-up view of the man and woman in the garden. This earlier, longer account, however, is much more global in its scope. This is the football play as seen from the Goodyear (or MetLife, or whoever's) blimp. It lacks the personal detail of the subsequent account, but it helps us to see the big picture.

Accordingly, since it is the big picture perspective that the author offers us at this point, it is the big picture that we should endeavor to see. To that end, I would try to cull this familiar passage in order to identify the recurring themes and patterns. Those are, after all, the most salient elements in the big picture.

The passage is, of course, most rich, and it has been mined by better minds than mine. But let me offer a few of my own big picture observations about the text that is before us. I will run out of space before the text runs out of insight. As we see the big picture, I believe we'll discover more good news to preach than a single Sunday will afford.

First, we observe the before-and-after quality of the account. From weight loss programs to personal makeovers to home remodeling, we are familiar with before-and-after pictures. It is its own kind of beautiful testimony, then, to use the creation story as a before-and-after picture that bears witness to the activity of God. What was it like before he began his work? What was it like once he was finished? That is the nature of his influence and that is what we may still expect when we allow him to work in our lives, in our homes, and in our churches.

Second, we note the profound meaning of the word "good" in scripture. In our day, "good" has become a kind of halfway compliment. Good as opposed to great. Good as one step short of better and two steps short of best. Good has become a lukewarm, easily achieved measure of a life, as in "I've always tried to be a basically good person." Ah, but in the creation story we see what good really looks like. Good means exactly the way God meant it to be. No wonder Jesus said, "No one is good but God alone" (Luke 18:19).

Third, we are challenged by the biblical definition of a day. Evening and morning is the pattern revealed here, though that is not how our calendars, our clocks, or our psyches reckon it. Perhaps we figure that a day begins at midnight or, more practically, it begins when we wake up. But the Old Testament urges us to recognize that tomorrow begins tonight. Perhaps that truth was in Paul's mind when he urged the Christians in Ephesus, "Do not let the sun go down on your anger" (Ephesians 4:26). We must not let today's anger spill over into tomorrow.

Fourth, we notice the doubling pattern of the account. The first day introduces light, while the fourth day brings the physical sources of light. The second day sees the separation of waters below from waters above, and the fifth day fills the waters and the sky with fish and birds. The third day focuses on the dry land and its vegetation, while the sixth day sees the formation of the creatures that dwell on that land and live off that vegetation.

Finally, we detect a sense of escalation in the story. The account suggests a climax, a finishing touch. Interestingly, God's finishing touch takes two forms: humankind and then rest.

2 Corinthians 13:11-13

What's your favorite movie? Imagine a person walking in and seeing just the final two minutes of that movie. How much would they understand? How much would they know?

Between 1 and 2 Corinthians, we have 29 chapters of correspondence from the apostle Paul to the Christians in Corinth. We enjoy greater insight into that church and Paul's relationship with it than any other of the New Testament era. Yet our New Testament lection for this week features just the final three verses of that considerable correspondence. If this is all that our people hear from Paul's letters to the Corinthians, how much will they understand? How much will they know?

You and I have seen the whole movie, of course, and so it is our happy task to try to help our people understand some of what has happened prior to these final two minutes. Then they can appreciate the passage within its larger, original context.

When we read Paul say to the Corinthians, "Put things in order," we recall his earlier appeal that "all things should be done decently and in order" (1 Corinthians 14:40). Perhaps enthusiasm and self-importance had conspired to create a certain disorder in the worship there at Corinth.

Meanwhile, when we hear the apostle encouraging them to "agree with one another" and to "live in peace," we are reminded of the friction and strife that evidently marked that congregation. They were dividing into sects (1 Corinthians 1:10-15; 3:1-4). Members were dragging each other to court (1 Corinthians 6:1-11). They were elbowing ahead of one another at the Lord's Supper (1 Corinthians 11:17-22). And clearly Paul himself struggled in his own relationship with them (2 Corinthians 2:1-4; 11:1-11; 12:11-21). One senses that the apostle is like the parent with a backseat full of bickering children. How he longs for them just to get along! How he yearns for them to be at peace!

When Paul references "the God of love," we think of the exquisite definition of love that Paul had given this congregation (1 Corinthians 13). He held it up before them as the most excellent gift and most desirable way. For all that they had going for them, it seems that the Corinthians were not characterized by the very trait that is God's essential attribute (1 John 4:8) and the hallmark of Christ's followers (John 13:35).

Yet these closing instructions from Paul to the Christians in Corinth should not be misunderstood as a thematic rehashing of the earlier grievances. No, the apostle attains something far higher here. He looks above and beyond the people's present patterns and behaviors and points them to the way things ought to be.

Surely this is a key ability of an effective leader. If all that we can see is how things are — the way that they aren't right — our tone and content will be all frustration and scolding. There will be nothing uplifting in our words or voices, for we will be focused entirely on the negative. The leader must be able to keep in view the perfect picture, even when it doesn't at all resemble the present.

In the end, Paul sketches out that perfect picture for his silly, bickering children. It is a picture of peace and order. It is a scene of welcome and embrace. It is a church infused with the love of God, the grace of Christ, and the fellowship of the Holy Spirit. The previous 28-plus chapters may not paint a pretty picture of the church at Corinth, but the final verses are a beautiful picture of the way that church — every church — ought to be.

Matthew 28:16-20

We are dealing with three endings this week. Our Old Testament lection takes us through to show us the end of creation when it is finished. Our epistle passage is the end of Paul's second letter to the Corinthians. And our gospel reading is Matthew's conclusion to his book. It is interesting to see how he chooses to bring his story to an end.

While Matthew's conclusion is climactic, it is not artificially so. He does not need to find this moment's importance in large numbers, for example. While so much of Jesus' ministry is characterized by crowds and multitudes, there are only eleven witnesses and companions for this moment. And the narrator does not even bother to airbrush his portrait of them, for even at this occasion Matthew reports that "some doubted."

In dramatic contrast to that small and blemished scene, then, are Jesus' words: "All authority in heaven and on earth has been given to me." We would expect such a grand claim to be surrounded by greater fanfare. Yet this is typical, is it not? For his birth was not fabulous and his resurrection was not witnessed. The God who could so easily overwhelm us continuously chooses not to.

Jesus' statement about himself is followed immediately by an assignment to his disciples. His use of "therefore" insists on a connection between the two. That is to say, it is because of what is true about him that his followers should go and do what they do. This is an important principle for his followers

— and perhaps particularly his preaching followers — to keep always in mind.

The assignment that Jesus gave becomes the church's mission statement. "Go and make disciples of all nations, baptizing them in the name of the Father and of the Son and of the Holy Spirit, and teaching them to obey everything that I have commanded you." It is the "standing order" under which we operate, and it is captured in four verbs: go, make disciples, baptize, and teach. It would be a worthwhile exercise for a church to contemplate each of these four verbs, and then to evaluate their own work in light of this "great commission."

Finally, Matthew's closing word for his gospel is Jesus' beautiful and characteristic promise: "I am with you always, to the end of the age." Throughout so many Old Testament stories, the guarantee that God would be "with" was the source of boldness and peace (e.g., Genesis 26:3; Exodus 3:12; Joshua 1:5; Judges 6:16; Psalm 23:4; Isaiah 43:2). Within the scope of just this gospel, this crowning promise brings to full circle the identity given to Jesus before his birth: Emmanuel (Matthew 1:23).

Application

Ask your people what is the first commandment. Some will turn instinctively to Exodus 20 and the Ten Commandments. Others will hear the question through the filter of the New Testament and say with Jesus that the first and greatest commandment is to love God. But there is arguably a third answer, and it is found in our Old Testament lection.

Chronologically, the first commandment that God gave to human beings was this: "Be fruitful and multiply." Now we live in a culture that recoils a bit from such an instruction. Abundant propagation and reproduction seems irresponsible to the modern, western mind. But whatever we make of the literal application of that commandment to our world today, we cannot deny that fruitfulness and multiplication were built into God's design.

When Genesis records God's purposeful design for plant life, for example, he says, "Let the earth put forth vegetation: plants yielding seed, and fruit trees of every kind on earth that bear fruit with the seed in it" (Genesis 1:11). See how prominent and deliberate the reproductive — indeed, the multiplicative — quality is. See the emphasis on yielding seed.

We know, of course, the tremendous potential for multiplication that those seeds represent. How many seeds are generated by a single apple tree in a single year? How many seeds are contained in a single stalk of grain? The proliferation implied by the design is staggering.

And what is true of plant life is indicated in the animal world as well. Before human beings came on the scene, God had commanded the fish and birds to "be fruitful and multiply." Just as humanity was later instructed to "fill the earth and subdue it," so the fish were called to fill the waters. We know that so many species — including human beings — have within their bodies the capacity to reproduce at a remarkable rate. Multiply, indeed!

Yet as we read on in scripture, we see that fruitfulness is God's desire across the board. That is to say, it is not merely biological reproduction. His will in all of life is embodied by the idea of fruitfulness. Thus the righteous are "like trees planted by streams of water, which yield their fruit in its season" (Psalm 1:3). Jesus told his disciples that abiding in him would make them fruitful and that their fruitfulness glorified God (John 14:1-8). Paul spoke of the Christian virtues as the natural produce of the Spirit's influence (Galatians 5:22-23). So it is that God looks for fruitfulness in people, but judgment awaits those who do not bear the good fruit (Luke 3:8-9).

It turns out that God's command in the beginning is Christ's standing order in the end. That is to say, God had made the plants, the fish, the birds, the animals, and the human beings, and he intended for them to reproduce as more of what he had made them to be in the first place. In the end, Jesus commanded his followers to do the same. He had made them disciples and now they were to reproduce what he had made them to be.

The will and design of God remain constant. "Be fruitful and multiply, fill the earth." "Go and make disciples of all nations." His desire is that we should reproduce in abundance, throughout the whole earth, what he himself began.

An Alternative Application

Matthew 28:16-20. "A Doubting Thomas by Any Other Name." They say that hope springs eternal. I am unwilling to give doubt equal credit, but it surely is durable. Doubt may not be eternal, but it does stay alive too long.

By the time we arrive at this juncture, the disciples have personally witnessed the multitudes fed, lepers cleansed, and storms calmed. They have watched the crippled walk and the dead raised. They have seen Jesus crucified and resurrected. And now, in this climactic moment from his gospel, Matthew reports, "But some doubted."

Who are these guys? Because of one episode in John's gospel, we have forever labeled Thomas as "doubting," but this reference from Matthew suggests that Thomas was not alone. After all that they had seen and heard, still some doubted.

Thomas, you recall, was away from the rest of the group when Jesus made his first resurrection appearance to the disciples. That gave rise to his infamous statement about not believing. Once he saw firsthand the risen Lord, however, Thomas was full of confidence about Jesus.

The folks gathered around here at the end of Matthew 28, on the other hand, are all privy to the risen Lord. They can all see him, touch him, hear him "but some doubted." I admit that they are an uninspiring lot at this moment. Yet I am grateful for Matthew's reference to them, for they remind us of several important truths.

First, they remind us that the first disciples of Jesus were as human as we are. We needn't imprison them in stained-glass windows or marble sculptures, for they are as flesh and blood and blemished as any of us. And given what God accomplished through them, we may be encouraged by that truth.

Second, they remind us of the reliability of the scriptures. If the New Testament were some early church concoction designed as pro-Jesus propaganda, it would not include this detail. Portraying some of his own followers still in doubt mode at the conclusion of the gospel story, after all, is not great salesmanship. And that brings us very naturally to the third point.

Third, this snapshot of the disciples reminds us that truth is not determined by public opinion polls. What the people around Jesus did or did not believe affected them, not him. He was risen whether they believed or not. He was the Son of God whether they doubted it or affirmed it. So it is that our proclamation of the gospel is to help people come to know the truth, not to garner support for it.

Proper 6 | Ordinary Time 11

Genesis 18:1-15 (21:1-7)

Romans 5:1-8

Matthew 9:35--10:8 (9-23)

Psalm 116:1-2, 12-19

by Wayne Brouwer and Schuyler Rhodes

Promises, promises

Psychiatrist, Viktor Frankl, often wrote about the meaninglessness of his patients' lives. He was able to sympathize with them in a powerful way, since he spent part of World War II in a concentration camp. He remembered the dark weeks of 1944 vividly: the numbness of the gray days, the cold sameness of every dreary morning.

Suddenly, like a bolt of bright colors, came the stunning whisper that the Allies had landed at Normandy. The push was on. The Germans were running. The tide of the war had turned. "By Christmas we'll be released!" they told each other.

Frankl recalls the changes that took place in the camp: Every day the workers went out to their same jobs but their hearts were lighter, and the work seemed a bit easier. Each mealtime they peered into the same cauldron of slop but somehow it seemed less difficult to swallow since every bite was a countdown to freedom. The stress in each barracks community was the same: people fighting for a little privacy; jealousies and dislikes aired in spicy retorts. Yet forgiveness came a little easier these days, for the ups and downs of the present dimmed as the future became a closer and closer reality.

It was interesting, says Frankl. Fewer people died in those months. Even the weakest ones began to cling tenaciously to life. But Christmas 1944 passed, and the Allied troops never came. There were setbacks and defeats, and the bits of news smuggled into the camp made no more promises.

Then, says Frankl, the people began to die. No new diseases came into the camp. Rations remained the same. There was no change in working conditions. But the people began to die one after the other, as if some terrible plague had struck.

And, indeed, it had. It was the plague of hopelessness, the epidemic of despair. Studies show that we can live forty to sixty days without food, eight to twelve days without water, and maybe three minutes without oxygen. But without hope we can't survive even a moment. Without hope we die. Without hope there's no reason to wake up in the morning.

Hope is at the heart of today's passages. Hope is the promise of God to Abram and Sarai that they will not die childless. Hope is the pledge of tomorrow given in the saving grace of Jesus Christ. Hope is the message of the disciples of Jesus, scattering throughout Palestine and beyond, bringing the message of the kingdom of God to all the villages and towns. There are times when hope is gone, when life is cruel, and when the future is a blank wall. Then, says the gospel, there is only one way to carry on. Hope in God.

Genesis 18:1-15 (21:1-7)

Abram is an Aramean from the heart of Mesopotamia whose father, Terah, begins a journey westward that Abram continues upon his father's death. Whatever Terah's reasons might have been for moving from the old family village — restlessness, treasure-seeking, displacement, wanderlust —

Genesis 12 informs us that Abram's continuation of the trek was motivated by a divine call to seek a land that would become his by providential appointment. This was the first of four similar divine declarations that occur in quick succession in chapters 12, 13, 15, and 17. Such repetition cues us to the importance of these theophanies, but they ought also cause us to look more closely at the forms in which the promises to Abram are made.

In brief, Abram's first three encounters with God are shaped as promises of gifts that God would bring into Abram's future: land, riches, and heirs. Only in Genesis 17, however, does the language of the dialogue alter and Abram is challenged to respond with visible acts of trust — his name is changed (along with Sarai's), and the covenant cutting of circumcision is introduced to mark the family as under new management. All of these elements form the background to today's lectionary reading. Now, in today's lectionary reading, the promises are reaffirmed in a visitation that calls on Abraham and Sarah to provide hospitality for God so that God might provide hospitality for them. The "laughter" of Isaac's miraculous birth is pledged.

For ancient Israel (and through scripture, for us, as well), the implications would be striking. First of all, the nation would see itself as the unique and miraculously born child fulfilling a divine promise. Israel could not exist were it not for God's unusual efforts at getting Abram and Sarai pregnant in a way that was humanly impossible. Second, they were the descendents of a man on a divine pilgrimage. Not only was Abram *en route* to a land of promise, but he was also the instrument of God for the blessing of all the nations of the earth. In other words, Israel was born with a mandate, and it was globally encompassing. Third, there was a selection in the process of creating their identity. They were children of Abraham, but so were a number of area tribes and nations descending from Ishmael. What made them special was the uniqueness of their lineage through Isaac, the miraculously born child of Abraham and Sarah's old age. Israel had international kinship relations, but she also retained a unique identity fostered by the divine distinctions between branches of the family.

In recalling the tale of father Abraham in this manner, Genesis places before Israel at Sinai the important element of unique identity: We came into this world miraculously as a result of a divine initiative to bless all the nations of the earth; therefore we are a unique people with the powerful backing of the Creator and participating in a mission that is still in progress. It is in the divine promises of unwarranted but hugely needed hope that laughter, whether in disbelief or the unbridled hilarity of fulfillment, is released.

Romans 5:1-8

In Romans 1:18-3:20, Paul describes the crippling effect of sin. But once the stage has been set for his readers to realize again the pervasive grip of evil in this world, including within their own divided and deluded hearts, Paul marches Abraham out onto the stage as a model of divine religious reconstruction. God does not wish to be distant from the world, judgmental and vengeful. Instead, as shown to Abraham, God desires an ever-renewing relationship with the people God made. Thus, as exhibited in Abraham's life (Romans 4), God initiates a relationship of favor and grace with us. In fact, according to Paul, this purpose of God is no less spectacular than the divine quest to re-create the world, undoing the effects that the cancer of sin has blighted upon us (Romans 5).

The language Paul uses to talk about salvation in Romans 5 is that of homecoming. We were alienated, but now we have come near. We were strangers, but now we have become the dwelling place of God's Spirit. We were sinners, but Jesus Christ has made us friends and family. When we actually begin to breathe the air of the gospel, we begin to smell the aromas of home.

Christopher Fry put it this way in one of his plays (*The Lady's Not for Burning*): Margaret and Nicholas are talking about a woman who seems to be acting strangely. Margaret says, "She must be lost."

Nicholas responds, wistfully, "Who isn't? The best thing we can do is to make whatever we're lost in look as much like home as we can."

That's what we do with our lives, isn't it? We have so many goals and dreams and hopes in life, yet so few of them turn out. We get old before we've done half of what we wanted. Somehow we never become what we thought we might. We make a few mistakes along the way. We disappoint some people, and they disappoint us. Even our best times have an edge of bitterness attached to them — when they end we walk away nursing our nostalgia. We're always a little bit away from home — from the home we remember, or the home we desire; from the dream we miss, or the dream we're still looking for. Especially in our relationship with God, we have become outsiders and foreigners. Then, in the mystery of grace, God steps into our world in Jesus, takes our alienation upon himself, and welcomes us back into the family.

That's what Nicholas is saying to Margaret in Christopher Fry's play. We're all a bit lost in life. We're all a bit away from home. The best we can do is make what we have look as much as possible like what we think "home" should be, until we can finally see our true home, and, like Paul suggests later in this letter, bring our friends along with us.

No matter where we go, no matter what we do, there must live in each of us a touch of that homesickness, or we die a horrible death. Our trips "home" are only a pale imitation of the place we belong and merely a wayside rest stop on a restless journey to the real home of God's love and God's eternity. More than we know, that is where we all truly want to go. And only in finding Jesus and the coming of God's kingdom will our desires find fulfillment, and our longings be satisfied. Only then will our homesickness end.

Matthew 9:35--10:8 (9-23)

If we began with Abraham and the promises of hope that launched God's great mission in our world, we come now to the culmination of that witness. Jesus has appeared and here affirms the great mission of God by empowering his disciples to speak the gospel of heaven on his behalf. Matthew ties this witness directly to Abraham, beginning the gospel by telling us that Jesus is the son of Abraham, the one who fulfills the greatest promises of God. It must have been a strange thing for Abraham to experience the call of Yahweh. It was a big call from a big God, for it set in motion a mission that echoes throughout the Bible and is still unfolding today. Through you, said God, I will bless all people on earth. For that reason Israel exists as a witness to its neighboring nations. For the same reason, the younger children of Abraham in the church of Jesus engage in global mission efforts, as our Lord himself commissions here.

A scene from Tony Campolo's life makes us think about it in fresh ways. When Tony spoke at a conference in Hawaii it took a while for his body to catch up with the move across five time zones. The first night at his hotel his internal clock buzzed at 3 a.m. and his stomach growled for attention.

Tony wandered quiet Honolulu streets looking for a place to get fried eggs and bacon. All the respectable places were closed, and Tony finally ended up at a greasy dive in a narrow and dim alley. The place reeked with grunge. Tony was afraid to touch the menu for fear that it would stick to his fingers and that if he opened it something with too many legs to count might crawl out.

Suddenly Tony wasn't hungry, no matter how much his stomach protested. He saw a stack of donuts under a cracked plastic cover. "I'll have a donut and a coffee," he said. That ought to be safe.

The guy poured a cup of dark, thick coffee. Then he wiped his greasy hand on his dirty apron, grabbed a donut with his fingers, and threw it on the counter in front of Tony. There sat Tony Campolo at 3:30 in the morning, gagging on sour coffee and a stale donut.

All at once the door slammed open and eight or nine prostitutes sauntered in, just finished with a night's work. The joint was small and when the women crowded at the counter they surrounded Tony, swearing, smoking, and gossiping tales of their johns. Another gulp and bite, and Tony would scram.

But something stopped his exit when the woman next to him turned to her friend and said, with a faraway look in her eye, "You know what? Tomorrow's my birthday. I'm gonna be 39...."

That got Tony thinking. He asked the owner if he knew the woman who sat next to him. "Sure, that's Agnes. She's been coming here for years. Comes every night about this time."

"Well," said Tony, "she just said that it was her birthday tomorrow. What do you think? Do you think you and I could do something about that — maybe throw her a birthday party right here tomorrow night?"

The man got a cute smile on his chubby cheeks. "That's great!" he said. So they made their plans. At 2:30 the next morning Tony was back. He brought crepe paper decorations and a foldout sign that said, "Happy Birthday, Agnes!" By three o'clock, the diner was looking pretty good. By 3:15, it was crowded with wall-to-wall prostitutes. At 3:30, Agnes and her group walked in. Tony had everyone ready to shout, "Happy birthday, Agnes!" She was flabbergasted. Her mouth fell open, her legs wobbled, she put her hands to her head, and almost fell over stunned. Her friend grabbed her by the arm and led her to the counter where her birthday cake rested on a pedestal. Tony led the room in an energetic chorus of "Happy Birthday to You."

Agnes began to cry. She saw the cake with all the candles and wept. Harry, who was not used to seeing a prostitute cry, said rather gruffly, "Blow out the candles, Agnes! Come on! Blow out the candles! If you don't blow 'em out, I'll have to do it!"

So Agnes composed herself, and after a minute or two she blew them out. Everyone cheered. "Cut the cake, Agnes," they yelled. "Cut the cake!"

But Agnes looked down at the cake and, without taking her eyes off it, said to Harry, "Look, Harry ... Would it be all right with you if I ... I mean, is it okay if I ... What I mean is, do you think it's okay if I just *kept* the cake for a little while? I mean, is it all right if we don't eat it right away?'

Harry didn't know what to say. He shrugged his shoulders and said, "Sure, if that's what you want. Go ahead and keep the cake. Take it home if you want to."

Agnes turned to Tony and asked again, "Is it okay? I live just down the street. Can I take the cake home for a minute? I'll be right back. Honest!"

Agnes picked up the cake like it was the Holy Grail itself. Slowly, she promenaded through the room with it high in front of her for everyone to see. She carried her treasure out the door and everyone there watched her in stunned silence. When she was gone nobody seemed to know what to do, so Tony got up on a chair and said, "What do you say we pray?"

There they were together in a hole-in-the-wall, greasy spoon, all the prostitutes of Honolulu's streets, at 3:30 in the morning, and Tony gathered them to pray for Agnes. He prayed for her life. He prayed for her health. He prayed for her soul and her relationship with God.

When Tony finished praying Harry leaned over the counter and said, accusingly, "Hey! You never told me you was a preacher! What kind of a church do you belong to anyway?"

Tony replied, "I belong to a church that throws parties for prostitutes at 3:30 in the morning."

Harry thought about that for a moment and then said, "Naw you don't! There ain't no church like that! If there was, I'd join it! Yessir, I'd be a member of a church like that!"

What do you think? Would you be a member of a church like that? Is that what God had in mind when talking with Abraham way back in Genesis? How does the Bible urge us to take the journey of Jesus' disciples and follow the mission of God?

Proper 6 / Ordinary Time 11

Application

Years ago, Dr. Arthur Gossip preached a sermon titled, "When Life Tumbles In, What Then?" He preached it the day after his beloved wife had suddenly died. No one could bring more powerfully than he the challenge of the closing lines:

"Our hearts are very frail, and there are places where the road is very steep and very lonely. Standing in the roaring Jordan, cold with its dreadful chill and very conscious of its terror, of its rushing, I ... call back to you who one day will have your turn to cross it, 'Be of good cheer, my brother, for I feel the bottom and it is sound!' "

That's the hope which breathes through today's readings.

Alternative Application

Romans 5:1-8. Paul's opening in Romans 5 is fresh with many sermon nuggets. Don Francisco's great lyrics in "I'll Never Let Go of Your Hand" might make wonderful poetry to flesh out the themes of this pregnant passage.

Preaching The Psalm

by Schuyler Rhodes

Psalm 116:1-2, 12-19. The words of this psalm emerge from a grateful heart. They flow from the consciousness of one who knows the saving power of God in concrete terms. More to the point, they reflect the experience of someone who has been rescued. Public safety professionals experience this kind of thing frequently. In the daily line of their work they rescue people, and the gratefulness of some of them is remarkable. A woman whose children have been rescued from a fire shows up at the fire station every week with gifts for the firefighters. She falls all over herself thanking them again and again. She becomes a booster for the fire station, raising funds and developing community support. She even remembers the rescuers in her will. This is the kind of gratefulness that flows from this psalm.

But here we have more than brave firefighters on the job. Here we have God as the rescuer.

In a culture where privilege and entitlement are the prevailing sentiments of the day, this is a hard thing to grasp. Most people can't imagine that they need rescuing, so being grateful for such a rescue isn't really within their emotional vocabulary. Yet the truth is that we do need rescuing. We need rescuing from this epidemic of consumerism, which is strangling our spirit and ruining the life of the planet. We need rescuing from the blindness that keeps us from being sensitive to the suffering of others. We need to be rescued from our participation in the wounding and death of millions of innocent people. There is no question about it. We're in trouble. Whether we wish to acknowledge it or not, we are a people who need rescuing. We are a people who need God.

The incredible part of it all is that our rescuer is here, present, ready. All we need do is reach out and grab the lifeline. All we need do is turn to God in our hearts. Once we are able to do this, our own voices will match that of this psalm. Once we accept and embrace this God who rescues we will know the power and wonder of a grateful heart. We will then understand what it means to be saved and our impulse, our desire will be to "offer a thanksgiving of sacrifice as we call upon the name of the Lord."

Proper 7 | Ordinary Time 12
Genesis 21:8-21
Romans 6:1b-11
Matthew 10:24-39
by Cathy Venkatesh

Family wounds and God's grace

In one of my former parishes, the wife of retired pastor led us in a Bible study of the book of Genesis. She was trained as a social worker and had previously led studies of Genesis in her work with prisoners. As we progressed through the stories, she told us how the complicated family relationships of the patriarchs prompted the incarcerated men in her Bible study to talk about their own families and the troubles so many of them had experienced growing up. Today's readings invite us to consider the families God has given us, how they may be sources both of wounding and grace, and how we are ultimately called to place our trust in God alone.

Genesis 21:8-21

This is the second of two stories in Genesis in which Hagar was cast out into the wilderness. In the first story (Genesis 16), Hagar is pregnant by Abram, runs away when she is ill-treated by Sarai, and is found by a spring in the wilderness by an angel who tells her to return to Abram and Sarai and bear her son Ishmael. The angel gives Hagar a promise similar to the one God gave to Abram that her offspring will be so many that they cannot be counted (Genesis 16:10). This first story is considered by scholars to come from the Jahwist source.

Today's story is attributed to the Elohist source and while it bears some striking parallels to the earlier story, it also differs in significant ways. Sarai and Abram have become Sarah and Abraham; Ishmael is now a child and Isaac has been born. Where the conflict in the first story is over the pregnant Hagar's contempt for her barren mistress Sarai and Sarai's subsequent mistreatment of Hagar, here Sarah becomes jealous of Hagar's son Ishmael and fears that he will share in or usurp Isaac's inheritance. When Hagar leaves this time, she does not run away; she is dismissed by Abraham at Sarah's bidding, and she does not come back. In casting her out, Abraham gives the Egyptian Hagar her freedom after years as a slave; yet she wanders in the wilderness where death is a certainty. The connections with the later Exodus story are striking. When the water Abraham has given them runs out, Hagar despairs of her own life and her son's. While we are told that Hagar was the one who raised up her voice in despair, the angel who responds says that God has heard the voice of her son, a wordplay on Ishmael's name, which means "God hears." Hagar receives the promise that Ishmael will become a great nation. And now both Jewish and Muslim traditions consider Ishmael the father of the Arab people.

Romans 6:1b-11

Today is the first of thirteen successive weeks reading through Paul's letter to the Romans from the beginning of chapter 6 through the end of chapter 12, skipping some sections along the way. In chapters 1-5, Paul has developed his argument that Jew and Gentile alike are justified by faith, not works. It is Christ's death that has saved sinful humanity and reconciled us with God. This is a free gift of grace, to be accepted with joy and gratitude, and which will rightly lead us to transformed lives. Freed from God's judgment for our sins, we no longer live in fear, but grace.

In chapter 6, Paul describes the transformation that comes when we accept God's justification through baptism. We die to the old ways, as Christ died, and rise to new life as he rose. Through Christ's death, our sins have been forgiven, so we, too, through his death must become dead to sin. When we accept this through baptism, we do not go on living in the same old way, confident that God will keep forgiving us over and over again. Instead, we are transformed from our old, sinful selves, united with God and live gladly according to his ways.

Matthew 10:24-39

Chapter 10 in Matthew describes Jesus sending out the twelve apostles to perform healings and exorcisms. Most of the chapter, including today's readings, reports his instructions to the twelve; this "missionary discourse" is the second of five major discourses in the gospel of Matthew, which together may reflect the five books of the Torah. (The other discourses appear in chapters 5-7, 13, 18, and 24-25.) Jesus tells the apostles to visit Jewish towns and offer their services freely to those who will accept them (10:5-15). He warns them to expect persecution (10:16-23) and verses 24-25 continue this warning, noting that if people call Jesus Beelzebul (master of the demons), then the apostles should expect similar or worse treatment. In the face of expected persecution, Jesus offers words of reassurance that God will preserve the souls of those who are faithful (vv. 26-32). The disciples should expect that following Jesus' instructions will produce conflict (not peace, but a sword) and division and he cites the prophet Micah in describing divisions even within households (vv. 35-36). These disturbing promises and the call to take up one's cross end with the promise of life for those who are willing to surrender all that they have and are to God's mission.

Application

Today's readings are all about placing our trust in God rather than human beings and even the closest of human relationships. In Genesis, Hagar and Ishmael are cast out into the wilderness by Ishmael's father Abraham where they are saved by an angel of God. In Romans, Paul has spent chapters describing the depravity to which humanity has sunk and counsels that we can never be saved by our own merit, but only through the sacrifice of Christ. In Matthew, Jesus warns his apostles to expect persecution, resistance, possibly even death for carrying his message to the surrounding countryside. Even family members may turn against the apostles or against one another when some hear and respond to their message while others do not. God will value the apostles and preserve their souls whatever comes, if they remain faithful, but what will come will be difficult indeed.

"Amen!" some will cry aloud or in their hearts to this message to trust only God and not even those closest to us. Those who have experienced betrayal, neglect, and abuse in intimate relationships may cling to these words. Others, sitting in the pews with loving or at least good-enough families may cringe and want to cover their ears against these very same words. I think of the prisoners my friend ministered with who found the difficult stories of Genesis an opening to talk about their own experiences of the harm family members can do to each other. I think of the homeless woman who this past week shared with me her own story of bouncing around the foster care system as a child, where the families who were charged with her care often neglected and sometimes outright abused her. There are people in this world who know in their very bones how little even those closest to them may be trusted; for them, finding a way to place their trust in God can be a monumental step toward wholeness and new life. But this same message may sound like hard news for those who do love mother and father, daughter and son.

It is worth remembering that neither Jesus nor Paul had any notion of a family in which spouses shared the Christian faith and raised their children in it. Adult converts, not infants, were baptized into the faith. The gospel of Matthew and Paul's letter to the Romans come out of the earliest years of the formation of Christian communities that now have lasted for 2,000 years. We live in a world that has been profoundly shaped by Jesus' teaching. Sin still abounds, yes, but Christian communities and families have also sought to practice *agape* love with one another in every generation since Matthew and Romans were written. What was true in Matthew and Paul's day may not be true for everyone in the same way today. Even so all of us, no matter how loving our relationships, are called to place our ultimate trust and devotion in God. If we expect other people to fill the place of God in our lives, we do them a disservice and we fail in our love for them and for God. It may be worth reflecting on the ways we can place our trust or hope inappropriately in others: by expecting them to love us perfectly, to never get sick or make mistakes, to never die, to read our minds, to know and meet all our needs. Children may do all these things, but mature Christians know better (though all but the wisest may need reminding from time to time). When we give our hearts to God, we are freed to truly love other people as they are, not as we wish them to be.

An Alternate Application

Next Sunday, June 29, marks the beginning of Ramadan, and the story of Hagar and Ishmael invites reflection on the troubled family relationships among the three Abrahamic religions of Judaism, Christianity, and Islam. More than one person has observed how our bitterest enemies are often those who are like us, not those who are different. Family grudges and hostilities can divide generations, where fallings-out among friends seldom persist for so long with such vigor. With sufficient planning, a guest speaker or preacher from an Islamic community may make sense for some congregations, while prayers for peace and unity among world religions may make sense for others. Peace-making efforts across religious lines in the Holy Land or elsewhere could be highlighted.

Proper 8 | Ordinary Time 13

Genesis 22:1-14

Romans 6:12-23

Matthew 10:40-42

Psalm 13

by Wayne Brouwer and Schuyler Rhodes

Defined by choices

Robert Maynard once told how he became a writer. The journey, he said, began when he was a young boy walking to school one morning. He came to a fresh patch of concrete in the sidewalk. Somebody had just finished troweling it smooth, and it was just waiting for him!

He bent over to write his name in the cement, when suddenly there was a hulking shadow engulfing him. Looking up in terror he saw the biggest construction mason he had ever seen in his life! The guy was holding a garbage can lid, ready to smash the first little kid who dared mess up his new sidewalk!

Maynard says he tried to run, but the guy caught him around the waist and shouted, "What do you think you're doing?! Why are you trying to spoil my work?!"

Maynard remembers babbling something about only wanting to write his name there for everyone to see. The man's eyes softened. He set young Maynard on the ground and said, "Look at me, son! What do you want to be when you grow up?!"

Maynard squeaked it out: "A writer, I think."

The man sat there with him for a moment, and then pointed to the school across the street. He said, "If you want to write your name where it really matters, then go to that school, and learn what it takes, and become a real writer. And then, someday, write your name on the cover of a book, and let the whole world see it!"

That, says Robert Maynard, was the day he became a writer. The first decision was made that day, and every choice he had to make along the way has been easier because someone helped him to know who he really was. Someone showed him how to make an early choice, taking his hand at a critical moment in his life, and leading him to the right door.

So it is in today's lectionary passages. Abraham is called to make a choice none of us should ever face, yet finds the one who asks it of him providing more grace than he ever imagined. Paul tells of the struggles we make in the choices of life, and the one who chose us first so that we might never fall too deeply in the mire of broken hopes. Jesus declares that our daily choices are essentially choices about him. Choose well and wisely!

Genesis 22:1-14

Abraham was a great old man, probably 125 or so! God had come to him in the past in strange and wonderful ways. When he wore a younger man's clothes, the voice had called him on a journey with no fixed destination. But the beckoning was always one of blessing: "I'll give you land beyond measure! I'll make sure you have a child, old as you are! Your descendants will populate these hills and valleys like rain!"

Well, the land sort of took him in. Moreover, after some fits and starts he and Sarai did get a child. And even though his pension plan was still not entirely clear, life in these later years was peaceful and prosperous. After all, there was Isaac. His boy's name meant "Laughter!" and that's certainly what he brought Abraham these days. Life had turned out okay.

Now the voice came to him again. But was it really the same voice? "Sacrifice your son Isaac on the altar to me!" it said. What kind of God was this? Or was it perhaps a demon's mocking mimic? "Kill your boy! Choke out the laughter!" God forbid! Please, God, let it not be so!

There would be no sleep this night. Abraham's mind whirls while his old bones crawl in pain. Get the servants... get the transportation... get provisions... get wood... get the son....

Three days travel they go, with every step harder than the last. Isaac chatters his usual banter, laughter echoing in Abraham's cold heart. Reluctantly, Abraham spies the high place, finally. The mountain of doom. The plateau of death.

Strangely gruff, Abraham orders the servants to stay. "The boy and I will go it alone from here." Two on a murderous mission. Only one will return. The father-son hike soured even more when Isaac's laughter lilted a deadly chilly question: "Where's the lamb, father?"

What could Abraham say? Does he tell Isaac the truth: "Son, the God who said he loved me enough to give you to your mother and I now says he wants you back, and I've got to do the dirty work!"? How do you lie with a straight face when heaven is ripped apart by hell? Is it a spiteful retort, spat out in unholy jest that finally clears his throat: "My son, God will provide..."?

So here they are, clearing, building, and preparing. And now the end creeps with horror into Isaac's eyes. His father binds him. His father thrusts him on the wood. His father stands over him with a glinting knife. And the laughter dies....

But not yet. In a miraculous moment, time stops and grace points to another sacrifice. The son is free, and faith is affirmed. And he calls the place Moriah.

Moriah is one of those delightfully ambiguous names that can mean several things at once. It probably has to do with seeing at this point, or knowing. Where God sees, he will be seen. Something like that.

But what is it that God sees on a mountain called Moriah? For one thing, he sees a man. A weak man. A stumbler on the earth. A businessman who got ahead in life. A husband who cheated on his wife. A father who knew the joy of bringing new life into being.

Even more than that God sees a man who was willing to put it all on the line. Here was someone who counted his relationship with the God of the voice to be the one thing that mattered, the one thing that put everything else together, the one thing that could raise even heaven out of this stench of hell.

Probably the most important thing about the moment of seeing is not only that God sees Abraham there on Mount Moriah. In some mysterious way, God is also seen by Abraham.

A geography lesson tells the rest of the story. On this same barren spot of ground, centuries later, David would urge Solomon to build the temple of God. It would stand as a doorway between earth and eternity. Then, in the mysterious design of the ages, one day another Father would walk these slopes with another son. That son, too, would raise his voice to his Father, and the Father, for a time, would be silent. The wood of the offering would be prepared, and the son would be lifted as a sacrifice. On what the world would later call "Good Friday," this other Father would shed tears of pain as his child died, this time with no escape.

Somehow history would repeat itself and more with a vengeance. Yet this Lamb would also be chosen by God for the altar. And laughter would be silenced for three days while all the world looked on in wonder.

Proper 8 / Ordinary Time 13

Romans 6:12-23

Good intentions aren't enough in life, according to Paul. I think of that sometimes when I am officiating at a marriage ceremony. What exciting times! Everyone smiles! Everybody is dressed up for a celebration! Everything is so beautiful, so radiant, so full of hope and promise!

I stand at the front of the church with the bride and groom, and in their eyes I see the best of intentions: theirs will be the perfect marriage! Theirs will be the strongest home! Theirs will be the deepest vows, the truest commitments, the richest promises, the surest future! Yet within me there is often this nagging uncertainty. Why for so many who think they are headed for heaven does the journey of marriage lead them to hell?

Good intentions aren't enough. Hector Berlioz, the great composer, was living in Paris in 1830. He loved a young woman named Camille, and they were engaged to be married.

But then Hector was awarded the Prix de Roma, the Prize of Rome. He could study and compose and perform his music in Italy for a year or two, and all of his financial needs would be covered!

Camille agreed with him that this was an opportunity he needed to take. Off he went, with a kiss and a promise that they would soon be married. His intentions never changed.

But life in Rome swallowed him up. And for Camille, life in Paris went on. Other suitors came. When Berlioz next heard from her, she was on her way to marriage with another! Hector, of course, caught the next coach to Paris. Only he got on the wrong one and ended up in Genoa. There he tried again. He booked passage to France once more, but his anxiety must have blinded him because he took the wrong coach again and ended up in Nice.

By this time Camille was married, and Hector quit his journey. That's what happens sometimes when you catch the wrong bus!

The world is full of good intentions. Nobody wants war! Everybody wants prosperity! There is a hope and a wish and a desire for love in every human breast! But read the morning newspaper or watch the evening news, and another picture emerges. The best of intentions isn't enough to heal racial scars. The highest ambitions can't lift the slums out of hell. The purest desires won't by themselves chart a course to peace, prosperity, and democracy among the countries in turmoil.

Having an ideal, or catching a vision, or knowing to city to which you want to go doesn't get you there! You know the old saying: "The road to hell is paved with good intentions!" That's what Paul speaks of here.

Do you think that those who sit in AA meetings dreamed, in their younger years, asked Harry Emerson Fosdick, that they would find themselves there some day? Of course not! And when they come to that point, when they find themselves in a city they didn't intend to visit, when they know that they took the wrong bus somewhere, what do they do? Do they wish for another city and imagine it into being? The City of Sobriety? The Metropolis of Second Chances?

If you have ever gone to an AA meeting you know it isn't so. The right bus comes for them only through hard work, and mutual support, and through watching every step of the journey. Late at night they call each other and say, "Get on the right bus! Stay on the wagon! Don't let your thirst take your feet where your heart knows it shouldn't go!"

Do you remember the story of the Minotaur in ancient Greek legends? The Minotaur was a terrible monster that lived deep underground in a labyrinth of caves and passages. Every year the Minotaur devoured young children. Ate them up!

Someone had to put a stop to it, so young Theseus did the work. He went down into the realms of darkness, took his sword, braved the beast, and slew it dead. But how would he get out of the labyrinth? How would he take the right turns and pass through the right gates in this maze? Everyone who saw him enter the deadly chasm was sure that he would never return to the surface, even though the Minotaur had stopped its fierce bellowing.

There was one person, however, who never stopped hoping. She loved Theseus, and knew that he would return. She knew it because she had handed Theseus a ball of string before he left on his mission. And there, in the land where he was loved, in the place where he belonged, he tied one end of that string.

When he destroyed the cruel beast in the maze all he had to do was follow the string of his love. It opened for him the right doors, and took him on the right paths. It marked for him the right gates, and led him to the place he knew he had to reach.

And that's the gospel for us. All our education, all our training, all our decision-making is, in some way, following the string that was handed to us by others. And one time, long ago, when the labyrinth of life around us was roaring with the rough meanness of the Minotaur, a young man came into our caves and our dark passages. He found the beast and slew it. Then he did one more thing. He handed us a golden string: the way out; the way of life; the ticket on the right bus.

Listen to the words of William Blake. They are really the words of Jesus. He says to us:

> *I give you the end of a golden string;*
> *Only wind it into a ball,*
> *It will lead you in at Heaven's gate,*
> *Built in Jerusalem's wall.*

Matthew 10:40-42

Jesus sends his disciples out as ambassadors of grace. While blessing them in these verses, he actually announces the impact of the choices people make. C.S. Lewis described our lives so well in *Mere Christianity*. In his chapter on "Christian Behavior" he talked about people who think that Christianity is a kind of one-time bargain with God: "You do this for me and I'll do that for you!" We bargain our way into heaven based on a one-time negotiation.

Not so, says Lewis. That's not the way of the Bible. We aren't people who have managed to bargain our way into heaven. Rather, we are people who make choices. We all start out at a similar point when we enter this world as babies. But then we begin to choose. We choose this way instead of that; we choose these friends instead of those; we pick this career rather than the other.

Little by little along the way, says Lewis, we begin to turn ourselves toward God or toward something else, something ultimately demonic. Each choice in life is a new gate. Which way will you go? Or perhaps more accurately, who are you becoming?

Says Lewis, "... every time you make a choice you are turning the central part of you, the part of you that chooses, into something a little different than it was before." He says that when you look at your life as a whole, with all of those innumerable choices you make from day to day, "all your life long you are slowly turning either into a heavenly creature or into a hellish creature."

Application

Robert Frost summarized this well in his famous poem. He talks about finding himself in a forest of trees on a glorious autumn afternoon. He›s walking down a path, and there's a fork in the way. Which direction should he go?

When he makes his choice and picks his direction, he says to himself:

I shall be telling this with a sigh
Somewhere ages and ages hence:
Two roads diverged in a wood, and I —
I took the one less traveled by,
And that has made all the difference.

That's the way it is in life. George Mueller was one of the finest persons who ever walked this earth. In the nineteenth century he set up orphanages around the world to care for the little ones who had no one else to look after them. He provided for the poor. He preached the love of Jesus, and he lived it every day.

Someone once called him a success. He said no, he wasn't a success; only a servant, a servant of his Master who had loved him to life.

Well, asked a reporter, how did you manage to do all you've done during the course of your life?

"I don't really know," replied Mueller. "As I look back on my life, I see that I was constantly brought to a crossroads which demanded a choice of which way I should go." He said that once he had started to follow in the steps of Jesus all the rest of the decisions that came after seemed easier. He caught the right bus. When he had done that the first time it became the start of a habit. The second time he knew which bus to take, and by the third and the fourth and the fifth choices, the way was much more clear. Earlier decisions made his later decisions easier.

Alternative Application

Genesis 22:1-14. This incident is identified as a test of Abraham's faith. In light of his response to earlier Royal Grant promises (12 — given land, he leaves the land; 13 — promised land, he tries to take the land by force; 15 — declared a soon-to-be father, he connives to get a son), Abraham is now called to declare his loyalty to the God who has ratified a Suzerain Vassal covenant with him (Genesis 17). While the test may seem overly demanding (*kill your only son, the one given miraculously and the heir to your identity and promises*), there are mitigating factors that help us understand it better.

First, it was not out of the ordinary for people at that time to believe that deities required human sacrifice. The unusual twist in this story is that Yahweh, by stopping the bloodshed of Isaac, chooses deliberately to distance himself from these other deities, and shows that he does not delight in human sacrifice.

Second, Yahweh provides an alternative offering, a ram divinely placed on the scene. Third, the place is named "Moriah," which can ambiguously mean either "Yahweh sees" or "Yahweh will be seen," both of which are correct (Yahweh sees the faith of Abraham; Yahweh is more clearly seen by Abraham) and thus illuminate the idea presented in the text that "Yahweh provides" the sacrifice.

Fourth, this idea is further confirmed by later references to the location of the site. In 2 Chronicles 3:1, this mountain is specified as the future location of Solomon's temple. Such a designation would tie the animal sacrifice to the temple rituals of a later century. It would also put the events of Genesis 22 on the very spot where Jesus would be crucified some twenty centuries hence, in another intense father/son engagement.

Preaching the Psalm

By Schuyler Rhodes

Psalm 13. "Hide and Seek." Children scatter in the backyard, finding shadows and crevices in which to hide as the one who is "it" counts ever more quickly. "1, 2, 3, 4, 5, 6, 7, 8, 9, 10... Ready or not! Here I come!" It is an epic tale of childhood. Hiding, seeking, finding; all the elements of real life wrapped up in a game played at dusk on a humid night in June. Sometimes it seems that God plays such a game with us. In this game we're "it," and God is hiding.

In times of deepest distress, it can feel like God has taken a hike. The contemporary language may put it a little differently, but the words "How long will you hide your face from me?" say it pretty well.

For everyone there comes a time when all the language about God's abiding presence melts away in the face of suffering and pain. In the midst of a horrific divorce, the abandoned and betrayed spouse cries out for God. From the grim chaos of a battlefield a terrified boy shrieks for God's salvation from a fetid trench lined with the corpses of his buddies. The list is very, very long. And this is no child's game.

Where is it that God goes sometimes? Why is it that there are times when we feel not Holy presence, but an empty void instead? Has God truly taken a powder? Or is something else happening?

A wise rabbi once said that when we feel that God is far away it might be a good idea to check and see who it is that really moved. Have we stepped so far away from the practice of God's presence that when the moment of need arrives we have no idea what to do?

There is also the matter of our need over against a universe we simply do not understand. The person, for example, who cried for God in the midst of a soul-crushing divorce is now blissfully remarried with several children. Perhaps God was in the details, after all?

It seems that John Wesley had it right when he urged his followers who felt faith slipping away to pray until faith would come. Even if the lights are out and we're wandering around looking for a God who seems to be hiding, it turns out that God is indeed there. God is indeed with us. And so, even through our unknowing and our confusion; through our weary tears and our pain we never stop falling to our knees and giving thanks and praise to God... even if we think God is playing hide and seek.

Proper 9 | Ordinary Time 14

Genesis 24:34-38, 42-49, 58-67

Romans 7:15-25a

Matthew 11:16-19, 25-30

by Ron Love

A faith journey

Two players. Two teammates. Same team. One is known for "Tebowing." One is known for murder. Tim Tebow. Aaron Hernandez. So it was for theNew England Patriots. One lives by the spirit. One lives by the flesh.

Though the struggle between the old and the new, between the former life of sin and the new life of grace seems to be lived separately in these two New England players, for the rest of us it is a constant internal battle of good versus evil, what we do versus what we desire to do.

There is a common theme in our three lectionary readings for this Sunday. It is being able to give up our former selves to become a new creation. It is the ability to give up the old for the new. It is the ability to accept God's call to welcome and celebrate a new life.

It was for Isaac the acceptance of a new wife and a new journey. For Paul it was giving up a life lived under the law for one lived by grace. For the Jews it was able to surrender the asceticism of John the Baptist for the celebration of Jesus. And for all of those involved, the transformation could only come by faith.

When Pope Francis was speaking at the World Youth Day in August 2013 he said children fall prey to the "false paradise" of drugs. But the false paradise we succumb to is not just drugs, for it is anything that keeps us under the vestige of sin and abhorrent of righteous living.

At the same rally in Rio de Janeiro the pope spoke of the importance of grandparents acting as a "bridge" to preserve our religious heritage. A bridge between the old and the new is the proclamation of all three lessons this day. Isaac was to be the bridge with Rebekah, a wife from his father's Abraham clan to continue the faithful adherence to the covenant. Paul was to bridge the gap from law to grace. Jesus was to bridge the gap from stoicism to the celebration of a living a redemptive life.

The bridge, for all three, could only be crossed over by faith. Isaac had to have faith in his trusted servant that the Lord would lead him to an honorable wife. Paul had to have the faith to accept the revelation experienced on the road to Damascus. Those who jeered at Jesus had to accept by faith that he represented the celebration of the coming kingdom of God.

Genesis 24:34-38, 42-49, 58-67

Isaac's mother has passed away. His father Abraham is on his death bed. As the patriarch of the family and the one to whom God had established his covenant with the chosen people, Abraham knew it was time to pass the mantle of leadership to his son. In order for the Hebrews to be numbered as the stars in the heavens and as the grains of sand on the shores of the sea, Isaac needed a wife. The honorable lady could not be a foreigner but had to come from Abraham's own tribe. To assure this Abraham sent his dutiful servant in search of a bride. It was for Abraham an act of faith for he knew he would be deceased before the betrothed returned to Isaac. Abraham's steadfast obedience and reliance on faith brought Rebekah to Isaac.

Romans 7:15-25a

Paul in this passage is reflecting on his old life lived under the law and his new life lived by grace. Yet even though he has become a new creation in Christ he still struggles with the oppressiveness of sin. He considers that sin has infected the members of his body, but his mind realizes that by grace he has been forgiven. Thus he is struggling between living a life beguiled by sin and one of righteousness. He realizes that he cannot with sure will power cast sin out of his life, for this can only be accomplished by living in faith. Therefore he so aptly describes his spiritual struggle.

Matthew 11:16-19, 25-30

Those gathered around Jesus live in a confused state of mind. They rejected John the Baptist for he was too stoic; yet, they are unable to entertain the celebratory disposition of Jesus. Because of their legalistic orientation they are unable to surrender their entrenched way of thinking and accept the grace that is offered to them by Jesus. They are hindered by hardness of heart to accept on faith that Jesus is the Messiah who will forgive sins and redeem the fallen world.

Application

The sermon could center on the struggle we have to live by faith. The message would be one of letting go and trusting in God's divine guidance. Abraham had to let go and trust God to bring a wife from his clan. Isaac had to let go and trust that Rebekah was the chosen wife for him. Paul had to let go of the law and be willing to live by faith. The followers of Jesus had to let go of their preconceived notions and celebrate that Jesus is the true Messiah.

An Alternate Application

In all three lectionary readings, there is a personal struggle to live by faith. Each character mentioned had to have to have the trust that can only come by faith. To acquire that trust, each had to exercise self-surrendering and self-discipline. In so doing they had to trust that faith would sustain them and that the promises of God were dependable.

Proper 10 | Ordinary Time 15

Genesis 25:19-34

Romans 8:1-11

Matthew 13:1-9, 18-23

by Wayne Brouwer

Choices

As parents, we want to influence our children. One pastor I know moved his family seven different times. During each of the last five moves, he left one or two children behind. Now, as he retires, he's trying to figure out what's become of his family, and what impact his life has had on his children. He mourns that the center is gone. They have no place to call home.

Parents make choices that affect the manner in which their children form their identities. Harry Chapin put it well in his song "Cat's in the Cradle." When he was a young father, he was too busy making a living to take time with his son. When he was finally old enough to enjoy time with the family, his son in turn had learned to be too busy for his dad.

Of course, parents can have a positive influence, too. Maurice Boyd remembers one incident that sealed the impact of his father on his life forever. His father worked in a shipyard in Belfast, Northern Ireland. During the Depression, work dried up. Times were tough, and for three years his father was out of a job.

Then one of his father's old bosses at the shipyard approached him. The important man would find work for Mr. Boyd. He would guarantee it, no matter how much worse things got. All Mr. Boyd would have to do would be to buy a life insurance policy from the man. It would work to their mutual benefit: the boss's income would increase, and Mr. Boyd's work income would be guaranteed!

It was a great deal except for one thing: it was illegal. Maurice Boyd remembers his father sitting at the kitchen table with the whole family surrounding him. There at the table his father counted the cost. He reviewed their desperate financial situation. He ticked off the outstanding bills and the money he would be making, *ought* to be making, if only he'd say yes to his boss.

His father wrote it all down on a sheet of paper: the gains and the losses, what he could make and what he could lose. Then he wrote down a category that Maurice Boyd will never forget: integrity. What did it matter if he gained the cash to pay the rent, but lost his ability to teach his children right from wrong? What did it matter if he gained the dignity of a job but lost it each morning when he looked at himself in the mirror and knew that the only one reason he could go off to work instead of someone else was because he cheated?

His father declined the job, and the family groveled through several more years of poverty. Yet, of his father, Maurice Boyd says, "He discovered that no one can make you feel inferior without your consent, and that one way you can keep your soul is by refusing to sell it. He realized that whatever else he lost... he didn't have to lose himself."

Today's passages are all about making choices, and the outcomes they bring. Already in the womb, Jacob was showing his hand as a conniver, cheat, and swindler; his choices would follow him through a lifetime of deceit, even though God would wrestle with him for higher purposes. God's wrestling with us is Paul's theme in his letter to the Romans — Jesus makes choices that forever lock us in a grace we do not deserve, but mightily revel. And Jesus himself reminds us that we need to choose and choose and choose again in reference to him; that is the only way his seed will grow in our soil.

Genesis 25:19-34

Only a few details of Isaac's life are told on the pages of Genesis, and they occur in the transitional paragraphs from the Abraham Story Cycle (Genesis 12–25) to the Jacob Story Cycle (Genesis 26–37). Isaac is to have a wife from within Terah's larger family back in the old country, and this is accomplished through clear divine intervention and leading (chapter 24). To Isaac and Rebecca are born twins who are opposites in character, and always in competition with one another (chapter 25). Rather than emerging with an identity of his own, Isaac seems doomed to repeat his father's mistakes (chapter 26).

After those few notes, Jacob takes center stage. As our passage for today clearly indicates, he is a conniver from birth (Genesis 25:21–34). This bent of character is further developed in the following stories, where it is shown that he is favored by his mother (Genesis 25:28; 27:12; 8:9), cheats his family (father Isaac — 27:1-39; brother Esau — 25:29-34, 27:1-39; Uncle Laban — 30:25-43; daughter Dinah — 34:1-31), works for his Uncle Laban to earn wives Leah and Rachel (Genesis 29:15-30) and cattle (Genesis 30:25-43), is cheated by his uncle (Genesis 29:25-27), afraid of his brother (Genesis 32:3-21), a cowardly wrestler with God (Genesis 32:22-32), and finally receives the covenant blessing and mandate (Genesis 35:1-15).

While all of these stories are fascinating in themselves, there are two significant themes that emerge as dominant. First, in the character of Jacob the nation of Israel will always find herself reflected. After all, it is Jacob who bequeaths his special covenant name "Israel" to the community formed by his descendants. Hearing about Jacob and his exploits would be like reading a secret diary mapping Israel's psychological profile. Even before leaving Egypt the people were wrangling with Moses about burdens and responsibilities, seeking ways to shift workloads and blames elsewhere. Once the wilderness trek began, a variety of conniving subterfuges showed up, including complaints about who really had a right to lead. The spirit of Jacob remained with his namesakes.

Second, the meaning of the name "Israel" and the circumstances surrounding it became a defining moment in Israel's theology. Rarely does the text of Genesis crack open to reveal an origin outside of its narrative timeline, but as the tale of Jacob's night-long wrestling match concludes, there is indeed a note that identifies the organized nation of Israel as the audience reviewing these matters (Genesis 32:32). The story itself is more sordid than it appears at first glance. Jacob and his amassed company are heading back home to Canaan. Jacob hopes that his brother Esau has miraculously had a bout of amnesia and is excited to welcome him with no dark thoughts about Jacob's nasty subterfuge a few decades earlier. But Esau has a good memory, and the report quickly arrives that the maligned brother is racing toward Jacob's retinue at the center of an aggressive army seeking revenge.

Always the manipulator, Jacob strategizes ways to save his skin. First he splits the caravan in two, hoping Esau will target the wrong camp. Then large gifts are sent ahead in the expectation that Esau will be slowed by the herds offered, and his men distracted by the feasts of fresh roasted meat they take. Perhaps a little drunkenness might accompany the barbecue rituals, and because of these subterfuges, Jacob's groups will be able to slip past in the night.

But Jacob knows the depth of his guilt, and his manic attempts at self-preservation continue. He sends his wives and children and remaining possessions across the Jabok River while he remains behind. This is a sinister and cowardly move, for it exposes Jacob's family to the possible onslaught of Esau's army without the moderate natural moat of the river to make their position more defensible. Meantime, Jacob himself would be sitting in the protection of the rearward hills, and will have the advantage of hearing the screams of his children and wives while they are slaughtered as a warning order to escape, even if they do not. Jacob is always the conniver, and a master of self-preservation.

Yet it is here, in the quarters where he had taken such pains to make himself safe, that he becomes most vulnerable. "A man wrestled with him till daybreak" (Genesis 32:24). We know even less about this figure than the little that Jacob seems to know. Nevertheless both he and we are to infer that this was a divine engagement, and that God would not allow Jacob's hiding to keep him aloof from the court of heaven or a confrontation with himself and the tests of righteousness. At the same time, there is a graciousness in the story which reminds us that the divine messenger does not overpower or overwhelm Jacob, but continues to grapple with him, and even provides a blessing he does not deserve. This, then, is the meaning of "Israel" — one who wrestles with God.

Looking back at Jacob, Israel at Mount Sinai would see herself. She carried the conniving DNA of her forebear in her social makeup. But here at Mount Sinai she also carried his divinely appointed name. In the Suzerain Vassal covenant Yahweh formulated with her, the wrestling continued. Yahweh and Israel were bound in an embrace that would change them both.

Romans 8:1-11

Somewhere around late 53 AD the social and economic impact of the Christian gospel began to be felt acutely in Ephesus. Among the many cultural and civic resources of that city was its shrine to Artemis (known among the Romans as Diana). This temple was considered to be one of the seven wonders of the world. In fact, a great portion of the economy of Ephesus was derived from the cultic activities surrounding the temple, along with the religious tourist trade it brought to the city. As Christian adherents multiplied in Ephesus, and numbers of participants in the religious and social services related to the temple decreased, the local business world felt deeply challenged.

In response, "a silversmith named Demetrius" called together other craftsmen, and incited a public riot that brought the city to a standstill (Acts 19:23-41). Local government officials eventually defused the situation, but Paul believed the time had come for him to move on. He traveled around the Aegean Sea, collecting the offerings that had been set aside in the churches for the large benevolence gift he was planning to bring to Jerusalem. Paul arrived in Corinth either late in 53 or early in 54, and stayed three months with his friend Gaius (Acts 19:1-3; Romans 16:23). When he found that another acquaintance (and a leader in the Christian congregation located in Cenchrea, one of Corinth's seaport suburbs) named Phoebe was making a trip to Rome (Romans 16:1), Paul quickly penned what has become the most orderly summary of early Christian theology.

Because Paul had not yet made a visit to Rome, this letter was less personal and more rationally organized than was often otherwise true. Paul intended this missive to be a working document; the congregation, already established in the capital city of the empire, would be able to read and discuss it together, in anticipation of Paul's arrival, which was planned for some months ahead (Romans 1:6-15). Paul summarized his working theme and emphasis up front: a new expression of the "righteousness of God" had been recently revealed, with great power, through the coming of Jesus Christ (Romans 1:17).

Paul moves directly from his brief declaration about the righteousness of God into an extended discourse on the wrath of God as revealed against wickedness (Romans 1:18). Because of this, many have interpreted Paul's understanding of God's righteousness as an unattainable standard, against which the whole human race is measured and fails miserably. Only then, in the context of this desperate human situation, would the grand salvation of Christ be appreciated and enjoyed.

But more scholars believe that Paul's assertions about the righteousness of God actually have a positive and missional thrust. In their understanding of what Paul says, it is precisely because of the obvious corruption and sinfulness in our world, which are demeaning and destroying humanity, that God needed again, as God did through Israel, to assert the divine will. In so doing, the focus of God's righteousness is not to heap judgment upon humankind; instead God's brilliant display of grace and power in Jesus ought to draw people back to the creational goodness God had originally intended for them. In other words, the Creator has never changed purpose or plan. The divine mission through Israel was to display the righteousness of God so that all nations might return to the goodness of Yahweh. Now again, in Jesus, the righteousness of God is revealed as a beacon of hope in a world ravaged by evil bullies. The power of God is our only sure bodyguard against the killing effects of sin and society and self.

Precisely in this context, says Paul, the power of the righteousness of God as our bodyguard is most clearly revealed Thankfully, God's righteousness grabs us and holds us, so that through Jesus and the Holy Spirit we are never separated from divine love(Romans 7:25-8:39). Hope floods through us because we know Jesus and what he has done for us (8:1-11). Hope whispers inside of us as the Holy Spirit reminds us who we truly are and whose we will always be (8:12-27). Hope thunders around us as God's faithfulness is shouted from the heavens right through the pages of history (8:28-39): "...we are more than conquerors through him who loved us. For I am convinced that neither death nor life, neither angels nor demons, neither the present nor the future, nor any powers, neither height or depth, nor anything else in all creation, will be able to separate us from the love of God that is in Christ Jesus our Lord."

Matthew 13:1-9, 18-23

Within the body of Matthew's gospel, after the lengthy "Sermon on the Mount" (Matthew 5-7), Jesus' first extended teaching is the parable of the sower and seeds, today's lectionary reading. Its placing and expansive size, in comparison to the snippets of teaching that came earlier, highlight it as distinctive and important. As one reads these pages in continuous narrative, the pace suddenly slows, and Jesus demands that we reflect on what has happened so far. We have been watching the Jesus of power and action through the eyes of those around Jesus, experiencing his healings and commissionings. Now we are all called to respond to the person of Jesus. How will the sower's seed find perch in our own lives? What kind of soil are we? Both for Jesus' initial audience and for those who encounter Jesus through this gospel, the multiple-layered metaphor serves as a call to self-assessment and belief. Reaching behind the literary origins of the gospel, it is clear to see that Matthew's summary of Jesus' teachings and actions was not preaching merely to communicate information, nor was he recording Jesus' parables as a nice collection of spiritual writings. This was a document intended for volitional reaction. One *must* respond to Jesus, and the outcome of that engagement would be seen in direct changes of lifestyle and behavior.

Application

Robert Coles, child psychiatrist and Harvard University professor, tried at one time to figure out why we do the things we do. In his book *The Call of Service*, Cole reflects on people who try to make a difference in life. People who seek to reform themselves, even when sinful tendencies oozed like tentacles through their inner marrow. People who attempt to better society, in spite of the fact that it stubbornly refused the challenge.

Why do they do it? Cole asks. The people themselves often have a hard time defining what makes them tick. One young teacher in an urban school gets challenged all the time by street-smart students. Weary of self-righteous do-gooders, they ask, "What's in it for you?" And he really can't say.

But all these compassionate volunteers have one thing in common: earlier in their lives, each of them ran into a crisis situation that tested their identity and their willingness to do something about it. In that crisis situation, each of them encountered someone who put his or her life on the line and taught them the meaning of service. Someone who gave of themselves in a way that bucks the trend of selfishness and of self-preservation. And the influence of that someone else made it possible for the person they helped to be greater than each of them had previously thought they could be.

This is what Erik Erikson called "greatness finding itself." In a troubled world, where the safest bet is self-preservation, Jesus would put it this way: "Blessed are the peacemakers, for they will be called children of God." Do you see them around you? Do you know the names of some whose last name is Father, and Son, and Holy Spirit? Do you know any "children of God"? Then you've been touched by greatness itself, and have begun to make the choices of life that truly matter.

An Alternative Application

Matthew 13:1-9, 18-23. There is a powerful scene in Robert Bolt's play *A Man for all Seasons*. The story is about Sir Thomas More, loyal subject of the English crown. King Henry VIII wants to change things to suit his own devious plans, so he requires all his nobles to swear an oath of allegiance which violates the conscience of Sir Thomas More before his God. Since he will not swear the oath, More is put in jail. His daughter Margaret comes to visit him. Meg, he calls her, with affection. She's his pride and joy, the one who things his thoughts after him.

Meg comes to plead with her father in prison. "Take the oath, Father!" she urges him. "Take it with your mouth, if you can't take it with your heart! Take it and return to us! You can't do us any good in here! And you can't be there for us if the king should execute you!"

She's right is so many ways. Yet her father answers her this way. "Meg, when a man swears an oath, he holds himself in his hands like water, and if he opens his fingers, how can he hope to find himself again?"

You know what he means, don't you? When our lives begin to fragment, it's like holding our lives like water in our hands, and then letting our fingers come apart, just a little bit. The water of our very selves dribbles away. We may look like the same people, but who we are inside has begun to change.

This is why we need to consider every day how we receive the seed of the sower, the word of Jesus. What kind of soil are we? We only truly know when we chart the choices we make in a compromised world.

Proper 11 | Ordinary Time 16

Genesis 28:10-19a

Romans 8:12-25

Matthew 13:24-30, 36-43

Psalm 139:1-12, 23-24

by R. Craig MacCreary and Schuyler Rhodes

Don't blow your inheritance

I suppose all of us have particular objects of our venom and disgust. Whenever said object comes up in conversation unless we are prepared for a battle royal, loss of friendship, and a potential conviction for felony assault, we find ourselves saying, "Don't get me started." When it comes to the matter at hand we better not get started because we have no idea how things might end. Here in New England you can easily make a conversation go nuclear by simply mentioning the New York Yankees and the Boston Red Sox in the same breath. I went to college in the south and a combination of Duke and the University of North Carolina produces similar combustible results. In the Old West it was cattlemen and sheepherders that wound up the voltage of any conversation. The principle is simply that the other is accorded no slack whatsoever and no allowance is made for the common humanity we presumably all share.

On a medical doctor's advice and on the advice of counsel, I try to keep as much distance as I can between me and such potential combustibility. However, one emotional accelerant to my mental state is people who manage to squander their inheritance. Drop this catalyst into conversation and you had better head for the hills before the reaction settles. Frankly, I cheer for the man who, in Jesus' story, buried his treasure. At least he did not blow it all. I am not a hard person. I can understand how not all of us are well suited to managing money, land, or the family business. Life can get us in over our heads. So, find someone who can take care of business, create an annuity, and get out of the way. Is this so much to ask? Certainly that would be my recommendation to the prodigal son — time for career and financial counseling.

My wife knows better than to read newspaper articles to me about the latest poor, little, rich girl who has gone through her inheritance in a matter of months — "Don't get me started." It is best not to bring up within my earshot the latest headline about how someone has gone through old money with newfangled notions — "Don't get me started." The seething rage in me is set off when Civil War battlefields are encroached upon by housing developments. I register on the Richter scale when I see the loss of birds and bears to the inevitable results of a prolific disregard of the conditions of their divine inheritance.

As I approach the lectionary for this Sunday I am a little leery that this catalyst might end in some sort of cataclysm. Each of these texts in their own way reflect Paul's words that we are "... heirs of God and joint heirs with Christ — if, in fact, we suffer with him so that we may also be glorified with him" (Romans 8:17). Certainly, one way to blow the inheritance is not to recognize that you have one. There seems to be an endless supply of people included in the legal listings of those who have failed to claim their inheritance or who are missing in action. Much more is at stake here than how the pie will be divided or how high the lawyers' fees will be to sort things out: "For the creation waits with eager longing for the revealing of the children of God" (Romans 8:19). The intentions of God will be stymied until we claim the inheritance that is ours. "... For the creation was subjected to futility, not of its own will but by the will of the one who subjected it, in hope that the creation itself will be set free from its bondage to decay and will obtain the freedom of the glory of the children of God" (Romans 8:20-21).

If ever there was a man who has gone missing it was Jacob, after claiming his brother's inheritance and the blessing of their father. After all that has gone on, does he have a rightful claim to anything? Is he claimed by anyone? Tune in! The slaves in Jesus' parable feel they are in danger of losing their harvest/inheritance in spite of all the hard work that they have done. Surprisingly, Jesus does not recommend good counsel to take up their cause. As a matter of fact, Jesus recommends doing nothing and waiting. It sounds like a bad legal strategy to me. Jesus recommends against doing what any gardener knows needs to be done. The usual plan of action might not be the thing that would get one into the Garden of Eden where "the righteous will shine like the sun in the kingdom of their Father. Let anyone with ears listen!" (Matthew 13:43). I think I am ready for my own catalytic converter.

Genesis 28:10-19a

Scholars remind us that the Hebrew testament in large part was brought together following the period of Babylonian exile. People found themselves in exile from their old certainties. They believed while history had its ups and downs, the institutions of law and religion and their faith in God would save them from falling into the same fate as other nations. In a sense, as I look back over my life, America has gone through much of the same experience. As a child, it was just assumed that we were number one and invincible because of our sacred history that proceeds from glory unto glory and from Plymouth Rock through July 4 up to now.

However, the exile was the time when it seemed that things were out of control and beyond control. Having your most-honored institution trashed will do that to you. The Hebrews had experienced the mocking of their most-sacred institution by foreigners and even by their own children who tried to pass into the surrounding Babylonian culture that certainly seemed a more solid reality than when their parents talked of the good old days.

Much as Vietnam, Watergate, and the Clinton impeachment has put a dent in American self-confidence, so the Hebrews were facing a crisis of faith and trust. Leslie Gelb, formerly of *The New York Times*, wrote in 1991 of what had become of the Washington DC: "Washington is largely indifferent to truth. Truth has been reduced to a conflict of press releases and a contest of handlers. Truth is judged not by evidence, but by theatrical performance. Truth is fear, fear of opinion polls, fear of special interests, fear of judging others for fear of being judged, and fear of losing power and prestige. Truth has become acceptance of untruths." Unhinged from the protective penumbra of sacred history and like Jacob who is on the run, many in Washington DC are on the make with little or no sense of the transcendent.

Like Jacob, many have in tough times, or in the chase of what they believe to be their natural inheritance, engaged in behavior they would not normally have pursued. What is it that has prompted people to engage in political and economic conduct that has lead to Enron, the current housing crises, and to take shortcuts in public life that have led to disastrous consequences? Like Jacob, whose name can be rendered, "he who supplants," many have been willing to supplant their usual loyalty to the law to gain what they believe is their right. As with Jacob who is egged on by his mother, Rebekah, many believe that empowered by their own cleverness they will be shielded from the consequences of their acts. It is not to be for they bring pain and sorrow into our midst.

Jacob must be on the run and the sooner the better. One wonders if this is the end of the story, because of Jacob's behavior the inheritance is now sacrificed to human perfidy. The text eloquently describes the moment, "He came to a certain place and stayed there for the night, because the sun had set. Taking one of the stones of the place, he put it under his head and lay down in that place" (v. 11). The reader ponders whether the sun has set on Jacob's future as he yields to his weariness and lies down.

Imagine what a comfort this story must have been to those who have lived in exile. While most of us cannot imagine what it is to be exiled in Babylon, we have more than a passing acquaintance with what it is to feel like your children are mocking your commitments as they pass into the allure of the surrounding culture. All married couples have lived through times when the emotional distance between each other is hard to overcome. Who has not had a knowing feeling that our nation is far from its potential of living out its creed when acts of terror and torture are justified at the highest level? We mourn the sense of communal commitment when pension funds disappear and insider trading leaves most of us feeling like we are on the outside.

Jacob's story tells us this is not the final word over our lives. And the Lord stood beside him and said, "I am the Lord, the God of Abraham your father and the God of Isaac; the land on which you lie I will give to you and to your offspring; and your offspring shall be like the dust of the earth, and you shall spread abroad to the west and to the east and to the north and to the south; and all the families of the earth shall be blessed in you and in your offspring. Know that I am with you and will keep you wherever you go, and will bring you back to this land; for I will not leave you until I have done what I have promised you" (vv. 13-15).

It reminds me of what Martha said to Jesus when her brother Lazarus died, Martha said to Jesus, "Lord, if you had been here, my brother would not have died. But even now I know that God will give you whatever you ask of him" (John 11:21-22). Even now God is present and active. Times apart can be used to bring wisdom and understanding. God has a way of intruding on our schemes to live as if we are not made in God's image. Churches find that God has plans for them to grow in wisdom and stature. The United Church of Christ, of which I am a member, says never put a period where God intends a comma — God is still speaking — *"even now."*

Then Jacob woke from his sleep and said, "Surely the Lord is in this place — and I did not know it!" And he was afraid, and said, "How awesome is this place! This is none other than the house of God, and this is the gate of heaven" (vv. 16-17). Broken marriages, parental struggles, church challenges, tough times can be the gateway to heaven. When we remember where we are standing and who is standing with us we will not lose our inheritance.

Romans 8:12-25

"We do not know what the future holds but we do know who holds the future." I would expand this old saying somewhat further. While we do not know what the future holds we do know what is being held out to us in the days to come. "I consider that the sufferings of this present time are not worth comparing with the glory about to be revealed to us." There is glory ahead, after all we are, "... children, then heirs, heirs of God and joint heirs with Christ — if, in fact, we suffer with him so that we may also be glorified with him" (Romans 8:17). Just don't blow it. Here Paul relies heavily on the family image of the church as he addresses the Romans, "So then, brothers and sisters, we are debtors, not to the flesh, to live according to the flesh" (v. 12). I often find the use of the family metaphor for church as overdrawn and overused. The self-description of many congregations as one big, happy family seems to hide misery as much as reveal the glory of the church. Rather than enter into the kind of new family relationships that Jesus advocated, we often seem stuck in the kind of relationships that seem to put our inheritance at risk.

Like many families, we often presume too much about each other and do too little to free each other from fixed roles that serve the interest of the community but not the individual. We count on folks to fulfill the needs of the community more than their own. We are not very good at fighting with each other. In order to avoid conflict we suppress differences and minimize diversity. Unfortunately, like many families, we do not know how to handle or confront abusive members. We have blamed victims rather than acknowledge that when abuse arises in a congregation, we are all victims in need of healing. Close knit, we have sometimes failed to see the face of God in those other than the "family."

All of this tends to put at risk an inheritance that is ours by virtue of being a member of the family of God. It is, according to Paul, to live according to the flesh. "For if you live according to the flesh, you will die; but if by the Spirit you put to death the deeds of the body, you will live" (v. 13). Elsewhere Paul describes the church as the body of Christ. In attempting to elucidate the resurrection he writes to the Corinthians, "So it is with the resurrection of the dead. What is sown is perishable, what is raised is imperishable. It is sown in dishonor, it is raised in glory. It is sown in weakness, it is raised in power. It is sown a physical body, it is raised a spiritual body. If there is a physical body, there is also a spiritual body" (1 Corinthians 15:42-44).

In order to receive our in heritance we must be given a new heavenly body: We must become part of a new body. This concept leaps beyond the intimate level of family relations to direct us to consider what bodies I am a part of that might put my inheritance at risk? Do I participate in organizations that make it easier for me to be a racist because of their membership practices? Am I a part of a body of flesh that in its style and ambience accepts the world as it is and mocks any alternative to things as they are — a political party, a corporation, a fraternal organization? Is my inheritance of a different world at risk by getting and going along so that I can no longer imagine an alternative world? Perhaps that is why the "whole creation is waiting with eager longing for the revelation of the children of God" (v. 19).

Matthew 13:24-30, 36-43

In this parable, it is assumed that the harvest is coming. In a sense there is an inheritance ahead. There can be no doubt about it for the sower uses good seed. It is clear that the harvest will come. The question is what may dilute or diminish the harvest. What happens next seems to be that nothing can be in doubt about unless one is prepared to stay awake 24 hours a day in order to prevent the inevitable from happening. Certainly there are those folks in life who just cannot help themselves as they are ready to pounce on any hated imperfection that might crop up in their lives. Such hypervigilance cannot prevent the usual crop of things that can come up.

Some churches are hypervigilant for any and all signs of conflict so they stand ready to pounce at the very first sign of trouble. All they wind up doing is advertising that they cannot handle conflict and they miss out on the harvest that might be garnered by working the conflict through. Other churches stand on guard against any doctrinal deviation from the norm. This often leaves them functioning out of head level with a harvest of heresy trials and splinter groups rather than finding strength in listening to each other. Others fear any sign of diversion from societal norms must be eliminated lest there be no harvest. Yet, the story indicates that there will be a harvest.

The reality is that somebody is going to sneak in and get things out of plumb, "move your cheese," and rearrange the day. The master has done nothing wrong here. The fact that everyone was asleep, suggests the inevitable and natural. Quite naturally the slaves wonder how these weeds could have cropped up after the master had sowed good seed. The slaves have a plan to fix the "problem," though they seem to not have a clue as to how all this has happened. I am no gardener or farmer but under most circumstances the plan would seem to work. After all, the "problem" has been caught fairly early. They are at a place where the problem is manageable. If things are allowed to go on who knows where they might wind up and how far things could get out of hand?

However, this is not our problem to solve. Indeed it is less of a problem to be solved than a reality to be lived. Indeed much of our efforts at uprooting the "weeds" actually leave us worse off by putting the harvest at risk. "He answered, 'An enemy has done this.' The slaves said to him, 'Then do you want us to go and gather them?' But he replied, 'No; for in gathering the weeds you would uproot the wheat along with them' " (vv. 28-29). This is a fact of life that is not to be overcome in this life but can only be resolved beyond this life. "Let both of them grow together until the harvest; and at harvest time I will tell the reapers, collect the weeds first and bind them in bundles to be burned, but gather the wheat into my barn" (v. 30).

The conclusion is inescapable — the only thing left to do for the slaves is to live faithfully with this undeniable reality. Only that will prevent them from blowing the harvest/inheritance.

Application

There are several principles that can be deduced from a joint reading of these texts. One, there is an inheritance and harvest that is coming that is not necessarily contingent on the moral integrity or action of the recipient. Jacob is overtaken in flight from the consequences of his actions. Paul's words clearly imply that there are some in the Roman faith community that have been living more by the flesh than the Spirit. The master in Jesus' story acts appropriately but nevertheless is confronted with weeds that have grown up in his life. Second, there are actions that are conducive to receiving the inheritance and actions that put the inheritance at risk. Jacob can remain on the run. The Romans can act as if they are not heirs and fall back into a spirit of slavery to the flesh. Whatever actions are taken there are consequences beyond the individual. The fulfillment of God's promise is not only to Jacob but to all Israel and through them to the world. All of creation hangs on the outcome of how Christians respond to their status as heirs. The action of the master is performed not merely on his behalf but will shape the future of his entire household. Any homiletical effort that leaves out any of these dimensions has left out something that is integral to the telling of these stories.

Alternative Application

Matthew 13:24-30, 36-43. Many pastors find it hard to enter the pulpit with a head full of scholarship but a heart full of trepidation at the prospect that such scholarship might puncture the foundation of faith many of their parishioners have. The explanation that Matthew has Jesus offer about his story in verses 37-43 gives somewhat of an opportunity to bridge the gap between the head and the heart of the preacher.

Certainly, the explanation does not seem to entirely conform to the principles offered above. The emphasis seems to be an elimination of the causes of sin and evildoers rather than on how to live faithfully with such realities that do not seem to go away. Certainly the explanation seems to be out of character for Jesus. Why is this parable explained as opposed to such stories as the good Samaritan or the prodigal son? Are those stories so obvious that we readily get their meaning?

This might be an opportunity for the preacher to talk about the ongoing effort to understand the meaning of Jesus' words that goes back to the New Testament itself. In a sense the explanation is its own alternative application of the Jesus' words in the context of the Matthean community. Proclaiming that Jesus' words have been a source of meaning and direction in a variety of contexts might usher in its own inheritance/harvest.

Preaching The Psalm

by Schuyler Rhodes

Psalm 139:1-12, 23-24. The definition of a true friend is someone who knows all there is to know about you, and still loves you. More than that, a true friend is always there for you. In the modern vernacular, a true friend, knowing all there is to know about you, still "has your back." Most people present a careful construct of themselves to the world. Most people maintain a trove of secrets unknown, they think, to anyone but themselves. But a true friend knows, and won't go away.

This is the kind of fealty we find in the description of God in this psalm. No matter where this writer goes, God is there. God discerns every thought, knows every action, and is aware of our vast capacity for self-delusion and untruth. God has a file on us that goes way back. God knows it all and, incredibly, still loves us utterly and completely.

This is nothing short of amazing. It is, in fact, almost too much to bear. So, with Jonah and a host of notable others, we try to flee. Like the psalmist, we choose a dizzying array of hiding places. Careers, drugs, sex, alcohol, serial relationships; the list is long, and through it all God is still there.

To accept a love this complete has to have ramifications. To accept a love like this means that we ourselves must abandon our carefully constructed sense of self. We must step back from our delusions of independence and power. We must lay down every ridiculous assumption and face God simply, truly, as we are. Then and only then can this unqualified and abundant love flow into our being and claim us. And most of us just don't want to go there. It is, or at least we believe it is easier to stay put. "Better the devil you know ..." or something like that.

This true friend, however, stays faithful. God continues to show up in the midst of our follies and wanderings. In the storm and stress of a fractured relationship, God is there. In the shame and disgrace of failure, God is there. No matter where we try to go, God travels with us, continuing to pour out abundant grace and love. This grace doesn't go away.

Perhaps it's time to stop hiding; time to stop running. Maybe the moment has arrived to turn and accept God's incredible love and to allow the delusions to fall away. Could it be that the moment of transformation in God's loving grace is upon us?

Proper 12 | Ordinary Time 17

Genesis 29:15-28

Romans 8:26-39

Matthew 13:31-33, 44-52

by David Coffin

Kingdom ambiguities

So a person believes they have gotten a job or are active in a community that calls itself "Christian." Is this place a snapshot of the kingdom of God (or heaven as St. Matthew calls it), or are we all in process of becoming the "kingdom of God?" Today's texts provide ambiguities of how God's kingdom comes together with varying personalities and concerns.

One can identify a joker, or trickster in a given organization. We wonder, "When will this person ever grow up?" But then we see God's hand at work when this same person reaps what he or she sows because of their tricks, white lies or secretive stunts comes to haunt them. This is the world of Jacob in Genesis 29. But there are other people at work within the organization also.

There might be a person who always seems to have bad luck in life. They might as well have Murphy's Law written above their desk, "If anything can go wrong it will go wrong — at the worst possible time." To such a person Paul in Romans addresses folks who are one of the "elect." To be "elected" by God is not exclusively about "privilege," but about trials in life. So where is God? Romans 8:31-19 is read at tragic events. Yet, Romans 8:28 can be used in a flippant, dismissive way or a caring manner.

Then we have the person is who always on the search for something in life that is more fulfilling. This person might say, "I am sorry but I do not find my identity or fulfillment working in this organization... I need something more to feel my life has meaning." Such a person can take counsel from the Matthew 13: 31-33; 44-52 text. Which if these snapshots depicts the kingdom of Heaven? Maybe all of them do. These texts describe the ambiguities of the kingdom.

Genesis 29:15-28

In every community I have served, there are local stories of two brothers who are farmers, business owners or some sort of professional who are bitter rivals. It is said that their families have been in conflict from birth like Jacob and Esau fighting to see who leaves the mother's womb first. These two people in the family have been in conflict before the pastor got there, and will continue in conflict after any pastor leaves! Genesis 29 picks up on larger story or journey of Jacob who has tricked and angered his brother on many occasions and is now in exile away from the elder brother's wrath. This is a very human story where family members play tricks and deceive one another in ways that appear to have a humorous tone them.

God uses scandal, deception, trickery, multiple wives, conflict, and playfulness to accomplish his will through these people. This narrative is claimed by both the southern (Yahwist, "J") and northern (Elohist, "E") traditions-combined in terms of and community stories and folklore.

In this text, Jacob the trickster now gets a dose of his own medicine as his Uncle Laban has Jacob work for seven years for the hand of daughter Rachel who is quite attractive. On the dark wedding night when all there are is late night, dimming campfires for lighting, Uncle Laban switches daughters and gives Jacob his elder and average looking daughter Leah. Is this a lesson to Jacob that the elder child deserves a break once in a while (as he deprived his brother Esau)? How did the sincere, good-hearted Leah get caught up in these two men's pranks? Is Rachel worth fighting for here?

When Jacob awakens the next morning, he finds out that he has been tricked in the switching of the women. So Laban allows Jacob to work another seven years so Jacob can have Rachel also, or two wives! Historically, Leah would produce the most children, and Rachel would have a difficult time having one child, whose name would be Joseph. Jacob would show preferential treatment to this son, while the others worked in the fields. This takes us into another story for another Sunday.

The point is that God works through all of these family stories, as humorous or bizarre as they may be. Possibly we know people in an office, place of study, community or yes-church with some pretty "colorful" characters in their family that stir the pot up frequently. Also, there might some tragedy, as well as irony in how these people try to outwit one another and may or may not get caught up in their own traps. To keep one's sanity with all of the shenanigans that goes on among certain families or tight-knit groups of people, the 12 Step groups have a tool of the "3 Cs." That is, "I did not cause it, I cannot control, nor can I cure it." We have to ultimately "Let go and let God." It is our job to care and love such people. It is God's job to actually change them. Such wisdom could apply to the family which Jacob lives in. Things are not as "cut and dry" or black and white in life. Ambiguities exist in families, but God's kingdom still comes to the surface.

For me, the telling of this family saga sort of preaches itself! Every family has some colorful characters or maybe "skeletons in the closet" they are hesitant to admit having in the family tree. The good news is God is still at work! God still has a plan for such people despite the schemes, and underhanded tricks they might pull on other people. One other direction I have heard preached well is to imagine one is Leah and her big night for her wedding day as bride is muddied by the pranks of Laban and Jacob. [source: Walter Brueggemann, *Interpretation a Bible Commentary for Teaching and Preaching: Genesis*(John Knox Press, 1982)]

Romans 8:26-39

If a person or community has gone through one cycle after another of tragedy, misfortune and loss, this text is a gold mine full of nuggets of: assurance, love, confidence and compassion. First, God hears the prayers of all believers who have the Holy Spirit within them (be the Christian's theology of sacramental or conversion method of receiving the Spirit). Rest assured that the Spirit does intercede in times of prayer, even if the Christian does not know the exact words to say. So God hears the prayers of believers in all situations are one piece of good news here (8:26-27).

Romans 8:28 is one of those passages that might be a good memory verse to take along life's journey, "We know that all things work together for good for those who love God, who are called according to his purpose." This text can be used inappropriately toward people who are currently in deep grief over the loss of a loved one. A time will come to apply this verse, but a caregiver needs to discern when the time of lament and grief is complete, then Romans 8:28 might be welcomed by those who experience loss. Another reading of this text might be, "all things work out for good for the one who endures suffering." So after endurance, an eventual positive outcome will occur. There is no timeline here. It may be in the long run that a person realizes, "I did not know it then, but I know it now, that God's hand was in the loss of a loved one." The key to using this verse is to seek a hopeful outcome to those who experience repeated losses, but not jump the gun in quoting Romans 8:28 amidst the lamenting process.

Romans 8:29-30, refers to God foreknowing and predestining people to be the "firstborn" in the family of faith. All commentators consulted agree that such election comes with responsibilities as well as privilege. Historically, it might entail suffering for one's faith. Also, this text could be used to argue the basic Calvinist "predestination" view (alongside other texts in the New Testament). This would be an individualist reading of the text (God foreknew persons Fred, Cletus, Lars, Ashley and Hannah) to be the "elect." Equally valid is to read the text collectively, that being God has elected a "people" such as the Church as God elected the nation of Israel to be his family. This does not necessarily have the Calvinist accent to it. The bottom line is that God has embraced a people to be in his family and nothing can separate them from God's love.

Romans 8:31-39, is used at many funerals as an assurance that nothing can separate us from the love of God. Romans 8:36 does insert Psalm 44:22 into the text to show one might have to suffer for following a king or monarch. Preaching on Psalm 44 might be an interesting direction for this text, if we have preached on the Romans 8:31-39 texts in past years. Worldly powers come and go, but not that of the God of the Hebrew Scriptures and New Testament.

The Romans 8 text itself contains eight parallel opposites as to areas where God's love is still found despite the forces of destruction: Death and life; angels and rulers; things present and things to come; height and depth; and any other creature. It is God's power (Greek word, *dunamis,* where we get "dynamite") which is on our side as believers. No human or cosmic forces will separate believers in Christ from the love of God. The bond is too great to be broken.

Another strand running through this testing is that of, "Who is to condemn?" This is a court metaphor. It is present because it implies a day of reckoning before some sort of divine judge. However, for those whose faith is in Christ, there is no accuser, only love and acceptance.

For the persons who have gone through many times of loss, crisis and tragedy, first God hears their prayers — regardless of whether they can pray like a preacher or not. Second, after the struggles in life, God will work things out in some manner, though we might not know the details now. Third, there is a sense that the people of God are secure in his love, but tragedy and testing has been part of the history of the people of faith as Psalm 44:22 in this text indicates. Fourth, God continues to be active in the world through divine election in whatever form one is comfortable understanding. God is still sovereign. Fifth, no forces will separate believers from God's love. Human power empires come and go. Cosmic forces are also part of God's domain. Sixth, to those who feel guilty, they are comforted that Christ who died on the cross for the sins of humanity will not condemn them as their faith is in this Christ.

For a sermon, I might quote the words of the popular song by Dan Powter, "So You Had A Bad Day," then plug this text into wherever I see people in the congregation have experienced setbacks in their lives. God is active in life's ambiguities! [source: Arland J. Hultgren, Arland J. *Paul's Letter to the Romans: A Commentary*(Wm B. Eerdmans, 2011)]

Matthew 13:31-33, 44-52

This text is part of a larger collection of teachings on the kingdom of Heaven (Matthew uses "kingdom of Heaven" as other synoptic writers use "kingdom of God"). How can God's kingdom emerge beside Satan's presence on earth? Since Matthew 4, when Jesus is tempted in the wilderness, this question persists throughout the gospel. How can the kingdom grow in such a world of evil and adversity? Again, there is a certain ambiguity in God's creation.

However, the smallest of seeds that being the mustard seed grows to become the largest of shrubs, so much so that birds make nests in its branches. The next metaphor is the leaven, which is usually a symbol of uncleanness can later feed up to one hundred people with bread. God works through the less obvious small and unclean elements to do great actions in Matthew 13:31-33.

What kind of treasures that are hidden are people willing to sacrifice much to obtain? We might see this in a parent or teacher who sees potential in a student who does not seem to be smartest child in the class. An artist could see a block of wood and see a sculpture in it, while a trash collector sees potential fire wood in the block of wood.

What will people sacrifice to find hidden treasures in their lives? This text illustrates the question with pearls and a great catching of fish. These parables suggest that people of faith have permission to break with old patterns of seeking out treasure and go down different paths. While evil and conflict exist, buried treasures also co-exist for those with the patience to seek them out.

There will come a time of reckoning and judgment according to this text. But for now "scribes of the kingdom" are like treasure hunters seeking out kings of the kingdom of Heaven (Matthew 13:49-52).

A "scribe" in the kingdom of Heaven is not necessarily a trained expert, but an ongoing disciple who seeks signs of the kingdom through smaller, less significant elements in God's creation. Despite signs of evil all around people of faith the news, God's rule often appears hidden, but it is approaching in God's due time. The ambiguity of the kingdom is that it appears small and insignificant to the naked eye, but it is also very potent. This text is a collection of such metaphors of the kingdom. [source: Robert Smith, *Augsburg Commentary on the New Testament: Matthew* Augsburg Fortress, 1989)]

Application

A retail business, store or restaurant usually prefers to have public friendly faces to greet the customers during the daily business hours. The corporate office recommends a sweet, well groomed, possibly energetic person creates a great first impression for any customers who come into the door. However, a certain supervisor has no such people working on the night shift of the business. The one person who was supposed to be the front office person called in "sick." However, an older, heavy set, single mother with some facial scars is more than willing to welcome the customers. This woman has a down-to-earth greeting, friendly personality and willingness to listen to customers. This more than makes up for her lack of the new, young looks of the preferred populist media image person. The supervisor has found a "treasure" or "pearl" in this worker. How many people come and go in the lives of businesses, communities and schools who may not "dress for success" or have the populist image, but are truly yeast that needs a little flour so they that can produce much for the community?

An Alternative Application

Is there an inner emptiness that people seem to have which materialism, more electronic devices, and more fancy meals and drinks cannot fulfill? If so, possibly the kingdom of Heaven is where they need to look. Theologian Paul Tillich argues that a person's inner emptiness cannot be satisfied by false gods, concupiscence (more recreational vehicle purchases, sex, or entertainment) or escapism through drugs and alcohol. This emptiness can only be filled by the God who creates humans and realizes that the treasures mentioned in Matthew 13 point to the kingdom of Heaven. For example, a man is able to retire in his early fifties of age as he sees others in his generation who will work well into their late sixties of age. He decides to buy himself a new pick-up truck, boat, and fishing equipment. After one year, he grows bored with these adult toys. He drinks too much alcohol at one of the local clubs and smokes heavily until he has a major aheart attack. Due to the medical insurance he had from the company he retired, he as a second chance at life. He has an opportunity to volunteer at the local church or boy scout troop or he can go back to the place where he drank and smoked for many years. How will he fill his inner emptiness in tough economic times? Matthew suggests there are treasure and pearls out there for those who seek the fulfillment of the kingdom. [source: Paul Tillich, *Courage to Be*(Yale University Press, 1952)]

Proper 13 | Ordinary Time 18
Genesis 32:22-31
Romans 9:1-5
Matthew 14:13-21
by Ron Love

Abundance

The wise old preacher hobbled up to the pulpit and made an announcement to the congregation. "I have some good news and I have some bad news," the preacher said. "Our fund-raising efforts have been successful. The capital campaign will more than pay off the educational wing. We'll even have enough money for all new toys for the nursery. The good news is, right here in this sanctuary, we have more than enough money!"

Thrilled, the congregation grinned, excited about the new life, but then, grew worried. What was the bad news?

The preacher continued, "The bad news is that the money is still in your pockets."

I have always enjoyed this joke. The brief journey our wallets travel from our back pockets into our hands and then into the collection plate is the hardest journey of all. It is not a joke to know that we have plenty but in our unwillingness to share, we impoverish our life together as a community.

The common theme in our three lectionary readings for this Sunday is the importance of understanding our blessings, then having a willingness to share those blessings with others. In all our readings it is Jesus as the Messiah that becomes the most prominent blessing we can give to others.

In the gospel lesson it is mentioned that a fish was lifted up before the people. The Greek letters for the word fish are *ichthus*, which were the initials of the full title of Jesus that the church worshiped; that is *Iesous Christos Theou Uios Soter* meaning "Jesus Christ God's Son, Savior." Paul wanted the Jews to continue to affirm their Jewish heritage, but he desperately wanted them to accept Jesus as their Messiah. Jacob was to fulfill the promise of going into the promised land of Canaan, but first he had to accept the blessing of the new name of Israel. Matthew, as he reports of Jesus feeding the 5,000, declares that the abundance of God's blessing is for all people, of all nationalities, in all countries.

Grace operates on a theology of abundance. There is more than enough if you can make that journey from billfold to collection plate, both literally and figuratively. There is more than enough grace. Share what you have. Share with a glad and generous heart. There is an abundance of grace. There is an overflowing of mercy. There is a profusion of forgiveness.

Genesis 32:22-31

Jacob's encounter with a spirit, who is described as a man, took place on one of the two mounds where you can cross the Jabbok River into the Jordan Valley. The spirit wanted to prevent Jacob from crossing into the promised land, and thus came out in darkness to wrestle him into submission. The spirit could have been a representative of the Canaanite god who inhabited the land. Jacob prevailed and in doing so was able to secure a blessing. Jacob would now be called Israel, which means "He has striven with God," or "He has been saved by God." The word Israel has come to represent all the Hebrew people, thus the abundant blessing of God.

Proper 13 / Ordinary Time 18

Romans 9:1-5

Paul is in anguish because the Jews will not accept Jesus as their Messiah. Paul recounts all the blessings the Jews have received as the chosen people. He does not dismiss these blessings, but authenticates them. But he is now preaching, almost pleading, with them to recognize Jesus. It is Paul's desire as a Jew and Pharisee to share the blessing he experienced on the road to Damascus.

Matthew 14:13-21

The story of the feeding of the 5,000 is reported in all four gospels. Each highlights the importance of this occasion. For Matthew the actual event is engulfed with symbolic meaning, all of which declare the blessing of God upon all people. That the blessing of God is abundant enough for everyone is seen in the number 5,000. A number that is representative of all people, of all nationalities, in all countries, who are able to receive the grace of God. The fish demonstrates that Christ is for all people. The loaf of bread and Jesus looking up into heaven then breaking the bread is symbolic of the Eucharist; the blessing received in the upper room is now available for all believers. When the meal was complete and there were leftovers confesses again the abundance of God's grace can never be completely expended.

Application

The sermon could center on no matter how difficult our lives are, God is present. For Jacob, God was present at the river's edge. For Paul, God was present on the road to Damascus. For the followers of Jesus, God was present in the miracle of the loaves and fishes. Whatever situation we may find ourselves, God in his abundance will care for us. But like Jacob and Paul and those gathered on the hillside, we must believe.

An Alternate Application

Each lectionary reading is a story of sharing. Jacob shared the blessing that came with his new name of Israel. Paul shared the blessing of his transformation on the road to Damascus. The people gathered on the hillside shared their blessing of food with one another. The message is that as we have come to understand how God has blessed us, we must go forth and be a blessing unto others.

Proper 14 | Ordinary Time 19

Genesis 37:1-4, 12-28

Romans 10:5-15

Matthew 14:22-33

by Wayne Brouwer

The calm at the center

One Chinese word-symbol for "doubt" is a caricature of a person with each foot in a different canoe. If the waters are calm and the canoes are tied securely, it is possible for the person to stand like that indefinitely. But if those canoes are adrift on the swelling tides of the sea or scrambling down the whitewaters of a raging torrent, someone positioned so precariously would topple quickly.

Cecil Beaton pictures it well in his short story *The Settee*. Violet and Dorothy prowl an antique shop and find a marvelous old French style long wooden bench called a settee. Dorothy thinks it is "Louise-Seize," and therefore extremely valuable. When she finds that she can get it for a very inexpensive price, she convinces Violet to allow her to buy it as a gift for Violet.

Of course, the value of the piece weighs heavily in Dorothy's mind, and soon she begins to dream of ways to get it back for herself. After all, she was the one who found it in the first place. Sharing her obsession with family friend Colonel Coddington, they scheme together to trick Violet into surrendering custody of the piece by declaring it a worthless imitation.

The tables are turned, however, when Colonel Coddington inspects the supposed antique and declares that it is, in fact, only a cheap copy of the famous Louis-Sieze style, and certainly not valuable at all. Dorothy's greed and obsession deflate rapidly.

The next day she laughingly relates the whole tale to George. Then the roller coaster ride begins all over again as George informs Dorothy that the Colonel's ability to appraise anything is sheer quackery, and he wouldn't know art from imitation. George, who has seen the settee, knows that it is indeed a rare and valuable piece. After all, he himself owns an antique shop where a bench twin to Violet's sits in the window with a huge price tag. Dorothy's obsessive greed is fired anew, and passionate covetousness surges through her veins.

There Beaton ends the story, allowing Dorothy's mood-swings to rip apart her heart.

The seas always roll, in life's journey, and the pounding waves beg their share of the soul's cargo. Those of us who have experienced significant doubts in the uncharted waters of our voyage find today's lectionary passages echoing themes we have rehearsed too well.

Certainly it is true that many Christians are single-minded and clearly aware of the brilliant sunshine of God's love, rarely deviating from paths of focused faith and purposeful existence. Yet while some folks have a "summery" sort of spirituality, according to Martin Marty in his devotional reflections on the Psalms, many of us know only or often *A Cry of Absence* (Harper & Row, 1983). For those who wrestle often the blasts of chilling doubt and wrestle for direction under gray and forbidding skies, the absence of God seems more apparent than his presence.

When the absence of God shouts louder than his presence, few who feel faith can escape the winds of doubt. Fortunately these verses are not all that James has to say on the subject. There will come moments of brilliance and insight further along in his letter of encouragement. Perhaps, even, the harshness of his judgment here will challenge those of us with wintry spirits to take a second look at our perennial insecurities of faith.

Without the larger context of grace binding the fraying edges of our souls, more ships of self would visit Davey Jones' locker than would reach the haven of rest. Fortunately the one who stilled the storms on the Sea of Galilee is able yet to tame the troubling tides for those who cry out in winter's night. This is the message of Joseph's tumultuous life mapped out by strange dreams. This is the promise of Paul in the middle of his most difficult exploration at the heart of Romans. And this is certainly the meaning of Matthew's reminder of what happened the night he and the other disciples were terrified on the high seas of Galilee. Jesus alone remains the calm at the center of every storm.

Genesis 37:1-4, 12-28

Although Abraham hears a disembodied voice and Jacob has a vision of heaven one night at Bethel, it is Joseph whose Genesis record is entirely shaped by dreams. He enters the narrative as a self-absorbed, privileged son, who foolishly antagonizes his family by reporting nighttime revelations that he is the most important among them, destined to become their lord and master (Genesis 37:2-11). His arrogance precipitates a plot among his siblings to get rid of him (Genesis 37:12-35), and this brings him to Egypt as a slave (Genesis 37:36; 38:1-6). Now the dreaming takes center stage again as Joseph is unjustly thrown in prison (Genesis 39:7-23) where he meets two men from the pharaoh's court who are awaiting adjudication on treason charges (Genesis 40:1-4). They each have dreams (Genesis 40:5-8) which Joseph is able to interpret (Genesis 40:9-19) in a way entirely consistent with the events that follow (Genesis 40:20-22).

Joseph's unique skills come to the attention of the pharaoh two years later, when the ruler's nighttime reveries plague him like a nightmare, and Joseph is brought in to make sense of it all (Genesis 40:23-41:36). This earns Joseph a spot as co-regent of Egypt (Genesis 41:37-57), and it is from this position that he becomes savior of his family during the ensuing famine (Genesis 42-46). Joseph's tale ends with his sons Manasseh and Ephraim gaining equal status with Jacob's other sons in the inheritance distributions (Genesis 48-49), and Joseph burying his father with honors in Canaan (Genesis 50:1-14) while keeping alive the dream of having the whole family return there one day when the current crisis had passed (Genesis 50:15-26).

In its focus on dreams, the Joseph story cycle that concludes Genesis deals with two issues. First, it answers the question of how this nation of Israel, springing from such illustrious stock, becomes an enslaved people in land not their own. Second, it creates a vision for the way in which the future is brighter than the past: along with their forebear Joseph, they need only take hold of the dream of God for them.

Romans 10:5-15

Romans 9-11 forms a kind of interlude in the progressive movement of Paul's otherwise arrow-straight discourse. The powerful "righteousness of God" (1:17) has recently been revealed in this world through the coming of Jesus. This righteousness is God's working out of a plan to recover and restore a universe that has been warped and twisted by evil (1:18-3:20). God's righteousness expresses itself through an ages-long redemptive history (3:21-8:39) that was first made manifest through Abraham (v. 4) and then powerfully consummated in Jesus (v. 5). Although the application of this righteousness has not connected easily with us as individual humans (vv. 6-7), the outcomes of God's plan are assured through the trinitarian initiatives (v. 8). "We are more than conquerors through him who loved us!" "... nothing shall separate us from the love of God in Christ Jesus our Lord!"

This powerful testimony now seems to cause Paul to reflect ruefully, however, on a truly knotty theological problem. If Paul can be so certain about God's strident grace toward us in this new age of the messiah, why did God's declarations of favor toward Israel in the previous age of revelation seem to fail? Why did Israel lose its privileged place in the divine plan, while the spreading church of Jesus Christ is suddenly God's favored child?

These questions become the research matters for Paul's internal intellectual debating team in Romans 9-11. First up, comes the standard reflection that God is sovereign. This means, for Paul, that God's special relationship with Israel was God's choice to make and is not undone now that God wishes also to use a new tactic in the divine attempt at recovering the whole of humanity back into a meaningful relationship with God.

Nevertheless, according to Paul, there has been something amiss about Israel's side of this relationship with God. Rather than understanding its favored position as enlisting it into the divine global mission, the nation tended to become myopic and self-centered. Instead of believing that she too needed to repent and find God's care through grace, Israel supposed that she had an inherent right to divine favor.

It is in this dynamic interaction, first between Israel and God, and more recently between the Gentiles of the early Christian church and God, that today's lectionary passage speaks. God is sovereign, yet Israel and we choose. God speaks, and Israel and we are called to respond. God remains in control, yet Israel and we exercise a freedom of choice.

The logic of it is impossible to nail down, any more than is the logic of selfless love or commitments of grace in the face of no reciprocation. Yet divine initiative and human volition are somehow inseparably connected in the drama of redemption.

In the end, Paul believes that partly through Israel's false presumptions, and partly because of God's temporary change of strategies in order to better fulfill the original divine redemptive mission, Gentiles have come to the center of God's attention, while Israel, though not forgotten, is partially sidelined for a time. But even this alteration in the temperature of God's relationship with Israel is a lover's game: Israel needs to feel the good jealousy for a partner that she has too long taken for granted, so that she will recover her passions of great love. In the meantime, however, all win. God wins in the divine missional enterprise. The Gentiles win because they have a renewed opportunity to get to know God. And Israel wins because she is never forgotten and is coming round to a renewed love affair with her beau. No wonder Paul ends these reflections with a passionate doxology culled from Isaiah 40:13 and Job 41:11 — "Oh, the depth of the riches of the wisdom and knowledge of God! How unsearchable his judgments, and his paths beyond tracing out! Who has known the mind of the Lord? Or who has been his counselor? Who has ever given to God, that God should repay him? For from him and through him and to him are all things. To him the glory forever! Amen."

Matthew 14:22-33

The storm that rose was a double whammy for Jesus' disciples, desperately traumatized on the Sea of Galilee. Only hours before they had been front and center in another of Jesus' amazing magical acts. The crowds had followed this young rabbi out into the wild places where he was wandering just to listen and look for miracles.

He certainly gave them a good one — it had been well past mealtime, with no fast-food restaurants in sight when Jesus took the lunch a mother packed for her young son and turned it into a feast that everyone could share. That's when they, Jesus' special deputies, were put in charge of the distribution. No one among the milling men could fail to notice that these fellows were important. They were hand-picked agents of this great man and got to spend all day every day with him. Envy skittered around them as they moved with humble pride to serve these poor folks.

But then Jesus had left them. He had just walked away and gone off into the hills by himself, as if he didn't want to be around them. As if they didn't really matter that much to him. So they retaliated

Proper 14 / Ordinary Time 19

and ran from him in the other direction, shoving off across the lake in a boat. Conversation among them over the waters must have skittered between rehearsals of their afternoon greatness and pouty uncertainties about Jesus.

They were fisherman, though, and this rowing across Galilee was good therapy. They knew these waters well. Some, like James and John, could probably see the lights in the windows of their parents' home over in Capernaum. Fickle fortunes may challenge them, but they could always come back to the sea. It was their home. They were masters of these acres.

That's when the second wallop hit them. Their friend Galilee rebelled. It caught them by surprise. The winds changed. The horizon melted and sky merged with sea in a toxic soup. They thought they could play this lake like a dance partner, but she kicked them in the shins and was coming back with a kidney punch. They turned the boat into the wind and rowed with passion. They were more than a little scared, even if they wouldn't admit it.

Then suddenly their fear turned up the volume. Like the bow of a ghost ship emerging from a fog bank, something was aiming for them out of the storm. Was it a phantom? Was it another boat about to be thrown at them by the wicked winds? Was it the premonition of death? They were terrified.

They were amazed as well, for there was an eerie calmness surrounding this apparition. No waves bounced it, no breezes billowed whatever rags it might own. Swirling about it were the claws of death, but they could neither claim nor impede this water walker.

Certainly it seemed to be striding across the surface, for there was no question now that it was headed toward them. Between gasps of futile rowing and spits to get rid of the spray, they began to make out the form of a man. "It's Jesus!" cried one, and the breathing of their oarsmanship hiccupped. Peter yelled out, "Is it you, my Lord?"

A familiar voice cut through the tempest, as if it were on a different frequency altogether. "It is I! Don't be afraid!"

Things like this don't happen every day, even for disciples of Jesus who are getting used to a winning string of miracles. Surprised by his own giddiness, Peter called out, "Is it really you, my Lord?"

Then, to confirm his passionate boldness, he begged for a chance to find the footing Jesus knew atop the waves. "Come!" commanded Jesus, and Peter stepped gingerly out of the boat.

It was amazing and intriguing to feel the cold softness against his bare feet form in place like a shoe's gel insert. He suddenly had an unusual place to stand!

He tested his left foot against the flood and found he could walk! Gingerly he shuffled toward Jesus wondering when he would come to the edge of the wet precipice. But the terra aqua held firm.

The storm still had not abated. In fact, it seemed almost as if the wind packed a new punch in its insistence that these strange events not take place. Peter was pummeled by gales that sneaked in from every direction without pattern. He bobbled and turned to beat back his enemy. It was then that his feet slid. The water became slippery, with pockets and holes that no longer supported his footfalls. He felt himself tipping and twisting and groped the air for non-existent supports. The deep knew his name and was laying claim to his body heel upward.

"Lord, save me!" he cried in panic. And Jesus took his hand. Jesus took his hand and the footing was firm. Jesus took his hand and the waves were tamed. Jesus took his hand and the winds calmed.

They chatted together as if it were a walk in the woods, nothing unusual. Jesus chided his friend for losing focus so quickly, and the two of them stepped into the boat together. Around them the others gaped wordlessly. What do you say when nothing makes sense and yet everything is okay?

More quickly than it had blown in the storm whimpered away. Suddenly the skies were clear, the stars bright, the air fresh and the sea shimmering as it reflected sentinel fires on the shore.

What were the disciples to make of this? Nothing, really. You just get on with your life and tell the tale over drinks every chance you get, for a while at least. But then you begin to hold it and review it and wonder at it. Not so much the freak storm or even the strange thing Peter did, although, looking back, you wonder how it ever happened. Who, in his right mind, would get out of a boat on a stormy sea and think he could walk on water?

But the recounting of the story would begin to feel weird, as if you were violating some sacred trust, because you told the story at first out of sheer exhilaration at the experience, and then later because it was such a good story and it made you kind of proud to have been there. But now you know that the story can't be about you. It was always about Jesus. The storm came because Jesus was not there. The winds blew in because the disciples were becoming overconfident in their Superman status. The seas rebelled because, for a moment, everyone and everything had lost focus when Jesus stepped up into the hills by himself. Without Jesus at the center, everything becomes dark and brooding and chaotic.

This then is why Matthew made sure to tell the story as he did. Not with great embellishments of flair or excitement, but in straightforward simplicity. For the meaning is not to be found in the extraordinary things that took occurred, but in the place Jesus must have at the center of every picture.

Application

Artists were once encouraged to submit their most descriptive canvases portraying "peace" to a painting contest. The offerings were as varied as the colors of the spectrum. One bright scene showed a pastoral countryside. Another found peace on the wide expanse of sea coast, drummed by the steadying rhythm of the waves. A third found its glow in the setting sun at day's end.

The winning painting, though, portrayed a chaotic and troubled scene. Torrents of water cascaded over jagged rocks. Black storm clouds reached down to earth with destructive claws of lightning. Fierce winds tore at the leafy clothing of trees. Hailstones mixed with rain punished the world with a sound beating.

But these were not the things that grabbed the viewer's attention. There, just to the right of center, in a nest supported by a gnarled old tree limb and sheltered by overhanging rocks, was a small bird. Singing. Peaceful.

This is the calm of God at the center of human storms. This is the peace of Christ.

Alternative Application

Matthew 14:22-33. Madeleine L'Engle's short story *Dance in the Desert* begins with a caravan of people traveling in hurried fear through a trackless wilderness. They seem to be running from something and turn furtively to check the movement of shadows at the edge of their peripheral vision. Particularly noticeable among them is a young family, a husband and wife along with their tiny boy.

Night falls and the travelers establish a camp. All gather around the huge bonfire that is lit as a repellent to the darkness and whatever beasts and demons it might hold. From huddled security near the flames, the community shivers at growls and hisses that emanate from the unseen world beyond the licking of the fire. Now and again the piercing reflection of strange eyes looks at them out of the black void and they quickly turn back to comforting small talk, which helps them pretend at safety.

But they will not be left alone. The shrieks and warning snarls edge closer. Then a paw appears or a sniffing nose only to be withdrawn before spears can poke or arrows be aimed. More faggots are thrown on the fire.

Yet the beasties and wild things will not be stopped. Growing more daring, a bear steps into their circle and a bold viper slithers in from the other direction. There is panic in the camp as all scatter and leap and search for weapons. In the commotion the young husband and his younger wife are separated, each believing the other has grabbed their little boy to safety.

But the child was left behind. He faces the wolf and the lion and the bear and the snake and the other wilderness creatures alone. Only there is no distress in his voice, no panic in his cry. Instead, he coos and clucks with delight at these mighty furry and scaly toys that have come to play. He claps his hands and bounces his feet and giggles with animation.

As the caravansary is suddenly pulled from its panicked zig zagging by the tinkle of the child's good humor, all the adults stop and turn, expecting the wild things to tear limb from limb and demolish this human plaything they have abandoned. But it is not so. Instead, the child has brought some kind of intelligent direction to its strange play. His chubby arms are actually orchestrating a symphony of animal cries, and his hands are directing the choreography of a marvelous beastly dance. The bear is on its hind legs, not to swipe and strike but to gyrate with the tempo of the child's clapping. The snakes slither in pairs forming artistic designs in the desert sands. Above, the vultures and hawks swoop and turn and bank and dive in aviary formation. The lions and tigers nod their heads as if in rhythm to celestial instrumentation.

Slowly, and with mesmerizing fascination, the adults creep back to their places by the bonfire. They become the audience in the greatest show on earth. The child whoops and tips and giggles and sways and claps his hands in time with the music of heaven, and the animals of earth dance around him with delight. Even the big people begin to hear transcendent melodies, and the night has become as friendly as dawn or daylight.

Eventually the child tires, as all children do, and the cooing stops, the clapping ceases, and the animals slink away. But they are no longer predators and the fear of both man and beast has vanished. All that is left is the child, and those who linger in awe know that there is a new center of gravity in the universe.

I cannot reflect back to all of you today what storms and beasts and dark places you fear. You know them all too well. They have become, for some of you, a house of horrors from which you would move if you could but you can't. You step out into the weather of each morning wearing a façade of faith and trust, believing you are able again to walk on water. Yet too often, before the day is half finished, and often in full sight of your friends and coworkers traveling with you, you slip and slide and sink.

I do not have any quick-fix solutions for you, no faith waders, no emergency life rafts, or instant pontoons. All I can say is what Matthew, in recounting this story for us, wished to affirm. You've got to keep your attention focused on Jesus. Not as an iconic talisman, but as the center of meaning around which everything else begins to revolve and resonate.

Proper 15 | Ordinary Time 20

Genesis 45:1-15

Romans 11:1-2a, 29-32

Matthew 15:(10-20) 21-28

by David Kalas

God in the rearview mirror

I was an Arminian in a Calvinist seminary. It was not a hostile relationship, and I was not in constant arguments. From time to time the underlying difference in outlook would percolate to the surface of some conversations, and I usually found the resulting dialogue most fruitful.

On one occasion, I engaged one of my theology professors on the subject of predestination. He was patient with me as I tried to explore for the first-time issues he had no doubt covered countless times. Along the way he offered a helpful, personal insight. "I like to think of predestination as a rearview mirror doctrine," he said. "God's sovereign choices may not be apparent at the time, but when you look back, you can't help but conclude that it was God who did it."

Salvation, election, predestination, and the sovereign choices of God are all at stake in the passages we consider together this week. Our purpose will not be to choose sides in a debate, however. Rather, we just want to meditate on and affirm God's work.

First we'll hear Joseph reflecting back on God's work in the circumstances of his life. He is not engaging in a formal theological discourse. He is just bearing witness to what he sees in his own rearview mirror.

Second, we'll read a small sampling from Paul's long and complex discussion of God's saving work among Jews and Gentiles. He wrestles with the fact that his own people seemed to be rejecting the plan and salvation of God. So the apostle sought to understand the Lord's providential plan and timing in it all.

Finally, we contemplate a strange episode from Jesus' ministry. It appears to be the lone occasion when Jesus declines someone's request for healing, at least initially. The Lord's various plans and purposes for Jews and Gentiles come to the fore again, and we are left to wonder at Jesus agreeing to do something that he originally indicated he would not.

I am not eager to build a case for either Jacob Arminius or John Calvin. Rather, I am eager for us to explore together the wondrous work of God. I believe that Joseph, Paul, and Matthew will help us and our people do that together this week.

Genesis 45:1-15

It almost seems a shame to separate this passage from all that comes before. When we read these verses from Genesis 45 out of their larger context, it is like watching only the end of a movie. The emotion and beauty of the scene cannot be understood and appreciated apart from the plot and dialogue that preceded it.

The story begins before any of the characters in this scene were even born. It began way back when a young Jacob fell in love with a young Rachel, but Rachel's father acted duplicitously on their wedding night. Laban had inserted his other daughter, Leah, into Rachel's place in Jacob's wedding bed, putting everyone in an awkward and unenviable position. The unhappy effects of that trickery kept rippling through the years and generations.

Rachel was more loved than Leah, but Leah was more fertile than Rachel. Eleven children were born to Jacob before Rachel finally became pregnant. When she finally did give birth to a son, therefore, he was almost destined to be his father's favorite.

The favoritism was overt and it bred violent resentment among all of Jacob's half-brothers. Their contempt for Joseph was so great that they considered killing him. Remarkably, selling their brother into slavery seemed like the compassionate choice. That sinister deed took Joseph to Egypt, which set the stage for God's providence there.

Meanwhile, back in Canaan, the remaining sons of Jacob lived with a father who was locked in his grief. When famine hit the region, they went to Egypt to buy grain. When both circumstances and the Egyptian leader turned against them, they regretted aloud how they had treated Joseph years earlier, reckoning that they deserved their present misfortune.

Finally, there was the accumulating emotion within Joseph himself. He had lived through so much undeserved suffering and mistreatment, only to have the tables turn completely for him one day in the presence of Pharaoh. In the midst of the prominence and authority of his new life, these members from his old life came calling. He toys with them. He finds out about home from them. He overhears them. He slyly arranges a reunion with his one full brother, Benjamin, through them.

Now with all of that behind them all, there comes this moment. It is filled with both human drama and divine providence. All the emotions and experiences that have been welling up in Joseph for years come to a head now, and he can no longer contain himself. He sends everyone but his unwitting relatives out of the room and then he begins to gush, expressing both his love and his testimony.

See all of the conversions that occur in this dramatic moment. Capricious Egyptian ruler suddenly becomes kid brother. Underrated dreamer becomes uncommonly wise and prophetic young man. Animosity is replaced by appreciation. Vengeance is disabled by forgiveness. Distance is closed by embrace.

At this moment, what was heretofore invisible instantly becomes clear: namely, that this is all the work of God. The brothers and Potiphar's wife, the baker and the wine stewards the jailer and the pharaoh — they all had their parts to play. Yet from Joseph's first young dream to this moment of revelation, we see in it all the hand of God. It is God's work, now clearly visible in the rearview mirror.

Romans 11:1-2a, 29-32

The selected passage is brief but the context from which it is excerpted is quite long. For several chapters in the second half of his letter to the Romans, the apostle Paul wrestles with a question that is for him both personal and theological. The question involves the salvation of the Jews — God's long-standing covenant with them and their response to the gospel.

The personal quality of this dilemma is poignant, indeed. We know a bit about Paul's proud Jewish heritage (see, for example, Philippians 3:4-6). And we know too that his missionary pattern was to go first to the synagogues (see, for example, Acts 9:20, 13:5). His own people, after all, were the most natural audience for this gospel, rooted in the covenants, promises, and prophecies of the Old Testament.

The record of Paul's experience in Pisidian Antioch, however, serves as a kind of microcosm of his larger ministry. "When the Jews saw the crowds, they were filled with jealousy... they contradicted what was spoken by Paul" (Acts 13:45). So Paul offered this bittersweet response: "It was necessary that the word of God should be spoken first to you. Since you reject it and judge yourselves to be unworthy of eternal life, we are now turning to the Gentiles" (v. 46).

Paul enjoyed a phenomenal ministry among the Gentiles, yet the joy of their responsiveness to the gospel could not outweigh the grief he felt over his own people. As you and I know, it is small comfort to lead others to Christ if we see that our own children are rejecting him. And the apostle Paul lived with that very sort of sorrow over his own people.

In addition to that personal struggle, there were also theological issues involved. As we see earlier in his letter to the Romans, Paul felt entirely resolved on the themes of law, circumcision, and righteousness. Although the Jews historically had a unique, covenant relationship with God and were the beneficiaries of special revelation, the problem of sin is universal and the salvation offered in Christ is identical for all, Jew and Gentile alike.

On the other hand, what of that covenant relationship? What of that chosen people status? Why should the most natural audience for the gospel so largely and so vigorously reject it?

As Paul contemplates the situation, he flatly refuses the possibility that God has "rejected his people." He is pained by the reality that they have rejected God's plan, yet he seems convinced that they remain part of God's plan. Indeed, Paul explores the possibility that even their present disobedience is itself part of God's plan.

Disobedience, of course, is never the will of God. To suggest that it is would render God's will a kind of empty set. But in the wisdom and power of God, even disobedience can be used to serve his purpose. The pool player may use one of the striped balls to knock in the desired solid ball. So it is that the Lord uses a tool of the enemy to his own advantage, for human disobedience becomes the avenue for his mercy.

In this particular matter, Paul reckons the human disobedience at two levels. First, there is the universal reality of human disobedience. As noted above, Jew and Gentile alike require and are offered the same salvation.

Second, Paul sees salvation history in broad strokes. The Gentiles were disobedient and unresponsive for a time, and the Lord's work was among the chosen people, Israel. In his own day, however, it was the Jews who were disobedient and unresponsive, making room for God's saving work among the Gentiles. The shift was not a permanent condition for the Jews, revoking forever their covenant relationship with God. Rather, it was a phase, with the prospect of both the natural and grafted vines existing together in God's saving grace.

Matthew 15:(10-20) 21-28

We carry in our mind's eye so many pictures from Jesus' ministry that we cherish. Here is a scene, though, that I don't remember hanging in any of my Sunday school classrooms when I was a child. I have not seen this moment captured in an illustrated Bible. For all of the portraits of Jesus that are available in Christian bookstores today, I have yet to see this depiction.

The scene is unfamiliar and seemingly out of character. First, it's a picture of Jesus ignoring someone. Then it shifts to what appears to be an unwillingness to help that someone. Then he makes what sounds to us like a racist statement. Admittedly, the story has a happy ending. But are we happy with the middle?

The scene features two main characters: Jesus and a Gentile woman from the region where Jesus and his disciples were briefly traveling. The woman is desperate. Any of us who are parents naturally sympathize with how she must have been feeling.

"But he did not answer her at all."

Perhaps at some time or another, we have counseled a child or a friend, saying, "You just have to ignore..." It may be a person or a group or a behavior or a circumstance, but we know there are times when the best thing to do is simply to ignore. This, however, is a mother in desperation, seeking help for her tortured daughter. Is this the sort of person and situation that you just have to ignore?

In addition to the two main characters, there is also a supporting cast. They are the disciples and they do not acquit themselves well in this moment. "Send her away," they urge Jesus, "for she keeps shouting after us." This is hardly the type of intercession that should characterize the followers of Jesus. They seem more annoyed than concerned.

It's at this moment that Jesus seems to establish the reason that he will not help the poor woman. He explains to his disciples that he was "sent only to the lost sheep of the house of Israel." We understand his later remark about "the dogs" against this backdrop. The guiding paradigm involves a distinction between Jews and Gentiles with an assumption that Jesus' mission, with all of its benefits, is for the former and not the latter.

The audience is so distracted by what the magician is doing with the one hand that they miss what he does with the other. Likewise, we may be so fixated on what Jesus does say that we overlook what he does not. When the disciples urge Jesus to send the woman away, you see, he doesn't do it. He seems to ignore her at first and he seems to be ruling her out next, but he never says "no" and he never sends her away.

My wife is famous for cutting off telephone solicitations quickly. The person on the other end is barely into his or her spiel before my wife kindly interrupts, saying, "We're not interested. Thank you. Good-bye." Her point is that if you know you're not going to say yes, it's just a waste of everyone's time to go through the wholesales pitch.

If Jesus intended to say no, wouldn't he have said it at the start? The fact that he didn't tells me that, perhaps, he never intended to. And so we end with another picture of Jesus that we may cherish: He is compelling enough to inspire in a Gentile great faith, compassionate enough to extend his ministry beyond its immediate boundaries, and powerful enough to heal at a distance with just his word.

Application

John Wesley did us the favor of introducing some of Paul Gerhardt's German hymns to the English-speaking world. Among them is a grand song about the providence of God. And along the way, Gerhardt encourages the Christian thus: "Leave to God's sovereign sway to choose and to command; so shalt thou, wondering, own that way, how wise, how strong this hand."

I can imagine Joseph singing that hymn 3,000 years before it was written. Indeed, I can imagine him writing that hymn, for Joseph had endured, as Gerhardt puts it, "waves and clouds and storms." Yet the mistreated brother, falsely accused servant, and wrongly imprisoned innocent, now sat on top of his world. He was free, promoted, and prosperous. He looked back on it all and said to his disreputable brothers, "It was not you who sent me here, but God."

A careful reader wants to put the bookmark in Genesis at that point in order to go back and review the preceding chapters. Where, exactly, do we see a reference to God sending Joseph to Egypt? We do not. It is entirely his brothers' doing. Yet in retrospect, what has human fingerprints is still recognized as the hand of God.

What Joseph looks back on, Paul is still in the midst of. That is to say, Joseph is able to reflect back on the work of God already accomplished. Paul, however, is living in the midst of the uncertainty and confusion that might have characterized Joseph while he sat in an Egyptian prison. How, we wonder, is this going to work out right?

As Paul grieves the behavior of his own people, he wonders. And still in the midst of it, he affirms a future he cannot see and a plan he cannot prove. The natural signals of circumstance do not point in a hopeful direction, but the character and promises of God do. So he trusts "how wise, how strong (God's) hand."

Finally there is the case of the Canaanite woman. Hers is the shortest of the stories. Paul is dealing with millennia-long salvation history. Joseph's experience of God's providence was decades in unfolding. But this woman's experience, while trying, was relatively short. She went from need to healing within a single day.

Yet, as with Joseph and Paul, the path from here to there was not always clear. She felt ignored and her request was deferred. What she wanted did not, it seemed, fit into the plan of God. But in the end, Gerhardt's counsel articulates her experience: "Wait thou God's time; so shall this night soon end in joyous day."

The end is the key, isn't it? We cannot always see the hand of God at work during the journey, but we recognize it in the end. We do not always understand the plan of God while we are living it out, yet we see it clearly in the end. More than that, we always find the distinctively wise and perfect will of God at the end as well. Joseph is enthroned. The woman's child is healed. And all Israel will be saved.

An Alternative Application

Matthew 15:21-28. "He did not answer her at all." We noted in our discussion of the gospel lection that this depiction of Jesus looks unfamiliar to us. But then again, perhaps it doesn't. Perhaps this is a very familiar scene that we and our people have seen again and again.

The reason that this story seems unfamiliar to us is because in the gospel accounts, Jesus is so consistently responsive to human needs. He touched and healed all of the sick (Luke 4:40). He cast out demons, fed the hungry, blessed the children, turned water into wine, and raised the dead. In light of all that, the episode with the Canaanite woman appears, at first blush, to be the lone exception to the rule.

Yet what seems inconsistent with the rest of the gospel accounts may resonate very personally with our own life experience. We may feel that we know this woman and her situation well. We have sought him out and we have called out to him for help. We have demonstrated the faith to come to him in the first place. We have presented to him our earnest and genuine need, and "he did not answer at all."

Sometimes people will tell us that the Lord always answers prayers, it's just that sometimes the answer is "no." We understand that and we believe it. Yet the explanation does not satisfy unless we have heard him say no.

We are at peace with the reality that the Lord will sometimes decline what we ask for. We do not presume to believe that our every request is perfect or that our wish is God's command. We know better. Yet we do not often hear him say "no." Are we to assume then that his silence is the same as "no"? Is seeming inaction a "no"? Is delay? If he told me "no," perhaps I would be able to move on. But if he doesn't seem to answer at all, then I don't know what I am supposed to do.

The woman's initial experience was that "he did not answer her at all." We sometimes carelessly apply to her the phrase "she wouldn't take no for an answer." But that is not the case. He didn't say no to her. What she chose was not to take *silence* for an answer, so she persisted and received what she needed.

Jesus said her faith was great. So too is her example. When he does not answer us at all, let us keep this Canaanite saint in mind and keep asking.

---

1. Paul Gerhardt, translated by John Wesley, "Give To The Winds Thy Fear," *United Methodist Hymnal* #129.

Proper 16 | Ordinary Time 21

Exodus 1:8--2:10

Romans 12:1-8

Matthew 16:13-20

by Cathy Venkatesh

The power of names

"What's in a name? That which we call a rose would by any other name smell as sweet." Shakespeare's Juliet bemoans Romeo's family name of Montague and begs him to cast it off, but all who have seen the play know that is not so easily done. Names have power, both the names we are given and the names that we choose. Each of our lessons today touches on the power of names and naming in our lives of faith. Are there names we need to cast off? Are there names we need to claim? Today's readings offer much to ponder.

Exodus 1:8--2:10

Today marks a transition in readings from the book of Genesis, begun on Trinity Sunday in June, to the book of Exodus, which we will read into late October. It can be worth marking this transition and reminding parishioners of the remarkable story of the Hebrew people that has been read through the summer: Abraham and Sarah; Isaac and Rebekah; Jacob, Leah, and Rachel; Joseph and his brothers. I have found that many parishioners do not realize that the Israelites became enslaved in Egypt because Joseph's brothers settled there. Through multiple twists of fate and circumstance, their decision to sell Joseph into slavery led to their own great-grandchildren becoming slaves of the Egyptians. Though it is not assigned for today, it could be worth reading Exodus 1:1-7 to help parishioners understand this transition from the stories of the patriarchs to the stories of Moses and the liberation of the Hebrew people from slavery. It is worth noting too that the great expansion of the Hebrew population in Egypt fulfills the repeated promises of a great family that God made to the patriarchs in Genesis (13:16, 15:5, 22:17, 26:4, 32:13).

Today's story has many characters but only three are named: the two Hebrew midwives Shiphrah and Puah, and Moses. The king/pharaoh is not named; neither are Moses' parents or sister or even the pharaoh's daughter. The Hebrew words describing the midwives may be interpreted either as the NRSV translation states, "Hebrew midwives" or as "midwives to the Hebrews," which would make Shiphrah and Puah Egyptians, who would certainly be more likely to be trusted by the pharaoh to carry out an order to kill Hebrew boys. If the midwives were Egyptians, they are all the more remarkable for recognizing and fearing the God of the enslaved Hebrew people (Exodus 1:17). The compassion of the midwives and Pharaoh's daughter stand in stark contrast to the fear-inspired genocide commanded by Pharaoh. It is noteworthy in these early stories of the faith to find women named in their own right and not simply in relation to the men to whom they were daughters, sisters, wives, concubines, or mothers. Whether Hebrew or Egyptian, Shiphrah and Puah are rightly remembered and named for their acts of courage and their defiance. Some Christian commentators have noted that their actions may be the earliest recorded example of civil disobedience toward an oppressive regime, though this would require an extensive knowledge of world literatures and history to verify.

Romans 12:1-8

As in today's reading from the Hebrew scriptures, today's epistle reading also marks an important transition. Though we are still reading from Romans, Paul's main theological arguments, which we have read through the summer from chapter 6 through chapter 11, have concluded. The "therefore" in Romans 12:1 refers to Paul's exposition in the prior chapters of the grace and saving mercies of God given to us in Christ. In chapters 12 to 15:13, he moves on to an exhortation of how we should live in response to God's grace. We are to present our bodies to God as living sacrifices, which may seem to modern readers a lovely metaphor, but to Paul's readers in a time when animals were regularly slain as sacrifices in temple worship, I suspect it resonated far more viscerally. No longer are we to offer objects or animals outside ourselves to God; we are to offer our own selves. We are not to follow the ways of the world and present age but to let God transform our minds and actions. In Romans 1:18-32, Paul outlined the wickedness and sinfulness of humanity; the life he describes in response to Christ in chapters 12-15 is its opposite. A note on the word "perfect" at the end of 12:2, which has proven a stumbling-block to more than one faithful Christian: The connotation of "perfect" here and elsewhere in the New Testament (as when Jesus advises his hearers in Matthew 5:48 to be perfect as his Father in heaven is perfect) is of completion and maturity, as a small acorn achieves its perfection in a majestic, full-grown oak tree. "Perfect" here does not mean without blemish but living fully into the God-given potential we have been given. And Paul is clear in Romans 12:6 that we are not all given the same gifts to realize. The diversity of fully realized gifts within the community of faith is what makes up the body of Christ, the church. For those who feel weak in faith, it may be helpful to note that faith itself is a gift that God assigns in unequal measures (12:3). Rather than fretting about personal shortcomings, Paul invites his hearers into trusting the shared gifts and graces of the Christian community: prophecy, ministry, teaching, exhorting, giving, leading, and showing compassion.

Matthew 16:13-20

Jesus and his disciples enter the district of Caesarea Philippi, one of the northern-most points of their shared travels. The city of Caesarea Philippi lies at the foot of Mount Hermon, a notable mountain range that straddles the current Syria-Lebanon border and is part of the Golan Heights. Long a place of worship of the Greek god Pan, it is here, far from Jerusalem that the disciples begin to receive a deeper knowledge of Jesus. Peter's confession that we hear today is followed immediately by Jesus' beginning to teach his disciples about his coming death and resurrection. The Transfiguration, which follows in chapter 17, may have occurred on Mount Hermon.

Jesus is beginning to prepare for his own end in Jerusalem, and the language in this reading comes from Jewish apocalyptic traditions. When Jesus asks, "Who do people say that the Son of Man is?" he alludes to Daniel 7:13-14, in which the Son of Man is given eternal dominion over the world after the final judgment. The disciples' initial answers of John the Baptist, Elijah, Jeremiah, or one of the prophets do not get to the truth Jesus seeks and in his next question he implicitly claims the title "Son of Man" that he has just used: "But who do you say that I am?" Simon Peter answers, "You are the Messiah [or the anointed one or Christ], the Son of the living God."

After 2,000 years of Christian usage, the word "Messiah" has more clarity of meaning than it did in Jesus' day. A messiah or anointed one was certainly an agent sent by God as a part of God's re-establishing rule on earth, but the notion of "The Messiah" claimed here by Peter is new. It may be worth noting Peter's attribution "Son of the living God" in contrast to the pagan (non-living) god of the region. Peter has named a truth about Jesus that Jesus is more than a prophet, healer, or teacher: He is one with a distinct and powerful relationship with God that has to do with ushering in the rule of God on earth.

It is even more than that, for Jesus responds by claiming not only the powers of earth but the powers of heaven for Peter. In giving Peter the keys of the kingdom of heaven, Jesus gives Peter the power to control entry into that kingdom. In giving Peter powers of binding and loosing, which are technical rabbinical terms, Jesus gives Peter authority to declare what is forbidden and what is permitted. Congruence between heaven and earth will be established in contrast to the conditions of their day. The name "Peter" from the Greek *petros* signifies more than simply a stone; it is more like bedrock or a huge rock outcropping like the Rock of Gibraltar. It is solid, foundational, and immoveable. Yet, after all this illumination and extraordinary promise, Jesus tells the disciples to keep it all quiet. No one else is to know that he is the Messiah. From our vantage point, we know that Jesus' living out of his messianic call was so different from anyone's expectations of a messiah that it made sense for the disciples not to proclaim it far and wide, but this order to keep quiet may have been confusing for the disciples. Indeed, immediately after this conversation, Jesus begins teaching them about his coming suffering, death, and resurrection (Matthew 16:21), which are not anticipated in any of the prophecies about a Jewish messiah.

Application

Last fall, my family visited Plymouth Plantation in Plymouth, Massachusetts, a "living museum" that seeks to present life as it was in the 1600s soon after the Pilgrims arrived. In the English village, costumed actors role-play historical characters, but in the neighboring Wampanaog homesite, modern-day members of the Wampanaog tribe demonstrate skills and answer questions about their culture and history. The center of the Wampanaog homesite is a bark-covered longhouse that seats several dozen people. When we visited, a tribal elder was there fielding questions from a motley collection of visitors. One person asked how names were chosen, and we learned that a member of the Wampanaog tribe might have several names in a lifetime, not just one. As a person grew and matured into new skills and responsibilities, and as the community identified and called out their gifts, the person would receive a new name. Over a lifetime, one person might have four or five distinct names, each name noting a season of their life, and each new name noting a transition in their status within the community.

We change names too in this culture, though seldom as often and fully as the Wampanoag. Titles may be added when we achieve a certain professional status; family names may be change upon marriage; nicknames may be claimed or discarded, but few of us actively choose to change our so-called Christian names: the names we were given at birth and again at our baptisms. Monks, nuns, and popes may take on new names as they profess their vows, but the rest of us usually trundle along with the names we were given as infants.

To name something or someone is to claim and define it in some deep way. There is good reason for the Jewish reluctance to speak the name of God — to say God's name is in some way to draw bounds around what is boundless, to attempt to pin down what is beyond all our knowledge. About a year ago, my father received a diagnosis of Parkinson's disease. This is a terrible illness, not one to wish upon anyone, but in giving his diffuse and troubling symptoms a name, he and our family received some power over them. He was able to begin treatment for a defined illness, find a support group for Parkinson's patients and their spouses, and begin to plan for a different future than he and my mother had imagined. Having this name, while terrible, has been empowering, and so it may be for anyone with a serious medical or psychological condition: having a name for their experience can simultaneously condemn and liberate.

Saint Paul names a host of gifts within the Christian community: prophecy, ministry, teaching, exhorting, giving, leading, and showing compassion. Reading his list, I instantly begin assessing which ones I have (and which ones I don't!) and thinking about others I know who demonstrate these gifts. In settings that are conducive to dialogue, a fruitful sermon time could be devoted to expanding on Paul's list with the gathered community and inviting the congregation to name the gifts they see in each other.

Our gospel today is a powerful story of naming: first of Jesus claiming the name of Messiah that Simon speaks, and then of Jesus giving Simon his new name of Peter. As stated above, at the time of Jesus, the notion and definition of Messiah was diffused. In claiming this name and living, dying, and rising as he did, Jesus created a new definition of what it is to be a messiah. Does a messiah by any other name smell as sweet? Perhaps not, if Jesus had chosen a title like king, emperor, or lord. Any name carries with it a set of expectations that shape our perceptions of the individual who carries it, even if that individual comes to transcend those expectations, as Jesus did.

Jesus' naming of Simon Peter is also notable. Simon was a voluble, perhaps impetuous follower of Jesus who showed promise but who also made grave mistakes more than once. In calling him "bedrock," Jesus gave Simon a name to live into, a name to cling to when times got tough, a name to fulfill for the rest of his days. Given another name by Jesus, would Simon have become the same leader that Peter did? The names and the nicknames that we give one another can have great power; they can become self-fulfilling prophecies. Moses, named from a root word meaning "take out," was taken out of the Nile River, but he also became the one who took his people out of Egypt. Surely his name, combined with the story of his rescue shaped the man that he became.

What names and nicknames have we been given? What names do we claim and what names do we need to discard because they do not serve us as children of God? This world is full of cruelty and some of the names we have been called and have called others are best put away where they can do no more harm. Some names we need to let go. And some names we need to claim. In an increasingly secular society and varying with local cultures, some members of our congregations may be reluctant to claim the name "Christian" because of negative associations they or others have with the name. Yet we should all be brave enough to claim the name Christian. As Jesus did with the name Messiah, by our living and dying, we can give it a new definition apart from the lingering triumphalism of other times and places. "See how these Christians love one another," Tertullian is reputed to have said. May it be so.

An Alternative Application

In multiple ways, today's readings mark turning points in the lives of the faithful: We mark the birth and rescue of the infant Moses, who will lead his people out of slavery; we mark Paul's movement in Romans from theological exposition to exhortation of faithful Christian response; and we mark Peter's confession of Jesus as Messiah, which sets Jesus and the disciples on the long march to Jerusalem. This last Sunday of summer before Labor Day weekend is also for many of us a season of turning and a fruitful moment to consider the question, "How then, shall we live?" The beginning of a new school and program year often feels like the start of a new year, and it can be an excellent time to set new habits and resolutions, to start anew in seeking to live more faithfully as children of God.

Proper 17 | Ordinary Time 22
Exodus 3:1-15
Romans 12:9-21
Matthew 16:21-28
by David Coffin

Coming off the sidelines

A certain congregation has many problems as they survey the community where they exist grows more secular and obsessed with school sports. Fewer volunteers want to do ministry work in the church and several building projects need to be completed before the year's end. The finances are tight, the pastor is spread out thin in terms of what is expected of him or her and many people wonder, "Why not just stay home and watch church on TV?" One group within the church believes they have some great ideas as to what should be in this church to improve things (as they remember them in times past). However, this group wants other people to carry out their ideas because they believe they have "done their time." Another group in the congregation believes they have some solutions to the church's problems but believes if they had the right pastor or if the current pastor would follow their directives, there would be much improvement. Still another group thinks hiring a consultant group may be of assistance. So when the weary pastor comes to the office after another hard week of work, he or she is greeted with a bulletin from another church that an anonymous person has placed on their desk with a note attached saying, "We visited this church, why not have some of the activities and worship order this church uses." In all of these situations, people who remain on the sidelines of the main activity of the congregational life have new ideas, but nobody is planning on coming off the sidelines. Each of the three texts for this Sunday is an invitation to come off the sidelines and get into the action of doing ministry in this season of the church called "Pentecost."

Exodus 3:1-15

A certain person says, "I would like to help out in the church ministry, but I do not have background or training for such jobs." Welcome to the world of Moses. He was neither a prophet nor a priest, but rather a shepherd. He is a wanted criminal in Egypt (Exodus 2:11-15), and he is working for his father-in-law Jethro. He is married to Zipporah and has a son named Gershom. In many modern organizations Moses would have a "tarnished" name. In scripture, God does mighty works through vulnerable humans such as Moses at Mount Horeb. For Christians who have had setbacks in their vocations, family situation, or education, this text reminds all people that God called Moses — who was hardly a person who would be invited to give a university commencement speech. Moses is being called off the sidelines of the wilderness and invited to be a major player in the game plan God has for Israel.

God appeared to Moses in fire amidst a bush, not a bush that is burning to a crisp. Rather than being frightened or repelled, Moses was curious, which lead to a calling. This account might be called a theophany experience, for which there will be more in the future (for example the Mount of Transfiguration with Moses, Elijah and Jesus, Matthew 17:1-9). Both sound and sight are used here by Moses, as God uses natural fire and a bush to act as messenger and a God who enters into world or creation of God's people. Moses could not look at God directly, as this could mean death. One theme for preaching here might be the "holiness" of God. Do people in our American culture regard anything as being "holy" these days? Possibly there has been "divine initiatives" taken in the lives of people, community, and work, but they are ignored.

God recognizes the suffering of the people in Egypt. God is not at the sidelines but actively suffering alongside the people who are in bondage in Egypt. God is commissioning Moses for this divine project of freeing the people. God remains good for God's promise to Israel's ancestors since Abraham (Genesis 12). Initially Moses hesitates as he does not see himself as a "transformational leader and turn-around pastoral" figure of his time. God's initiative to enlist Moses persists. God still wishes to maintain Moses' and the nation's integrity. God does work alongside his creation to deliver people from bondage and provide gifts of freedom. It is part of creation theology. Some have argued this could be called a "God in process" or "process theology" (see writings of, John Cobb, Terence Fretheim, and Tyrone Inbody). God not only calls people from something to some new life as well.

Exodus 3:7-9 is where God identifies the plight of his people and enters into this suffering alongside them. Exodus 3:10 is God asking Moses to come off the sidelines and get directly involved by way of confronting the Egyptian pharaoh. Who are the powerbrokers in any given community the people in our congregations exist in and at what level dare we challenge them? Is there a time to "fight city hall" in any particular town? Moses protests! Does God have to send Moses to a "leadership" workshop or does God work with what he has in Moses? Are there problems and issues in our community that continue to stand like a big elephant in the room, which many people are afraid to address? This text is an invitation to reflect on such mission of the church. God persists in the effort to invite Moses to participate in the same suffering relationship with the people of Israel as God experiences. [source: Terence Fretheim, *Interpretation a Bible Commentary for Teaching and Preaching: Exodus*(Westminster John Knox, 1991)]

Romans 12:9-21

The next time some careless driver who is text messaging in a crowded parking lot and they run into your shiny, clean car, consider the final verse of this text, "Do not be overcome by evil, but overcome evil with good" (Romans 12:21). This whole passage can give anybody's spiritual muscles a good work out! For those who protest that they do not seem to be growing "spiritually" from the pastor's sermons, here is a real feast of mature spirituality to consider! "Let love be genuine; hate what is evil, hold fast to what is good" (Romans 12:9). These texts invite people to grow as disciples themselves — rather than sit at the sidelines to watch other Christians stretch their own faith muscles.

These ethical traditions of the early church are grounded in the Old Testament or Hebrew Bible in passages such as Proverbs 12:13, 20:29, and 25:22 (heaping coals of fire by being kind). To practice love and hate evil without hypocrisy usually took a concrete form in welcoming the stranger or hospitality ministry because the roads and countryside were dangerous. How could this be accomplished today? Today suppose a new family moved into the community and they did not have an income. Are there people who will try to get them a job at their place of work?

Actually, when I was a child in southeast Michigan, this sort of thing happened often. A neighbor would get a new family's mother or father a job at a factory, driving a truck, or at a local small shop. This also became the "entrance card" to invite this same family to church on Sunday. Believe it or not, many churches grew in leaps and bounds among the poorer families then. As the economy worsened, families became more tribal and only pointed their immediate relatives to job openings. Paul would say that a mature Christian looks out for the whole community.

Christians are called to rejoice with those who rejoice and weep with those who weep. We are to be "little Christs" in this respect as Martin Luther put it. The only "Christ" people may see is in us. This is quite a challenge in times when people prefer to create "gods" of victory; success and "I got mine, so you get yours" type thinking. Paul is preaching a totally countercultural message in this regard.

Not seeking revenge, living in harmony with the community at all costs, being ardent, serving the Lord, and helping those who otherwise might despise you — is not the formula to get ahead in a "dog eat dog; rat race" world. Yet Paul is preaching to an urban audience in Rome. So why do we live in such a way? After all, this book of Romans is often viewed as uncontested "vintage Paul!"

For Paul, "[the just] shall live by faith (alone)" (Romans 1:17). This was the cry of the Reformation (also found in Habakkuk 2:4). Paul also quotes Deuteronomy 32:35, "Vengeance is mine, and recompense, for the time when their foot shall slip; because the day of their calamity is at hand, their doom comes swiftly." One of the recurring assumptions here is that one day there will be a day of reckoning or judgment with God for those who continue to act in wicked ways toward other people. Therefore, the best outcome a disciple can have in any situation of conflict is toward reconciliation or to seek peace. Rather than sitting at the race track hoping for the next car wreck to destroy metal or a person, Paul would say to get into the pit crew and help the team out. This happens in church also.

If there is a conflict on church council over a property manner, Paul would suggest that everybody has a chance to share their views. There might come a vote and the people who lose can either try again some other time or get mad, carry grudges, seek revenge, or leave the council and speak negative words about certain individuals. The other view is to find ways to compromise, seek "win-win" solutions to problems, and do not attack the "person but the problem." This could be difficult when dealing with people who thrive on adversity, confrontation, and must always be the winners. It is indeed coming off the sidelines and stretching one's faith muscles. [source: Arland J. Hultgren, *Paul's Letter to the Romans: A Commentary*(Wm. B. Eerdmans, 2011)]

Matthew 16:21-28

"If any want to become my followers, let them deny themselves and take up their cross and follow me" (Matthew 16:24). This is an invitation *par excellence* to get off the sidelines and become part of the kingdom of heaven in Matthew's gospel. Jesus assumes that he and his followers will be criticized and abused like the Hebrew prophets were as they carried out their mission from God. Matthew's audience knew the dangers of standing up to the government and government supported powers of the times.

After Peter's confession, Jesus has a passion announcement regarding suffering, being killed, and being raised on the third day. Peter rebukes this and Jesus in turn rebukes Peter for being on the side of Satan (Mathew 16:22-23). In order to have a fulfilled life on earth and for eternity, those who follow Jesus the Christ will indeed have eternal life. Disciples will not be insulated from trials, and yes suffering for what they believe to be the true God that gives meaning and life.

Matthew asks those who sit at life's sidelines if they either wish to come and follow Jesus with the dangers that accompany this spiritual journey, or do they wish to sit this one out and save their lives for now? This is a daily question for each believer to consider. Christianity continues to be a religion of second chances for those who err. However, suffering is definitely a part of being in the kingdom of heaven here in Matthew's gospel. Part of the confession in which the church is built on with Peter's words is also one must "deny themselves and take up their cross" (Matthew 16:24). For those in any broader community who do not like to hear about suffering as a part of the maturing spiritual journey, one can point out, it is right here in the Bible! There is also new life after every death. This is the gospel of the Christian church as well. [source: Craig S. Keener, *The Gospel of Matthew: A Socio-Rhetorical Commentary*(Wm. B Eerdmans, 2009)]

Application

All three of these texts are basically a challenge to "put up or shut up" when it comes to brainstorming, visioning, and planning for Christian ministry within the church. For instance, starting any type of small group might be a good idea (12 Step, Bible Study, Missionary project). However, which core group of four to five people is going to commit their time and effort beyond a couple months even a year or so to see this ministry to its fruition? Maybe a Bible study needs to be limited for seven weeks and then revisited. Maybe a support group has a life of six months then revisited. What sort of time and money commitments are people themselves willing to give to the community to see the mission of the church carried out?

How often does the cry go out in any given church, "We need a growing Sunday school program or the church will die within one generation?" With that said, will these same voices get up early on Sunday mornings to start a driving or bus ministry for such children? Will these same people call up the parents on Saturday night to remind them that they will be in front of the house early in the morning for Sunday school? Then there is the frustration of possibly a bigger, more heavily financed church in the next town that is already carrying on a bus ministry. That does not let the other smaller churches off the hook. What is our congregation doing that is unique to the kingdom and makes it worth it for children and their families to check out? How are people growing and maturing in their Christian faith in our congregation? All three of these texts address such questions in their own ways.

An Alternative Application

The books like Proverbs have wisdom in them that have lasted for centuries and have served all of the Abraham-based religions in many situations. Monotheism itself was not the only religion show on the block in the days of the Ancient Near East. A pastor could select texts from books such as Proverbs to suggest that competing views of the gods, and people who like to sit at the sidelines while criticizing, have been around for years. Proverbs might call such behaviors names such as "folly and foolishness." Today, just like Paul used various verses from Proverbs in Romans 12, what sort of texts can God be using to inform our ministry where we are in our communities?

Proper 18 | Ordinary Time 23

Exodus 12:1-14

Romans 13:8-14

Matthew 18:15-20

Psalm 149

by Wayne Brouwer

Kill or be killed?

Gilbert and Sullivan, the dynamic duo of the stage, created fun-filled musicals and light operas a generation ago, giving high school drama departments and community theaters plenty of material to dazzle and delight. Their names always appeared in tandem on the programs. It was as if they were a married couple. Indeed, much of their career felt like that. It was only right that their names be wedded together in common speech.

At the height of their success they even purchased a theater together so they could exert full creative control over their new works. Then came the nasty disagreement. Sullivan ordered the installation of new carpets. When the bill arrived, Gilbert hit the roof at the cost and refused to share in payment. They argued and fought about it and finally took the case to court. A legal judgment settled the claim, but it did nothing to heal the breach between them.

These grown men never spoke to one another again as long as they lived. When Sullivan wrote the music for a new production he would mail it to Gilbert. Then, when Gilbert finished the libretto, he would post it back to Sullivan again.

One time, they were requested to make a curtain call together. Although they normally refused such things because of their ongoing animosity, this time it was a benefit honoring their joint work, and they couldn't get out of it with grace. So they stayed at opposite sides backstage, entered from the far edges of the curtain, ensured that there were props in between them so that they could not see one another on the platform, and waved in isolation to opposite portions of the gathered audience.

Gilbert quarantined Sullivan in the prison of his mind, and Sullivan banished Gilbert from his social continent. Eventually they each became wardens for the prison of the other. Yet, like the guards who traveled to Australia on the first convict ships, it became apparent all too soon that there was little difference between the jailer and the jailed. Both came ashore onto a deserted island in the middle of an alien sea with no way to escape.

We are social creatures who cannot live in isolation. Yet, because of the sin and stupidity that trouble our human condition, we do not live well with those around us. The German philosopher, Schopenhauer, compared us to porcupines trying to nest together on a cold winter's night. We crouch toward one another because we need the heat of other bodies to survive. Yet the closer we huddle, the more we prick each other with our porcupine quills. Today's lectionary passages probe that conflict. When "Israel" was created as a nation in the original Passover, a brooding tempest of resentment roiled that has spilled over in ethnic bloodshed ever since. Paul, in his letter to the Romans, tries to steer Christians through the tumultuous seas of social chaos. As Jesus indicates in the gospel reading, each of us must deal with problems of social tension on a personal level, for it is most often those who are closest to us, our "brother" or our "sister," who feel the pain of our presence and we theirs.

Exodus 12:1-14

There are defining moments in every life. These are the occasions when identity is up for grabs and at least several strong contenders vie to acquire the rights to our purpose and values. We are at a crossroads, either as individuals or societies. We could go left. We might go right. The road ahead, with its sameness, may numb us into continuing as we are. Or the trackless hills beckon to vistas we had never considered before, off the highway completely. Even a valley, with its cool death of defeat, is a lure to our spirits.

Which way will we go? What pressures will force us, what attractions will draw us, what opportunities for redefinition will entice us?

Today's lectionary reading from Exodus 12 is the greatest defining moment in the life of ancient Israel. Everything changes after this point. Nothing remains the same. Suddenly, in the space of twelve hours, the path ahead is blocked and discontinuity demands a new identity. From this point forward, for thousands of generations, those who attach themselves to this small community of slaves, either by historical accidents of ethnicity or through faith commitments that rearrange international religious boundaries, will breathe a single word and it will shimmer as a paradigm-shifting talisman: *Passover*!

There are a number of levels of significance to that term. First, "Passover" contains memories of an action of divine intervention in Egyptian and Israelite history. The unique sociological role of the firstborn male was given new religious significance. Whereas the firstborn son was typically the recipient of the primary hereditary blessing, it was also this person's lot to carry on the family name, values, and traditions. Suddenly, in a single, decisive act, Egyptian culture was cut off. All who were supposed to receive the cultural mandate of continuity within the communities along the never-changing Nile were instantly set adrift, and all ties to the past were severed. In effect, Egypt died that night and could only hope to go into the future by reinventing itself. The standardized umbilical cord had been lopped as the destroying angel flew through, and old Egypt was gone. At the same time, this very act of discontinuity produced a new version of Israel. Previously, she was the identity-less under-caste of Egyptian society, working behind the scenes without voice or recognition; now, suddenly, she became an entire firstborn nation sired by Yahweh and heir to land and purpose and meaning and destiny that were being thrust upon her. In the Passover event, society was turned upside-down, so that the "haves" ceased to exist, and the "have-nots" became the defining oligarchy of a new civilization that was not merely gaining notoriety through revolution or comeuppance through evolution, but rather replacing human valuation systems with a divinely re-imposed social ordering.

Second, "Passover" redefined time for Israel. "This month is to be for you the first month, the first month of your year," said Yahweh (v. 2). Thus Israel was to explain the meaning of life by this event of release. Although the act of release from tyranny is not unusual in national celebrations ("Cinco de Mayo" in Mexico, for instance, or the American or Russian Revolutions, or "Bastille Day" and the French Revolution), what made this event unique is that all of time itself was to be reordered as originating from this day. It was the new way to think about the structure of daily life and the cycle of the seasons. This Passover redefined more than a nation; it was the new cosmology for understanding existence.

Third, "Passover" brought judgment and grace together in a strange way that would linger with Hebrew religion and Judaism and Christianity and Islam in an unending paradox. "We" become the favored people only because "they" are killed by God. Although "we" are probably not worthy, "they" were clearly in the wrong and deserved to be slaughtered. Each future branch of this religious tree would deal with this psychological conundrum in differing ways. Israel would presume on the "most favored nation" status and lose its religious moorings through ritual pride. Judaism would become self-doubting and introspective, believing that it retained a unique relationship with Yahweh, but was perplexed by the holy one's increasing silence and seeming forgetfulness of the passionate beginnings of their partnership. Christianity would package the problem of judgment's symbiotic twinship with grace into a new understanding of messianic mediatorship, combining both in the person of Jesus Christ. And Islam would declare that the lines between the chosen and the not-chosen remain clear throughout history, affirming divine vengeance as a necessary corollary to Allah's graciousness to some.

Romans 13:8-14

In the last chapters of his letter to the Romans, Paul outlined general principles of Christian social behavior. First, he urged a lifestyle of service rooted in sacrifice to Jesus, shaped by spiritual giftedness, and energized by love (Romans 12). Then Paul made this servant behavior specific by nodding to its public expressions (Romans 13). Finally, Paul revisited the issues surrounding the matter of the purchase and consumption of meat offered to idols (Romans 14:1--15:13), just has he had probed it in 1 Corinthians 8:1--11:1.

Paul's letter addressed a couple of specific issues — the nature of civil government, for instance (13:1-7), and a rehearsal of the ethical options available in a community where faith seemed to come in differing strengths (14:1--15:13). But mostly he painted in vibrant colors the character of moral choices in a world that is compromised and broken. Darkness and light are the key metaphors. Evil has wrapped a blanket of pain and harm around all that takes place in the human arena. Jesus is the brilliant light of God, penetrating earth's atmosphere with grace and reconciliation. Because of his physical departure at the ascension, Jesus' followers now must step in and become 10,000 points of light, restoring relationships and renewing meaning. The key element in this witness is love. Jesus is great, and because of our connection with him, we can be, too. Not for our own sakes, of course, but in the eschatological hope that we already participate in the world of tomorrow today. That is why Christianity is the religion of the dawn, and its adherents are ambassadors of love.

Matthew 18:15-20

Jesus' words to his disciples in Matthew 18 about conflict resolution and forgiveness are wonderful on paper. We read them and nod with understanding and trust. Yet they are some of the most difficult words of challenge that face us anywhere in scripture. Jesus outlines a strategy for addressing our troubled relationships with one another. It is important to follow him down this difficult path in our attempts to restore relational glue to our fractured worlds, for the alternatives are much more destructive.

First, Jesus reminds us that we have to make the process of restoration a very personal matter. When we are hurt and when our pride has been damaged we often become vindictive and belligerent. We charge about and spew venom and seek to build polarized communities of those who are for "us" against "them." The weapon of response most readily available to us is gossip and rumor. If I can send a toxic word to poison the atmosphere around the person who has hurt me, I hold a new advantage over her or him. In so doing, of course, I demote the other person from humankind and relegate her or him to animal status or lower. She is no longer my equal; she is a slut or a witch or a bimbo. He has become a pariah or a jackass or a scoundrel.

When my friend becomes my enemy, I feel the need to degrade him or her until they no longer deserve respect and have ceased to be bound with me by the rules of gentlemanly conduct or even the combat and prisoner of war stipulations of the Geneva Convention. Then I can blast them with excessive force and hit below the belt.

Second, Jesus challenges us to keep these matters under the eye of the community. It is hard for us to think communally in our highly individualized societies, yet this is precisely what we need to do. To keep these matters under the eye of the community means to place ourselves in submission to at least some form of group identity. This is not easy. Our consumerist way of life constantly tells us that all of reality revolves around us, our tastes and schedules and desires. In stark contrast, to enter a community means that I give up some of my personal agenda for the sake of the greater good.

We cannot claim fidelity with God and at the same time play cavalierly in our daily relations with those around us. Each person and each congregation will have to be part of the process of determining how the community and its leadership will invest in reconciliation and restoration.

If we know this, then when we experience tension and broken bonds with someone else in the community, it is not ours or theirs to resolve in isolation. The community itself has a stake in all lives and their interactions. Therefore, says Jesus, it is absolutely imperative that we engage the power of the community in addressing the hurts that affect any of its members. Failing to do so does not so much destroy community as it does isolate us from it. We become impoverished when we think we have all the resources to force others into obedience to our way of thinking or living.

One more thing that becomes apparent in Jesus' teaching is that the entire emotional content of our relational difficulties needs to be reframed. Jesus says that our goal is to have a brother restored. Moreover, if that does not happen through our own initiatives and those of the community, the outcome must be that we treat the other person in the broken relationship as if he were a "pagan or a tax collector."

These designations sound ominous to us. They are off-putting to our sensibilities of associating with "nice" people. But we need to recall that Jesus was accused of spending too much time with tax collectors and sinners. To treat people in this manner is not to throw stones at them or to turn away in disgust. Rather it is a call to re-engage with them as those whom God is seeking and saving.

When Bill Hybels was a college student in Iowa, he had a roommate who trained his pet dog to growl whenever the town mayor's name was mentioned. No matter what might be happening at any time, if someone happened to say the mayor's name in passing, the little mutt would bristle and growl.

So it is with each of us, when relationships have become strained or undone by someone's carelessness, craft, or calumny. We bristle and growl. In the middle of other conversations, the name might be mentioned and we can feel our stomachs tighten and our breath catch. There is an autonomic response that drives us to pain and frustration.

Only if we can somehow reframe the other person's image in our senses as a "pagan or tax collector" — that is, someone who needs to experience the grace of God — can we still the inner growls and get the beast of our hatred to stop bristling. It is only then that we can hear Jesus saying, "You have gained again your sister. You have found again your brother." And something in the world smells sweeter because of it.

Application

Thomas Merton, when writing about the religious community with which he spent many years, noted that every prospective participant was initially brought in and made to stand in the center of a circle formed by current members. There he was asked by the abbot, "What do you come seeking?"

The answers varied, of course, in line with the individual's recent experiences. Some said, "I come seeking a deeper relationship with God." Others were more pragmatic: "I desire to become more disciplined in my practices of life." And there were always a few who were simply running away: "I hope to find solace from the world and refuge from the problems that have plagued me."

Merton said that there was really only one answer, which all needed to voice before they could take up residence. "I need mercy!" was the true cry of the heart. "I need mercy!"

Merton said that any other answer betrayed our prideful assertion of self-determination. We wanted, we planned, we were running away from, we desired ... But the person who knew his need of mercy had stepped out of the myopic circle of self-interest long enough to begin to see the fragile interdependence of all who were taken into the larger fellowship of faith. We cannot create community, for it does not revolve around us. We can only enter community or receive it as a gift. Hence, we need mercy in order to walk through its door.

This, of course, is the message of the lectionary texts today. Israel was created out of an act of mercy that she would forever remember in the Passover. Paul saw mercy as the public show of redemptive love. And Jesus announced that the antagonisms of our world can only truly find redemptive conclusion in the mercy of forgiveness.

Alternative Application

Matthew 18:15-20. Today's gospel reading is always good to preach on its own. After the tragedy of September 11, 2001, our nation experienced something of intentional, projected dehumanization. Those who hijacked the planes, according to many speeches and articles, were not humans but terrorists. They did not play by the rules. They did not value life as we did. They were schooled in barbarianism. For all these reasons and others like them our nation uttered cries for vengeance, many of which exceeded limits of human respect. It was General Philip Sheridan who gave us the striking reflection in 1869 that, "The only good Indian is a dead Indian." Post 9/11 there were many voices that seemed to echo his advice in the new and painful context.

However, Jesus demands that we keep our hurting relationship and all its parties personal. "If your brother sins against you go and show him his fault, just between the two of you." This instruction strips me of my most destructive weapons and forces me to rehumanize the very one from whom my heart wants to pull away in disgust. Jesus does not claim it will be an easy thing to do. No psychologist would pretend the process is a lark, or carries us along like a carnival ride. Hurt is painful, and so is restoration.

Preaching The Psalm

by Schuyler Rhodes

Psalm 149. The very words, "Praise the Lord," have, in some circles, taken on a tone of mockery and scorn. In certain quarters, one can hear the high nasal satiric voice as it bleats out the opening words to this psalm. "Praaaise the Lorrrrd!" It's true. Making fun of Christian faith is quite fashionable these days. From comedians to songwriters to self-proclaimed spiritual-but-not-religious folk, a steady stream of ridicule flows unabated.

The taunting disrespect comes for a lot of reasons. It is aimed at hypocritical television preachers who are quick to judge the moral turpitude of others, only to themselves be found severely wanting. It is leveled at religious institutions that are far more engaged in the maintenance of the institution than in actually praising the Lord. Yes, the mockery comes from many places, but it is generated by what the world clearly sees as a religious community unable to live up to its own teachings.

Maybe, as this psalm suggests, it's time to sing a "new song." Perhaps this song brings with it the melody of humility, tolerance, and hope. How does it go? Could there be harmonies of forgiveness, grace, and openness? What's the beat? Is it the rhythm of generosity and peace? Does it have a backbeat of compassion and justice?

There's no question about it. Listening to the rising tide of critique and outright condemnation of Christian faith raises the hackles. Yet, if honesty prevails, it must be admitted that much of the negative energy directed at the Christian community is richly deserved. We have not lived by the teachings of Jesus. We have not stood up for the poor and the weak. We are not good at loving our enemies, and we do not make a real great showing at offering forgiveness. We have uttered empty pious judgments and held to legalistic rulings while grace has been discarded and left behind. And we have looked the other way while people waving the cross of Christ have used his name for economic and political gain.

Yes indeed. It is time to sing a new song. But let the song come, not as a way to stem the tide of criticism. Let it come instead as a true and powerful symphony of praise to the holy creating God of Israel! Let this new song call the "assembly" to faithfulness and the leaders to integrity and passion. Let the notes of new life pour forth as the whole community joins with one voice to sing a new song.

Proper 19 | Ordinary Time 24

Exodus 14:19-31

Romans 14:1-12

Matthew 18:21-35

by Wayne Brouwer

Living as if faith matters

When Eric Lomax was posted to Singapore in 1941 he knew nothing of the horror that lay ahead of him. With hundreds of other soldiers he was taken captive, and then declared a spy by the Japanese victors. They broke both his arms and smashed several ribs, and left him barely alive. Yet somehow he survived the death camps and returned home, albeit a damaged man. For fifty years his seething bitterness poisoned his relationships, first with his father and then with his wife. The former died and the latter was divorced.

In 1985, Lomax received a letter from a former army chaplain who had made contact with Nagase Takashi, the man who had served as interpreter at Lomax's cruel interrogation. Nagase was deeply offended by his nation's treatment of war prisoners and had devoted the rest of his life to whatever restitution or recompense could be made. He even built a Buddhist temple near the place where Lomax and others had been severely beaten or killed.

Lomax felt the anger of boiling vengeance swell through him. He shared his frustrations with Patti, his second wife. She was indignant that Nagase could write about feeling forgiven and at peace, when she knew the troubles that had dogged her husband for decades. In irritation she wrote to Nagase about Eric's ongoing emotional pain.

To her surprise, she received a letter of response from Nagase. At first she was almost afraid to open it but with trembling curiosity she finally relented. What spilled into her lap was "an extraordinarily beautiful letter," as she put it. Even Lomax found himself moved deeply by its compassion and desire for reconciliation.

A year later Eric and Patti Lomax met Nagase at the location of the famous River Kwai Bridge. In halting English Nagase repeated over and over, "I am very, very sorry."

Lomax, in tears, took him by the arm and said, "That's very kind of you to say so."

They met for hours, and Lomax gave Nagase a short letter. In it he said that he could not forget what happened in 1943 but that he had chosen to offer Nagase "total forgiveness." Nagase wept with emotion.

When interviewed later, Lomax said simply, "Sometime the hating has to stop."

There is no end to the hostilities that can erupt between good friends or neighbors or relatives when a slight is incurred or a tragedy can be laid to someone's blame. No end, that is, until someone chooses to say, "Sometime the hating has to stop." That is the very personal moment of forgiveness. It does not come easily. But if we live under the umbrella of God's mercy, it can come.

In today's gospel reading, Jesus steps outside of the numbers game of blame and negotiation and creates a new playing field which is so large that no scores can be kept. In effect, the message Jesus sends is not "You must try harder to learn the discipline of forgiving!" but rather "You must continually remember who you are!"

But forgiveness is only one dimension of acting as if faith matters. The Israelites faced a life-threatening challenge that tested the depths of their commitment to acting on faith. The apostle Paul challenges first-century Christians in Rome to take their beliefs even into the small choices of life.

Exodus 14:19-31

Exodus 1-19 forms an extended "historical prologue" to the Sinai covenant by declaring Israel's precarious situation in Egypt (chapter 1), the birth and training of the leader who would become Yahweh's agent for recovering Yahweh's enslaved people (chapter 2), the calling of this deliverer (chapters 3-4), and the battle of the superpowers (the Pharaoh and Yahweh) who each lay claim to suzerain status over this vassal nation (chapters 5-19). Exodus 20-24 is the original covenant document of the Old Testament, binding Israel to her God in a suzerain-vassal treaty. Exodus 25-40 focuses on the creation of a suitable residence for Israel's suzerain. Thus the whole of Exodus may be quickly outlined as Struggles (1-19), Stipulations (20-24), and Symbols (25-40) surrounding the Sinai covenant-making event.

The struggles of chapters 1-19 involve a number of things. At the start there is the nasty relationship that has developed between the Pharaoh of Egypt and the Israelites. An editorial note declares that "Joseph" has been forgotten, and this small reference forms the bridge that later draws Genesis into an even more broadly extended historical prologue to the Sinai covenant. We will find out, by reading backward, that Joseph was the critical link between the Egyptians and this other ethnic community living within its borders. When the good that Joseph did for both races was forgotten, the dominant Egyptian culture attempted to dehumanize and then destroy these Israelite aliens.

Israel belongs to Yahweh both because of historic promises made to Abraham, and also by way of chivalrous combat in which Yahweh won back the prize of lover and human companion from the usurper who had stolen her away from the divine heart. Furthermore, Yahweh accomplished this act *without* the help of Israel's own resources (no armies, no resistance movements, no terrorist tactics, no great escape plans), and in a decisive manner that announced the limitations of the Egyptian religious and cultural resources.

This is why the final plague is paired with the institution of the Passover festival (Exodus 12). The annual festival would become an ongoing reminder that Israel was bought back by way of a blood-price redemption, and that the nation owed its very existence to the love and fighting jealousy of its divine champion. In one momentous confrontation, Egypt lost its firstborn and its cultural heritage, while Israel became Yahweh's firstborn and rightful inheritance.

Related to this divinely-initiated ownership theme is the miraculous deliverance of Israel through the Red Sea, coupled with the annihilation of the Egyptian army and its national military prowess in the same incidents. While Exodus 14 narrates the episode in the nail-biting urgency of a documentary, chapter 15 is given over largely to the ancient song of Moses, which unmistakably identifies the entire exodus event as divine combat against Pharaoh over the possession of Israel. Furthermore, the victory ballad also clearly anticipates the effect of this battle on the other near eastern nations, with the result that Yahweh is able to march the Israelites through many hostile territories and eventually settle the nation in Canaan as an ongoing testimony to Yahweh's rightful prestige. So it is that the exodus itself is not the divine goal, but only the first stage toward something else.

Romans 14:1-12

The matter of dietary choices in the early church, as probed by Paul in Romans 14, is very interesting. Paul spent the winter of 53-54 AD in Corinth, and it might well have been this setting that prompted the inclusion of this ethical discussion in his letter to the Roman church. After all, only a year or so earlier Paul had been required to address this same issue for the Corinthian congregation (see 1 Corinthians 8-10). What makes this discussion particularly compelling is that it arises from confusion about the instructions issued by the Jerusalem council several years before (Acts 15). Gentiles were told that they did not have to first become practicing Jews in order to become believing Christians. But some social and dietary suggestions were offered so that Gentiles and Jews might be able to share table fellowship, particularly when commemorating the Last Supper together. The brief instruction issued by the Jerusalem council several years before was to "abstain from food sacrificed to idols" (Acts 15:29).

Already now that command was being interpreted in various ways. When animal sacrifices were made at cultic shrines, particularly on well-attended public occasions, there was often too much flesh either for burning or for eating at the time. Without refrigeration, since the meat was destined to spoil quickly, much of the excess was dumped into the markets at bargain-basement prices. Because many of the Christians in Rome were slaves or from lower classes, this inexpensive meat offered a lot of meal for the money. And that is where the controversy began.

Some folks, who had taken a strong hold on the freedoms offered by Christ, knew that idols were not rival gods and therefore any meat purchased in this way was simply a wise use of funds. Others, however, who had emerged into Christianity from prior work at the shrines and former participation in the cultic practices of these non-Christian religions, found it scandalous for Christians to buy and eat such meat. Another group remembered the instructions of the Jerusalem council, and thought it a matter of principle not to engage in this act that had specifically been prohibited by the church leaders.

Paul's response sorts through these differing reflections on Christian freedoms and interpersonal responsibilities and leaves the final decisions up to maturing believers who are wise enough to understand how their behavior can impact others. Once again, as with his instructions in his letters to the Corinthians and earlier the Galatians, Paul places the goal of a loving response to Jesus as primary in the making of all moral and ethical choices and follows that closely with a sense of obligation to serve and help others. In effect, Paul's ethical code is essentially that which Jesus espoused: love God above all, and love your neighbor as yourself (Matthew 22:37-40).

Matthew 18:21-35

Several themes emerge from Jesus' story. First, it becomes obvious that forgiveness is always personal because pain is personal. Peter asks about what he should do when his "brother" sins against him. That makes sense to us, even if we don't want to admit it. It is far easier to pretend to deal with people and matters that are at a distance. We can choose to hate terrorists and then choose to talk with politically correct understanding about them because few of us have ever actually been terrorized firsthand. But if a murder has happened in our family, or if a drunk driver has destroyed our property or our health or the life of a loved one, things become highly personal and our glib forgiving spirit runs away.

A second thing Jesus teaches us in his parable is that forgiveness is essentially one-sided. While we hope for reconciliation — a two-sided outcome — in matters of hurt and broken relationships, forgiveness is not the same thing. Forgiveness is initiated by one party and is often rebuffed or rejected by the other. That does not undo forgiveness, but it does remind us that forgiveness is essentially one-sided. Forgiveness is what I do or he does or she does. If it leads to mutual restoration, only then does the one-sided forgiveness become two-sided reconciliation.

Jesus emphasizes this in his teaching by showing that when the rich creditor chose to cancel the initial debt, it was neither required nor expected. It happened only because of the choice made by the king. The outcome of the debt cancellation was two-sided, to be sure, but it was initiated as a one-sided movement on the part of the king.

This is a very important point to remember. If we can't have our way in some matter, we often want to make sure that at least the other person can't have her way either. If I hurt, he has to hurt. If I have been wronged, at minimum the other person should be required to make a public show of sorrow. Tit for tat. We want the scales to be balanced somehow, even if it is by way of some kind of mutual expressions that hurt has been caused.

But Jesus is not asking us to be fair people. He is asking that we become excessively unfair in mercy, in the same way that our Father in heaven is merciful with us. It begins as a one-sided initiative.

There is a third element of meaning to note in Jesus' teaching parable and that is that forgiveness is not merely a one-time event but rather a growing disposition of graciousness. Matthew makes this clear by placing the parable in the middle section of his gospel. Those events leading up to the Transfiguration in chapter 17 show Jesus focusing most of his attention on the crowds who gather around, and emphasizing the character of the kingdom of heaven. Later, following the entry into Jerusalem on Palm Sunday (chapter 21), most of Jesus' teachings will anticipate his death and resurrection and the Messianic Age that these usher in. But here, in between, Jesus spends most of his time with his disciples and tries to help them understand the character of a committed spiritual lifestyle. We call it discipleship.

Jesus makes it clear in his story to Peter that there are others looking on as they practice their piety. It is a group of otherwise undescribed folks who notice how the forgiven debtor treats the man who owes him a little. These people also report the man's actions to the king, who had originally laid aside the huge obligation that could never have been paid.

In telling this part of the story, Jesus reminds his disciples and us that the goal of any spiritual formation in our lives is not merely to make us feel good or to give us a sense of accomplishment. This is quite important, since it was Peter's question that sparked the teaching in the first place. Peter had come asking what it would take for him to know that he had done enough, he was good enough, and he had arrived at some new level of spiritual graduation.

But accomplishments that become self-serving and occasions for self-congratulations are not the goal of discipleship. Jesus, in fact, had said earlier in the Sermon on the Mount, that those who pray in public and make a big show of giving to the poor have their immediate gratification, but it holds no heavenly value. The goal of spiritual growth is transformation, not arrival. We are to be engaged in a process whereby we become different people and through which our world begins to look more like the kingdom God intended it to be.

So forgiveness is not merely an act that is repeated on occasion to make us feel good in our accomplishments. Rather, it is a growing disposition of graciousness that is an unfolding process of discipleship identity and lifestyle. Peter ought not to think about how many times he forgives one person or a hundred. Instead, the question is whether his character is continually evolving to become more reflective of God.

Application

Michael Christopher probed the actions of faith well in his play *The Black Angel*. He told of Hermann Engel, a German general who was sentenced to thirty years in prison by the Nuremberg court for war crimes. Nearly forgotten by the time he was released, Engel escaped from society and built a small mountain cabin near Alsace to live out his final years in obscurity.

But a journalist named Morrieaux would not let the story die so easily. After all, it had been his village and his family who were destroyed by Engel's brutality. Working carefully by spreading rumor and stirring up old feelings of bitterness, Morrieaux fomented a plot to burn the man's house down around him and sear him painfully to death.

Even this, though, was not enough. Morrieaux had a thirst for revenge. He wanted to hear a confession from Engel. Then he wanted Engel to understand what was about to happen to him. Morrieaux desired to watch the horror invade Engel's eyes at the moment when his destruction was assured.

So Morrieaux sneaked ahead of the mob he had stirred up and connived to enter the general's cottage on pretense. But the person he met there was not at all what he expected. There was no gruesomeness about him; he held no monster-like qualities. This was just a feeble old man. In fact, as Morrieaux tried to draw out from him the awful details of his war experiences and crimes, Engel was halting and confused. He could not fully remember all that took place. Dates had blurred and incidents were lost or rewoven.

Morrieaux began to realize that his vengeance would not be sweet, and that the plot he had instigated against the old man was a terrible act of murder. In desperation he revealed himself and his intentions to Engel, begging that the general escape quickly with him. Even as they spoke there were distant sounds of the mob climbing to do the nasty deed.

Engel finally understood what was going on. But before he would leave with Morrieaux he required one condition. "What is it?" asked Morrieaux.

"Forgive me," replied Engel.

The journalist was frozen. What should he do?

As the lights come down Morrieaux slipped out of the cottage alone. The mob did its work and the horrible war criminal died. But the journalist remained forever locked in his own prison of unforgiveness.

An Alternative Application

Matthew 18:21-35. In February of 1982, Max Lindeman and Harold Wells were sentenced to modest prison terms by a New York judge. Police had booked the pair on rape and assault charges in a highly publicized case. Four months earlier, they had entered a convent in New York City and had brutally victimized a thirty-year-old nun. Not only had they repeatedly raped her, they had also beaten her and then used a nail file to carve 27 crosses into her body. It was a crime that brought even the insensitive to tears.

But when it came time to press charges, the nun refused. She was fully aware that these were the men who attacked her. Nor did she deny that something evil had happened to her at their hand. Yet when it came time to overtly accuse the men of their crimes, she chose instead to tell the police and the reporters that after the model of Jesus, she forgave them. She hoped, she said, that they would learn something from this act of one-sided forgiveness and change their ways.

The police were almost livid. Here were two rotten scoundrels who needed to be punished, yet the nun had tied their hands. Social outrage mounted as the two were tried on lesser charges and jailed for significantly shorter sentences than their basest crimes really demanded.

Did it work? Did the nun's forgiving spirit soften the hearts of Lindeman and Wells? Did they change?

The nun believes that is the wrong question to ask. In her heart, forgiveness works. She is more like Christ and lives in greater harmony with the Spirit of God than if she had followed through on the requests to press charges.

We cannot know, of course, whether the nun's actions are better or worse for the men or for society generally. We probably could not endure a world where no justice was meted and where the fabric of social responsibility became a mockery through expectations of convenient unilateral forgiveness.

Nevertheless, the wisdom of Jesus' words is found precisely in their unusual instruction. Jesus himself would die upon a cross that he did not deserve, and while hanging there would breathe words of divine forgiveness. It is the very contrary nature of forgiveness that requires of us respect. To forgive is an unusual way of life that cuts across our otherwise jaded senses and renegotiates the character of power in our world.

Forgiveness is a choice and a unilateral one at that. It cannot go on the bargaining block or it becomes something other than its essential character. Forgiveness is not fair. It is mercy offered and that act alone sets aside certain demands of justice. It does not negate justice, but it says that a higher power will be entered to trump the ordinary scheme of things for extraordinary purposes.

Proper 20 | Ordinary Time 25
Exodus 16:2-15
Philippians 1:21-30
Matthew 20:1-16
by David Kalas

Who's On First?

I heard a story once of a custodian who worked at a certain university. Among his responsibilities, he emptied the wastebaskets in the administration building where the president of the university had his office. The school underwent a change in presidents during this custodian's time there, and he found that his experience of his job changed. "I didn't mind emptying Dr. Wilson's garbage," he remarked, referring to the former president.

Dr. Wilson, you see, was a most gracious man. He was as solicitous of the custodian as he was of the multimillion-dollar donor. His successor, however, was cut from a different cloth. He busily passed by much of the staff without more than a nod most days. And the man who emptied his wastebasket found that it was harder to do with joy than it had been for the previous president.

It was an interesting and insightful remark by the custodian. After all, the actual job was the same as it had always been. The problem was not that the second president made a bigger mess or had smellier trash. No, it was about the style and the character of the men involved. And the custodian confessed that it was easier to do his job for the more humble and winsome man than it was for his successor.

In some arenas of life, the cynical wisdom when it comes to getting ahead says "It's not what you know, it's who you know." I'm sure that is an accurate assessment in some settings. Perhaps when it comes to being happy in your work, meanwhile, the adage might be slightly different. Perhaps we might say instead: "It's not what you do, it's for whom you do it."

This, of course, is the Christian's key. And it goes far beyond mere employment. For us as followers of Christ, this is our joy and our peace, our purpose and our satisfaction — not what we do, but for whom we do it.If it is Christ's wastebaskets that I get to empty, you see, then I am a fortunate man and happy to do it.

Exodus 16:2-15

Whenever God is in the picture, there is always the capacity for the routine to turn miraculous, for the ordinary to become extraordinary. The scriptures are full of stories that bear witness to that truth. So are our own lives and testimonies.

In the case of our Old Testament reading, see the remarkable transition from the beginning to the end.

The beginning is about as ordinary as it gets: hunger. This is a daily affair. It is built into the universal human experience. One wouldn't expect so humdrum a starting place to turn into something so monumental.

In addition to the universal quality of this very ordinary starting place, there is also something very familiar about it in the immediate context of the exodus story. "The whole congregation of the Israelites complained," the writer reports. Well, there's nothing new about that. Even a person very well-versed in scripture would be hard-pressed to identify the chapter and verse of that line, for it occurs so often in the story. Again and again, the people complain. And more than just a bad attitude, their chronic complaining indicates an underlying faithlessness on the part of the people.

We also see in the early verses of this episode an element that may be personally familiar to us. Observe the content of the people's complaint, for it lacks all sense of perspective. They cried out that they wished they had died back in Egypt. And their memory of Egypt is summarized as "we sat by the fleshpots and ate our fill." Do either of those matters square with reality?

First, of course, they didn't want to die back in Egypt. After Moses and Aaron's first encounter with Pharaoh, you recall, the edict came down to make bricks without straw. And in the wake of that difficulty, the Israelites complained to Moses: "You have made us obnoxious to Pharaoh and his officials and have put a sword in their hand to kill us" (Exodus 5:21 NIV).

Meanwhile, their recollection about sitting around eating all that they wanted sounds unlikely. They were slaves in Egypt, after all, not passengers on a cruise. And when Moses appeared on the scene to deliver them, there's no indication in the story that the people were saying, "No, thanks. We like it just fine here!"

Nevertheless, oftentimes when we are desperate we lose our ability to see clearly. They were hungry, discouraged, and overwhelmed. And in that clouded condition, slavery looked better than freedom, death looked better than life.

Well, the Lord provided for their need there in the wilderness. Within 24 hours, it seems, he miraculously furnished two staples for the hungry multitude: meat and bread. And the bread, of course, was the famous desert diet that came to be known as "manna" — a name born out of their question "What is it?"

The introduction of that manna, then, marks the end of the episode. And what do we know about that manna? It was the original "daily bread," for God sustained them with it throughout their generation of wilderness wanderings. It became a symbol of both God's providence and the people's obedience, inasmuch as it could not be kept overnight except in preparation for the sabbath, when there would be no manna to gather. It embodied God's faithfulness, as the manna continued regularly until the people transitioned to eating the produce of the Promised Land (Joshua 5:11-12). And ultimately that manna foreshadowed "the real bread from heaven" (see John 6:31-35, 48-58).

We see, then, how the routine turns miraculous under the hand of God. We see how the ordinary becomes extraordinary. The commonplace stuff of life — hunger and growling, needing and fussing — becomes the context for God's power, kindness, faithfulness, and salvation.

Philippians 1:21-30

Hamlet's famous "to be or not to be" speech was born out of despair. In his letter to the Philippians, Paul is pondering a similar sort of "whether 'tis better" dilemma; yet for him it is not a tortured decision. Rather, it seems that he is torn between two good options. Indeed, as he expresses each it becomes clear to us that these are two beautiful options.

And these two beautiful options may be ours as well.

On the one hand, there is the beauty of remaining in this world, in this life. It is "more necessary" for the Philippians (and, no doubt, for so many other believers across the Mediterranean world). That choice is marked by participating in their "progress and joy in faith." This, you see, is the lovely option of working for the Lord and accomplishing his work in the lives of his people. It is clearly the privilege that you and I enjoy as ministers of the gospel. And more broadly, it is the rewarding option available to anyone who is willing to be used by God.

On the other hand, there is the beauty of "departing." Paul regards it as "far better," for to die is "gain," it is to "be with Christ." This is a beauty that goes unrecognized by most of us most of the time. We so instinctively cling to this life and this world, you see. We do all that we can to avoid death, failing to see what awaits us on the other side. That's not to say that the Christian should have a death wish. Quite the contrary: it is a life wish! We should be characterized by the perspective that anticipates with joy the fullness of our destination. How silly it is to linger at the rest stop when the end of the journey is so perfect and so good!

And so we observe that the apostle is faced with two excellent options. What a nice problem to have! And the same enviable problem is available to anyone and everyone. The recipe is simple, and Paul reveals it at the outset. "For to me," he writes, "living is Christ"; or, as the old King James Version rendered it, "For to me to live is Christ."

If, for me, life is devoted to something else — family, career, possessions, pleasures, causes, or you name it — then I will not enjoy Paul's happy dilemma. But when life is all about Christ, then life in the flesh is suddenly endowed with an ultimate meaning and purpose. And at the same time, death offers to us the greatest fulfillment, for it unites us with the one who is our first love and reason for being.

Matthew 20:1-16

Life is not fair. God is not fair. Both of those statements are true, yet the truths are quite different.

We make a mistake when we equate God with life. It's not a conscious or deliberate thing, but it's a very common one. When life is good, it is easy for us to affirm that God is good. When life is bad, however, we find ourselves questioning the goodness of God. It is as though God is the chef in the kitchen of a restaurant, and so we credit or blame him for the quality of the meal we are served.

But let us be purposeful about separating the issues. The goodness of God is not identical with the goodness of life. I am reminded in this regard of the psalmist's profound affirmation that God's love is better than life (Psalm 63:3). And likewise, the fairness of life is a different question from the fairness of God. Both are unfair, but in different ways.

We need not invest any time in trying to prove that life is unfair. Keep your eyes open for ten minutes and you will likely see proof enough. And we are often grieved by the ways in which life is unfair, whether to us or to others.

The parable that Jesus tells in our gospel lection, meanwhile, illustrates beautifully the truth of God's unfairness. It is the unfairness that the main character in the story calls generosity. It is the unfairness that you and I know as grace.

The story has many nuances and details worth preaching or teaching. The bottom line, however, is Jesus' surprise ending. At the end of a work day, a landowner who has employed a great many workers in his vineyard over the course of the day pays them all the same wage. It is the day's wage agreed upon by those hired at the very beginning. Fair enough. But he pays that same amount even to those who were hired as the day's work was winding down.

Tellingly, the workers hired first were not unhappy with their pay until they saw their juniors receiving the same amount. This is the ugliness of envy, of course. Left on my own, I may be content. But when the green eye looks around and sees what others have, what others get, what others enjoy, suddenly I am no longer content with what I have. The position of those first workers is arguable, to be sure, but not defensible.

We may see ourselves in those first workers. We may also recognize in them Jonah or the prodigal son's older brother. They too were famously unhappy with the unfairness of God.

The generous master, of course, is the character that reveals God to us. He is not unfair in the traditional sense of the term. That is, he never cheats anyone, never gives someone less than he or she deserves. Ah, but the Lord is renowned for giving people more than they have earned, giving them better than they deserve. He was not unfair in his treatment of the first workers hired. He was profligately unfair, however, in his treatment of the last workers hired.

See the long line of workers. And see how many, many of them — of us — are among those who receive from the Master better than we deserve, so much more than we have earned. Life is unfair, to be sure. But God is unfair too, and we call his unfairness grace.

Application

This week's selected passages furnish us with an assortment of variously happy and unhappy people. The hungry children of Israel are unhappy, and they let their complaints be known. The workers hired first in Jesus' parable, likewise, are an unhappy group, and they too voice their complaint. Standing in contrast to all those folks, however, is the apostle Paul.

To say that Paul was happy is to do an injustice to what Paul was. The letter from which our New Testament lection is taken is sometimes nicknamed "the joyful epistle." This in spite of the fact that Paul was in prison when he wrote it.

The children of Israel were in an unhappy circumstance. So was Paul. But while they were marked by complaining, he was filled with rejoicing.

The servants hired first felt that they had been treated unjustly. As the landowner pointed out, they had not. The apostle Paul, meanwhile, had almost certainly been treated unjustly. While we don't know the circumstance of his imprisonment at the time he wrote to the Philippians, we may be quite sure that he was no criminal. Yet while the workers were feeling cheated, Paul was feeling joyful.

We make a great mistake, albeit a natural and common one, when we rely on our circumstances for our happiness, our contentment, our sense of satisfaction. There will always be something wrong, after all. There will always be something that isn't quite right, not quite to our liking, not fair or pleasing to us. And so we will find ourselves perpetually in the camp of the Israelites or the grumbling workers.

I would rather align myself with Paul. But how? "For to me," he revealed, "living is Christ." It was not what he did — or more broadly, what he experienced — that was finally the issue for him. It was for whom he did it.

Alternative Application

Exodus 16:2-15. "The Complaint Department" The customer service desk, the suggestion box, the support line, the "tell us what you think" survey — these are all standard practices used by businesses and other organizations to deal with the needs of their customers. Many times, of course, the needy customer is a complaining customer. He or she is frustrated or dissatisfied with the product or service, and so the business has to provide some proper way of channeling and processing those complaints. A happy customer, after all, is your best advertisement. But an unhappy customer — especially in the day of online reviews — can be devastating to a business.

And so a million times a day two old adages are affirmed and reinforced: "The customer is always right" and "The squeaky wheel gets the grease." The unhappy customer registers his or her complaint, and if the customer service department is functioning properly, that customer walks away satisfied.

A common error of the unhappy customer, of course, is taking the complaint to the wrong person or place. The server in the restaurant, for example, has to field a lot of complaints that really belong to the cook or the manager. The salesperson may get an earful about problems that belong to the manufacturer. (We as preachers, too, may have to hear more than our share of misplaced complaints. It was the choir, the organist, the youth minister, or the bishop that made this parishioner unhappy, but you and I hear about it and are forced to answer for it.)

That same phenomenon may be in play with our Old Testament story. The Israelites had complaints, but they were misplaced. It's a small enough detail in the text that we may gloss over it, but relationally it is a huge detail. "The whole congregation of the Israelites," the narrator reports, "complained against Moses and Aaron in the wilderness."

This is a classic case of the server paying the price for what did or did not happen back in the kitchen. What, after all, had been the role of Moses and Aaron in all of this? Had they initiated the process? Was it their idea, their plan? Were they mapping out the itinerary? Were they making the rules?

Time and again throughout the story the Israelites complained about Moses and Aaron, and they complained to Moses and Aaron. But the people were going to the wrong place in terms of both cause and effect. It was God who had been the cause of their exodus, their journey, and their provisions. And the effect of complaining against God compared with complaining to God is a night-and-day difference.

The pages of the Bible are full of people who complain to God. Moses himself does it. So does Job, the psalmist, Jeremiah, Habakkuk, Jonah, and more. And remarkably, there is no penalty for such candor. It's when the people of God take their complaints elsewhere — which the children of Israel do as a matter of course — that the hammer comes down.

That seems counterintuitive to us. After all, wouldn't you and I rather not hear than hear people's complaints? Why should we fare better with God when we complain to him instead of not?

In the context of a relationship, a complaint is a beautiful thing. The content of what is being said may be unpleasant enough, but the meaning of what is unsaid is marvelous. For the complaints we bring to God carry with them these unspoken messages. First, that he is there. Second, that he cares enough to listen. Third, that he loves us so much that our circumstances and our feelings matter to him. And fourth, that he is powerful enough to do something about it all.

In any relationship, candor is a compliment. And the candor of a complaint offered in prayer carries with it significant affirmations about God. The children of Israel needed to find the right complaint department.

Proper 21 | Ordinary Time 26

Exodus 17:1-7

Philippians 2:1-13

Matthew 21:23-32

Psalm 78:1-4, 12-16

by Wayne Brouwer and Schuyler Rhodes

Obedience

When Sadie and Bessie, the famed "Delany Sisters," were in the early years of their second centuries (103 and 105, respectively) they told interviewers, "God only gave you one body, so you better be nice to it. Exercise, because if you don't, by the time you're our age, you'll be pushing up daisies." Fitness gymnasiums ought to put the Delany Sisters on their billboards and quote them into larger profit margins.

Some people know when enough is enough. Others never seem to quit. What separates an athlete from a couch potato quarterback is the same thing that divides between pilgrimage disciples and religious tourists: The former are participants while the latter are consumers. This is the key element probed in each of today's lectionary passages. Will the ancient Israelites make it to the promised land, or will they die of cancerous consumption in the wilderness? Will the congregation in Philippi express itself the mind of Christ or the spirit of the age? Will those who hear Jesus actually obey the will of the Father, or are they only in the business of religion to rub some mythical magic genie's lamp in self-serving experientialism?

The difference between the two in each case comes down to obedience: not slavish legalism, but rather a commitment to a higher cause (and a higher power) that acts on its values. As Rabindranath Tagore put it: "I slept and dreamt that life was Joy. I woke and saw that life was Duty. I acted, and behold, Duty was Joy."

Exodus 17:1-7

The stories of Israel's early days in the wilderness after their wonderful release from captivity are heartbreakingly current. Wowed by Yahweh's great acts of deliverance, the people are soon cantankerous and crabby because life is hard. True, they were in desperate need of water, but still it is amazing how quickly trust evaporated with the press of changing circumstances.

What is bothersome to us today is that we see ourselves mirrored quickly in their lack of faithfulness. Eugene Peterson put it this way in his book, *A Long Obedience* (InterVarsity, 1980, p. 12): "Religion" in our time has been captured by the tourist mindset. Religion is understood as a visit to an attractive site to be made when we have adequate leisure. For some it is a weekly jaunt to church. For others, occasional visits to special services. Some, with a bent for religious entertainment and sacred diversion, plan their lives around special events like retreats, rallies, and conferences.

"We go," he says, "to see a new personality, to hear a new truth, to get a new experience, and so, somehow, expand our otherwise humdrum lives. The religious life is defined as the latest and the newest: We'll try anything — until something else comes along."

That is a tragic indictment of our spiritual expressions. Particularly so, since the Bible uses two words to describe the character of religion in its truest form, shaped far differently than by either the consumer mindset or the tourist mentality.

The first word is "disciple." This is the term by which the followers of Jesus are known. A disciple is someone who is apprenticed to a master — someone who will stick close to him. Someone who will follow him through thick and thin. Someone who will not lose energy too quickly, or seek to go his or her own way too soon.

A disciple is a learner, but not in the classroom or a schoolhouse. A disciple is one who follows the master craftsman as he shapes his world. Such an education is not something completed in five hours in an afternoon, or even during a term at college or university. It is something that involves a whole-life commitment, surrounding every motive of our hearts and every choice of our minds. This is what Jesus expected of his relationship with the twelve when he called them to himself as "disciples."

The other word in the Bible for those who take religion seriously is "pilgrim." A pilgrim is someone who is on a journey in life. Someone who has a past in which she is not wallowing. Some one who has a present to which he is not tied. Someone who has a future that is not certain, but which is very specific and very real; a future that belongs to God.

It is easy to fault the ancient Israelites for their consumerist religion. But we do not fare much better today. This passage calls on us again to assess the commitments of God's people, and the religious pandering that reduces discipleship to new forms of Sunday entertainment. "Is the Lord with us or not?" they asked. The answer is not always found in some miraculous sign.

Philippians 2:1-13

Paul grew up in the world of Greek games and Roman contests. Around him there were people constantly exercising to increase their strength, sharpen their abilities, and win contests. The language of training enters Paul's writings often, and this great hymn of Jesus from the early church is one of the finest examples. While it is certainly a theological testimony of "Christology from above," it is much more. We need to pay particular attention to the opening verses where Paul urges and encourages Christians to develop habits readily apparent in the mind of Christ. This is spiritual training at its best. So the flow of Paul's words about Jesus' descension and ascension are not just grist for theological investigation into confessional nuance; they are, in fact, a record of the commitments made by those who would be obedient in a regimen of spiritual training.

Joni Dunn entered the Ironman Triathlon (a 2.4 mile swim in the ocean as appetizer, a main course of bicycling for 112 miles, and then a desert marathon run of 26 miles to finish things off) in 1985 at the age of 43, and managed to come in first in her division. Not only that — she set a new record time.

Two things made Joni Dunn's win a real surprise. First, Joni nearly died in a skiing accident a dozen years earlier. She plunged over a cliff and fell more than 100 feet into a deep ravine. Her spine was fractured in seven places and her neck was broken. Joni also suffered several fractures to her head.

At first, doctors held little hope for Joni's survival. She would later remember lying on her hospital bed catching whispers of concerned professional conversation through a blanket of morphine haze. "I heard them say, 'She won't live through the night.' I knew that if I stopped concentrating on living I would die."

But live she did. It took countless operations to put Joni back together. She emerged from the hospital two inches shorter, and so hunchbacked that when she first saw herself in a mirror she didn't recognize the image.

It was during her long years of therapy that the idea of competing in the Ironman Triathlon began. Still, it took Joni a decade to work up the courage and stamina to enter.

That is the first thing that makes Joni's win in 1985 so surprising — moving from near death to sports endurance triumph. Here is the second — Joni Dunn says there is only one thing that pulled her through the torture of the grueling race: her religion. "Just moving caused me incredible pain," Joni told her interviewers. "But I knew I had to do this. I come from a very disciplined Dutch Reformed family in Illinois. That discipline has always been with me, and it makes me strong."

That is a surprising testimony, isn't it? Joni Dunn says her religious identity gave her the determination necessary to see her through a life-threatening accident and then pushed her down the road to win the grueling Ironman Triathlon.

Most North American Christians lack such discipline and focus, according to social researcher Reginald Bibby. His book *Fragmented Gods*(Irwin, 1987) declared that historic Christianity was all but dead. People today are consumers, he reminded his readers. They go shopping for this and that, a new toy here, a new emotion there, a new sensation each time around. When one pastime doesn't excite them anymore, they move on to a new one.

Those same people have become religious consumers in the vast array of church supermarkets, said Bibby. A ritual here, a prayer there, a cause in the next parish, an entertaining preacher on the other side of town, and the Christian population grazes through the cafeteria of weekly specials. Bibby said that most Christians treat religion like a wardrobe — they take different garments out of the closet each Sunday, depending on their spiritual moods, and then they put them all back in the closet on Monday when they take out their "secular" clothes and get on with the real business of life.

Matthew 21:23-32

When Jesus was questioned by the religious leaders of his day to give credentials for his growing public prominence, he would not comply. It was not because Jesus had no credentials to offer, but because those who were asking for such documents were themselves in no mood to become either disciples or pilgrims. They did not want to submit to religious authorities other than those they believed were already theirs to manipulate. This had become obvious in their interaction with John the Baptist, as Jesus reminded them.

Although this silenced Jesus' would-be accusers, Jesus himself took the matter one step further. He told them a story and then demanded that they explain it for him. Two sons were asked by their father to work the fields. One quickly said yes, but didn't make a move and never stepped out to do the labor. The other was belligerent and immediately refused to be part of his father's livelihood; yet later he realized who he truly was and what he had become, and then went out to the field to do the work.

What was the point? Jesus' detractors understood quickly that he was speaking about them. It is one thing to parade religious values as high-minded ideals, but quite another thing to put them into practice. No one who refuses to be a disciple can ever become a pilgrim. The disciple gives up his will for the sake of the master's teachings and good graces. The pilgrim sets out on the road of the kingdom in a journey of obedience.

Therein lies the rub, of course, because the wandering steps of pilgrims only reach hallowed ground by first experiencing the bruising of walking too long on the jagged stones of unholy territory. To become a pilgrim means first to become a disciple. Moreover, it requires that one get to work.

To become this follower of Jesus starts with the sob of a soul that no longer believes the lie of society. We hear the lie every day in its subtle forms: "Things are really getting better and better all the time." "Everyone has an equal opportunity in life." "Education will conquer all our ills." "If you just try hard enough, you can make it on your own."

The advertisements tell us that people are really pretty good, and that the world itself is a rather pleasant and harmless place when we dress right, smell right, eat right, exercise right, and drive the right cars or invest in the right companies. Everything will work out well for the nice people.

Cornelius Plantinga Jr. documented the leaching power of evil well when he called his "breviary of sin" a reflection on life that is *Not the Way It's Supposed to Be*(Eerdmans, 1995). Like a stranded motorist in the wrong part of town being hustled by ominous turf lords brandishing Saturday night specials, we feel the creeping cancer of a world coming undone.

The way of the disciple takes its first step with confession. She cries for help. He confesses that he cannot make it on his own. This was the call and invitation of John the Baptist, which too many had refused to heed. From Jesus' perspective, John was the first hint of dawn calling to minds newly awakening from the twisted darkness of the world in which we are trapped: the advertiser who claims to know what I need and what I want and who can make everything better with just a single credit card; the entertainer who promises me a quick fix, a cheap trick, a sensuous fling that really *is* love; the politician who has my best interests at stake, and who will make me ruler with him if I just give him my vote; the psychiatrist who will help me achieve gain without pain by lowering my standards to the mud around me.

A disciple sees the world through different eyes and begins the journey of the pilgrim with a cry of repentance. Such people have been caught up in the fashions of their day, majoring in minors and having no direction or purpose or real meaning for what they are doing. They find themselves like alcoholics who have been warned by every friend and challenged by every enemy, but remain blind to the dangers of their drinking habits until one morning they struggle awake in an unknown bed, family gone, reputation destroyed, with all their begged and stolen income bargained insanely away for another hangover. "Woe is me!" they cry, in the first note of repentance.

It is then, and then alone, that dawns a ray of hope. The journey begins in that moment, just as Bill W. testified in *The Big Book* of Alcoholics Anonymous. It starts at the bottom.

It is like the old Shaker song:

> *When true simplicity is gained,*
> *To bow and to bend we shan't be ashamed.*
> *To turn, turn will be our delight*
> *Till by turning, turning, we come 'round right.*

Application

Some years ago Madeleine L'Engle explained how she came, one day, to understand the meaning of her life. At the time she was the "Writer in Residence" at the Cathedral of St. John the Divine on Fifth Avenue in New York City. She met regularly with the rest of the staff at the church and developed a fast friendship with the Cathedral bishop.

One day the two of them were talking about the times in their lives when they felt they had grown the most in terms of inner graces and spiritual depth. It did not take long for each to realize that the most creative energies had come to life only at the end of periods of great struggle, often filled with agonizing mental and emotional torment. In fact, said Madeleine L'Engle, the best of her books were written just after the worst times of her life!

As they talked, each experienced the growing realization of what poet and hymn-writer Margaret Clarkson identified when she penned *Grace Grows Best in Winter* (Eerdmans, 1984). More than that, they also found that the turning point leading out of the dark night of the soul was, for each of them, always a moment of repentance.

After some tender moments of further sharing, the bishop got up to leave. At the door, said L'Engle, he stopped for a moment and then turned round to face her. "Madeleine," he said to her, "I don't know how to say this, but have a *bad* day!"

He was the best kind of friend, Madeleine told us, for he truly cared about her. He did not wish for her to experience the nastiness of life. Yet he did wish for her to find the grace of God that only emerges with power out of the repentance that comes to those who realize the insufficient, incomplete, inept, and inconsistent state of their hearts. Only a very kind and truly great friend could see that sometimes what we need most is a bad day that will help us turn our hearts toward home and remind us of the depth of spirituality sometimes only found through obedience as an antidote to the wash of consumerism.

Alternative Application
Philippians 2:1-13. The epistle reading is powerful and needs to be preached regularly. Most important when doing so is to be careful not to focus overmuch on the wonderful Christology in the passage, but use Jesus' actions as guides by which to gain the mind of Christ. This is, after all, what Paul intended when he wrote the letter.

Paul's letter to the Philippians is the most joyful and uplifting note of the entire New Testament. Even in Paul's confinement, he is filled with delight in his relationships and amazed at what God is doing (Philippians 1). Almost without needing to do so, Paul reminds the congregation of the great example of Jesus, who gave up everything in order to express the love of God to us (Philippians 2:1-18). Another example of this selfless care is found in both Timothy and Epaphroditus, each of whom had given up much in order to serve others, especially the faith community in Philippi (Philippians 2:19-30). More encouragement to serve follows, with Paul reflecting on his own changes of behavior and value systems, once he was gripped by the love of God in Jesus (Philippians 3). A few personal instructions and notes of appreciation round out the letter (Philippians 4).

Although other letters of Paul are more intentionally "theological," this small epistle has a particularly wonderful poetic reflection encapsulating the entire ministry of Christ in a few lines (Philippians 2:6-11). Because of its condensed and hymnic character, some think Paul brought these verses in from an early popular Christian song or creedal statement. Perhaps so. Nevertheless, the whole of this short book is lyrical and reaches for the superlatives in life through lines that are both economical and majestic.

Preaching The Psalm

by Schuyler Rhodes

Psalm 78:1-4, 12-16. What are the stories we pass on to our children? Every family has them. My own father concocted an elaborate set of stories based on the adventures of an elf who lived in the forest around my childhood home. This elf had all kinds of adventures with the various animals, with each story a moral that somehow fit into the particular childhood struggle occurring. I always marveled at how this elf led a life so parallel to my own.

Aside from family fairy tales and lore, we also pass on and tell other stories, don't we? Caught up, as we are, in our national mythos, we pass along stories of patriots and great leaders. We pass along tales of heroism and valor, and we pass on the narrative of our culture. One cultural narrative here in the United States would be the story line that says everyone has an equal shot at success. Another narrative would be that if we only work hard enough, success will be ours. True or not, these are the background stories for who we are as a nation.

How does this work for us as a people of faith? What stories about God do we hear and pass on to our children? More to the point, what stories do you pass on to your children about God? At dinner with family, at prayer time, on those long car journeys to Grandma's house, what is it that you tell your children about God?

The question is asked because it seems that the stories are told less these days. It's not that God's activity in the world has lessened. Indeed, look around and see everywhere the evidence of a loving and powerful God! Still, the stories don't seem to come to — or from — us very much. Why, one is left to wonder, are we not telling our stories about God?

In an evermore secular climate some people, of course, are a little embarrassed to talk about God. Indeed, one church member who was putting on a benefit for a noble cause and was using the church sanctuary recently came and asked the pastor if he could cover up the cross and Christian symbols because he was afraid they might offend someone. Thankfully, the pastor politely declined to have the cross covered.

We also decline to tell the stories of God because we have so nicely compartmentalized our faith. Church or Christianity is what we do one morning a week and perhaps one evening for a committee or Bible study. It is seldom something that dominates our whole being. No, such extremism is for zealots.

So the question remains, not to be answered here, but by our daily living. How do the stories of God's mighty acts in history get told? Who tells them? Who is there to hear? Perhaps the call comes today for us to begin to share our stories; with our children, our friends, with anyone who will listen.

Proper 22 | Ordinary Time 27

Exodus 20:1-4, 7-9, 12-20

Philippians 3:4b-14

Matthew 21:33-46

by Ron Love

We shall be as a city upon a hill

Over fifty years ago on January 9, John Fitzgerald Kennedy gave his farewell speech to the Massachusetts legislature before departing to Washington DC to prepare for his presidency. Kennedy opened his speech with these words: "We shall be as a city upon a hill." Kennedy was quoting John Winthrop, who used that phrase in his speech abroad the ship *Arbella* in 1630 as the Puritans were preparing to land in the New World. Kennedy was implying that the eyes of the world would be upon the new administration, and in so doing his presidency must be like a city upon a hill. Ronald Reagan, in his first inaugural address used the same words from Winthrop's speech, in reference that the United States under his administration would become the guiding light for the free world and the antithesis to communism.

The three lectionary readings for this Sunday carry the common theme that we are to live our lives as a witness to our obedience to the teachings of God. That witness will make us like a light set upon a hill for those with whom we come in contact on a daily basis. Though, as Paul recounts we may not be a perfect witness, we will be an adequate witness.

In a meditation written by Billy Graham, he noted that it is "never hopeless to bear witness to unbelievers." He went on to conclude that there are two major barriers keeping people from believing in Jesus Christ. Graham wrote, "The first is the barrier of self-will — that is, their determination to control their life instead of letting Christ control it." The evangelist went on to write, "The second major barrier is harder for us to see — but it's even more powerful. This is Satan's hold on the world, and his commitment to do everything he can to keep us from Christ."

The three lectionary readings address the cautions lifted up by Billy Graham. We surrender self-will when we accept living by the commandments set before us by God as outlined by Moses. We surrender the power of Satan when, like Paul in his reference to himself and like Jesus in his reference to Israel, we reject the old order and accept the new: that Jesus is the cornerstone of our lives. Having done this, we will be as a city set upon a hill. It will be a Christian city but never should we presuppose that it will be a perfect city.

Exodus 20:1-4, 7-9, 12-20

The Ten Commandments along with the Golden Rule have become the standard bearers as to how we are to live as Christians. The Ten Commandments outline for us the simple fundamentals of our religious duties, both to God and our neighbor. It is important to see the commandments listed in the order in which they appeared on the two tablets presented to Moses:

1. I am the Lord, your God.
2. Thou shall bring no false idols before me.
3. Do not take the name of the Lord in vain.

4. Remember the Sabbath and keep it holy.
5. Honor thy father and thy mother.
6. Thou shall not kill/murder.
7. Thou shall not commit adultery.
8. Thou shall not steal.
9. Thou shall not bear false witness against your neighbor.
10. Thou shall not covet your neighbor's wife (or anything that belongs to your neighbor).

As a youngster I would look at the commandments engraved in the stained-glass window of our sanctuary and I was always perplexed why one tablet had four commandments listed and the other six. Why were they not printed in perfect symmetry, five and five, I always wondered. The disparity was made clear to me in a sermon when I learned the first four commandants discuss our relationship to God, and the last six discuss our relationship to our neighbor. I have always said the teachings of the Bible are simple, but they are not simplistic. The Ten Commandments may seem simple, just plain common sense, but they are anything but simple to practice.

Philippians 3:4b-14

Paul does not discount his former life lived under the law, nor does he make any apologies for being a keeper of the law as a Pharisee. He now counts that as "rubbish," possibly a harsh word used as an overstatement to emphasize his new life lived in grace. He realizes that even though he has accepted Jesus as his Lord and Savior and now lives by faith, his life is far from perfect. That is why he pushes on to make Jesus more of a part of his life lived daily among his neighbors.

Matthew 21:33-46

In this parable Jesus is speaking to the Jewish people and their inability to accept the new creation brought forth. In rejecting Jesus they have rejected God and in so doing have rejected the meaning of the law. The Jewish leaders have failed to see that Jesus has fulfilled the law and the words of the prophets. Jesus declares himself to be the cornerstone of the new creation upon which all are to place their faith. As with Paul the law is not rejected outright for it still guides, but a new precedent has come with the gift of grace.

Application

The sermon should discuss the meaning of having religious guidelines to live by. It should be emphasized that the Old Testament still holds a great deal of credence for us, but it will never be a substitute for a life lived by grace. The sermon should center on the teachings of the Ten Commandments. Like Paul, we should discuss that we do not discount the commandments, but we struggle to live a life that is reflective of the commandments. In reference to Jesus, we must always see the teachings of Judaism in compliance to the teachings of Jesus.

An Alternate Application

The sermon should begin by discussing the struggles of Paul to live as Jesus lived. The sermon then should move to each of the Ten Commandments in order of appearance and what each means for us in our daily living. The sermon should conclude that if we struggle as Paul has struggled, then we will not have rejected the cornerstone of the new covenant.

Proper 23 | Ordinary Time 28

Exodus 32:1-14

Philippians 4:1-9

Matthew 22:1-14

by Wayne Brouwer

The music of grace

His shrunken frame and age-diminished voice were almost lost at the front of our large church auditorium. He had been a medical intern at a small hospital in Arnhem when Hitler's war machine rolled through the Netherlands and set up a puppet Nazi government. Radios were destroyed to prevent BBC "propaganda" from demoralizing folks who needed nothing other than German "truth."

But among the clutter of equipment in one surgical suite, someone had managed to hide a shortwave set. At 5 p.m. each Sunday afternoon, the doctors and nurses gathered secretly and tuned in softly to the worship service of St. Martin's-in-the-Fields on the edge of London. My friend could not remember a single sermon heard in those covert assemblies, but one thing he never forgot. At the close of each broadcast swelled the choral power of Henry Lyte's magnificent melody, "Abide With Me."

"In the distance we could hear the guns," the old doctor whispered, "and the cupboards of medical supplies rattled with falling bombs. We huddled together, standing close to the single speaker, weeping as we were transported for a few moments into the congregation in London, and with it to the very throne of God."

"This," he said, as we turned our own hymnbooks to the song, "is how we survived those dark and awful hours." And so we sang with him:

> *Abide with me! Fast falls the eventide!*
> *The darkness deepens; Lord, with me abide!*
> *When other helpers fail, and comforts flee,*
> *O Thou who changest not, abide with me!*

I think of him often when my students walk into class with buds in their ears linked to phones. "What are you listening to?" I ask them, and they tell me of the latest hits and greatest groups and hottest tunes and newest metal. I love music and share their passions, often playing videos of recent songs for classroom discussions.

But in the noisy archives of all the wonderful melodies I've loved and sung with pounding intensity or heart-throbbing intimacy, I wonder sometimes what music actually changes my life or places me in the company of those who need to enter another realm in order to remember what this one is truly all about. What are you listening to?

Each of today's lectionary passages echoes with the song of grace. For the Israelites at Mount Sinai, it was wedding bells that confirmed their relationship with Yahweh, even when the marriage got off to a rocky start. For Paul in his letter to the Philippians, it is the joy of dancing grace that lifts the spirit to transcendent places. And for Jesus when describing the kingdom of heaven, it is the haunting call of grace from the banqueting hall of eternity, causing folks on the highways and byways of life to stop and turn and long and hope for something that makes sense in an upside-down world.

Proper 23 / Ordinary Time 28

Exodus 32:1-14

The tabernacle existed uniquely in its world, representing the physical home of Israel's deity as a residence within its own spatial and temporal context. Israel was not a people who needed to create representations of powers that it then idolized; instead, the very society in which it lived emanated from the identity of the chief citizen who lived at its heart.

It is in this context that the golden calf incident of Exodus 32-34 must be understood. Moses' delay on the mountain while talking with Yahweh on behalf of the people bred frustration and anxiety within the community. So they begged Aaron for symbols around which to rally, and what emerged was a bull calf made of gold. The Israelites were probably not seeking to worship something other than the God who brought them out of Egypt so recently; instead they were trying to find a representation of that God within their cultural frame of reference, so that they could cajole (or manipulate) this deity into further meaningful actions rather than wasting time in the seeming stall of their current lethargy. Since the bull calf was revered among the Egyptians for its ability to portray the liveliness of sentient power, it could well serve the Israelites in their quest to display national adolescent brash energy.

The problem for Yahweh, however, was twofold. First, the calf was an *Egyptian* symbol, and thus essentially blasphemous in light of Yahweh's recent decisive victory over all aspects of Egyptian power and civilization. Second, the calf reflected brute strength in the natural order and of a kind that could be controlled by human will. A bull was meant to be yoked, harnessed, and guided by whips and goads. True, it was more powerful than its human driver but at the same time it became a tool in service to the human will. For Yahweh to be represented in this manner undermined the significance of the divine defeat of Egypt and its culture and appeared to turn Yahweh into a mighty, albeit controllable, source of energy serving the Israelite will.

Under Moses' leadership his own tribe, the Levites, rallied to avenge Yahweh's disgrace. Because of that action they were appointed to the honored position of keepers of the house of God. Meanwhile, Yahweh himself wished to break covenant with Israel and instead start over with Moses' family; after all, Moses and Yahweh had become great partners and almost friends over the past few years and especially through their time on the mountain. Moses argued against this divine turnabout, however, for two reasons. First, he reminded the great one that Yahweh had sealed this suzerain-vassal covenant with Israel, and it could not so easily be discarded or broken. Yahweh had deliberately invested Yahweh's own destiny into this people, and while they might wrestle with the chafing fit of the new relationship, Yahweh no longer had a right to deny it. Second, Moses raised the card of shame. What would the nations say if Yahweh quit this project now? The peoples of the ancient near east had begun to tremble because of Yahweh's decisive victory over Pharaoh; if the God of Israel was able so clearly and convincingly to topple the deities of Egypt and their power in both the natural and supernatural realms, what hope could there be for any other mere national interest or powers? But if Yahweh now suddenly left the Israelites to die in the wilderness, the nations around would see that this god was no more than a flash-bang, a one-hit wonder, a dog with more bark than bite. Moses used Yahweh's own covenant to make the deity toe the line and get back into bed with Israel on this honeymoon night.

Philippians 4:1-9

Sometime in the spring of 57 AD Paul arrived in Rome. While he was clearly a prisoner awaiting adjudication before Caesar himself, Paul was also a Roman citizen with rights and freedoms. Since the charges against him were sectarian (related to Jewish religious practices) rather than capital crimes, Paul was able to establish his own living circumstances within the larger palace precincts while remaining under a type of house arrest.

Probably late in 57 AD or early in 58, Epaphroditus, who had been serving as pastor or congregational leader in Philippi, brought Paul a rather significant gift from that church (Philippians 2:25; 4:10). It may have included both money and supplies; in any case, it greatly enhanced Paul's comfort in his limited circumstances.

Epaphroditus stayed on with Paul for some time, assisting him as a servant. Unfortunately, Epaphroditus became ill and nearly died (Philippians 2:25-30) and only very recently had returned to full health.

Paul believed that homesickness for Philippi and the congregation there might have contributed to Epaphroditus' grave malady and vowed to send him back home as soon as he was able to travel. Of course, a letter of appreciation and encouragement was a necessary part of all these things, so Paul penned Philippians, probably sometime in early 58 AD.

Paul's letter to the Philippians is the most joyful and uplifting note of the entire New Testament. Even in Paul's confinement, he is filled with delight in his relationships and amazed at what God is doing (Philippians 1). Almost without needing to do so, Paul reminds the congregation of the great example of Jesus, who gave up everything in order to express the love of God to us (Philippians 2:1-18). Another example of this selfless care is found in both Timothy and Epaphroditus, each of whom had sacrificed much in order to serve others, especially the faith community in Philippi (Philippians 2:19-30). More encouragement to serve follows, with Paul reflecting on his own changes of behavior and value systems once he was gripped by the love of God in Jesus (Philippians 3). There are a few personal instructions and notes of appreciation to round out the letter (Philippians 4).

Although other letters of Paul are more intentionally "theological," this small epistle has a particularly wonderful poetic reflection encapsulating the entire ministry of Christ in a few lines (Philippians 2:6-11). Because of its condensed and hymnic character, some think Paul brought these verses into his letter from an early popular Christian song or creedal statement. Perhaps so. Nevertheless, the whole of this short book is lyrical and reaches for the superlatives in life through lines that are both economical and majestic:

> *Finally, brothers, whatever is true, whatever is noble, whatever is right, whatever is pure, whatever is lovely, whatever is admirable — if anything is excellent or praiseworthy — think about such things.*
> — Philippians 4:8

Matthew 22:1-14

The idea of "kingdom of heaven" is central to Jesus' teachings, and a common theme throughout the gospel of Matthew. It implies citizenship or at least allegiance to a governing authority. In today's gospel reading, Jesus shows the gentle but ultimate compulsion it has in our lives.

It is the kind of thing that J.R.R. Tolkien tried to picture in his powerful trilogy *The Lord of the Rings*. Writing in the recovery years after World War II, Tolkien imagined what powers there are in this world that can possess peoples and nations, for good or for ill. His tale of the struggles of Middle Earth allegorically reflected the biblical idea of kingdoms in conflict.

Either, as Jesus indicates, we play games with little treasures, buying and selling them on world markets and moving among commercial districts that hold our attraction for a while, or we are sold out to a greater power. We sell all and buy it. We give up our claims in order that we might be claimed.

Our youngest daughter was born in Nigeria while I was teaching at the Reformed Theological College in Mkar. Because the Nigerian government does not automatically grant citizenship to all who are born on its soil, Kaitlyn was truly a person without a country in her earliest days. Until I could process her existence with the United States consulate in Kaduna she had no official identity, no traveling permissions, and no rights in society outside of our home. We took a picture of her at five days old, sleeping in my hands, and this became the photograph used on her passport for the first ten years of her life. The snapshot may have become outdated quickly as she grew through the stages of childhood, but the passport to which it was affixed declared that she belonged to the United States of America. She had rights. She had privileges. She had protection under the law. When the time came for us to leave Nigeria and travel through three continents to get back to North America, that little passport opened doors and prepared the way for her. She had never lived in the U.S., but the U.S. knew her by name and kept watch over her.

So it is and more with the kingdom of heaven, according to Jesus. It becomes the badge of identification for us, as well as the symbol of our protection and care. When we choose other pearls or dig around for treasures in our own backyards we get from them what we are looking for — things that we can possess. But when the great prize of the hidden treasure comes our way, or we stumble onto the pearl of great price, we realize that our little hordes are insufficient. It is not enough to own a piece of fading substance; we need to be owned by something that transcends our time. We need God to lay hold on us.

This is why, in many of the earliest liturgical forms for baptism, those who were newly coming into the fellowship of believers were asked if they renounced the devil and all his works. Early on it was recognized that entering the kingdom of God was more than just adding another spiritual talisman to the mix of superstitious hex warders; it was a fundamental commitment of identity that could not be shared. No dual passports in this kingdom! The truly great treasure demands that one sell everything else. It is exclusive. And when it is purchased, it actually purchases you.

Some time ago I talked with a pastor of a large congregation in a major city. He was pleased with the worship and the ministries of his church. Everything seemed to operate with care, good taste, and competence. He had the right staff in place and they all were able to find dedicated, trained volunteers to shape a marvelous network of programs. Yet something didn't sit right with him. In his words, it was a very, very nice church. And therein was the problem. It was a church that looked after itself so well that it had forgotten that it was under orders to be about the missionary business of the kingdom of heaven.

If people wanted wonderful worship, all they had to do was join the congregation on Sundays. If they wanted terrific children's ministries and youth programs, all they had to do was drop their sons and daughters off at the right times. If anyone wanted a little diaconal assistance, just stop by the office and a secretary would arrange for a modest handout.

But the onus was on others to come and find the church. The congregation itself had little use for going out to search for the lost and the last and the least. It had given up being a net. It had lost its marching orders. It had gained the corner on "nice" but was losing the ability to call itself "church."

We are not saved so that we may politely pat ourselves on the back and smile at one another in the tiny corners we occupy. No, we are part of a mandate issued by the Lord of our estate that seeks and engages the fish of this world who might be swimming to their own destruction.

When we hear Jesus tell us about the kingdom of heaven, we recover our sense of values and outcomes in the quagmire of daily events. We carry the passport of heaven. We live as those who are under orders to be and do and make a difference. And we know who writes the last chapter, because the kingdom of heaven is growing tenaciously around us in spite of reports to the contrary.

Application

God is good, creation is good, and human alienation from the good is a late introduction brought about by our sinful choices. Throughout scripture, the message communicated is that all of humanity had the same opportunities to remain in fellowship with the Creator and all are equally responsible for their distance from God.

But the prophets and apostles, and certainly Jesus himself, also couched the story in swaddling folds of never-ending grace. Time after time, God initiated a restoration of relationships with humanity.

All are welcome to be part of the team. As part of our latter days, in fact, God sent in Jesus to spur the team to new spiritual victories. Jesus is the expression of God's righteousness inserted recently into our world, and the means by which we are attached to the righteous endeavors of God. He is the glue that binds the team together and keeps them connected both to the owner and the game.

It is like the "deep magic" of Aslan in C.S. Lewis' great tale *The Lion, the Witch, and the Wardrobe*. Most don't understand it but without it the game becomes a never-ending cycle of violence in which there are only losers.

An Alternative Application

Matthew 22:1-14. Savannah, Georgia, is a beautiful city of gardens and cemeteries and parks. Our youngest daughter went to college in Savannah just as *Midnight in the Garden of Good and Evil* became popular in both book and movie versions. She even had a job for a summer working in one of the cemeteries where she reset gravestones and restored family monuments. Some of them had been looted and reconfigured by General Sherman's troops after his infamous Civil War "March to the Sea" from Atlanta to Savannah wasted many communities.

Sherman loved Savannah, however, and we could understand why. When platted in 1769, Savannah's founders created four "squares" of public park space to enhance the social life of its residents. As the city grew, the "squares" multiplied to 24, enhanced by other larger parkland areas and marvelously crafted cemeteries. Today Savannah's southern charm is enhanced by ghost stories and haunting sightings in its ancient buildings and sultry public places lined by Spanish moss-hung oaks.

John Wesley preached his first sermons in the New World in the squares of Savannah, cementing the gospel link between gardens and cemeteries and parks. Today his image stands in bronze downtown still crying out about eternity among those plagued by the fatal human disease of death. Interestingly, the story of our race, according to the Bible, begins in a garden, ends in a park-like city, and is focused in between on a cemetery.

Gardens speak of well-sculptured horticulture and minimal human engagement. Friends walk through parks and gardens. Lovers stroll secluded paths, picking flowers for one another and hiding smooches from public view. Birders relish the quiet of muted breezes carrying fowl calls of the wild.

Cities, on the other hand, rush and roil, bump and burn, stomp and shout, push and pluck, and assault every sense all at once. Cities are made for crime, particularly if you read of their origins in Genesis 5. The sons of Adam and daughters of Eve, who heard from their first parents of the delights of communion with God and one another, once ejected from the garden of bliss tried to re-create the great societies by building cities. They didn't work then, and rarely to the present have they ever been agents of great grace.

Yet it was to the city that rural Jesus came when he brought home the divine message of salvation. It was to the cities that Paul and others traveled with the good news about Jesus. In fact, the word "pagan" originally meant "farmer" or "rural person" in Greek, only picking up its negative connotations when the cities of the Roman world had become "Christianized" by the fourth century and those out in the country were left behind in the evangelization process.

Today the cities of our world cry for renewal. There are many social programs that seek to address small or great needs. But above all stands the call for the rebuilding of the city of humanity into the city of God. Though the final design and construction will require another mighty act of God at the end of time, today we participate in the global quest through restoring communities of faith, redeeming social structures, and renewing urban blight into blessing. This is what Jesus has in mind when he speaks of the kingdom of heaven, and its urgent invitation to people everywhere in the countryside of humanity. Come now, for the banquet of life is prepared in the city of God.

Proper 24 | Ordinary Time 29

Exodus 33:12-23

1 Thessalonians 1:1-10

Matthew 22:15-22

by David Kalas

Do I dare to preach this?

The preacher lives in a privileged place. He or she has the incalculable honor of standing as the intermediary between the word of God and the people of God. That's not to say, of course, that the people cannot read and receive it on their own. Certainly they can. Yet you and I both know that they look to us.

I see it in the body language and energy level as we transition each Sunday from the scripture reading to the sermon. The attention given to the liturgist who reads the scripture is so passive and half-hearted. I sometimes think that the liturgist could read the ingredients for pizza into the midst of the passage and half the congregation wouldn't notice. Yet when it's time for the sermon, the attention level perks up. This, they think, is what they really came to listen to.

It's not that the sermon is better than the scripture. Not remotely. But there remains for so many laypeople a sense of distance from the Bible. They do not feel that they understand it without help. They do not immediately see the interest or the relevance. So they look to us. Just as our doctor or mechanic or IT consultant is expected to understand all the technical stuff and then be able to tell us what we need to know, so too the preacher.

But just as soon as we take on that privilege, the preacher also lives in a vulnerable place. For who is worthy to be that intermediary between God's word and God's people? What human being is adequate for that task? And which one of us lives up to the words that we proclaim?

Sunday after Sunday, I offer to show how the scripture speaks to my people and how it applies to their lives. This Sunday, will I have the courage to show how it speaks to me? Will I share candidly how it applies to my life?

Exodus 33:12-23

Few passages manage to capture in so few verses both the immanence and transcendence of God. Those words may not be the ones to use with your people this Sunday, but those are the key principles involved. Each time God's people gather for worship, these are important principles to bear in mind. Taken together, they express lovely and profound truths about our God.

On the one hand, there is something almost scandalously approachable about this God of Moses. It is almost as though Moses bursts into the Lord's office making demands. The man knows he is the underling in the relationship; yet still he is bold enough to do some insisting before the Lord. He reasons with God and presses his point.

Of course the behavior could be a reflection only on the character of Moses, not the Lord. See how the Lord responds to Moses' boldness and requests. He does not strike down the man for presumption. He does not condemn the man for audacity. Rather, the Lord gives tacit approval to Moses' method by responding favorably to Moses' requests.

Meanwhile, for as approachable as the Lord God seems to be at the beginning of this episode, we are quickly reminded of his mysterious otherness by the end of the encounter. Moses desires to see more of the Lord than he can. That desire is altogether good — a far cry better than the more common human tendency to shrink away and stay at a distance. Yet Moses seeks more current than his breaker can accommodate. He wants to see God's glory, yet "no one shall see me and live."

In our day, it seems to me, we need to rediscover the transcendence of God. For a variety of reasons, we have become so very casual. That's not to say that formality equals reverence. But our casual attitudes and approaches do tend toward irreverence. We come and go at our convenience, we think and act like consumers, and we take lightly the things of God. And in the process, we forget — or never learn — with whom we are dealing.

Only when we open our eyes to his transcendence do we recognize the grace of his approachability. Only when we are reminded of the second part of Moses' encounter do we perceive the grace and loveliness of the first part.

A significant part of God's grace in the first part, meanwhile, is not just in the candid and forthright way that Moses is permitted to approach him, but also in the promise of his presence with his people. This is, of course, the great and recurring promise of God through scripture. Moses was wise enough to ask for it, and God is gracious enough to offer it. It was his word of assurance to many a reluctant servant (e.g., Genesis 31:3; Exodus 3:12; Joshua 1:9; Judges 6:16). It was the psalmist's profound and sufficient comfort in the valley (Psalm 23:4). It is the promise and meaning of Emmanuel. And it is the eternal hope for Jesus' followers (John 14:3; 1 Thessalonians 4:17; Revelation 21:3).

Finally, the second part of this episode also recalls a larger biblical theme: God's glory. Its brilliance and accompanying smoke occasionally kept people from the place of worship (Exodus 40:35; 1 Kings 8:11; 2 Chronicles 5:14). Some approximate reflection of it was the fabulous vision that Ezekiel saw (Ezekiel 1:28b). Isaiah promised that it would one day be revealed and that all flesh would see it together (Isaiah 40:5). The gospel writer testified that in Jesus "we beheld his glory" (John 1:14). In the end, the Lord's glory will be the source of light for the New Jerusalem (Revelation 21:23). And that glory of the Lord is what Moses is eager to see in our selected passage.

1 Thessalonians 1:1-10

Many New Testament scholars believe that Paul's first letter to the Christians in Thessalonica is the earliest of all his letters. While some are more difficult to place on the apostle's time line, 1 Thessalonians is comparatively straightforward. He writes to this freshly founded church during his second missionary journey, not long after circumstances forced him to leave Thessalonica and move on toward points south. These first verses of 1 Thessalonians, therefore, are perhaps the earliest recorded words from Paul that we have.

The first sentences are familiar in genre, for they resemble what we see at the outset of all of Paul's letters. He identifies both authors and audience, followed by his statement of thanksgiving for the people. That statement, while customary, was not without meaning. The absence of such a statement in Paul's letter to the Galatians, for example, proves that it was not a mindless gesture or pleasantry on the part of the apostle.

In this specific instance, Paul expresses his gratitude for what the Thessalonians have become. It is not gratitude to them, of course, but to God. God, after all, is the one who has initiated and cultivated the work. But the Thessalonian Christians are to be commended and encouraged for their responsiveness to the Lord's work in their lives and in their midst.

Paul's profound sense of thanks is best understood in context. I currently serve a church in Green Bay, Wisconsin, that was established in 1826. Wisconsin itself didn't become a state until 1848. So the congregation I serve is well-established and has been working for the kingdom in this place for generations.

By contrast, Paul was writing to a congregation that was perhaps just a few months old. It had none of the historic stability that most of our churches enjoy. Rather, it was as fragile as a newborn. And Paul had not even been permitted to stay in Thessalonica long enough to wean it properly. They were left on their own from a very young age. So when he observed and heard of their faith and faithfulness, he was thankful indeed!

Particularly remarkable is the fact that the Thessalonians had even earned a reputation beyond their own walls. Others in their own region — and others still even beyond their region — had heard the news of their faith. This is a beautiful thing and especially in that ancient context where churches did not engage in the sort of publicity and self-promotion that is common in our day. No, Thessalonica's growing reputation was purely organic. They were not trying to puff themselves up, but the sheer reality of what they were was sufficient to have become the talk of the town, as it were.

Finally, Paul reminds the Christians in that early church of the transition that they made and thus articulates for us the fundamental nature of their conversion. "You turned to God from idols, to serve a living and true God." That was surely the story in the ancient Mediterranean world. Though we think ourselves far removed from such primitive practices as idolatry, the same central issue is at play in our day as well, for we all serve someone or something. The question is to what extent we have turned completely from serving what is, at its core, manmade to serving the true and living God.

Matthew 22:15-22

The writer of Ecclesiastes noted that there is nothing new under the sun (Ecclesiastes 1:9), and the setting for this episode is a case in point. Jesus' opponents "plotted to entrap him in what he said." And 2,000 years later we are no more sophisticated than that, for still so much of our political gamesmanship is predicated on the same old strategy.

The larger context of the passage is Matthew's account of holy week. Jesus entered Jerusalem on Palm Sunday in the previous chapter, and now the next few eventful days are filled with tension and teaching. The ongoing conflict between Jesus and his antagonists intensifies, and many of his teachings become more pointed in his condemnation of those Jewish leaders in Jerusalem. Even a newcomer to the story would sense the escalating pressure, moving inevitably toward some climax.

So it was that the Pharisees sent emissaries to trick Jesus with a question. We note that their words are incongruous with their intentions, for while they endeavor to trap him, they appear to be praising him. This is the duplicitous speech of the flatterer (see Proverbs 29:5), and it is reminiscent of the serpent's diabolical conversation in Eden.

The question is an ingenious conundrum. There in a public setting Jesus is asked about paying taxes to the emperor. In order to appreciate how clever the question is, it will be important for our people to understand the historical context.

No one likes taxes much, of course, but taxes for us and taxes for Jesus' countrymen are completely different affairs. We may not always approve of how our government uses our money or how much of our money they take, but at least it is our own duly elected government. For the Jews of Jesus' day, however, the taxes were imposed by a foreign empire. They were an occupied nation, and they had to pay the freight for their own occupation. It was a noxious business indeed, and the people of Israel naturally resented it.

Some of them, in fact, harbored dreams of overthrowing that Roman presence in their midst. Many people no doubt associated Jesus' popularity and power with the prospect of such a God-ordained revolution. So for Jesus to encourage paying taxes to the emperor would, his opponents reckoned, take much of the wind out of the sail of his popular support.

On the other hand, if Jesus were to do the impolitic thing and discourage paying taxes to the emperor, then the trap would really be sprung. His Jewish opponents could hand him over to their

Roman occupiers, and he would be treated as a troublemaker and insurrectionist against the empire. The Pharisees' Jesus-problem would be solved.

So they have him caught between the proverbial rock and a hard place. Two answers seem to be available to Jesus, and each one is risky. Yet he, with unflappable wisdom, offers an answer that not only sets him free from the trap but also reveals the truth of God.

Seeking a visual aid to make his point, Jesus asks for a coin. Then he asks his audience to identify the image and the name on the coin. They are, of course, both Caesar's. So Jesus famously concludes: "Render unto Caesar..." "Give therefore to the emperor the things that are the emperor's, and to God the things that are God's."

This brilliant answer has often been a motto for folks trying to capture the Christian's dual responsibilities to church and state. There is more beauty in the teaching than that, and it completely reorients the believer from the world to the kingdom.

In great economy of reasoning and language, Jesus surmises from the name and image on the coin that it must come from Caesar and must belong to Caesar. Therefore, since it is clearly his, we simply ought to give back to him what belongs to him. Just like that our attitude toward and grip on money is loosened. Jesus effectively trivializes it, and we see how contrived and temporary it is.

But the principle he established with the coin positioned Jesus to make a larger point. We know now what belongs to Caesar and is therefore due to him. What, though, belongs to God? What is due to him? The answer comes by implied analogy: Whatever it is that bears God's name and image. In short, we come from him, and we belong to him. And so we are called to give ourselves to him.

Application

In both the episode from Exodus and the excerpt from 1 Thessalonians, we are given a glimpse of intermediaries. Moses is manifestly that in the Old Testament passage, for he takes to the Lord his deep concern about the responsibility to lead the people in his care. And every letter from Paul, of course, implies that intermediary role — especially those letters addressed to churches that he himself founded.

Moses and Paul are go-betweens. They are the individuals who spoke to people on God's behalf, sharing his word with them. God is fully capable of speaking to those individuals directly, of course, but he consistently uses human beings as the vessels of his work and word. Both Moses and Paul function as preachers and teachers in the midst of their respective congregations. They certainly serve as pastors to those people as well. And so — swallow hard — you and I find ourselves in the company of Moses and of Paul.

But we do not connect those dots this Sunday in order to exalt ourselves or to inflate our own sense of importance. On the contrary, we humble ourselves before God, his word, and his people this week. We take the examples of Moses and Paul as challenging models of our high calling, and we pledge to our people our own resolve to answer that call.

See Moses there, alone with God, praying for the people entrusted to his care. And see him moving ever nearer to God, seeking his face. That is the model set before us.

Likewise, see Paul, following up with the folks he has had to leave behind. No out-of-sight-out-of-mind with him. They are on his mind and in his prayers. See how he nearly equates his example and Christ's, for he knows that he is a vicar, a flesh-and-blood, visible example to his people.

Our sermons often invite our people to respond to God's word, to apply it to their circumstances, and to live more faithfully in response. But this Sunday we preach to ourselves. We respond to our own altar call, pledging ourselves to live more faithfully in response to God's word.

An Alternative Application
1 Thessalonians 1:1-10. "The Power of Example." When I meet with a couple before baptizing their baby, I talk through with them the vows that we will ask them to make on that occasion. Among them is a promise to nurture their child spiritually "by your instruction and example." The task of Christian parenting is captured as a two-part process: instruction and example.

We don't have any record of the apostle Paul having biological children, but it's clear that he saw himself as a spiritual parent to many people. We see in this week's excerpt from his relationship to the Thessalonians some of his spiritual parenting. For while he may not use the language of parent and child here, we certainly see that two-part parenting process in place.

The instruction is the part of Paul's ministry that we think of first. We picture him traveling from place to place, preaching in the streets and teaching in the synagogues. When we read the New Testament letters, of course, we read his abundant instructions to the earliest Christians on matters such as spiritual gifts, church discipline, holy living, law and gospel, faith and works, and on and on. But the part of his ministry we don't see so clearly, of course, is the example part.

Yet that is precisely what the Thessalonians — and others like them in the first-century Mediterranean world — saw most clearly. They lived with Paul. They watched him, and thus they learned not just from his instruction but from his example.

Paul was conscious of the influence of his example. He did not shy away from it or apologize for it. On the contrary, he emphasized it. "You know what kind of people we proved to be among you," he wrote to those Christians in Thessalonica, "and you became imitators of us and of the Lord."

That is the nature of an example, of course, whether good or bad. Examples breed imitators. We see abundant evidence of that both in individual cases and in the broad trends of a whole culture. And the principle was true in Thessalonica as well.

Paul's juxtaposition of "us" and "the Lord" is a compelling one. He seems to equate the two examples. We would hesitate to make such a claim, and yet we know it is precisely to that that you and I are called.

Meanwhile, the ripple effects of Christian example do not end in Thessalonica. Rather, Paul commends those people because they in turn "became an example to all the believers in Macedonia and in Achaia." And so it goes.

We do a lot of instructing in the church. That we think is our most high-profile ministry. Yet that is not what our people see most clearly. They see our example, and they learn from it, for better or for worse. They go into their homes and schools and businesses without much opportunity to instruct, but with constant occasion to become an example to all.

Proper 25 | Ordinary Time 30

Deuteronomy 34:1-12

1 Thessalonians 2:1-8

Matthew 22:34-46

Psalm 90:1-6, 13-17

by David Kalas

Life on the level

I've been doing some around-the-house projects lately, and it seems each project has required at least one more new tool. Not that I mind. I have discovered the truth that having the right tool for the job can make all the difference. And I have found, too, that the tool aisle in hardware and home improvement stores makes me feel like the toy aisle used to when I was a boy.

One of the tools I have discovered recently is called a post level.

A level is a device that helps you detect whether an object is straight or not. A level can be fairly short or rather long, depending on its usage. At first glance, it might look like a heavy-duty yardstick. Whether long or short, this rectangular piece of wood or metal uses a bubble floating in a small, transparent case to identify whether the picture frame, the ceiling beam, the countertop, or whatever, is straight. When the bubble is left-of-center in the little transparent gauge, then you know that you need to raise the right side of the object, and vice versa.

The post level, meanwhile, is a slightly more involved device. Designed to help a builder guarantee that the fence post, the flagpole, or the baluster is properly upright, the post level features more than one bubble. As you hold the post in place in front of you, it needs not only to be straight in terms of its east-west orientation; it needs to be straight in terms of its north-south orientation, too. While an ordinary level is a rectangular object that rests along just one side of the object being straightened, the post level looks like half of a small box. It is designed to rest against two sides of a post to guarantee that it is upright in both directions.

It turns out that life requires a post level. It is insufficient to measure whether my life is upright in just one direction; I must be straight in two directions. For when Jesus was asked what the greatest commandment was, he didn't offer just one; he offered two. And those two commandments are the two bubbles we can use to detect whether our lives are on the level.

Deuteronomy 34:1-12

Frederick William Faber, a nineteenth-century English cleric, wrote a hymn titled "There's A Wideness In God's Mercy" about the nature of God that includes this insightful line: "There's a kindness in his justice, which is more than liberty."

We recognize that justice can be unkind. Our long-standing concern about "cruel and unusual punishment" reflects our recognition that justice can cross some undesirable line. We know that it can be unkind.

By contrast, Faber's witness is that God's justice has a certain kindness in it. That should not be confused with unvirtuous softness with compromised justice. Rather, it is the property of the wisdom of God that even his justice has a quality of kindness to it: as surely must be the case with a God who is love (1 John 4:8) and who disciplines like a loving parent (Proverbs 3:12).

So it is with this final chapter from Moses' life. He is permitted to see the promised land from afar, but he is not permitted to enter it. If we have followed Moses from his insecurity at the burning bush, through the painful vicissitudes of Egypt's pharaoh, amidst the complaining, ungrateful, and rebellious Israelites, and through the generation of wandering due to the faithlessness of other people, we will be inclined to feel sorry for Moses. If anyone deserves the reward of the land flowing with milk and honey, it is Moses. Yet, for what may seem to us a rather small and momentary lapse in faithfulness - - small, at least, in comparison to his larger body of work — it seemed quite unkind that God would prevent him from entering the promised land.

Yet, "there's a kindness in his justice." For what awaits immediately on the other side of the Jordan is not milk and honey, but battles and blood. For Moses to cross over with the rest of the Israelites would not be to enter into his rest, but to embark on the long military campaigns described in the book of Joshua. That would have been no favor to the 120-year-old man of God.

You and I have known people, cities, lawns, and bodies of water that look better at a distance than they do up close. And for old Moses, the promised land would look far better from the panoramic view of Pisgah than from the battle lines of Bethel and Ai. There is, indeed, a kindness in God's justice.

Meanwhile, the epitaph for Moses that is provided here at the end of Deuteronomy invites a certain kind of looking back. How far removed is this strong and accomplished old man from the edict that would have had him killed as a baby? How much has God accomplished in this man, now regarded as a peerless prophet, who once stammered and resisted at the burning bush? And how far has he come from not even knowing God's name to knowing the Lord "face-to-face"?

Finally, we may want to observe the paradigm for succession that is reflected in this passage. Moses had not been popularly elected by the people, and neither would his successor, Joshua, be. Nor was this a matter of royal lineage. It is not Moses' son who will rise to become the next leader of Israel. Instead, "Joshua son of Nun was full of the spirit of wisdom, because Moses had laid his hands on him." And we recall that a similar sort of method eventually brought the nation its greatest king, David.

1 Thessalonians 2:1-8

The apostle Paul was originally from Tarsus, which was in the ancient region we sometimes call Asia Minor, or modern-day Turkey. That region includes several of the churches to which Paul later wrote epistles (such as Galatians, Ephesians, Colossians), as well as the seven cities to which the letters in the book of Revelation are addressed.

When Paul and Barnabas set out on their first missionary journey together, they set an understandable itinerary: They went home. First they traveled in Cyprus, which had been Barnabas' home. Then they went into Asia Minor, which was Paul's old stomping ground.

Likewise, on Paul's second missionary journey, he returned to Asia Minor. But it was while he was there, in that familiar territory, that he had his vision of a Macedonian man saying, "Come over and help us." Paul left the familiar terrain of Asia Minor to cross the Aegean and enter into Macedonia. After landing at Neapolis, they traveled inland to Philippi. After Philippi, they went on to Thessalonica — the home of the Christians to whom this letter is addressed. We read the eventful story of Paul's missionary visit to Philippi in Acts 16:11-40.

This background is important to our passage because Paul makes quick reference to it. "Though we had already suffered and been shamefully mistreated at Philippi," Paul recalls. They did not leave their difficulties behind in Philippi, for they met with "great opposition" in Thessalonica, as well (see Acts 17:5-9).

Yet, "we had the courage in our God to declare to you the gospel of God," Paul writes. That is a significant claim, and it deserves our attention.

We know the end of the story, and so we may be inclined to overlook the details in the middle. We know all about Paul's three missionary journeys. We know him as the greatest evangelist of his age and one of the greatest of all time. We know the impact that he had, not only on individual lives, but on the entire Christian church.

Paul did not know the end of the story. He was living in the middle of it and being mistreated on foreign soil by unresponsive and antagonistic people. It must have been a desperate experience. How many of us have been stripped, beaten, and imprisoned for sharing the gospel? Again, because we know the end of the story, we pass too lightly over the details in the middle. And yet, after such a debilitating experience in Philippi, still "we had the courage in our God to declare to you the gospel of God." That detail — that response to God instead of to circumstances — is an example to us all.

Meanwhile, in the particulars of this passage, Paul is especially an example to you and me as preachers.

First, he refers to himself and his companions as having been "entrusted with the message of the gospel." The image must surely be seen against the backdrop of the time: a day when communication was not nearly so instant, so technologically enabled, and so legally guaranteed. If you wanted to get a message from here to there, you had to entrust it into the hands of some messenger.

What is the most important letter or package you have sent, say, in the past five years? Imagine if you had had to place that parcel in the hands of another human being, and then send him off, left only to trust that he would get it where it needed to go when it needed to get there.

Such is the confidence God had placed in Paul and his colleagues. God had a message — the good news — that needed to be delivered. It was of ultimate importance. And he entrusted it into the hands of Paul, and now, so much more recently, into your hands and mine.

Second, Paul notes, "We were gentle among you, like a nurse tenderly caring for her own children." Is this how we would be characterized in our pastoral work? Are we like a tender nurse caring for her own children, or might we sometimes resemble instead a distracted teenage babysitter, impatient, and easily irritated by the brats she has to watch? The children are God's children, and they deserve therefore our care, not our exasperation.

Finally, Paul said that he and his companions were "determined to share with you not only the gospel of God but also our own selves." That's a pricey calling. It's a rare Jonah who gets to walk in, deliver God's word, and then step back and watch the results. No, more often than not, being his messenger means a more demanding investment. To share the gospel is a somewhat easier task, for I can share it without it being diminished. But when I make the move to share of my own self, I make myself vulnerable to loss.

Matthew 22:34-46

In order to appreciate the passage, our people will need to know the larger context. Matthew 22 comes from the eventful final week of Jesus' life and ministry in Jerusalem. Palm Sunday is just past. Good Friday is just ahead. In between, we find an escalating tension between Jesus and the Jewish leaders who seek to do him in. A part of that tension is typified by the questions designed to trap him. The Sadducees had struck out in their attempt. In our selected passage, the Pharisees step to the plate.

The question posed to Jesus by one of their representatives was this: "Teacher, which commandment in the law is the greatest?"

The question is, at once, both daunting and harmless. Daunting because the scope of the law was so broad and the accumulated layers of tradition atop it so deep that it could not possibly be answered easily. The questioner might as well have asked which flower is the loveliest, which food the tastiest, or which sunrise the most brilliant. At the same time, the question seems harmless inasmuch as it is not as immediately tied to controversy as, say, the question about paying taxes (Matthew 22:15-17). Still, British scholar, R.V.G. Tasker, argues that "they hoped that Jesus in his reply would say something unorthodox and startling, which would render him liable to a charge of blasphemy."

Meanwhile, apart from the tactics of the question, we must be stunned by the content of the answer. After all, how impractical is it to command love above all else? And how improbable is it that an almighty and eternal God should want that, above all, from his puny, erratic, mortal creatures?

At the practical level, I think I would have suggested "obey" in the place of "love." After all, if we were to obey the Lord our God with all we've got, wouldn't that cover everything? Doesn't "obey" serve as the most logical, and most adequate catch-all commandment?

Evidently not, for the Pharisees prided themselves on their careful, deliberate, and thorough obedience to God. We gather from Jesus' critiques that they were clearly inadequate. Specifically, we think of the infamous Pharisee, Simon, who was quite attentive to matters of obedience and righteousness, but who lacked love (see Luke 7:36-47).

Furthermore, while human logic suggests that all righteousness would flow out of simple obedience, Jesus posited that simple obedience flows out of love (see John 14:15). Perhaps this is why Jesus referred to the love commandment as "the greatest and first commandment." The lawyer had only asked about the greatest, but love is greatest, in part, because it must come first.

Also, we come eventually to recognize that there can be no greater obedience to the God who is love (1 John 4:8) than to love. Naturally, love would be the first commandment. And, we discover, it is the second commandment, as well.

Jesus is only asked for the greatest commandment, but he offers two for the price of one. "A second is like it," he continues. "You shall love your neighbor as yourself."

Evidently it is insufficient to offer only the "love the Lord your God" commandment, for it is inseparable from its natural companion: love of neighbor. And it is inseparable, as we see from the preaching of the prophet (Isaiah 1:13-17) to the teaching of Jesus (Matthew 5:23-24) to the logic of the apostle (1 John 3:17; 4:20-21).

After offering the two-part answer to the Pharisees' question, Jesus observes: "On these two commandments hang all the law and the prophets." It is a testimony to the basic coherency of the word of God that all the elaborate and detailed instructions and corrections can be distilled down to two fundamental and complementary principles.

Finally, having been challenged by their various questions, Jesus turns the tables and asks a question of his own to his antagonists. It is a question that quotes the scriptures — so he's playing on their field — yet it is a question that befuddles them. They had not anticipated the doctrine of the preexistence of Christ, and so "from that day (they did not) dare to ask him any more questions."

Application

I come from the United Methodist tradition: We are heirs of the work and theology of John Wesley. Wesley was noteworthy, among other things, for his wholesome balance between personal piety and social gospel. We continue to see that balance reflected in our United Methodist hymnals, for right after 25 hymns under the heading of "personal holiness" we have 24 hymns under the heading of "social holiness." The first set features hymns of personal devotion, like "I Am Thine, O Lord" and "Close To Thee." The second set features hymns of challenge and social action, like "Forth In Thy Name, O Lord" and "Let There Be Peace On Earth."

Perhaps these are the two bubbles on the Christian's post level. Perhaps these are the two commandments that Jesus called greatest.

The individual (or church) who is entirely devoted to the love and worship of God but neglects the needs of his neighbor, is only halfway there. From one perspective, he seems entirely upright. Walk around to the other side, however, and you see how badly he is listing.

Likewise, the individual (or church) who spends himself in social causes but whose heart is far from God, does not fully pass the test, either.

The inquirer wanted to know which commandment was the greatest of all. He sought a simple level by which to judge and guide a person's life. But a simple, one-bubble level is not enough. Godly living has two dimensions, and we are called to be upright in both. Love of God and love of neighbor: This is the look of a life that's on the level.

Alternative Applications

Deuteronomy 34:1-12; 1 Thessalonians 2:1-8. "Pastor And Preacher." Perhaps this Sunday we might try something new. And perhaps our people will appreciate it.

I expect that most of us do a fair amount of preaching that might broadly fall under the heading of "what our people ought to do or to be." There is no malice in this and perhaps no criticism, either. It simply comes with the territory: for if we are to preach faithfully the challenges of discipleship and godly living, then our people will sense the theme — whether explicit or subtle — that they are invited to do and to be more than they are.

This Sunday, therefore, we might do well to turn the tables. Perhaps this Sunday we might let them overhear a sermon that we preach to ourselves. This is not to say that we are exempt from what we preach on every other Sunday; not at all. They might be refreshed by our challenge to ourselves and our pledge to them to do better and to be more of what we are called to: namely, pastor and preacher.

The apostle Paul is our model for preacher. We have examined his example a bit above: the courageous perseverance, even in the face of frustration and hardship; the profound sense of privilege and responsibility that comes from being entrusted with an important message; the nurturing gentility with which we must conduct ourselves in our work; and the costly selflessness that is required to share the gospel effectively.

Moses, meanwhile, is our model for pastor. His epitaph at the end of Deuteronomy reminds us of his core achievement: leading a group of people from where God found them to where God wanted them to be. He spent an entire generation doing it, often in inhospitable and thankless circumstances. He watched the older generation die; he watched the younger generation grow up. He felt every pain that they felt along the way. And he faithfully followed God, while the people fitfully followed him.

So let me preach to myself this Sunday, with my congregation eavesdropping on the sermon. Let me preach about Paul, about Moses, and about the kind of servant of God I ought to be.

Preaching The Psalm

by Schuyler Rhodes

Psalm 90:1-6, 13-17. It was Rene Descartes who said, "I think, therefore I am." While not wishing to enter the questionable theological ground of this statement, it is interesting to note that such ability to reason has plagued humanity for centuries. We are capable of discerning our place in the universe and at once are both awed and overwhelmed by it. It is with similar confusion that we approach the comprehension of the reality of God.

From our finite and limited point of view it is virtually impossible to imagine God. Yet this psalm attempts it with beauty, calling up images of eons before mountains were formed, and even a nod to the formation of the earth itself. Mortality, dust, time, all of it enters into these few verses and spills forth with a sense of muted awe.

Even though the practice of pulling Christian images and thoughts from pre-Christian texts is frowned upon by scholars, there is a point to be made here.

It is this very inability to comprehend God that makes the incarnation in Jesus so very powerful. Even the beautiful language and poetry of this psalm does not give the heart a grasping place to touch the holy. But in Christ Jesus we have a God with handles. In his humanity, Jesus is accessible in unbelievably wonderful ways.

Jesus in the scriptures is seen as very human. One moment he is gentle, the next racked with frustration. Another time he rolls his eyes in vexation at his followers while yet another he pulls out a bullwhip and drives the money changers from the temple. This Jesus kneels in love to heal. This Jesus grows harsh as he condemns those who make a mockery of faith. This Jesus asks out loud if the cup can pass from him. This so very human reflection is someone that we all can relate to in deep and life changing ways.

While the psalm blazes with beauty in its attempt to relate the wonder of God, this writer is thankful for the revelation that has come to us in Christ. Still, God is unsearchable, unfathomable, unknowable. But now in Christ, he has come near.

Reformation Sunday

Jeremiah 31:31-34

Romans 3:19-28

John 8:31-36

by David Coffin

Tradition reworked

It finally has happened! The elder Sunday school teacher, who has taught the adult class annual Bible study series from Genesis to Revelation every year for many decades, has submitted his letter of resignation. He is tired and has seen declining numbers in class attendance for a number of years. His fonder memories were several decades earlier, when the Sunday school class tables were full and adults were busily turning pages to look up Bible passages related to the book of the Bible they were studying that week. Now, the teacher feels at times that his class preparations are no longer as highly valued as in times past when older adults could not get enough of "studying God's Word in the Bible." In that same congregation, there is a live-wire junior high class coming into catechism that has much energy and has exhausted every Sunday school teacher they have had. In fact, the Sunday school superintendent has stepped down. On Reformation Sunday, how does one rework the cherished traditions of the church that have their roots in the Protestant tradition in Europe? Each of the texts today might provide some insights for any congregation that needs some level of change, yet has highly valued biblical traditions that have shaped many generations in the Christian community.

Jeremiah 31:31-34

"See, today I appoint you over nations and over kingdoms, to pluck up and to pull down, to destroy and to overthrow, to build and to plant" (Jeremiah 1:10). This is one interpretative lens for the Book of Jeremiah (Stulman, p. 42). The basic "theodicy" question was everpresent as Judah saw its city walls invaded, temple destroyed, and people taken into exile. "Theodicy" literally means "justice of God" (assuming that the monotheistic God is "sovereign or all-powerful"). Israel's God has been defeated in the minds of the nations who witnessed this sacking of the nation's temple city. Obadiah the prophet chastens Edom, Israel's neighbor, for any gloating over the loss of Jacob (Edom being of Esau, a longtime family feud since Genesis 25:29). Is God good for God's promises to preserve the throne of David and bless the family of Abraham (Genesis 12)?

Jeremiah's proposal is that God remains sovereign and is simply reworking the promise to write it onto the people's hearts in a new covenant. Is this supportive of a supersession view God's reign over Israel? In this case, there are no requirements to "repent," as one might see in the Deuteronomy writings. Instead, God remains with God's people and is starting all over again (building up and planting 1:10; Brueggemann, pp. 126-127). As this might apply to the opening illustration above, the pastor and Sunday school department concluded that each adult who attends the Sunday school class will take turns in leading the lesson. Each baptized (or as the case may be, "converted") Christian should have enough of the word written on his or her heart to be the leader for that particular hour of the class. They still follow the basic Genesis-Revelation Bible sequence, but this is tradition reworked. Like the people of Judah (Southern Israel), God's sovereignty remains intact. God is still the keeper of the people. God's word contained in the Bible is still a dynamic force to be reckoned with in daily discipleship. But now, the entire class is invited to become part of the instruction. Each person is invited to be the "team leader" instead of one constant teacher or instructor leading the whole year. On this Sunday, this is the spirit of an incremental change that reflects the spirit of the Reformation in Europe in the 1500s. [Sources: Walter Brueggemann, *Old Testament Theology: The Theology of the Book of Jeremiah*, (Cambridge University Press, 2007); Louis Stulman, *Abingdon Old Testament Commentaries:Jeremiah*(Abingdon Press, 2005)]

Romans 3:19-28

It is Reformation Sunday in a given traditional church. The color of the day is red; the hymn "A Mighty Fortress" is sung. But the preacher has to find new ways to address this special day. Then to his or her sudden dread, there sits a former Roman Catholic worshiper. In fact, due to a local family reunion there are many Roman Catholic worshipers present. How does one remain true to this Romans 3 text without using it as an opportunity to revisit age-old frictions between Roman Catholicism and traditional Protestant churches?

One helpful approach is discussed in N.T. Wright's two-volume set *Paul and the Faithfulness of God* (Augsburg Fortress Press, 2013). Rather than privileging "justification by faith" as Paul's central focus (though it is indeed present there and nobody will dispute it as an option to explore in preaching!), Wright suggests that Paul is simply reworking traditional Jewish monotheism to reflect a new world view that God has fulfilled the promise that Abraham will become a blessing to all nations in a new way (Genesis 12:3). That is, this is the Messiah who embodies the servant of the Isaiah texts. So the real issue here is finding ways to include all people who are born into or have committed "sin" in the covenant and inheritance as one of God's people.

Catholics, Protestants, and actually all of humanity have experienced "sin." The God of monotheism or traditional Judaism has included all peoples within the new covenant (cross-reference the Jeremiah 31:31-34 texts above) in a new way. Nobody should boast, as all people need God's grace through this new covenant every day. Paul is calling people of faith to transcend the current reality of sin and work toward a new world based on God's saving power, force, and justification of sin (by grace). Whether or not this is to be a forensic or court-framed discussion is contested and will remain contested, depending on the commentator one consults. Sin is what hurts humankind, and God's saving power through faith in Jesus the risen Christ is what unites the church (Kasemann, pp. 93-94).

In the case of the new catechism class in the opening illustration, the condition of being in junior high school and the transitional life changes that accompany this age group might mean another tradition to be reworked. Possibly, the discussion/small group-based curriculum might have to be replaced with a more structured set of books requiring a measured outcome of pages completed in the study book based on suggested Bible verses. If the class shows some maturity in the process, then a discussion and breakout group format could be part of a further reworking of tradition.

As one preaching direction to pursue, what areas in the tradition of the church could use some subtle or incremental change before the season of Advent is upon us? Many communities have ecumenical Thanksgiving services in some form. Is there a way to plan and arrange them with a given theme in mind about assisting those in the world or larger community who need to see new light from the church? Also, this is an opportune time to remind Christians that salvation is more than about each of us being regenerated, baptized, or saved from damnation. It is a time to reflect on how each of us are a blessing to those we come into contact with during the week. [Source: Ernst Kasemann, *Commentary on Romans* (Eerdmans, 1980)]

John 8:31-36

A key word in this text is that of "truth." The Greek root word of *alaythia* indicates a consistency and stability which is more than the reception of information about Jesus; it describes a relationship with God as a result of Jesus' unique and ultimate revelation from God. Truth that is reliable stands up and therefore has proven itself worthy of one's trust under testing (Powell, pp. 1072-1073). This is a challenge for a mature, seasoned type of discipleship from a Johannine perspective. It is eternal (John 3:16-17). For example, a person might feel insecure in their faith or spiritual matters as they become aware of their relatively short time on earth (also, "finitude" or awareness of anxiety of death, limitations, and possibility that their lives will amount to nothing upon their death [Tillich, pp. 189-195]). Therefore, John's gospel is an invitation to become part of a word (Jesus) that was pre-existent before creation (John 1:1-14; Matera, pp. 263-266).

A favorite biblical text during times surrounded by the possibility of death is John 14:1-6. Jesus says "I am the way, and the truth, and the life" (John 14:6), and this John 8:31-38 text could be one way to elaborate more benefits of this "truth" that is in Jesus the Christ. One of the hurdles any Christian preacher must overcome is the use of this text as a means to discredit Judaism in this time or any era. Judaism has changed much throughout the centuries; a more helpful way of identifying the Jewish temple leadership in John's day would be to call them "Judeans."

Jesus is the new king of Israel not because he renews a political monarchy, but because he brings the Father or God and the Spirit into the world. Whereas in the synoptic gospels the controversy is often surrounding the message of Jesus, in John one must decide whether they believe that Jesus embodies God the Creator. What does it take to elicit the response of Thomas in John 20:28: "My Lord and my God!?" [Sources: Andrew T. Lincoln, *Black's New Testament Commentary: The Gospel According to Saint John* (Hendrickson Publishers, 2005); Frank J. Matera, *New Testament Theology: Exploring Diversity and Unity* (Westminster John Knox Press, 2007); Mark Allen Powell, editor, *Harper Collins Bible Dictionary, Revised and Updated* (HarperOne, 2011); Paul Tillich, *Systematic Theology, Volume One* (University of Chicago Press, 1951)]

Application

What do people in our congregations need liberation from in these days? For Martin Luther and the reformers it was guilt and the burdens that come with such guilt. Could it be that idolatry in its latest entertainment, high-tech, or consumer form has many people in bondage? If so, Jesus is the reliable truth that sets us free.

Worry is another possible source of anxiety and bondage. A mother talks to her pastor about sending their son away to college. She sees other college graduates returning home and unable to find jobs for up to a year or so after graduation. She observes that some of the "safe" STEMM (Science, Technology, Engineering, Math, and Medicine) degrees no longer reap the promised career plans discussed back in the high school guidance counselors' office. John's gospel reminds people that being part of the community of faith that has been ejected from the Jewish synagogue of their day is as painful as not finding a gainful place in the job market (J. Louis Martyn argues this view). This could also be the reality of the parent who now discovers their age, experience, and education are barriers as much as assets to employment. Yet Jesus remains the truth that sets us free, remains the good news of the text.

Another direction is the congregation faces? What are the most effective ways to proclaim the gospel or the to point to the truths or reliable teachings that have impacted the lives in the past of the people who helped create the current congregation, and how might that (tradition) be reworked for current realities as well as honoring the emphasis of the gospel that this particular church has represented throughout its history? Being a "mission church" might look different than what it did when the church was first built. Yet there is a truth of how Jesus embodies God's life (and pre-existent creation) that is very authentic and relevant for any time. [Source: J. Louis. Martyn, *History and Theology of the Fourth Gospel* (Westminster John Knox Press, 2013)]

Alternative Application

One might take the posture of Jeremiah or even some in the Johannine circles to say: "I did not want to be born in this time and I do not like these circumstances. Why can't I be part of the golden era instead of having all of these complications in life to preach on?" That is, how is one faithful to any ministry when the rules have changed so radically that we no longer recognize the place we work, worship, or live? What is the central covenant or truth that has held communities (of faith) together when unprecedented (if not apocalyptic) changes have occurred? How do we maintain a belief in a good and sovereign God when all of the evidence around us suggests the contrary (the theodicy issue Jeremiah wrestles with in his time)?

All Saints Day

Revelation 7:9-17

1 John 3:1-3

Matthew 5:1-12

by Ron Love

White grave markers — white robes

The Arlington House was a mansion built as a living memorial to George Washington by the first president's adopted grandson. The estate was built on a 1,100-acre tract of land across the Potomac River from Washington DC. Decades later a distant cousin, Robert E. Lee, became the resident of the home. Between 1841 and 1857, Lee was away from Arlington House for several extended periods while serving in the Mexican War, and then as superintendent of the U.S. Military Academy at West Point, his alma mater. In 1857 Lee returned to Arlington to join his family and to serve as executor of the estate. Robert E. Lee and his wife, Mary Anna, lived at Arlington House until 1861, when Virginia ratified an alliance with the Confederacy and seceded from the Union. Lee, who had been named a major general for the Virginia military forces in April 1861, feared for his wife's safety and anticipated the loss of their family inheritance, so he moved to a new residence. Following the ratification of secession by Virginia, federal troops crossed the Potomac and took up positions around Arlington. Following the occupation, military installations were erected. In punishment for his allegiance to the South, the land was then made into a cemetery so Robert E. Lee would never be able to claim the Arlington House as a residency again. The Arlington National Cemetery was established on June 15, 1864.

Though Arlington National Cemetery may have been created as an act of retribution, it has become a tribute to our fallen warriors in battle. The 400,000 graves are a remembrance of those who made the supreme sacrifice for our country, both casualties of war and veterans. The white tombs arranged in straight lines as soldiers in formation are not unlike those who wore the white robes of martyrdom that surrounded the throne of God.

The parallel message in our three lectionary readings is one of sacrifice. It is a message of believing so much in a cause that no sacrifice is too great, even that of surrendering one's life. There are many noble causes for which one can make the supreme sacrifice, and on All Saints Day we recognize those who died in service to our Lord and Savior Jesus Christ.

"I did it!" Those are the words we would like to be able to say, knowing we have accomplished something both difficult and important. It is what Donny Osmond said when it was announced that he was the celebrity winner of the ninth competition *Dancing with the Stars* in 2009. But those three little words, "I did it," were not easy to come by.

For the final seven weeks of the ten-week competition, Donny danced on a broken toe. It took a physical toll on Donny as he related, "I don't think I've worked harder for any accolade than I have this one. When you record an album and it goes platinum... yeah, you're in the studio and you work hard for months, but it's not like your whole body hurts." The competition was emotionally draining. He noted on his blog that "the culmination of nine weeks filled with blood, sweat, and tears comes down to this — the finals." So disturbing were the finals that his professional dance partner, Kym Johnson, had to encourage Donny to continue. On the Sunday night before Tuesday's final performance, Donny was lying down and lamenting that he could not continue, only to have Kym revitalize him by saying,

All Saints Day

"We have to do it one more time." And one more time they did do it, and at the age of 51 Donny Osmond became the oldest winner of *Dancing with the Stars*.

There is no secret to Donny's success. The goal was important to him. He practiced hard, to the point that his body ached. He listened to the advice of his experienced instructor Kym, who had danced on five previous shows. He was not afraid of admitting his doubts and seeking encouragement. Persevering, Donny was able to hold high the *DWTS* mirror ball trophy.

Perseverance is the message that comes to us on All Saints Day. It is the willingness and fortitude to endure any hardship for both the defense and proclamation of our faith. When one thinks of Peter being crucified upside down because he felt unworthy to be crucified right side up like his Lord, something must have happened in the upper room in the days following the resurrection that placed such commitment upon Peter and all the followers and not just in the first decades but, for centuries to come.

Revelation 7:9-17

This passage of scripture is very picturesque as it describes those who have been marty red for the faith. They are wearing white robes. They are gathered about the throne. Angels are present. There is singing. The lamb is at the center of the throne. But amidst this celebratory expression of those who were victorious in never relinquishing their faith, the sacrifice that was made should never be forgotten. "They fell on their faces" describes their dedication and commitment. It is a testimony of the reverence they always had for Christ.

1 John 34:1-10, 22

John confesses that we are children of God, but the world does not fully understand us for it never fully understood Jesus. Though we can rejoice in our status of being adopted into God's family, we cannot be satisfied until everyone realizes we are God's children. This means we must be willing to testify to our faith. This may not be a popular thing to do, but it is an unavoidable requirement of being a Christian, which means "Christ follower."

Matthew 5:1-12

The Beatitudes speak of the joy of knowing Jesus, especially if we live a marginalized life. But the passage finishes with some very sobering words: "Blessed are those who are persecuted for righteousness' sake." The joy of persecution should not be equated with happiness but with the sense of self-satisfaction that accompanies being faithful. The Beatitudes give us a totality of the Christ message. We are to feed the hungry and comfort those who mourn, but equally so we are to witness against the sins of the world. People may not take notice of our food pantries, but they will take notice when we speak out for social justice.

Application

It is traditional on this Sunday to recognize those members of our congregation who have died in the past year. As we commemorate their dying, we should be sure to outline the services they provided for the church. This means that we do more than just read their names; we authenticate the work they did on behalf of the congregation. We then should speak to how these fallen were Christian warriors who are now wearing the white robes of sainthood. It should be mentioned how they understood what it meant to be a child of God. Their ministry and sacrifice should be placed in the context of the Beatitudes.

An Alternate Application

The sermon should open by discussing the teaching of John and what it means to be a child of God. As a child of God the world must recognize the conviction of our faith. This conviction can be seen as we discuss the teaching of Jesus and the Beatitudes. We should use the Beatitudes as an outline for ministry, and emphasize that if this is done conspicuously and with enthusiasm we will be persecuted for our faith. Realizing we will be persecuted for our ministry of social justice, we conclude by discussing the teaching from Revelation and how one day we will find ourselves before the throne of God

Proper 26 | Ordinary Time 31
Joshua 3:7-17
1 Thessalonians 2:9-13
Matthew 23:1-12
by Cathy Venkatesh

Law and life

God gives the law to the Israelites as a blessing and guidance for new life after generations of promise, care, and saving grace. And yet so often we get caught up in the law and forget the God who made it. In the life of faith, God comes first, and the law follows. When we put the law first, trouble eventually ensues.

Joshua 3:7-17

At long last, the Israelites enter the promised land. In our lectionary we have been reading since June through the stories of the Patriarchs in Genesis, then Moses' leadership of the people through the Exodus experience, culminating in his death on Mount Nebo, overlooking the promised land in Deuteronomy 34. Finally in our reading today, under Joshua's leadership, the people of Israel cross the Jordan River in a scene reminiscent of their crossing of the Red Sea upon their escape from Egypt a generation before. The story of God's fulfillment of his promise to Abraham is almost complete as we near the end of Year A in the lectionary cycle. The closing chapter of Joshua comes next Sunday, revisiting this long story of salvation history and renewing the covenant between God and the people. But much has been skipped over along the way, including all but one chapter of Deuteronomy, all of Numbers and Leviticus, and the stories of the conquest of Canaan in Joshua. Though we may have learned the story of the fall of Jericho in Sunday school as children, as adults we will not hear it read in church in our present lectionary cycle. The only other reading from Joshua in all of the lectionary cycle comes on Lent 4C — a very brief description of the first Passover observed after crossing the Jordan.

And so today of any day is one to wrestle with the militarism of Israel's entry into the promised land as recounted in the Hebrew scriptures and to consider the fates of those people listed in Joshua 3:10 who will be driven out by the Israelites: the Canaanites, Hittites, Hivites, Perizzites, Girgashites, Amorites, and Jebusites. As I write this in the summer of 2014, this morning's paper announces that John Kerry has arrived in the Mideast in an attempt to broker a ceasefire between Israel and Hamas given escalating violence in the Gaza strip. Thousands of years later, battles connected to God's promise to Abraham are still being fought. Some preachers may wish to focus on contemporary crises in the promised land, though this can be a delicate task in parish ministry. In some contexts, it may be more suited to the conversational setting of an adult forum where many voices may be heard, compared with the solo voice of a preacher in the pulpit. With sufficient planning time, both a forum and sermon on historic and contemporary conflict in the Middle East could be offered this Sunday.

For those who wish to explore the biblical story and its implications more deeply, there are several points to consider. The first (which may work better in some congregations than others) is to wonder whether Joshua recounts actual history versus the stories Israel came to tell itself about its origins. Most scholars and archaeologists find little or no evidence for the conquest battles recounted in Joshua, and it is notable that in each battle, divine intervention is a driving force for victory. The book of Joshua is very much a book about the power of the Israelites' God; not about the might of armies.

This brings us back to today's reading and the central role of the ark of the covenant in the people's crossing of the Jordan. Without it, the crossing into the promised land would not have been accomplished. Indeed, this crossing is very much a religious procession, which is followed in chapters 4 and 5 by the religious rituals of placing of the twelve stones at Gilgal, the circumcision of the new generation (to honor the Abrahamic covenant — Genesis 17:11), and the observance of the Passover — all this before marching on Jericho in chapter 6. The ark of the covenant, containing the tablets of the law, symbolically contains all that the lectionary has passed over in Leviticus, Numbers, and Deuteronomy — that is, the incredibly detailed explication of the law that was the foundation for the new society the Israelites were to create in the promised land. Throughout the rest of the Hebrew scriptures, when Israel honors God and keeps the law they live peaceably in the land God has given them. When they forget the covenant and God, things fall apart, and they lose the land. Walter Brueggemann in his biblical study *The Land* notes that when Israel accepts the land as the gift from God, they are blessed. When Israel grasps the land to itself and does not honor it as a gift, they lose it. This may be the insight we need to move from events in Israel, both ancient and modern, to reflecting on our own lives of faith. How do we receive and honor the gifts God has given us? What, to us, is our own "Promised Land"? Are we still on the way there, have we already entered it, have we been there and lost it again? We can consider this question as individuals, as families, as communities, as a nation. In the law, God provides Israel with the guidance it needs to accept the gift of the promised land and live graciously in it. Broadly writ, the law asks us to honor God and our forebears, to refrain from actions that harm others in body or spirit, to keep the sabbath, and to live justly with one another and all creation. Does this describe our own lives right now? Where are we lacking in keeping the covenant, and how is God calling us to renew our faith and commitment so that we may live graciously in the land God has given us or is preparing us to receive? While it may be tempting to polemicize about violence and injustices in the holy land, it may be that we are better served by examining our own lives and sending our heartfelt prayers for peace.

1 Thessalonians 2:9-13

Propers 24 through 28 in Year A represent the greatest attention 1 Thessalonians receives in the three-year lectionary cycle — the only other times it is read are Advent 1B and Advent 3C. In this, the oldest book of the New Testament, Paul reassures the Thessalonians of his devotion to them in his forced absence, commends them for their faith, and offers guidance for living in what he and his readers perceived to be the end times.

Acts 17:1-10 describes the brief time Paul and Silas spent in Thessalonica before a mob organized by the Jews of the synagogue drove them out of town. Even as they moved on to Beroea, they were persecuted and driven out by the same Thessalonian Jews, and Paul escaped to Athens, asking that Silas and Timothy join him there (Acts 17:10-15). Once they were reunited in Athens, Paul was able to send Timothy back to Thessalonica to check on the new church, but he was unable himself to return — "Satan blocked our way" (1 Thessalonians 2:18). First Thessalonians is Paul's response to Timothy's positive report from this visit, and in chapter 2:1-13 he reminds the Thessalonians of his faithful ministry among them as a precursor to assuring them of his continued care for them. From his words in today's reading we may imagine some of the charges laid against him by his opponents in Thessalonica, but Paul reminds his hearers that he earned his own keep, not asking them for any payment, and that he used persuasion, not demands, to convince his hearers of the truth of his message.

Matthew 23:1-12

After his entry into Jerusalem on Palm Sunday and cleansing the temple (Matthew 21:1-17), Jesus returned the next day to the temple to teach. First he told parables that condemned the Pharisees (Matthew 21:28--22:14). Then when they challenged him, he bested both the Sadducees and the Pharisees in rabbinic debates (Matthew 22:15-46). After Jesus' rhetorical triumph ("nor from that day did anyone dare to ask him any more questions" — Matthew 22:46), he launched into the condemnation of the scribes and Pharisees we encounter in today's reading. We actually get only the first part of it, for it goes on for the rest of chapter 23 and represents Jesus' parting words at the Jerusalem temple before he left with his disciples, telling them as they departed that the temple itself would be destroyed: "not one stone will be left here upon another" (Matthew 24:2). We have already been told that the chief priests and Pharisees wanted to arrest Jesus (Matthew 21:46); surely his parting diatribe did much to seal his fate.

Jesus upheld the mosaic law while challenging the scribes and Pharisees. This is consistent with his attitude throughout the gospel of Matthew ("Do not think I have come to abolish the law or the prophets; I have come not to abolish but to fulfill" — Matthew 5:17). When it is given appropriate weight, Jesus sees the law as a gift from God that brings life. But when one's focus becomes the minutiae of the law such that one no longer sees the loving God who created us and gifted it to us to help us live peaceably together, problems ensue. The law which was meant as gift becomes a burden. The Pharisees were an especially observant sect of Judaism and at the time were arbiters of questions about the law for many Jews. They also were politically and socially powerful within the constraints of Roman rule. Jesus' continued message of reversal — the last shall become first and the first last, the humbled exalted and exalted humbled — makes them obvious targets for his teaching. The term "rabbi" literally means "great one"; thus, an obvious title to avoid in Jesus' teaching, and a title used often by the Pharisees.

Application

Leadership is not for the faint of heart. Jesus lambastes the Pharisees for being so wrapped up in interpreting the details of the law that they forget its true spirit. Paul may on first glance sound like he is bragging, but in fact he is defending himself and his message after attacks on his character. And we know what happened to Jesus. All of these men were in their own way doing their best to lead their people in a difficult time full of violence. They did not have absolute power — the Romans did — but they had some power, by virtue of their calling and character, and people looked to them for insight and guidance on how to live in a perilous age.

There is such a temptation to believe that if we just do things right, things will turn out okay. The Pharisees fed into this temptation as they spent their days interpreting the law for the people who came to them. Follow the rules and God will love you and protect you! Or at least not punish you... For so many people, their experience of religion is of a set of rules to follow and fear of what will happen if they transgress. As I watch my daughter and her friends grow and as I ponder how pervasive this law/fear sense of religion is among adults, it really seems to me as if it is a developmental stage that many of us need some help passing through. How many young adults these days discard religion because they no longer believe in the law/fear understanding of God? And yet, in discarding religion and God at this stage they miss out on all the glories of a more mature faith and understanding. Yes, God is love. And the law is God's gift to help us love one another.

It is interesting that we look to science now for laws, and with God removed from the equation the fear, shame, and guilt associated with divine law seem to be removed. We all generally accept the law of gravity, and understand that if we try to do something incongruent with gravity, we will fall and possibly be hurt. That's just the way the world is. No judgment, no shame, no guilt. Yet we can get tied up in knots over transgressing divine law, which also describes how to live safely and generously in the world. If we do something against divine law, we or others will quite possibly be hurt — that's just the way the world is. Dishonor hurts. Theft hurts. Adultery hurts. Jealousy hurts. Forgetting God hurts. Working without pause hurts.

It is worth noting that in the long story of salvation history we have been reading through the summer and fall that God comes first, as a promising, guiding, rescuing, feeding protector, and it is a very long way into the story before God gives the law, which the Israelites then revere because it comes from the God who saved, fed, and guided them. Time and again through human history, people have put the law before personal encounters with God and each time this happens, things get out of whack. When we are out of touch with God, the law brings fear and legalism, not life. Jesus chastised the Pharisees; Martin Luther rebelled against the church leaders of his day; countless prophets, saints, and ordinary people found their way past overly scrupulous religious upbringings to genuine and generous love of God and neighbor. When the laws of our age serve love, they are congruent with God's will. When they do not, it is the Christian's call to bring them into alignment with the generous and gracious community God wills for all humanity. Ask Martin Luther. And Martin Luther King Jr. Ask everyone you know who has stood up for love of God and neighbor in fearful times. God comes first; the law follows.

Proper 27 | Ordinary Time 32

Joshua 24:1-3a, 14-25

1 Thessalonians 4:13-18

Matthew 25:1-13

by Wayne Brouwer

Live like you were dying

A well-rounded biblical moral lifestyle is established on four primary foundational principles:

Creational Norms: How did God intend for things to be?
- Here is where the portraits of life on earth in Genesis 1-2 establish the original dimensions of human behavior.

Restraint of Sin: What evil has infested the world that needs to be restrained and counteracted?
- Included in this category of scripture are the negative expression of the Ten Commandments and the laws for Israel. The point of these injunctions is to push back at the darker temptations and intentions of evil and depravity, even in the human heart. It is in this light that Joshua's final instructions to the Israelites in our Old Testament reading must be heard and read.

The Mind of Christ/God: What is the heart and passion and will of God?
- Paul's letter to the Philippians is perhaps the most concise call for Christians to put on the "mind of Christ," but throughout the Bible there are calls to "be holy, because I, the Lord, your God, am holy" (Leviticus 19:1-2, with amplifications in the Sermon on the Mount of Matthew 5-7). In other words, if we love God, we will be particularly interested in the unique revelation of God's heart and character in Jesus Christ.

Eschatological Hope: What goals, plans, or expectations is God drawing us toward in the consummation of all things?
- It is in this light that Paul's ethical urgings in 1 and 2 Thessalonians (as noted in our New Testament reading for today) comes to expression. But these are based on Jesus' own injunctions in the great eschatological visions of Matthew 24-25 (our gospel reading; along with Mark 13 and Luke 21). The point is that Christian behavior should be tempered by the confidence that Jesus will return soon to bring in the judgment day and that our actions are to be shaped by the urgency of this looming event.

Perhaps one of the most pointed contemporary reflections on this is Tim McGraw's song "Live Like You Were Dying." That might make a good title for a message encompassing the common themes of today's lectionary readings.

Joshua 24:1-3a, 14-25

Three incidents round out the book Joshua, each of which addresses some dimension of the future of the land and Israel's place in it. First there is the story of the tension produced when the warriors from the trans-Jordan tribes return home in chapter 22. While the early intent of taking and settling Canaan seems to have been limited to the area between the Jordan River and the Mediterranean Sea (cf. Numbers 32), several tribes found the lands just east of the Jordan to be to their liking. They requested the right to settle in this territory that had previously belonged to the Ammonites and Moabites. Moses gave them permission, with the stipulation that their soldiers must first accompany the rest of the tribes in the looming conquest of Canaan proper. This they agreed to do.

Now in Joshua 22, these warriors go back to their settlements east of the Jordan. As they forded the river, they built a huge altar and ignited a great blaze on it. Neighboring Israelite tribes grew suspicious, thinking that these trans-Jordan relatives were already bowing to other gods. In the ensuing conversations, all fears were quelled and Joshua heard testimony that they were not seeking a shrine for worship other than the tabernacle. Instead they only wanted to set up a monument that would help them remember their ties with the rest of the tribes. In this way a pledge was made for national unity that transcended tribal identities.

Second, as he grew old and neared death, Joshua called together the elders who had shaped community life for the Israelites at his side (Joshua 23). He took them on a verbal tour of their remembered history and called from them a pledge to keep their villages and cities true to the identity promulgated in the Sinai covenant.

Third, in a final covenant renewal ceremony (and our Old Testament lectionary reading for today), Joshua gathered the whole nation together shortly before he died (Joshua 24). Once again, he reminded them *who* they were and *whose* they were. The Israelites did not exist as an independent tribe negotiating its own way among the other nations of the ancient near east, nor were they free agents determining their religious allegiance by taking offers from the open market. They were the people of Yahweh, the nation of the Sinai covenant, the human agency of God's mission to recover a relationship with the residents of planet Earth as communicated to Abraham many centuries before.

The concluding appendix to the book (Joshua 24:28-33) lists three graves: those of Joshua, Joseph, and Eleazer. Each is uniquely significant. Graves are a symbol of settlement and homeland. Abraham and his wives were buried in this land, as were Isaac and his wives. When Jacob died in Egypt, his family made sure to bring his body back to Canaan to bury it there. Now the generations are passing again and upon their deaths Joshua the leader, Joseph the ancestor, and Eleazer the religious head are all buried in this land. It is a fitting reminder that the land has finally achieved its intended rest and its rightful owners can rest there as well. They are truly home.

It is in this light that the location of the "promised land" must be considered. Why was Canaan the land promised to Abraham? Why did Israel wrestle these acres away from other clans in order to establish its own settlements?

Without question, there are many geographical areas of the world that would have appeared to be far more desirable. Mesopotamia, with its well-watered valleys surrounding the Tigris and Euphrates rivers, had a much better agricultural base than did Canaan. Egypt experienced a more stable climate and a more secluded location. Anatolia was better suited to permanent settlement, because of its mountain-ringed highlands, than was the open strip of countryside between the Jordan River and the Mediterranean Sea. In fact, Canaan was largely a rock pile, very indefensible, lacking any natural harbor for trade, and geographically splintered, so that it would be very difficult to forge a national identity across high mountainous ridges and deep separating valleys.

What made this piece of property so valuable, at least in Yahweh's eyes? In the words of every real estate salesman: location, location, location. Canaan was the unparalleled single piece of territory in the ancient world that connected the various civilizations with each other. It was the bridge between Africa and Asia. It was the rest stop on the trade routes from what would become Europe to both the Orient and Egypt. It served as the primary highway for marshaling troops in the military campaigns of its world and formed a key segment in every major communication line or caravan trek.

Canaan was precisely the one spot in the world of that day where the nation of Israel could not be hidden from other tribes and countries and clans and peoples. In other words, the promised land was, for Israel, not a secluded sanctuary or retreat where the pastoral scenes of Eden could be replayed but rather the busiest street in town. Here Israel was placed as the divine billboard, calling all nations back to a relationship with the Creator. Here Israel's unique community character and moral ethos were on display to attract other civilizations to inquire and seek after the God of this people.

The choice of Canaan as the promised land was no accident, when seen in the larger perspectives of the Sinai covenant and its missional foregrounding provided by the book of Genesis. If the Creator was going to find a way back into the hearts of humans who had long ago forgotten their maker, it would require the formation of a community shaped by the Sinai covenant, and then displayed in the most prominent location possible in the world of the day: Canaan. In this sense, the mission of God was not first built out of Jesus and the New Testament church but was resident in the religion of the Bible from its very beginning. This is why Jesus would say that his disciples were to be like a city set on a hill (Matthew 5:13-16), for that is exactly what his ancient kin, the Israelites, were intended to be. That is why the Israelites have come home to this land they never knew, and why Joshua challenged them to buy into God's mission or get lost among the other nations, limping into oblivion.

1 Thessalonians 4:13-18

After the Jerusalem council of Acts 15, Paul and Barnabas were eager to visit the Galatian congregations and inform them personally of the good outcomes in this early Christian theological debate that had affected them so deeply (Acts 15:36). But tensions flamed between them when they argued whether John Mark should be invited along (Acts 15:37). Paul was still very upset that the younger man had suddenly "deserted" them on their first mission journey (Acts 13:13). In the end, Barnabas felt a family obligation to give it a try with Mark again, while Paul chose a new partner, named Silas, to join him in these travels (Acts 15:39-41).

It was probably late in 49 AD when Paul and Silas left Syrian Antioch, their home base. They traveled overland to the communities in central Asia Minor where Paul and Barnabas had established Christian congregations more than a year earlier. At Lystra, they were joined by Timothy (Acts 16:1-2), a promising young man whose mother was Christian but whose father was not. Together this growing company of itinerant preachers had in mind an itinerary taking them farther north in Asia Minor (Acts 16:6-8). There were other new areas where Jewish settlements in Hellenic cities might give them an open door for talking about Jesus.

While pondering their options at Troas, Paul may have had some medical problems. The text of Acts 16 shows a shift at that point from third-person references to first-person recollections (note vv. 6-10). It seems obvious that Doctor Luke, the man who would author this book, joined the band at Troas. It might well be that he came to Paul as a healer and stayed with Paul as a new believer and fellow evangelist. Also in this city a divine directive illumined Paul in a vision (Acts 16:9-10), with the result that the company headed next across the Aegean Sea to Macedonia. Philippi was their first major stop, a fairly new Roman colony established by military personnel who received parcels of land as their pensions. As of yet there was no sizeable Jewish population in the city, since Paul and Silas found a small group of Jews worshiping at the river's edge on a sabbath (Acts 16:13). Once there were ten Jewish males in any town a synagogue had to be established, so the river gathering meant that Jews had not come to Philippi in any significant numbers. As was his custom, Paul spoke to the small group about Jesus, and a new Christian congregation was formed in the home of Lydia (Acts 16:14-15).

Paul and Silas stayed in Philippi for some time but eventually encountered trouble that landed them in jail. A young fortune-teller began to follow them, shouting out to the crowds about them (Acts 16:16-17), perhaps in a mean-spirited or nasty manner. Paul became grieved by her evident demon possession and exorcised her (Acts 16:18). The girl's masters were very upset and threw Paul and Silas into prison (Acts 16:19-24). A midnight earthquake rocked the place and led to the jailer's conversion (Acts 16:25-34). In the morning, the Roman citizenship of Paul and Silas was discovered, and the magistrates were beside themselves in efforts to undo the unlawful treatment these two had received (Acts 16:35-40).

It was on to Thessalonica next, for Paul and Silas and their team (Acts 17:1-9). For three weeks, Paul preached about Jesus in the Jewish synagogue. When Gentiles swelled the crowd of Christ-believers, however, some Jews became jealous and formed a mob to disrupt civic life. The uproar caused city officials to arrest leading members of the new Christian congregation, and the group sent Paul and Silas out of town that evening under the cover of darkness. With brief stops in Berea (Acts 17:10-15) and Athens (Acts 17:16-34), Paul eventually arrived in Corinth, where he met Aquila and Priscilla for the first time (Acts 18:1-3). This couple would become fast friends with Paul, keeping in touch for the rest of his life.

Although Paul would spend the next year and a half in Corinth, at the outset his heart remained back in Thessalonica. Already when he was traveling through Athens, Paul worried about how the fledgling Thessalonian congregation was faring (1 Thessalonians 2:17-20), and sent Timothy back to find out more and make a report (1 Thessalonians 3:1-5). Paul had already continued on to Corinth by the time Timothy caught up with him and was elated at the good word his younger associate brought (1 Thessalonians 3:6-10). With emotions running high, Paul dashed off a letter of appreciation and encouragement to his new friends (1 Thessalonians).

Most of this short letter is given to expressions of praise for the great testimony already being talked about from those who observed the grace and spiritual energy of this newborn congregation. Paul rehearsed briefly (1 Thessalonians 1-3) the recent history that had deeply connected them and told of his aching heart now that they were so quickly "torn away" from one another (1 Thessalonians 2:17). Only after these passionate confessions does Paul spill some ink on a few notes of instruction (1 Thessalonians 4-5). While most of what Paul has to say are typical exhortations toward quiet and godly living, a surprising topic suddenly jumps out as prelude to a new and unique trajectory in Christian doctrinal development. Paul suddenly declares a new and powerful idea: Jesus will soon return and all who die in faith will rise to live with him.

The central message of Paul's missionary preaching focused on the resurrection of Jesus. This was, for Paul, the astounding confirmation of Jesus' divine character. It was the undeniable proof that Jesus was the Messiah and that his words and teachings had ushered in the new age of God's final revelation and redemptive activity.

Paul understood that Jesus was the great "Day of the Lord" event foretold by the Old Testament prophets (1 Thessalonians 5:1), and that out of gracious forbearance, Jesus had split this cataclysmic occurrence in two, so that the beginning of eternal blessings could be experienced before the final judgment fell (1 Thessalonians 5:2-11). This meant that Jesus had gone back to heaven only briefly and would be returning to earth very soon — probably next week, but maybe next month. It was the generous grace of God that had provided this brief window of opportunity, allowing Jesus' disciples a chance quickly to tell others the good news, so that those who believed would also reap the benefits of the looming messianic age. Neither Paul nor God wanted anyone to be destroyed in the judgments that were still ahead.

Matthew 25:1-13

The three parables of Matthew 25 are Jesus' amplification of his eschatological visions and challenges to his disciples in Matthew 24. After the Last Supper, Jesus and his disciples walked through the temple courts on their way to a time of prayer on the Mount of Olives. The buildings of the temple had gone through a massive renovation by Herod the Great, one of the most astounding builders of human history. The construction work was completed only a few years before and these rather rural Galilee folk were astounded by the immense structures and their marvelous beauty. This is the background to the introductory notes at the beginning of Matthew 24.

Proper 27 / Ordinary Time 32

While his disciples are agape at the splendor of the renewed temple buildings, Jesus quickly tosses water on their ardor by announcing the coming destruction of these great structures in the Roman campaign only a generation into the future (70 AD). Then Jesus springboards from that prophecy to more complex and frightening scenes from the end of time.

As his disciples shake their heads in disbelief and wonder, Jesus moves on quickly to this trilogy of parables in Matthew 25. All three are part of the great eschatological teachings that meander through both the Old and New Testaments. While each segment of the Bible contains a lot of moral instruction and guidelines to ethical behavior, addressing many dimensions of life and behavior, the grand culmination of behavior modification in the faith community is the challenge: What should we be doing at the end of time?

It is in that light that we need to read and interpret this first of Jesus' three Matthew 25 parables. No indication is given by our Lord as to when the final morning of human history will break. In fact, it is precisely the unknown hour that makes this parable tug at us. What will be the driving forces that shape our behavior? How will looming expectations of eternity keep time organized and schedules written with meaning and purpose?

Application

Until Jesus returns, we will debate issues of holiness. Few of us will be completely satisfied with others' perspectives. Part of the problem is that there is no concrete "code of ethics" in scripture that defines behavior in all situations of life. The Ten Commandments brush colors in broad strokes, which, as Jesus says in the Sermon on the Mount, have a variety of more specific applications. Even Joshua's injunctions to Israel in Joshua 24 are too general to be a final code of conduct. He speaks of the heart and expects some change in lifestyle. But the emphasis is on the heart. The person who lives with God carries himself or herself with a certain air in society. It's hard to define in exact terms, but others can sense it. And they can sense its absence too.

One morning in 1872, David Livingstone wrote this in his diary:

> *March 19, my birthday. My Jesus, my King, my Life, my All, I again dedicate my whole self to Thee. Accept me, and grant, O gracious Father, that ere the year is gone I may finish my work. In Jesus' name I ask it. Amen.*

Just one year later, to the day, servants came to check on their master's delay. They found him on his knees in prayer. He was dead. Friends in England provided a final resting place for his body and posted this note that testifies yet today:

> *He needs no epitaph to guard a name*
> *Which men will prize while worthy work is known;*
> *He lived and died for good — that is his fame;*
> *Let marble crumble: this is Living-stone!*

Perhaps that is a fitting testimony about all who seek to live like they were dying, confident of God's good purpose and direction in their lives.

An Alternative Application

1 Thessalonians 4:13-18. Paul's letters to the Thessalonian congregation occurred early in his ministry with both epistles most likely penned in 50 AD. These writings are very short and do not spell out a fully explored eschatology. But in their brief exhortations they contain some of Paul's most direct and explicit eschatological teachings.

First, it is clear that the emphasis in Paul's preaching was on the resurrection of Jesus. This was the confirmation that Jesus was the messiah foretold by the prophets. It was also the most profound sign that the new messianic age had arrived. Since the messianic age was part of the promised "Day of the Lord," a time of divine judgment was sure to arrive soon.

Second, Jesus' first coming brought the beginnings of the blessings of the messianic age, but it delayed the judgments of God for a time so that the followers of Jesus could spread the news of salvation far and wide. Splitting the "Day of the Lord" in two was an act of kindness on God's part, providing more opportunity for people to respond in faith. It also placed upon the church a missionary urgency. The reason Jesus left his followers behind during the gap between his ascension and return was to send them as ambassadors of hope to the nations.

Third, the return of Jesus was imminent and likely to take place within weeks or months. This was the expectation that made any trials, persecutions, or difficulties durable. Knowing that one can outlast an opponent, no matter how nasty or strong, gives great resilience to hang on and survive with dignity.

Fourth, all who trusted in Jesus when he returned would share in his glory and power. But so too would those who had believed in Jesus and then died before Jesus had made his return. This teaching profoundly changed the burial habits of Christians and altered expectations at dying. Rather than closing doors to human existence, death instead opened them to eternal life. Many early Christians welcomed death by martyrdom, knowing that through this act they were immediately secure in resurrection hope.

Fifth, the yawning gap of time that had been widening since Jesus' ascension required meaningful explanations for the delay of his return. Answers came in three major varieties. Some saw this lengthening "in-between" age as evidence of divine grace: God was not going to bring final judgment until more people could respond to the gospel message in faith. Others declared that the delay was a tool for testing the faithfulness of those who said they believed in Jesus. A final group called to mind Jesus' words about signs that would appear before the final days and tried more closely to define the number of specific events that must still take place prior to his return.

Intertwined together, these three dimensions of eschatological expectations became hardwired into the church and infused it, for Paul, with a missionary urgency and an uncompromising ethic. The church must speak to everyone with loving passion about Jesus. At the same time, Christians were responsible to live in a profound moral simplicity that assessed every behavior by the question "What should we be doing when Jesus returns?"

Proper 28 | Ordinary Time 33
Judges 4:1-7
1 Thessalonians 5:1-11
Matthew 25:14-30
by David Kalas

Here comes the judge

In the 1970s, comedian Flip Wilson made famous a series of routines that featured the phrase "Here comes the judge!" It was meant to sound like an ominous warning, though in the context of his skits, of course, it was always light-hearted and humorous.

As we ponder the three texts that come before us this morning, however, we are presented with a much more serious prospect. This is no comic charade. There really is a judge. And he really is coming.

It seems to me that Flip Wilson was onto something though, even in his clownish portrayal. While we typically think of the criminal having to come before the judge, the image of the judge coming to the outlaw is appropriate to scripture. And for the offender, the coming of "the judge" surely does suggest something frightening, for he represents the implementation of justice and that is bad news for anyone who is on the wrong side of the law.

So it is with the coming judgment of God. In a world that is full of wrong, the judge will come to make it right. In the big picture, of course, that's good news — we long for wrongs to be made right. But it is not good news if you're on the wrong side of right.

Julia Ward Howe articulated that sense of the vigorous, coming judgment of God in her epic poem *The Battle Hymn of the Republic*. She envisions the Lord coming in glory and his coming is accompanied by "the grapes of wrath," "fateful lightning," and "his terrible swift sword." Further, "he is sifting out the hearts of men before his judgment seat," with the end result that "the world shall be his footstool, and the soul of wrong his slave."[1]

So exploring three very different passages of scripture, we will see three different images that bear witness to the same, single truth: namely, here comes the judge!

Judges 4:1-7

Perhaps the most important single word in this selected text from the Old Testament book of Judges is "again." The author candidly reports, "The Israelites again did what was evil in the sight of the Lord." And the whole story that follows is a story of "again."

If we are familiar with the book of Judges, we are familiar with the pattern. But then, of course, the pattern is not limited to just that slice of Old Testament history. It is the story of all of Old Testament history and it is very likely the story of our own lives as well.

In broad outline, the story goes like this: The people of God sin. It's not just a foot fault, an inadvertent or accidental sin. No, it seems rather to be a case of the prodigal son's complete loss of perspective, foolishly thinking that squandering life beyond the Father's boundaries is better than truly living within them. In the case of the Israelites of Judges 4, we do not know the details but that variable makes the story easier to apply to ourselves.

---
1. Julia Ward Howe, "The Battle Hymn of the Republic" (United Methodist Hymnal #717).

That folly is followed by the chastening of God. In this case, "the Lord sold them into the hand of King Jabin of Canaan." This is no cruelty, mind you; it is mercy. If we choose to reject the Lord as our king, then we are due to discover what it is to belong to a different king. So the poet prays for wandering God's sheep, "Who chose the company of wolves, let them taste the companionship wolves give to helpless strays; but, oh! let them live — wiser, though torn!"[2]

Predictably, the miserable wanderers "cried out to the Lord for help." There is no faster cure for a latent prayer life than trouble. In this particular instance, the trouble is that Israel's cruel enemy "had 900 chariots of iron." That's a detail that changes, of course, from one prodigal's circumstance to the next. For the lost son in Jesus' story, hunger and poverty drove him home. Someone else will find sin's cruelty in the addiction that it has created — the brokenness, sadness, emptiness. Whether 900 iron chariots or the weariness of sin's disappointing detours, something always reminds God's people that his yoke is easier and his burden is lighter.

As predictable as the human routine is — disobedience, regret, and the cry for help — God's mercy toward us is untiring. As in the story of Judges 4, he responds to their desperate need by sending a deliverer. At one point in history that was Moses. At another point, it was Gideon, Cyrus, or Judas Maccabaeus. Ultimately and universally, the deliverer God has sent to rescue his people is Jesus Christ. Every other deliverer is just a pale and finite imitation. In this particular instance, God's agent of rescue was the judge Deborah.

Deborah may remind us of the character Samuel, who comes a few generations later. For she, like Samuel, is identified in a kind of dual role: prophet and judge. We see evidence throughout Israel's history that "prophet" seems to be the highest rank in the land. The prophets can correct the priest. The prophets can correct the kings. Indeed, in a number of cases it is the prophet who anoints the king! So Deborah represents that seat of highest authority in Israel and it is from that perch that she directs the battle plan against the Canaanites.

Our brief excerpt from Judges does not give us Deborah's entire story. In the end, it is a story of faith, obedience, God's divine assistance, and a great victory for Israel. It is also a story with a familiar plot line, which bears witness to the power, providence, and grace of God.

1 Thessalonians 5:1-11

In a culture that is increasingly illiterate of scripture, a reference to 1 Thessalonians is not likely to mean much to people. Genesis, Psalms, Job, and Revelation may all still at least conjure some images or impressions in people's minds but what do they know about Paul's letters to the Thessalonians?

Many New Testament scholars contend that this epistle is the earliest we have from Paul's hand and, for that matter, perhaps the earliest text in the entire New Testament corpus. It seems that Paul wrote the letter during his second missionary journey: perhaps very shortly after he had been chased out of town by his opponents (Acts 17:13-15).

That historical context is useful to know because it reminds us that Paul is writing to a rather new church and to rather young Christians. It is essential for him, therefore, to answer their questions, address their concerns, and encourage them in the way they should go. Throughout the two letters we have from the apostle to those new believers, we see that a primary concern in Thessalonica was this matter of "the times and seasons," specifically the end of the age and Christ's return.

To address that theme from 1 Thessalonians will be an instructive exercise for many of our congregations. The reflex of so many contemporary American Christians is to think exclusively of the book of Revelation when pondering the end times but the last book is not necessarily the last word on the subject. So we welcome the apostle Paul's insights into the eschaton.

---

2. Ruth Bell Graham, "For All Who Knew the Shelter of the Fold," *Prodigals and Those Who Love Them* (Colorado Springs: Focus on the Family Publishing, 1991), p. 15.

The first point to be observed is Paul's use of the phrase "the day of the Lord." Students of the Old Testament will immediately recognize the significance of the phrase. Further, we should note that Paul employs it elsewhere (e.g., 1 Corinthians 5:5; 2 Corinthians 2:14; 2 Thessalonians 2:2) and that Peter also uses the phrase with reference to coming "like a thief" (2 Peter 3:10). For the Jews, it was a term packed with meaning and that meaning deserves to be explored.

The second observation to be made is the theme of suddenness. While scripture gives ample notice that the day is coming, still, its arrival will evidently be a surprise to many. We see that theme in numerous New Testament references and that is the spirit of Paul's "thief in the night" image as well. Yet the apostle does not expect that to be the Thessalonians' experience. After all, that sudden event can only come "like a thief in the night" if it is nighttime. But nighttime suggests darkness, and this darkness is not ubiquitous. Paul makes a distinction — reminiscent of the distinction between the Egyptians and the Israelites (Exodus 10:21-23) — between those who are in light and those who are in darkness. Since the Thessalonians, spiritually speaking, "are not of the night or of darkness," they will not experience the suddenness of the end as those for whom it will mean "sudden destruction."

Finally, we discover that the day-vs.-night paradigm carries implications for more than just that future "day of the Lord"; it also has ramifications for today. In other words, if in fact the people of God are in the light rather than the darkness, then they should live accordingly. Behaviors that are associated with darkness and night include drunkenness and drowsiness. The daytime, however, is characterized by sobriety and alertness and those should be the hallmarks of Christ's disciples as they await his at-any-moment return.

Matthew 25:14-30

We are all acquainted with the helpful maps located in certain large public places — airports, malls, and so on — which include a little arrow saying "You are here!" Perhaps such a map-and-arrow technique might be helpful for our congregations when considering the gospel lection this Sunday.

Our selected passage comes from Matthew 25. By itself that detail may have very little meaning for most folks. So it is worth noting that the entire gospel has just 28 chapters. That means this comes toward the end. More specifically, the story of Jesus entering Jerusalem on Palm Sunday is recorded in Matthew 21 and the story of his arrest, suffering, and crucifixion is found in Matthew 26 and 27. Therefore we recognize that this particular teaching comes during that eventful final week in Jerusalem and it comes very near the climactic end of that week.

Meanwhile, there is a context within the chapter itself, which also deserves consideration. In a red-letter Bible, Matthew 25 would be printed entirely in red. The whole chapter is Jesus talking. Specifically, it is comprised of three long teachings. First, he tells the story of the wise and foolish bridesmaids (vv. 1-13), then our passage, and then the familiar story of the sheep and the goats (vv. 31-46). All three teachings, we observe, make either implicit allusion or explicit reference to the final judgment. As Jesus approaches the culmination of his earthly ministry, he talks a good deal about the events at the culmination of the age and our particular lection must be read in that light.

We'll consider below this strange marriage of original context and contemporary usage: namely, that a parable about the Judgment Day should be so routinely used as the text for local church financial campaigns. The relative scope of those two themes seems quite incongruous. For this space, however, let us turn our attention to a few very important details of the passage.

First, we cannot miss — and our people must not miss — the symbolism of a master who goes away for a long time and then returns. Perhaps your church does not spend a great deal of time thinking or talking about the Master's return but that neglect of the subject merely plays into the profile that Jesus himself predicted (e.g., Matthew 24:50; Luke 12:40). The inescapable fact is that this parable forces us to ponder the prospect of Christ's return and the accounting he will demand of his servants at that time.

Second, we should note that the master gave "to each according to his ability." While our contemporary culture is so prone to confuse the concepts of "fair," "equal," and "same," this parable does not pretend that the master treats his servants identically. Rather, Jesus is unapologetic in acknowledging different levels of ability and so those servants are given different levels of responsibility.

Right on the heels of that seeming inequity, however, comes the heroic but neglected example of the second servant. He is, the figures suggest, less than half as capable as the first servant and yet he shows an equal return: that is, both the first and second servants double their master's money. The mid-level ability does not prevent this servant from achieving top-level results.

We should note also the fabulous wealth of this master. He tells the first servant, for example, that he had "been trustworthy with a few things." Those "few things," you recall, were "five talents," which was actually quite a fortune. Scholars offer a variety of estimates about the value of a talent, which was a unit of weight measurement in New Testament times. A conservative estimate is that those five talents would have been perhaps 400 pounds of silver or gold. That considerable treasure is what our Master calls "a few things" — testament to the truth that "the cattle on a thousand hills" belong to him (Psalm 50:10).

Finally, there is the tragic case of the third servant. He might well be the subject of several sober sermons. For the present, however, suffice it to say of him that what he thought was being careful and cautious, his master reckoned as "wicked and lazy." From the very beginning, we recall, the Creator's first instruction to human beings was to "be fruitful" (Genesis 1:28). Fruitfulness, we discover, is the hallmark of the repentant (Matthew 3:8), the righteous (Psalm 1:3), and the godly (Galatians 5:22-23; John 15:8, 16). Unfruitfulness, meanwhile, invokes judgment (Luke 3:9; Matthew 21:19). Our high calling, therefore, is to produce for him — for that is what we are designed, commanded, and entrusted to do.

Application

The Old Testament episode recorded in the obscurity of Judges does not immediately seem to fit with the end-times theme of our two New Testament passages. For as long as we are dealing with the same unchanging God, however, there is certain to be profound continuity from one situation to the next. (And I should add that it is important for us to seek out that continuity lest we fall prey to the sloppy Marcionism that plagues so much of mainline American Christianity.)

The story from Judges is a small, specific event in the past — the long ago past at that. The subject of the two New Testament texts, on the other hand, is the climactic event of the universe's future. What could they possibly share in common? Well, it seems to me that the former serves as a kind of microcosm of the latter. There is an enemy of God's people. He is powerful, oppressive, and the people themselves are no match for him. Yet God assists his people and in the end that enemy is vanquished. The judge in this case is a human being but still serves as an agent of the God who comes onto the scene and makes things right.

The Thessalonians passage, meanwhile, has much of the same spirit as the old Flip Wilson line. The ultimate judge is coming and that is bad news for whoever is on the wrong side of right: "sudden destruction will come upon them." And the prospect of his arrival serves as no-nonsense encouragement for the rest of us to live in readiness.

Finally, the teaching of Jesus in Matthew 25 tells the same fundamental story. The master has gone away on a long journey but he is coming back. When he comes back, we see that he will come as a judge. He sits in judgment. Interestingly, however, this is not a judgment of his avowed enemies but rather of those who call him "Master." Even in that group, there are distinctions to be made.

For congregations that are accustomed to reciting the Apostles' Creed, the prospect should be a familiar one: "He shall come to judge the living and the dead." The gospel truth is that there is a judge and he is coming. Therefore, you and I are encouraged to do all that we have been instructed to do in order that we will be ready when he comes.

Alternative Application

Matthew 25:14-30. "The Bottom Line." The story of the three servants in Matthew 25 is favorite preaching material for Stewardship Sundays. The servants in Jesus' parable are functioning as stewards — managers of their master's resources — and so the parable is perfectly matched for a church's stewardship emphasis.

The only problem is that so many of our stewardship campaigns are not perfectly matched for a stewardship emphasis.

Play a word-association game with most church folks and include "stewardship" on the list of words used as triggers. What responses are we likely to get? For so many of the folks in our pews, I'm afraid, the word conjures associations with money, charitable giving, pledge drives, and the church budget.

My, how terribly we have demoted the stewards in our churches! God has given them such tremendous responsibility and yet we have whittled down their understanding of their profound job description to such a narrow and temporal slice of life. So they think that "stewardship" is all about what they give, while the grand truth is of this passage is quite the opposite: namely, that stewardship is actually about what they have been given.

The stewards are those individuals who have been entrusted with portions of the master's property. His interest is not in how they give back to him 2, 5, 10, or 12% of what he has given them. Rather, his interest is in how they manage everything that he has given them.

It might seem heavy-handed to tie this year's stewardship campaign to judgment day but the unavoidable truth is that this stewardship parable is a story that anticipates and depicts that day — the day when the Master shall return and demand an accounting of what we have done with his stuff. That's the bottom line in this story and it is essential for our people to understand, therefore, that the primary issue with stewardship is neither the church's bottom line nor their individual bottom line. Instead, we are dealing with the Master's bottom line and our opportunity as his servants to improve it.

Christ The King (Proper 29)

Ezekiel 34:11-16, 20-24

Ephesians 1:15-23

Matthew 25:31-46

by David Coffin

How Christ rules

Reign of Christ or Christ the King Sunday lends itself to the narration of stories as to how people experience God and God's kingdom breaking into our world. Karen D. Scheib's book titled *Pastoral Care: Telling Stories of our Lives* (Abingdon Press, 2016) makes some practical sense. "Narrative identity provides a means to hold together our various beliefs, hopes, dreams, and roles in a coherent way. The story you tell about yourself, for example, at that church retreat or in the classroom, interprets your past, conveys beliefs about how you developed over time into the person you are now, and projects anticipated in the future. This story also communicates your convictions, values and commitments." (Scheib, pp. 8-9). In the Ezekiel 34 text, if one's life plans have relied on the ruling shepherds of Israel to look after the well-being of the nation and its people, they will be bitterly disappointed. The prophet identifies the disappointments one would have if they trusted such ruling shepherds to reflect the reality of the Lord's reign. Ephesians 1:15-23 is a prayer for those who have placed their trust in a Christ who triumphs over the powers of evil. Does such a thanksgiving square with how people in the church view the world they live in everyday? The theme of the day remains "Reign of Christ," despite evidence to the contrary in personal life narratives people might experience. Paul is unshakable in this conviction. Finally, Matthew 25:31-46 portrays Christ as judge upon his return. If one has life narratives suggesting that nobody is in charge of the chaotic existence they eke a living in, who is this judge that is now separating the sheep from the goats? How do our personal life narratives support or detract from the three textual themes of this "Christ the King" or "Reign of Christ" Sunday?

Ezekiel 34:11-16; 20-24

The master narrative that Ezekiel and his generation were raised on to shape their lives has crumbled into pieces along with the city buildings and walls of Jerusalem. The prophet was trained to be a temple priest during a stable monarchy, as this was his family heritage. God, through the ruling kings, was to watch over and protect the city and its temple. Instead, Ezekiel's wife died in 588 BCE during the Babylonian siege of Jerusalem, as the nation was sent into exile. This tragic life narrative has resulted in the prophet speaking ecstatic words that have made some scholars question his sanity throughout the ages. The prophet's location is disputed, but it is probable he spent most of his life in the Babylon diaspora, after he was deported around 598 BCE (cf. 2 Kings 24:12-16). Babylon's conquest of the nation put an end to the 400-year monarchy. Private or individual faith was not widely practiced, so community worship was endangered with mass deportations of key people within the nations. Many people put faith in the prediction of short-term exile by the prophet Hananiah, but it proved to be false (Jeremiah 28). A major crisis of faith occurred on many fronts for the people. The specific portion of the overall crisis of faith in this particular section of the (uncontested) book of Elijah relates to their leaders, or shepherds (Blenkinsopp, pp. 9-13).

"Shepherds" in the Hebrew Bible (Old Testament) are usually people of power who are responsible for the well-being of those whom they serve and rule. These are the kings of Judah (Southern Israel). Not only did these monarchs or kings fail to protect the people from foreign powers, but many of them also proved to be corrupt, unfaithful to God, and unjust in the ruling of the peoples. In this text, God promises to one day act as a shepherd to search and seek out his sheep (Ezekiel 34:11-12), He will gather them, feed them, and bind up the weak or heal those who are despised. There will also be a judgment component of a shepherd who will restore justice. The key text to work from is Ezekiel 34:24 — "And I, the Lord, will be their God, and my servant David shall be prince among them; I, the Lord, have spoken."

On Christ the King Sunday, this text suggests a messianic leader of the family of King David who will gather the lost, heal the wounded, and restore justice. If one is comfortable aligning the Servant Songs of Isaiah 42:1-4, then the Jesus of Nazareth whom the Christian church confesses as the new Messiah can fill this role in a fuller way than a political or military leader. This is the basic theme of Reign of Christ Sunday. This messianic king serves God, Israel, and the world. He would demonstrate ultimate service through self-sacrifice on a cross for the sins of humanity (Matthew 1:21, "he will save his people from their sins").

Preaching on this text suggests one ask what exactly is the community looking for in a "leader"? One can utilize the term "servant leader" on paper as quickly as a person could claim to be a ruling king or monarch back in the ancient Middle East. However, this text would prompt us ask to see how the leader actually seeks, feeds, unites, and pursues justice. Ezekiel says God will do this through another type of shepherd of God's own choosing.

On Reign of Christ Sunday, what leadership traits are communities of faith seeking? For example, a person who has had experience in a top-down organization where subordinates must comply with orders and directives for fear of losing pay and health care benefits is to be distinguished from a leader who has to use volunteers who are not dependent on organizational pay and benefits. It might be the difference between selecting a former CEO of a company or government service manager vs. the person who must organize a volunteer cancer walk, soup kitchen, or disaster cleanup project. On Reign of Christ Sunday, what sort of "skill set" does the church and community of faith need?

Would a former CEO of a successful corporation even be able to lead a group of church volunteers who have already done a day's work and serve on the finance committee on their own free time? What would motivate a person to serve for a church organization without pay? What happens when a church leader embezzles money and the new leader is under much more scrutiny than leaders in times past? The good news of this text is that the values of the Servant of Isaiah tend to inform vision for such a leader. Which pastors have the most faithful stories in the history of a given church would be a path I would pursue. I would ask: "Why was this pastor well-liked?" Then maybe cite another example of a not-so-popular pastor or church leader. What was memorable about the reign of any given pastor or church leader? [Sources: Joseph Blenkinsopp, *Interpretation, a Bible Commentary for Teaching and Preaching: Ezekiel* (Westminster John Knox Press, 1990); Walther Eichrodt, *The Old Testament Library: Ezekiel* (Westminster Press, 1970)]

Ephesians 1:15-23

An alcoholic head of the family makes all sorts of promises to console his or her offspring, who have suffered much, but (each) will receive a hefty inheritance upon the parent's death. This narrative is one which many of the offspring count on for their future plans. Upon the death of the parent, it is discovered that not only is there no inheritance, but the estate is in debt and the family now has to find a way to pay for the funeral. Such is a narrative of how a promised inheritance can be a disappointment. How will one interpret future promises of an inheritance?

Ephesians is a circular letter addressed to many churches. Its authorship is contested, but this article will simply use the name "Paul." The text is intended to be a prayer of thanksgiving to faithful Christians who must also endure the false teachings of early Gnostic heresies. Terms such as "wisdom," "knowledge," and "revelation" could have Gnostic meanings, but this is not the intention of Paul. All has been accomplished when "God put this power to work in Christ when he raised him from the dead and seated him at his right hand in the heavenly places" (Ephesians 1:20). There is a certain security in the inheritance with this promise.

God has done everything with this death and resurrection. It could be a further fulfilling of Psalm 110:1: "The Lord says to my lord,'Sit at my right hand until I make your enemies your footstool.'" The victory is accomplished, the inheritance is untouchable! This might be a proposed counternarrative to the broken promises of human inheritances suggested above.

So if Christ has done it all, why are there wicked and evil powers still at work? The Christian church is an extension of Christ's body. The kingdom that is in the future is now being collapsed into the present as the church lives out the intentions of its crucified and risen Christ. For Paul, the church is doing a "rehearsal" for the age to come when the final king who sits at the right hand of heavenly places will one day rule all nations. This suggests a universal mission of the church outside the realms of traditional Judeo-Christian communities.

How does any particular congregation energize believers with the power to live out the vision of the kingdom? Whether a person be baptized or converted, Paul in Ephesians believes those who have the inheritance of eternal life and its riches are to live their lives as if the king, who is seated at the right hand, will return tomorrow or any day in the future. One direction I might pursue is "How does the church respond to being filled by Christ's blessings?" If somebody watched our daily lives and walk with God, what sort of kingdom are we reflecting? The Christians of the church are blazing the trails as to how Christ rules on this Sunday. [Sources: Ralph Martin, *Interpretation, a Bible Commentary for Teaching and Preaching: Ephesians, Colossians, and Philemon* (Westminster John Knox Press, 1991); Walter F. Taylor and John H.P. Reumann, *Augsburg Commentary on the New Testament: Ephesians, Colossians* (Augsburg Fortress, 1985)]

Matthew 25:31-46

This text could refer to the Hebrew Bible verses for today of Ezekiel 34:23-24:"I will set up over them one shepherd, my servant David, and he shall feed them: he shall feed them and be their shepherd. And I, the Lord, will be their God, and my servant David shall be prince among them; I, the Lord, have spoken." Jesus fulfills the words of the prophet Ezekiel in a deeper and meaningful way than any proposed political or military leader. The bottom line in this last judgment parable is that the way we treat other people will be judged by Christ the King. It is contested whether the specific ones who are being fed, given drink, welcomed, clothed, and visited while in prison are fellow Christians or all peoples of the world in need. The latter view supports the social gospel movement. If one is to ignore anybody in need it results in an ultimate judgment by the son of man (Schweizer, pp. 477-480). The former view still holds people responsible for how they treated others, but is limited to church people and particularly the servants of Christ. To attack a follower of the god or deity is to attack the deity himself (Talbert, p. 277). Whichever direction one decides to go with this text, to help those servants in need is to minister to the son of man or Christ as King on this Sunday.

Another insight one might include is how do we treat the messengers (teachers, pastors, missionaries, etc.) that God has sent us? To persecute the followers of Christ the King is to persecute the king himself as Saul heard in Acts 9:4; 22:7 (Talbert, p. 277). This text could be of comfort for those who suffer at the hands of religious people who say one thing on Sunday but act in a cold and mean-spirited way throughout the week. The preacher only needs to read this text and allow hearers to read in between the lines. Today Jesus is still launching all believers onto a mission that might result in some level of persecution. However, Christ the final king will bring justice to all people according to how they are or are not living out the kingdom of God (Wright, pp. 142-144). The gospel is that Christianity is a religion of second chances. One still can live and feed, welcome, and clothe those in need.

The consequences of such decisions could have long-lasting results, such as for eternity (Hill, p. 331). That the choices one makes on earth will have results is a basic agreement of all authors consulted. "The deeds of mercy in the present passage [Matthew 25 passage] are symbolic of a deeper reality... the main point of the parable is the acceptance or rejection of the Christian faith" (Hagner, p. 747).

Another sideline reflection to this text might be for those who have not come to a point where they confess Jesus as Lord, actually acting kinder, more mercifully toward the poor and welcoming than those who profess a faith in Christ. Could this text be a theological "loophole" for people who have little need for organized religion due to its past indiscretions, but who still practice all that this son of man has cited? That is, might the group who are surprised be unchurched people who actually live out the kingdom? [Sources: Donald A. Hagner, *Word Biblical Commentary: Matthew 14-28* (Thomas Nelson, 1995); David Hill, *The New Century Bible Commentary: The Gospel of Matthew* (Wm. B. Eerdmanns, 1972); Eduard Schweizer, *The Good News According to Matthew,* (John Knox Press, 1975); Charles H. Talbert, *Paideia Commentaries on the New Testament: Matthew* (Baker Academic, 2010); Tom Wright, *Matthew for Everyone: Part Two* (Westminster John Knox Press, 2002)]

Alternative Application

Ephesians 1:15-23. Ephesians 1:20 could be used to make a case for a portion of second article of the Apostles Creed: "On the third day he rose again; he ascended at the right hand of the Father, and he will come to judge the living and the dead" (Wengert, p. 29). Creeds were often employed as ways to discern what were the intended meanings of terms in the early church — in the interpretation of certain teachings on Jesus, God, the Spirit, etc., and what was outside the commonly accepted understanding of a particular teaching about the triune God. [Source: Timothy Wengert, translator, *Luther's Small Catechism: 500 Years of Reformation* (Augsburg Fortress, 2016)]

Alternative Application

Matthew 25:31-46. Is Matthew suggesting "salvation by works"? That is, if one is accepted into the kingdom and its rewards through baptism/conversion, does this text suggest that further acts of kindness are required by the believer? All authors consulted do not believe that responding to salvation with performing acts of mercy, care, and kindness need not contradict a basic theology of grace. The good works are to be a natural outpouring or result of the salvation by grace. My "pushback" here might be the thief on the cross in Luke 23:43, who undoubtedly did some pretty mean things before he suffered for his crimes. But Jesus still tells him, "today you will be with me in paradise." [Source: Charles H. Talbert, *Paideia Commentaries on the New Testament: Matthew* (Baker Academic, 2010)]

Thanksgiving Day
Deuteronomy 26:1-11
Philippians 4:4-9
John 6:25-35
by Wayne Brouwer

Party time!

During the Middle Ages, parts of Europe had a wonderfully unusual annual celebration called the Feast of Fools. It didn't occur, as one might expect, on April 1; most often it was celebrated at the turn of the year, the same time as our modern New Year's Eve parties.

At the Feast of Fools, everyone put on masks, sang outrageous songs, and made as much noise as possible. Society was turned upside down: those of low social position put on the clothing of rulers; they were in charge of church and state for a few brief hours. Every "normal" convention of serious life was mocked and lampooned.

Theologian Harvey Cox wrote about the Feast of Fools in a book by that title, calling people in our serious world to find time to celebrate life and love and God again. The pace of our workaday world is a killer, he says. Often the only thing we know how to do is take rushed "vacations" from it all in a mad dash for rest that never comes. What we need, he claims, is a sense of fun and celebration in our lives that keeps us from taking ourselves too seriously and that reminds us on a regular basis of grace and freedom.

You only have to read today's lectionary passages to know that that is good theology. In fact, when God introduced himself to Israel at Mount Sinai, God not only gave them a code of behavior to shape society; God also mandated a regular routine of parties — weekly sabbaths, seasonal celebrations, and special events that might occur only once in a lifetime. For some, life is a burden. For others, life is putting in time. But for Israel, life was meant to be a party, a festival, a celebration of the grand things an intimate relationship with God could mean.

The idea of life as a celebration is constant throughout scripture. Jesus often compared the kingdom of God to a banquet. He instituted a fellowship meal as the identifying feature of his community. And no picture of eternity could fully describe the visions of glory seen by John from the island of Patmos as well as that of a wedding reception. Those who know God's love and care often say "It is party time!" in the best sense of the term.

Deuteronomy 26:1-11

The festival calendar of daily, weekly, monthly, and yearly markers was not for Israel so much a schedule of holidays that broke up the work seasons into manageable pieces. Rather, it was the rhythm of married life with Yahweh. It was the way in which the covenant relationship was acknowledged daily and weekly, and then encouraged the deep permeation of the relationship as a kind of living testimony through the multiple anniversary remembrances throughout the year.

An ancient Jewish legend declares: "Pentecost is the day on which Torah was given." According to this teaching, it was on the day that eventually became the feast of Pentecost that God gave birth to the Hebrew nation by speaking the divine covenant to them at Mount Sinai.

As the book of Acts makes clear, Pentecost was the day on which the New Testament church was given birth. Just as God spoke through Moses to bring the nation of Israel into being at Mount Sinai, so God spoke through Peter to create the first elements of the new faith community.

It was symbolically powerful for these events to take place on Pentecost. In its first use "Pentecost" was essentially a nickname or label. The feast of Passover was one of the most significant holidays in the Jewish community, since it recalled the manner in which God miraculously brought the nation out of Egypt. Seven Sabbaths and a day later (7 x 7 + 1 = 50), the people celebrated this next major religious event as harvest season began in Palestine. Since it occurred fifty days after the Passover, people started referring to it as the "Feast after Fifty" or Pentecost.

Yet the real significance of the event was more clearly understood through its original name --**Feast of Firstfruits**. Regulations for the celebration, briefly stated in today's lectionary reading and fleshed out more fully in Leviticus 23, required all Israelites to assemble at the temple in Jerusalem, bringing with them the first sheaf of grain from their fields. As the time of harvest approached across the land, even before the regular reaping started, a single bundle of grain was cut on each farm and toted off to the temple.

There it was "waved" before the Lord as an offering (Leviticus 23:11), along with two loaves of bread that were baked from the newly harvested grain (Leviticus 23:17). Furthermore, to broaden the impact of the event two male lambs were also brought from the first castings of each flock (Leviticus 23:12).

As these gifts were presented to God in the temple courts, all of the men danced around the altar that carried the smoke of the gifts toward heaven. The crowds of women, children, and elderly men too old to jump around wildly formed a large circle around these revelers and sang Psalms 113-118. According to historical reports, the celebration was often wild and uninhibited.

We might ask what the purpose was behind these religious revelries. The instructions of Moses declared that the feast was a theological testimony. The nation was making a confession that no general harvesting for profit would begin until God had laid claim to the "firstfruits" of the fields and the flocks. By devoting the first of the new produce to God, the people were acknowledging that everything came from God and belonged to God. Whatever benefit they might receive from the harvest that year was a direct result of God's care and providential intervention.

With that background, the significance of Pentecost as the birthday of the Christian church takes on new meaning. A new era of God's kingdom began that day, as God claimed the firstfruits of a worldwide faith harvest. The mission of the church began only after God had first miraculously owned the original converts from each nation represented in Jerusalem that day.

God has big plans for the world and the church. At the dawn of creation, God sowed a world of hope and possibility. Evil storms and tragic seasons may have slowed the harvest of greatness on planet earth. But if anyone wants to know what the true and best harvest will look like, she should check out the church.

That may seem funny to us. We would have a hard time seeing the church as a picture of God's profit margins. Yet for God, the church is the firstfruits of the great harvest.

Maybe that's why we ought to take ourselves in the church less seriously and more seriously at the same time. Less seriously because there is an awful lot of humor in what God is up to. More seriously because God's humor is the first smile of love that the rest of creation around us needs desperately to see.

Philippians 4:4-9

Paul's reference to the "whole palace" in Philippians 1:13 could possibly indicate a provenance of Caesarea as well as Rome (though not as likely), but his specific note about fellow Christians "who belong to Caesar's household" (4:22) can hardly be taken as anything other than the royal courts of the empire capital. Because of such clues, it is very reasonable to understand that Paul's letter to the Philippians was written while he was in Rome between 57 and 59 AD.

There are also some hints that Philippians was written earlier in this stay, and the other "Prison Letters" (Philemon, Colossians, Ephesians) were penned near the end of it. Paul appears to be somewhat settled into prison life as he writes to the Philippians, while it is clear in his note to Philemon that Paul expects to be released soon and free again to travel.

- Sometime in the spring of 57 AD Paul arrived in Rome. Although he was clearly a prisoner, awaiting adjudication before Caesar himself, Paul was also a Roman citizen with rights and freedoms. And since the charges against him were sectarian (Jewish religious practices) rather than capital crimes, Paul was able to establish his own living circumstances within the larger palace precincts while remaining under a type of house arrest.
- Probably late in 57 AD or early in 58, Epaphroditus, who had been serving as pastor or congregational leader in Philippi, brought Paul a rather significant gift from that church (Philippians 2:25; 4:10). It may have included both money and supplies, and greatly enhanced Paul's comfort in his limited circumstances.
- Epaphroditus stayed on with Paul for some time, assisting him as a servant. Unfortunately, Epaphroditus became ill and nearly died (Philippians 2:25-30), and only very recently had returned to full health.
- Paul believed that homesickness for Philippi and the congregation there might have contributed to Epaphroditus' grave malady, and vowed to send him back home as soon as he was able to travel. Of course, a letter of appreciation and encouragement was a necessary part of all these things, so Paul penned Philippians, probably sometime in early 58 AD.
- Paul's letter to the Philippians is the most joyful and uplifting note of the entire New Testament. Even in Paul's confinement, he is filled with delight in his relationships and amazed at what God is doing (Philippians 1). Almost without needing to do so, Paul reminds the congregation of the great example of Jesus, who gave up everything in order to express the love of God to us (Philippians 2:1-18). Another example of this selfless care is found in both Timothy and Epaphroditus, each of whom had given up much in order to serve others, especially the faith community in Philippi (Philippians 2:19-30). More encouragement to serve follows, with Paul reflecting on his own changes of behavior and value systems, once he was gripped by the love of God in Jesus (Philippians 3). A few personal instructions and notes of appreciation round out the letter (Philippians 4).

Although other letters of Paul are more intentionally "theological," this small epistle has a particularly wonderful poetic reflection encapsulating the entire ministry of Christ in a few lines (Philippians 2:6-11). Because of its condensed and hymnic character, some think Paul brought these verses in from an early popular Christian song or creedal statement. Perhaps so. Nevertheless, the whole of this short book is lyrical and reaches for the superlatives in life through lines that are both economical and majestic in today's lectionary passage.

John 6:25-35

Food is a very big part of our lives. Hunger can be a time clock ticking inside, regulating the hours of our days with calculated passion. Or it can be a biologic need, demanding fuel stops on our restless race. Even more, hunger functions as a psychological drive, forcing us to crave chocolate when we lack love, or driving us to drink, drugs, and sex.

But deeper than all of these things is our search for meaning beyond the drudgery and repetition of our daily activities. It is the spiritual need each person has to know that she is not alone in this gigantic and sometimes unkind maze of life.

Hunger is what the writer of Ecclesiastes means when he said that God has "set eternity in the hearts of men" (3:11). Hunger is the pilgrimage of the soul. In other words, the old adage is true: "You are what you eat."

So life beckons us to follow the latest fad, to search for the newest fulfillment, to seek the richest treasure. We consume and devour until we are fed up with life, so to speak. And still we want more.

Then a word comes to us from heaven. In part it is a word of judgment against us: since you are what you eat, take a look at what it is that you are consuming. If you eat garbage, you become garbage. If you feast on pornography, as Ted Bundy said in his dying confessions to James Dobson, you become filthy. If you think that wealth can satisfy the cravings of your soul, you will become a calculator and a penny-pincher. If the adoration of the community feeds the hunger of your psyche, you refashion yourself into a code of law and ethics, toeing the line without compassion. If another high is what it takes to get you through the stomach cramps of another day you will shoot up or smoke up or pop some more or tease yourself with illicit sex, and end up becoming a bag of used chemicals and a bottle of cheap thrills.

You are hungry, and you are what you eat. The cravings of your soul will not be stilled. A meal will reset the alarm of your biological clock. Food will keep your hungry body going. Potato chips and a soda will stop the munchies for a while. But what are you eating for your soul?

This is the beauty and simplicity of what Jesus told people in today's gospel reading: "I am the bread of life. He who comes to me will never go hungry, and he who believes in me will never be thirsty." Through the symbolic nourishment of spiritual depth and richness, something satisfying begins to grow inside. Tasting the things that make heaven shine and earth blossom, we begin to find the values and goals and visions and dreams of God giving shape to our lives.

I thought of that when my daughters asked me who knew me better than anyone else in life. They suggested several possibilities: my colleagues at work, my parents, my friends. All along, of course, they knew that it was their mother, my wife, who knew me best. Yet *how* did she know me so well, they asked. As we probed the matter further we finally agreed that it had to be by my actions and attitudes toward her. Whatever lives in me eventually comes out from me in words, deeds, and perspectives. I cannot hide long what grows powerfully inside.

Augustine knew this as he reflected on the spiritual character of our race. "Man is one of your creatures, Lord," he said, "and his instinct is to praise you. The thought of you stirs him so deeply that he cannot be content unless he praises you, because you made us for yourself and our hearts find no peace until they rest in you."

What are you eating today? Tomorrow and next week, those who are close to you will know whether there was any eternal nourishment in your diet.

Application

Sometimes we distort what it means to party, particularly on "secular" holidays like Thanksgiving. Trimalchio's banquet, staged for the Emperor Nero in AD 60, was outlandish in its overabundance of food — guests were required to regurgitate what they'd eaten in between each of the four courses in order to be able to go back to the table and gorge again. In like manner, the overwhelming proportions of a feast celebrating the installation of the Archbishop of York, England, in 1470 (10 fat oxen, 6 wild bulls, 300 pigs, 300 hogs, 3,000 calves, plus approximately 25,000 deer, birds, and rabbits, just to mention the meat dishes) led to a later prohibition guarding against clerical excess at the table. Too often our celebrations of Thanksgiving begin and end only with food.

That party does not focus on one's own accomplishments. When the hostess noticed George Bernard Shaw standing alone in a corner at her celebration, she worriedly asked him if he was enjoying himself. "Certainly," he replied, "there's nothing else here to enjoy!"

The Bible's idea of a party involves keeping our eyes on life as God's gift and love as God's treat. It doesn't take away all the inconveniences and hurts we experience from day to day. Nor does it keep us from being drained at times by the dullness of some of our routines. It does put a framework around life that calls for joy in living, hope in expectation, and delight in salvation.

And that may be the best reason of all to celebrate Thanksgiving today.

An Alternative Application

Philippians 4:4-9. In the east, the story is told of an extremely wealthy king who ruled a vast domain from magnificent palaces. He had the respect of his citizens and peace within his borders.

But for some perplexing reason he was quite unhappy. The king's doctors could find no medical problem. Neither could psychiatrists figure it out. But one old wise man, an advisor to the king's late father, had this advice: "There is but a single cure for the king. Your majesty must sleep one night in the shirt of a happy man!"

Strange advice, to be sure! But the desperate king needed only a hint of finding release from his malady to command that the search begin. So his messengers scoured the land, looking for one truly happy person.

The messengers could find no one. Not one happy person! Everyone had experienced days of sorrow and times of mourning. Many could laugh for a moment, but sooner or later each person would settle back to reflect on the pain in his or her life.

Finally, the messengers happened upon a beggar next to the road leading back to the palace. He wore a smile. He giggled uncontrollably. He laughed at life as it surrounded him. Here was a truly happy man!

"Give us your shirt," the messengers demanded. "The king has need of it!"

But the fellow only doubled over with spasms of hilarity. "I'm sorry!" he gasped, between fits of laughter. "You see, I have no shirt."

The English language has a number of similar words that relate to good feelings inside. *Pleasure*, for instance, reflects our delighted response to sensations that stimulate us. *Happiness* surrounds us because of certain happenings in our lives. And then there's *joy*.

In a sense, *pleasure* is an "it" word; it mostly has to do with *things* that touch our senses. And *happiness* is a "me" word; its primary focus is *my* response to events that come and go in my life. But *joy* is really a "we" word; it usually reflects what happens between people, between me and you, between me and God.

Joy starts in the heart. It's a relational word. Robert Rainy, one-time head of New College in Edinburgh, Scotland, used to say that "joy is the flag which is flown from the castle of the heart when the king is in residence there!"

Paul would agree.

If joy starts in the heart, it is refined in the mind. It is more than an emotion that comes and goes. It is deeper than a reflexive response that needs the right kind of stimulation. It is an act of the will. "Rejoice in the LORD!" commands Paul. Joy grows from heartfelt relationships. But it is also a choice of the mind.

Someone once attributed to the Christian church "the haunting fear that someone, somewhere may be happy!" How sad! And in 1769, Alexander Cruden, who was one of the most meticulous Bible students of his day, wrote: "To laugh is to be merry in a sinful manner." How tedious and tasteless!

John Wesley was more on track with Paul when he said, "Sour godliness is the devil's religion." Such an attitude doesn't belong in a heart responsive to God's love. It has no place in a mind that hears the psalmist's command.

Every language reflects the culture that produces it. Some Eskimo languages have more than thirty different words for "snow." Some African tribal tongues have no word for "ocean." And Hebrew, the language of Paul's Jewish background, has 27 different words for "joy" and "rejoicing." Can you imagine that? Joy was as much a part of the Israelite culture as life itself!

That is the heritage of the Christian church. What other religion in the world has such a tradition of music and singing and joyful worship? Some time ago a woman came to our church on a Sunday for the very first time. She had never been to a Christian worship service before in her life. What struck her most? "You sing so much!" she said.

About the Authors

Wayne Brouwer is a pastor of the Christian Reformed Church in North America and is an Associate Professor of Religion at Hope College in Holland, Michigan, as well as a member of the faculty of Western Theological Seminary. Brouwer has been the lead pastor in three different congregations. He is a graduate of Dordt College and holds degrees from Calvin Theological Seminary and McMaster University. Over 700 of his articles have been published as well as over a dozen books. Previous CSS Publishing titles by Pastor Bouwer include Political Christianity and Humming Till the Music Returns. He has been a consistent contributor to Emphasis: A Preaching Journal since 2004 and is one of several authors featured in Navigating the Sermon. Pastor Brouwer resides in Holland, Michigan, with his wife Brenda and they are the parents of three daughters.

Herbert W. Chilstrom was the first Presiding Bishop of the Evangelical Lutheran Church in America, being elected and installed in 1987. He held the position for two consecutive, four-year terms. Prior to his election as presiding bishop, he was the bishop of the Minnesota synod of the Lutheran Church in America. As a pastor, Chilstrom served three different congregations in Minnesota. He was a professor of religion and served as academic dean of Luther College in Teaneck, NJ. Bishop Chilstrom also served as vice president of the Lutheran World Federation as well as heading a committee exploring special ecumenical relationships for the National Council of Churches. He holds degrees from Augsburg College, Augustana Theological Seminary, Princeton Theological Seminary and New York University.

David Coffin is pastor of Elgin/Highland Lutheran Parish in Elgin, Iowa. David is a graduate of Ferris State University with a BS degree in printing. He earned his Master of Divinity degree from Trinity Lutheran Seminary (Ohio) and his Doctor of Ministry Degree from Winebrenner Seminary. He enjoys bike riding and working with small group ministries. He also eats lots of pizza, so he needs to ride the bike.

David Kalas is pastor of First United Methodist Church in Green Bay, Wisconsin. Before moving to Green Bay, he pastored churches in Whitewater, Wisconsin; Appleton, Wisconsin; and Hurt, Virginia. He also lead youth ministries in Cleveland, Ohio, and Richmond, Virginia. David eared his undergraduate degree from the University of Virginia and his Master of Divinity degree from Union Theological Seminary in Richmond, Virginia. He has also done coursework at Pittsburgh Theological Seminary and Asbury Theological Seminary.

In addition to the present volume, David has also contributed to other preaching resources published by CSS, is a regular contributor to *Emphasis: A Lectionary Preaching Journal* (CSS Publishing Company, Inc.), and has also written curriculum materials for the United Methodist Publishing House. David and his wife, Karen, haave been married 30 years and have three daughters, Angela, Lydia, and Susanna.

The late **Arthur Kolsti**, Matinicus, Maine, is a graduate of Harvard University and Andover Newton Theological School. He has served United Church of Christ congregations in Illinois, Indiana, Kansas, Connecticut and Massachusetts. He wrote of *Lyrics for the Century*, (CSS Publishing Company, Inc.).

The late **R. Craig Maccreary** was pastor of South Congregational Church, United Church of Christ in Newport, New Hampshire. He held pastorates in Pennsylvania, West Virginia, and Massachusetts. He earned degrees from Elon University (B.A.), Lancaster Theological Seminary (M.Div.), and Hartford Seminary (D. Min.). His work appeared in *Colleague*, *Pulpit Disgest*, and *The United Church News*. He was a guest on National Public Radio and was a contributor to *Candles in the Dark: Preaching and Poetry in Times of Crises*, edited by James Randolph.

James Nestingen is an ordained pastor of the Evangelical Lutheran Church in America. He served as pastor of Faith Lutheran Church in Coquille, OR following his ordination and later served the congregation of St. Ansgar Lutheran Church in Toronto, Canada as assistant to the pastor. He is a graduate of Concordia College and earned two masters degrees from Luther Seminary as well as his doctorate from St. Michael's College at the University of Toronto. Nestingen has also served as curriculum editor at Augsburg Publishing House. His teaching career includes multiple professorships of church history at Luther Seminary where he is now professor emeritus.

Ronald H. Love was called into the ordained ministry from a career as a state trooper. He has served Methodist churches in rural, inner-city and suburban settings for 20 years, and also served for four years as an Army chaplain. Dr. Love has also been a corporate librarian for a Fortune 500 company and been a university professor for ten years, teaching history and theology. His writing experience includes denominational publications, magazine articles on religion, and a newspaper devotional column. He holds a bachelor's degree in sociology (Slippery Rock State College), master's degrees in library and information science (University of Pittsburgh), secondary education (Duquesne University), church history (Indiana University of Pennsylvania), and theology (Wesley Theological Seminary), as well as a doctorate in homiletics (Pittsburgh Theological Seminary). Dr. Love now resides in South Carolina.

Schuyler Rhodes is the pastor of Temple United Methodist Church in San Francisco, California. He previously pastored Washington Square United Methodist Church in New York City, and served as executive director and campus pastor for the Wesley Foundation, a broad-based campus ministry at the University of California (Berkeley). Rhodes' commitment to social justice and peace has taken him around the globe. Over the last decade, he has traveled to more than a dozen countries, serving as a delegate to several consultations of the World Council of Churches, as the secretary of the Social and International Affairs Committee of the World Methodist Council, and as the chair of the board of directors for Pastors for Peace and the Interreligious Foundation for Community Organizing. He has also been a consultant on Peace and Justice Ministries for the Methodist Church's General Board of Global Ministries, developing liturgical and training materials as well as representing the General Board at numerous national and international gatherings. A prolific writer, Rhodes is an honors graduate of Drew University Theological School (M.Div.) and the State University of New York at Potsdam (B.A.).

Catherine Venkatesh has served congregations in Michigan and Massachusetts. She now works at a local ecumenical retreat center, as a naturalist at a local nature sanctuary, and as a supply priest and Deanery Co-Convener with the Episcopal Diocese of Massachusetts. A graduate of Williams College and the Church Divinity School of the Pacific, she completed additional degrees in Development Economics and Forestry. Prior to entering the ordained ministry, she worked in environmental research and policy. She lives with her family outside Boston and travels regularly to India, where her husband's extended family resides.

www.ingramcontent.com/pod-product-compliance
Lightning Source LLC
Chambersburg PA
CBHW081802300426
44116CB00014B/2216